Frommer's®

San Antonio & Austin

6th Edition

by Edie Jarolim

Here's what the critics say about Frommer's:

"Amazingly easy to use. Very portable, very complete."

—*Booklist*

"Detailed, accurate, and easy-to-read information for all price ranges."
—*Glamour Magazine*

"Hotel information is close to encyclopedic."
—*Des Moines Sunday Register*

"Frommer's Guides have a way of giving you a real feel for a place."
—*Knight Ridder Newspapers*

WILEY

Wiley Publishing, Inc.

About the Author

Edie Jarolim is the author of *Arizona For Dummies* and one of the coauthors of *Frommer's Texas*. She has written for a variety of national publications, including the *New York Times Book Review*, *America West Airlines Magazine*, *Art & Antiques*, *Bride's*, *National Geographic Traveler*, and the *Wall Street Journal*.

Published by:

Wiley Publishing, Inc.

111 River St.
Hoboken, NJ 07030-5774

ISBN-13: 978-0-7645-7764-2
ISBN-10: 0-7645-7764-6

Editor: William Gibson
Production Editor: Ian Skinnari
Cartographer: Roberta Stockwell
Photo Editor: Richard Fox
Production by Wiley Indianapolis Composition Services

Front cover photo: Alamo Mission exterior
Back cover photo: Racks of J.R. specials at Paris Hatters, San Antonio

For information on our other products and services or to obtain technical support, please contact our Customer Care Department within the U.S. at 800/762-2974, outside the U.S. at 317/572-3993 or fax 317/572-4002.

Wiley also publishes its books in a variety of electronic formats. Some content that appears in print may not be available in electronic formats.

Manufactured in the United States of America

5   4   3   2   1

Contents

List of Maps

An Invitation to the Reader

In researching this book, we discovered many wonderful places—hotels, restaurants, shops, and more. We're sure you'll find others. Please tell us about them, so we can share the information with your fellow travelers in upcoming editions. If you were disappointed with a recommendation, we'd love to know that, too. Please write to:

Frommer's San Antonio & Austin, 6th Edition
Wiley Publishing, Inc. • 111 River St. • Hoboken, NJ 07030

An Additional Note

Please be advised that travel information is subject to change at any time—and this is especially true of prices. We therefore suggest that you write or call ahead for confirmation when making your travel plans. The authors, editors, and publisher cannot be held responsible for the experiences of readers while traveling. Your safety is important to us, however, so we encourage you to stay alert and be aware of your surroundings. Keep a close eye on cameras, purses, and wallets, all favorite targets of thieves and pickpockets.

Other Great Guides for Your Trip:

Frommer's Texas

Frommer's USA

Frommer's Exploring America by RV

Frommer's National Parks of the American West

Frommer's Star Ratings, Icons & Abbreviations

Every hotel, restaurant, and attraction listing in this guide has been ranked for quality, value, service, amenities, and special features using a **star-rating system.** In country, state, and regional guides, we also rate towns and regions to help you narrow down your choices and budget your time accordingly. Hotels and restaurants are rated on a scale of zero (recommended) to three stars (exceptional). Attractions, shopping, nightlife, towns, and regions are rated according to the following scale: zero stars (recommended), one star (highly recommended), two stars (very highly recommended), and three stars (must-see).

In addition to the star-rating system, we also use **seven feature icons** that point you to the great deals, in-the-know advice, and unique experiences that separate travelers from tourists. Throughout the book, look for:

Finds	Special finds—those places only insiders know about
Fun Fact	Fun facts—details that make travelers more informed and their trips more fun
Kids	Best bets for kids, and advice for the whole family
Moments	Special moments—those experiences that memories are made of
Overrated	Places or experiences not worth your time or money
Tips	Insider tips—great ways to save time and money
Value	Great values—where to get the best deals

The following **abbreviations** are used for credit cards:

AE	American Express	DISC	Discover	V	Visa
DC	Diners Club	MC	MasterCard		

Frommers.com

Now that you have the guidebook to a great trip, visit our website at **www.frommers.com** for travel information on more than 3,000 destinations. With features updated regularly, we give you instant access to the most current trip-planning information available. At Frommers.com, you'll also find the best prices on airfares, accommodations, and car rentals—and you can even book travel online through our travel booking partners. At Frommers.com, you'll also find the following:

- Online updates to our most popular guidebooks
- Vacation sweepstakes and contest giveaways
- Newsletter highlighting the hottest travel trends
- Online travel message boards with featured travel discussions

What's New in San Antonio & Austin

Following a slowdown at the beginning of the new millennium, several major projects in San Antonio and Austin are back on track. As always, the hotel and restaurant scenes are where most of the shape-shifting occurs.

SAN ANTONIO

ACCOMMODATIONS New lodgings that sit directly on the River Walk are always a big deal, and this time there are two major ones to report. (Maybe the bigger news is that neither is part of a corporate chain.) The superhip **Hotel Valencia Riverwalk,** 405 N. St. Mary's, San Antonio, TX 78205 (*Ⓒ* **866/842-0100;** www.hotelvalencia.com), brought the interior of a historic building into the present—perhaps the future. **The Watermark,** 212 W. Crockett St., San Antonio, TX 78205 (*Ⓒ* **866/605-1212;** www.watermarkhotel.com), sister property to La Mansión del Río, right across the river, is especially noteworthy for its expansive spa. Both hotels fall into the "very expensive" category.

Several notable nonchain properties that don't sit right on the river opened recently, too. Its name notwithstanding—well, maybe you can see the water from a block away—the intimate **Riverwalk Vista,** 262 Losoya, San Antonio, TX 78205 (*Ⓒ* **866/898-4782;** www.riverwalkvista.com), occupies a beautifully restored historic structure. Only the facade of the **O'Brien Historic Hotel,** 116 Navarro St. (at St. Mary's), San Antonio, TX 78205 (*Ⓒ* **800/257-6058;** www.obrienhotel.com), is old—again, what's in a name?—but these up-to-date digs near the Convention Center and La Villita are very appealing. Both properties are excellent values in their respective (expensive, moderate) price categories.

In addition, several big chain hotels underwent major renovations. The city's two Hyatts—the **Hyatt Regency San Antonio on the River Walk,** 123 Losoya St., San Antonio, TX 78205 (*Ⓒ* **800/233-1234;** www.sanantonioregency.hyatt.com), and the **Hyatt Regency Hill Country Resort,** 9800 Hyatt Resort Dr., San Antonio, TX 78251 (*Ⓒ* **800/233-1234;** http://hillcountry.hyatt.com)—spent mega-bucks in 2004 on, among other things, morphing the guest rooms from country-cute to Texas sophisticated. **The San Antonio Airport Hilton,** 611 NW Loop 410, San Antonio, TX 78216 (*Ⓒ* **800/HILTONS;** www.hilton.com), devoted multimillions to spiffing up its image, too, trading in Lone Star chairs for earth-tone lounges. Hmmm . . . don't y'all want to be associated with cowboys anymore?

We're not entirely sure what the $6 million that the **Marriott Plaza San Antonio,** 555 S. Alamo St., San Antonio, TX 78205 (*Ⓒ* **800/228-9290;**

www.plazasa.com), spent on a revamp went to—the work wasn't completed by the time we went to press and no photos were available—but the property always had an elegant air, so odds are it was more of a Botox injection than an extreme makeover.

For additional information, see chapter 4.

DINING   A couple of San Antonio's most recent arrivals on the dining scene are hot, hot, hot. The "New Tex-Mex" fare, the wildly colorful dining rooms, and the creators—Lisa Wong of Rosario and Bruce Auden of Biga, both longtime local celebrity chefs—have made **Acenar,** 146 E. Houston St. (© **210/222-CENA**), an instant River Walk success. And whoever doubted that Southtown was still happening need only check out the Latin rhythms, the mix-it-up Latin American menu, and the sharply dressed crowd at **Azuca,** 713 S. Alamo (© **210/225-5550**).

Pesca, 212 W. Crockett St. (© **210/ 396-5817**), at the Watermark Hotel, isn't as hip as the aforementioned two new spots, but who cares when you find fish this fresh and well prepared? (Besides, it's *way* too pricey to attract starving-artist types.) In contrast, **Ciao Lavanderia,** 226 E. Olmos (© **210/822-3990**), the sister restaurant to Bistro Vatel and in the same strip mall, serves stylish Italian food that's a great bargain to boot.

Like your scene with a French accent? Drop into chic **Metropolitain,** 255 E. Basse, #940 (© **210/ 822-8227**), for a café au lait and croissant next time you're shopping at the Alamo Quarry Mall.

Find out more about all these restaurants in chapter 5.

SIGHTSEEING   The most important—or at least longest-heralded—entry on the attractions scene, the **Museo Americano Smithsonian,** 101 S. Santa Rosa Blvd. (© **210/458-2300**), hasn't opened yet, but after years of delay there's a definite date for its debut: July 4, 2005. A cornerstone of the Centro Alamada project, devoted to exploring the city's Hispanic roots, MAS—get it?—is positioned at the entryway to Market Square.

Having expanded its Latin American holdings in the 1990s, the **San Antonio Museum of Art,** 200 W. Jones Ave. (© **210/978-8100**), is looking eastward: Once the Lenora and Walter F. Brown Asian Art Wing opens in spring 2005, the institution will boast the largest Asian art collection in Texas and one of the most extensive in the Southwest.

Although the two theme parks at the outskirts of town, **SeaWorld San Antonio,** 10500 SeaWorld Dr. (© **800/700-7786**), and **Six Flags Fiesta Texas,** 17000 I-10 W. (© **800/ 473-4378**), continue to compete to outdo each other with splashy new shows and thrill rides, the biggest news in family fun is downtown: **Davy Crockett's Tall Tales Ride,** the last piece in the new multimillion-dollar **Ripley's Haunted Adventure** and **Guinness World Records Museum** complex, 329 Alamo Plaza (© **210/ 226-2828**), will be completed in early 2005, combining a (very loose) history lesson with a lot of fun.

Learn more about all these tourist lures in chapter 6.

AUSTIN

ACCOMMODATIONS   The expansion of Austin's convention center to double its previous size, completed in 2002, resulted in an accompanying increase in the number of downtown hotel rooms. That the high-rise **Hilton Austin,** 500 E. Fourth Street, Austin, TX 78701 (© **800/HILTONS;** www. hilton.com), should offer a good fitness center and stylish rooms comes as no surprise. More unexpected are the upscale extras—such as room service from P.F. Chang's and Fleming's—at the new **Hampton Inn & Suites**

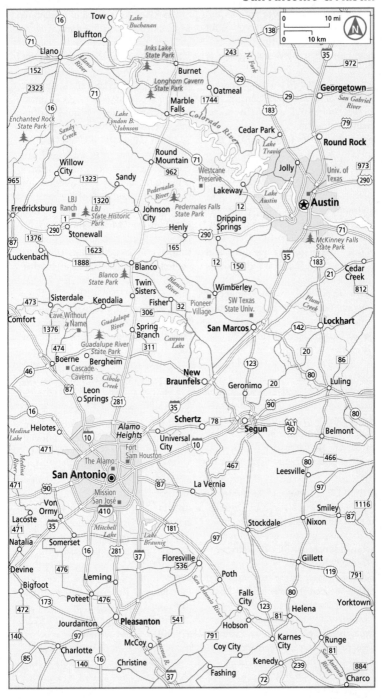

Austin-Downtown, 200 San Jacinto Blvd., Austin, TX 78701 (© **800/ HAMPTON;** www.hamptoninn.com).

In contrast, near the University of Texas, old is in. Not long after its 2003 debut, the **Mansion at Judges Hill,** 1900 Rio Grande, Austin, TX 78705 (© **800/311-1619;** www. mansionatjudgeshill.com), a converted late-19th-century home with a 1980s annex, became *the* place to stay in town. Not far away, the owner of the excellent Austin Folk House purchased the historic Governor's Mansion B&B; rechristened it the **Star of Texas,** 611 W. 22nd St., Austin, TX 78705 (© **866/472-6700;** http://staroftexasinn.com); and performed her magic on the rooms and public areas.

For those keener on pampering than sightseeing, the biggest scoop is the completion of the new spa at the **Lake Austin Spa Resort** 1705 S. Quinlan Park Rd., Austin, TX 78732 (© **800/847-5637;** www.lakeaustin. com), about a half-hour from the center of town. The 25,000-square-foot facility, opened in 2004, finally gives the property treatment rooms to match its idyllic setting and myriad nature-oriented activities.

See chapter 12 for more information.

DINING   It's tough to keep track of the culinary comings and goings around Austin—and especially downtown. Recently it was bye-bye Emilia's, hello **Moonshine,** 303 Red River St. (© **512/236-9599**). The haute comfort food served isn't as exciting as the cuisine offered by the former occupant—or as expensive, to be fair—but the setting, an 1850s complex with a tree-shaded yard, is as pleasant as ever. One of the most interesting recent arrivals, **Roaring Fork,** 701 Congress Ave. (© **512/583-0000**), was first introduced in Scottsdale, but chef Robert McGrath is a Texan, so his exciting New Texas cuisine deserves to be heralded on its home turf.

Proof that the hip South Austin scene has moved beyond Congress Avenue (but not far), **Uchi,** 801 S. Lamar (© **512/916-4808**), may be the most dazzling new eatery in town, with its Japan–meets–New American menu. The far more low-key **Habana,** 2728 S. Congress (© **512/443-4252**), which serves Cuban/Caribbean food, extends the sway of South Congress coolness beyond Oltdorf Avenue, once the southern boundary of the scene.

The hip are also hopping to East Austin, where Manor Road may be the next South Congress Avenue—at least as far as restaurants are concerned. Of the new eateries that opened on the strip east of I-35 that the East Side Café first staked out, **Vivo,** 2015 Manor Rd. (© **512/482-0300**), is our favorite, featuring excellent—and health-oriented—Mexican food and a fun patio.

Chapter 13 provides details on all.

SIGHTSEEING   Most of the recent news in the Austin sightseeing arena is arts- and culture-oriented. The long-awaited reopening of the **Austin Museum of Art–Laguna Gloria,** 3809 W. 35th St. (© **512/458-8191**), in 2003 surprised many with its shift of focus away from the art that hangs on the walls of the institution's historic structure to the historic building itself and its lovely grounds. Shows are now pleasant and low profile, not the big blockbusters as in the past. In contrast, the refurbishing of the facility and opening of two new galleries in the **Harry Ransom Humanities Research Center,** University of Texas, 21st and Guadalupe streets (© **512/ 471-8944**), has provided a better showcase for some of its flashier holdings—if you can call the world's first photograph and a rare Gutenberg Bible flashy. And to reflect its metamorphosis from relic of another era to cutting-edge art space, the gallery of the Texas Fine Art Association, created in 1911, changed its name to **Art-House at Jones Center,** 700 Congress Ave. (✆ **512/453-5312**). But Austin's major cultural event—from both a financial and an artistic standpoint—isn't going to occur until February 2006, when the **Blanton Museum of Art** debuts in a new building on the University of Texas campus.

As anyone who's been in town on a football weekend can attest, Austin's interests are far from exclusively effete. Witness the introduction in 2004 of the **Austin Wranglers** (✆ **512/491-6600;** www.austinwranglers.com), the newest members of the professional Arena Football League.

SHOPPING   The first link in what is now the world's largest organic and natural foods supermarket, **Whole Foods Market,** 525 N. Lamar (✆ **512/476-1206**), celebrated its 25th birthday in early 2005 by opening a huge new store near its original downtown location. Features include a 600-seat amphitheater, a cooking school, and on-site massages. And to fill an apparently insatiable local appetite for fresh produce—and culinary-related activities—the city saw the recent debut of the **Austin Farmers' Market,** held downtown at Republic Square Park, Fourth Street at Guadalupe, every Saturday from 9am to 1pm March to November (✆ **512/236-0074**).

THE TEXAS HILL COUNTRY

The relatively rural region around San Antonio and Austin changes less readily and steadily than the big cities, but that doesn't mean *nothing* ever happens here. For one thing, the area has a new central information resource that's actual—as opposed to existing only on the Internet or telephone—unlike similar such organizations in the past. The **Texas Hill Country Visitor Center,** 803 W. Hwy. 281 S. (✆ **830/868-5700,** www.hillcountry info.com), can be found just outside downtown Johnson City.

In addition, several interesting new restaurants and lodgings have cropped up in the region—as well as a couple of attractions. Here are some highlights.

The Silver Spur Guest Ranch in **Bandera** isn't new, but its owners are—which has led to major refurbishings and improvements, from individually redecorating the rooms to resurfacing the huge swimming pool. The hottest arrival on the dining scene—such as it is—is not in Bandera itself: **Mac and Ernie's** serves updated comfort food in a shack some 12 miles west of town.

One of the major tourist draws in **Kerrville** changed its name from the Cowboy Artists of America Museum to the **Museum of Western Art** to reflect a slight shift of focus in its holdings, but it remains as high quality as ever. The renovation of the town's old railroad depot is far more dramatic: **Rails,** the restaurant that now occupies the space, serves some of the freshest and most interesting food in the Hill Country.

Surprise: In **Fredericksburg,** a town best known for its B&Bs (more than 300 of them at last count), most in historic structures, the most interesting new place to lay your head is at the tiny airport. The **Hangar Hotel** does a delightful spin on 1940s flyboy style, replete with adjoining officers club. More typical of what's happening, tourist magnet–wise, is **Cuvee,** a wine bar, restaurant, and lounge that opened on the newly developing west end of Main Street.

New Braunfels has always touted its Germanic past and left tourists to discover its great river scene on their own. Now the local chamber of commerce has changed its website address to **www.nbjumpin.com** to reflect the town's interest in letting everyone know about its watery attractions. It doesn't hurt that the **Texas Ski Ranch,** a 70-acre complex with two lakes and water toys galore—as well as a track and skate park—opened on the outskirts of town. Both sports enthusiasts who've worked up an appetite and sophisticates who haven't will welcome the arrival of **Myron's,** a big-city–style steakhouse in a converted theater.

See chapter 17 for details on these and other Hill Country towns.

1

The Best of San Antonio

No matter if you call it the Fiesta City or the Alamo City, each of San Antonio's nicknames reveals a different truth. Visitors come here to kick back and party, but they also come to seek Texas's history—some would say its soul. They come to sit on the banks of a glittering river and sip cactus margaritas, but also to view Franciscan missions that rose along the same river more than 2½ centuries ago.

Multiculturalism isn't just an academic buzzword in San Antonio, the only major Texan city founded before Texas won its independence from Mexico. During its early days, it was populated by diverse groups with distinct goals: Spanish missionaries and militiamen, German merchants, Southern plantation owners, Western cattle ranchers, and Eastern architects. All have left their mark, both tangibly on San Antonio's downtown and subtly on the city's culture and cuisine.

With its German, Southern, Western, and, above all, Hispanic influences— at the 2000 census, the city was nearly 60% Mexican-American—San Antonio's cultural life is rich and complex. At the New Orleans–like Fiesta, for example, San Antonians might break confetti eggs called *cascarones,* listen to oompah bands, and cheer rodeo bull riders. Countless country-and-western ballads twang on about "San Antone"—no doubt because the name rhymes with "alone"—which is also America's capital for Tejano music, a unique blend of Mexican and German sounds. And no self-respecting San Antonio festival would be complete without Mexican tamales and tacos, Texan chili and barbecue, Southern hush puppies and glazed ham, and German beer and bratwurst.

The city's architecture also reflects its multiethnic history. After the Texas revolution, Spanish viga beams began to be replaced by southern Greek revival columns, German *fachwerk* (half-wooden) pitched roofs, and East Coast Victorian gingerbread facades. San Antonio, like the rest of the Southwest, has now returned to its Hispanic architectural roots—even chain hotels in the area have red-clay roofs, Saltillo tile floors, and central patios—but updated versions of other indigenous building styles are also popular. The rustic yet elegant Hill Country look, for example, might use native limestone in structures that combine sprawling Texas ranch features with more intricate German details.

These days, San Antonio is simultaneously moving backward and forward. The city is succumbing to the proliferation of highways, faceless housing developments, and homogeneous restaurant and lodging chains that so many Southwestern cities seem to equate with progress; in fact, early in the 20th century it almost paved over the river on which the city was founded. But it's also making a concerted effort to preserve its past, and for economic, and not sentimental, reasons: Cultural tourism sells, after all. Amid San Antonio's sprawl, it's the winding downtown streets that most visitors recall, and that once-endangered river. Few who come here leave without a memory of a moment, quiet or heart quickening, sunlit or sparkling with tiny tree-draped lights, when the river somehow worked its magic on them.

1 Frommer's Favorite San Antonio Experiences

- **Recapturing Texas's Fight for Independence at the Alamo:** It's hard to imagine the state's prime attraction as a battle site, surrounded as it is now by hotels and shops—that is, until you step inside the Long Barrack, where Texas's most famous fighters prepared to fight General Santa Anna's troops. Here, you just might shut out those modern images (if not the crowds) for a moment. See p. 84.

- **Attending a Mariachi Mass at Mission San José:** It's very moving to watch members of the congregation of this largest of the mission churches raise their voices in spirited musical prayer each Sunday at noon. Come early, as seats are limited and this is a popular thing to do. See p. 92.

- **Strolling Along San Antonio's River Walk:** Whether you opt for the buzz of the busy South Bank portion of the River Walk, or decide to escape to one of its quieter stretches, the green, lush banks of San Antonio's river will match your mood, day or night. See p. 105.

- **Seeing a Show at the Majestic Theatre:** As it happens, the restored Majestic offers top-notch shows of all kinds, but the venue itself is worth the price of admission alone. Book a seat in the front rows, or try the upstairs mezzanine so you can gaze at the star-studded ceiling. See p. 124.

- **Climbing into a Treehouse at the Witte Museum:** You can recapture your youth (or enjoy your kids relishing theirs) at the Witte, where the HEB Treehouse has interactive science exhibits galore. See p. 91.

- **Lazing in the Courtyard at the Marion Koogler McNay Art Museum:** As fine as many of the paintings here are, when it comes to transcendent experiences, you can't beat sitting out on the lovely tree-shaded patio of the McNay. See p. 91.

- **Pretending You Live in the King William District:** The opulent mansion homes built here by German merchants in the 19th century are eye-popping. You can't enter most of them (unless you're staying at one of the area's many B&Bs), but the fantasizing is free. See chapter 6.

- **Ascending the Tower of the Americas:** In the daytime, the tower provides a great way to get the lay of the land. At sunset, it's transformed from pragmatic to romantic as you sip a drink and watch the city lights wink on. See chapter 6.

- **Buying Day of the Dead Souvenirs in Southtown:** The Day of the Dead (actually 2 days, Nov 1 and 2) is commemorated throughout the largely Hispanic Southtown, but you can buy T-shirts with dancing skeletons and folk-art tableau typical of the holiday at Tienda Guadalupe year-round. See chapter 7.

- **Checking Out the Headgear at Paris Hatters:** Even if you're not in the market for a Stetson, you should at least wander over to this San Antonio institution that has sold hats to everyone from Pope John Paul II and Queen Elizabeth to lesser lights like TV's Jimmy

Smits. See how big your head is compared to those of the stars. See p. 120.

- **Grooving to Jazz at The Landing:** Jim Cullum and his band play cool jazz at a cool location on the River Walk. A groove doesn't get much mellower than this. See p. 126.

2 Best San Antonio Hotel Bets

- **Best Place for the Trendy to Be Seen:** The **Hotel Valencia Riverwalk,** 150 E. Houston St. (© **866/842-0100** or 210/227-9700), hosts Vbar and Citrus, two of the hottest hangouts in town. And flanking the hotel are Acenar and Sip (rhymes with hip), two other top styling spots. See p. 45.

- **Best Value for Business Travelers:** Such features as a location near the convention center and high-speed Internet access in the room make the **O'Brien Historic Hotel,** 116 Navarro St. (© **800/257-6058** or 210/527-1111), convenient for all business travelers, while low rates and perks such as free local phone calls make it especially appealing to those whose companies aren't picking up the tab. See p. 52.

- **The Best Place to See (or Feel) a Ghost:** San Antonio's got plenty of historic hotels—the kind where haunts tend to linger—but only **The Menger,** 204 Alamo Plaza (© **800/345-9285** or 210/223-4361), claims to have 32 ghosts. You can take your pick of the spirits you want to sleep with—or drink with. The bar where Teddy Roosevelt recruited his Rough Riders is in this hotel, too. See p. 50.

- **Best for Families:** If you can afford it, the **Hyatt Regency Hill Country Resort,** 9800 Hyatt Resort Dr. (© **800/233-1234** or 210/647-1234), just down the road from SeaWorld, is ideal for a family getaway. Kids get to splash in their own shallow pool, go tubing on a little river, and be entertained in a kids' camp—and you get to relax in the resort's spa or play a few holes on its expanding golf course. See p. 61.

- **Best Riverside Bargain:** The **Drury Inn & Suites,** 201 N. St. Mary's St. (© **800/DRURY-INN** or 210/212-5200), is a good, economical downtown bet located in a historic building right on the river. Breakfast and afternoon cocktails are included in the room rate, and in-room fridges and microwaves mean you can cut down on food costs in this pricey area even further. See p. 51.

- **Best Budget Lodging:** How do I love the savings at the **Best Western Sunset Suites,** 1103 E. Commerce St. (© **866/560-6000** or 210/223-4400)? Let me count the ways: Low room rates, lots of freebies, and a convenient location near downtown, plus very attractive rooms, make staying here a super deal. See p. 53.

- **Best B&B:** The King William area abounds with B&Bs, but the **Ogé House,** 209 Washington St. (© **800/242-2770** or 210/223-2353), stands out as much for its professionalism as for its gorgeous mansion and lovely rooms. New management has added modern amenities such as wi-fi, too. It's hard to beat this mix of the old and the new. See p. 53.

- **Best One-Stop Lodging:** You never have to wander far from the **Marriott Rivercenter,** 101 Bowie

St. (✆ **800/228-9290** or 210/223-1000), what with its excellent health club (on the same floor as the hotel's free washers and dryers, no less); its proximity to the Rivercenter Mall and to water taxis that take you along the River Walk; and its abundant on-site eateries. See p. 48.

- **Best Place to Spot Celebrities:** Everyone from Paula Abdul to ZZ Top (hey, they're big in Texas) has stayed at **La Mansión del Río,** 112 College St. (✆ **800/292-7300** or 210/518-1000); discretion, a willingness to cater to special requests, and a location that's just slightly away from the action might explain why. See p. 46.
- **Best for River Views:** La Mansión del Río, the Marriott Rivercenter,

the Watermark, and the Westin Riverwalk each boast prime watery views from some of their rooms, but if you stay at the **Hyatt Regency San Antonio on the River Walk,** 123 Losoya St. (✆ **800/233-1234** or 210/222-1234), you can book less expensive atrium-view lodgings and still glimpse a bit of the river running through the lobby. See p. 46.

- **Best New Hotel:** With its top-notch spa and health club, spacious, Zen-chic guest rooms, and excellent service, the **Watermark Hotel,** 212 W. Crockett St. (✆ **866/605-1212** or 210/396-5800), did what didn't seem possible: made a splash on the crowded high-end River Walk lodging scene. See p. 48.

3 Best San Antonio Dining Bets

- **Best for a Romantic Dinner:** On a quiet stretch of the River Walk, **Las Canarias,** at La Mansión del Río, 112 College St. (✆ **210/518-1063**), avoids the noise that plagues most waterview restaurants. You'll enjoy candlelight and superb, discreet service. See p. 68.
- **Best Movable Feast:** It used to be that you could dine on the river only if you were with a group, but among the restaurants that now offer reservations on communal tables to individuals and couples, **Boudro's,** 421 E. Commerce St./ River Walk (✆ **210/224-8484**), tops the meals-on-river-barge-wheels list. See p. 69.
- **Best for Serious Foodies:** After several years on the fine dining scene, **Le Rêve,** 152 E. Pecan St. (✆ **210/212-2221**), has proved that it's got staying power—there were rumbles about the chef moving to Dallas a while back—and that San Antonio is ready for a

place where men have to wear jackets and there is seating for dinner. The reward is stellar French food. See p. 68.

- **Best Seafood:** You'd think that serving brain food on the river would have been a no-brainer, but it wasn't until the arrival of **Pesca,** 212 W. Crockett St. (✆ **210/396-5817**), that there was a real contender. *Shark alert:* This place will take a bite out of your dining budget. See p. 69.
- **Best Italian Cuisine:** The risotto, potato gnocchi, and saltimbocca are among the dishes perfected by a chef from Rome that make it worth the trip to **Massimo,** 1896 Nacogdoches Rd. (✆ **210/342-8556**), in the Alamo Heights area. See p. 77.
- **Best Place to Listen to Music While You Eat:** Enjoy creative South American, Mexican, and Caribbean fare at Southtown's **Azuca,** 713 S. Alamo St. (✆ **210/ 225-5550**), while listening to

salsa, merengue, and other Latin sounds. See p. 73.

- **Best Blast from the Past: Schilo's,** 424 E. Commerce St. (© **210/223-6692**), not only serves up German deli in portions that date back to pre-cholesterol-conscious days but also retains prices from that era. See p. 73.

- **Best New Restaurant:** It's a tie this time: I love the innovative Tex-Mex food and the party atmosphere at **Acenar,** 146 E. Houston St. (© **210/222-CENA**), a sizzling addition to the River Walk, but I'd drive much farther than Olmos Park, just a few minutes north of downtown, to take advantage of the great Italian food and great prices at **Ciao Lavanderia,** 226 E. Olmos Dr. © **210/ 822-3990**). See p. 71.

- **Best Place to Encounter Artists:** Terrific food, a nice selection of libations, good prices, and a fun, funky atmosphere draw creative types of all kinds to the **Liberty Bar,** 328 E. Josephine St. (© **210/ 227-1187**). See p. 75.

2

Planning Your Trip to San Antonio

Spontaneity is all well and good once you get to where you're going, but advance planning can make or break a trip. San Antonio is becoming more and more popular, so it's best to book your vacation here well in advance. If you're thinking of coming for April's huge Fiesta bash, for example, try to reserve accommodations at least 6 months ahead of time to avoid disappointment.

1 Visitor Information

For a useful pretrip information packet, including a visitors' guide and map, lodging guide, detailed calendar of events, arts brochure, and *SAVE San Antonio* booklet with discount coupons for a number of hotels and attractions, call © **800/252-6609.** You can also get pretrip information, sans discount coupons, online at the San Antonio Convention and Visitor's Bureau website, **www.sanantonio visit.com**.

Phone or fill out an online form on the website of the **Texas Department of Tourism** (© **800/8888-TEX;** www.traveltex.com) to receive the *Texas State Travel Guide,* a glossy book chock-full of information about the state, along with a statewide accommodations booklet and map. The **Texas Travel Information Center** has a toll-free number (© **800/452-9292**) to call for the latest on road conditions, special events, and general attractions in the areas you're interested in visiting. Traveler counselors will even advise you on the quickest or most scenic route to your intended destination. *Texas Monthly* magazine, another good source of information, can be accessed at **www.texasmonthly. com**.

2 Money

Like most tourist-oriented cities, San Antonio has two price structures: one for locals, and another for visitors. You can expect everything from food to hotels to souvenirs to be fairly pricey on the River Walk and at theme parks such as SeaWorld. In general, however, the average San Antonio salary is not terribly high, and the cost of living is about 10% lower than the country's average, so prices tend to be moderate.

Minimal cash is required, since credit cards are accepted nearly universally, and automatic teller machines linked to national networks are strewn around tourist destinations and, increasingly, within hotels. **Cirrus** (© **800/424-7787;** www.master card.com) and **PLUS** (© **800/843-7587;** www.visa.com) are the two most popular networks. Call or check online for ATM locations in San Antonio.

What Things Cost in San Antonio	US$	UK£
Taxi from the airport to the city center	18.00	9.30
Streetcar ride between any two downtown points	0.80	0.40
Local telephone call	0.50	0.30
Long-neck beer	2.50–3.50	1.40–1.80
Double at Westin Riverwalk Inn (very expensive)	359.00	186.00
Double at Drury Inn & Suites San Antonio Riverwalk (moderate)	129.00	67.00
Double at Best Western Sunset Suites (inexpensive)	89.00	45.00
Lunch for one at Rosario's (moderate)	12.00	6.00
Lunch for one at Twin Sisters (inexpensive)	6.00	3.00
Dinner for one, without wine, at Las Canarias (very expensive)	55.00	29.00
Dinner for one, without beer, at La Fonda on Main (moderate)	16.00	8.00
Dinner for one, without beer, at Schilo's (inexpensive)	10.00	5.00
Coca-Cola	1.25–2.00	0.65–1.00
Cup of espresso	1.75–2.50	0.90–1.30
Roll of ASA 100 Kodacolor film, 24 exposures	5.00	2.60
Adult admission to the Witte Museum	7.00	3.60
Movie ticket	8.00	4.00
Ticket to the San Antonio Symphony	16.00–61.00	8.30–32.00
Ticket to a Spurs game	10.00–100.00	5.20–52.00

The three major traveler's checks agencies are **American Express** (© 800/221-7282), **MasterCard** (© **800/223-9920**), and **Visa** (© **800/ 732-1322**). See also Appendix B, "For International Visitors," p. 297.

3 When to Go

Most tourists visit San Antonio in summer, though it's not the ideal season. The weather is often steamy, and restaurants and attractions tend to be crowded. That said, there are plenty of places to cool off around town, and hotel rates are generally lower (conventioneers come in the fall, winter, and spring) during this time of year.

Also consider that some of the most popular outdoor attractions, such as SeaWorld and Six Flags Fiesta Texas, either open only in summer or keep far longer opening hours in summer. Fall and spring are less crowded with tourists, and the weather is much more pleasant. San Antonio is the single most popular destination in the state for Texans, many of whom drive in just for the weekend, so hotels fill up faster and rates may be higher on weekends. The city's business hotels are busy during the week, so consider booking a B&B or hotel that's not business oriented if you'll be staying weekdays.

CLIMATE

Complain to San Antonians about their city's heat on a sultry summer day and you're likely to be assured that it's far more humid in say, Houston, or anywhere in East Texas. This may be true, but it won't make you feel any less sweaty. From late May through September, expect regular high temperatures and high humidity.

Fall and spring are generally prime times to visit; the days are pleasantly warm and, if you come in late March or early April, the wildflowers in the nearby Hill Country will be in glorious bloom. Temperate weather combined with the lively celebrations surrounding Christmas also make November and December good months to visit. January and February can be a bit raw, relatively speaking—though, if you're from up north, you probably won't even notice.

San Antonio's Average DaytimeTemperature (°F & °C) & Monthly Rainfall (Inches)

	Jan	Feb	Mar	Apr	May	June	July	Aug	Sept	Oct	Nov	Dec
Avg. Temp. (°F)	52	55	61	68	75	82	84	84	80	71	60	53
Avg. Temp. (°C)	11	13	16	20	24	28	29	29	26	21	15	12
Rainfall (in.)	1.7	2.1	1.5	2.5	3.1	2.8	1.7	2.4	3.7	2.8	1.8	1.5

SAN ANTONIO CALENDAR OF EVENTS

Please note that the information contained below is always subject to change. For the most up-to-date information on these events, call the number provided, or check with the Convention and Visitors Bureau (© **800/447-3372**, ext. 4; www.SanAntonio Visit.com). You can also find a detailed calendar of downtown events on the website for the Downtown Alliance San Antonio, **http://downtownsanantonio.org/ calendar.html**.

January

Michelob ULTRA Riverwalk Mud Festival, River Walk. Every year, when the horseshoe bend of the San Antonio River Walk is drained for maintenance purposes, San Antonians cheer themselves up by electing a king and queen to reign over such events as Mud Stunts Day and the Mud Pie Ball. © **210/227-4262;** www.thesan antonioriverwalk.com. Mid-January.

February

Stock Show and Rodeo, SBC Center. In early February, San Antonio hosts more than 2 weeks of rodeo events, livestock judging, country-and-western bands, and carnivals. It's been going (and growing) since 1949. © **210/225-5851;** www.sa rodeo.com. Early February.

San Antonio CineFestival, Guadalupe Cultural Arts Center. The nation's oldest and largest Chicano/Latino film festival screens more than 70 films and videos. © **210/271-3151;** www.guadalupe culturalarts.org. Mid- to late February.

March

Dyeing O' the River Green Parade. Are leprechauns responsible for turning the San Antonio River into the green River Shannon? Irish dance and music fill the Arneson River Theatre from the afternoon on. © **210/227-4262;** www.thesanantonioriverwalk.com. St. Patrick's Day weekend.

April

Starving Artist Show, River Walk and La Villita. Part of the proceeds

---

Fun Fact **The Fiesta City**

San Antonio's nickname refers to its huge April bash, but it also touches on the city's tendency to party at the drop of a sombrero. It's only natural that a place with strong Southern, Western, and Hispanic roots would know how to have a good time, and elaborately costumed festival queens, wild-and-woolly rodeos, and Mexican food and mariachis are rolled out year-round. And where else but San Antonio would something as potentially dull as draining a river turn into a cause for celebration?

---

of the works sold by nearly 900 local artists goes to benefit the Little Church of La Villita's program to feed the hungry. ℂ **210/226-3593;** www.lavillita.com. First weekend of the month.

Fiesta San Antonio. What started as a modest marking of Texas's independence in 1891 is now a huge event, with an elaborately costumed royal court presiding for 9 or 10 days of revelry: parades, balls, food-fests, sporting events, concerts, and art shows all over town. Call ℂ **877/723-4378** or 210/227-5191for details on tickets and events, or log on to www.fiesta-sa. org. Late April (always includes Apr. 21, San Jacinto Day).

May

Tejano Conjunto Festival, Rosedale Park and Guadalupe Theater. This annual festival, sponsored by the Guadalupe Cultural Arts Center, celebrates the lively and unique blend of Mexican and German music born in south Texas. The best *conjunto* musicians perform at the largest event of its kind in the world. Call ℂ **210/271-3151** for schedules and ticket information, or check the website, www.guadalupeculturalarts.org. Early May.

Return of the Chili Queens, Market Square. An annual tribute to chili, said to have originated in San Antonio, with music, dancing, crafts demonstrations, and (of course) chili aplenty. Bring the Tums. ℂ **210/207-8600;** jessemo@ sanantonio.gov. Memorial Day weekend.

June

Texas Folklife Festival, Institute of Texas Cultures. Ethnic foods, dances, crafts demonstrations, and games celebrate the diversity of Texas's heritage. ℂ **210/458-2224;** www.texancultures.utsa.edu. Four days in June.

Juneteenth, various venues. The anniversary of the announcement of the Emancipation Proclamation in Texas in 1865 is the occasion for a series of African-American celebrations, including an outdoor jazz concert, gospelfest, parade, picnic, and more. Call the San Antonio Convention and Visitors Bureau for details at ℂ **800/447-3372;** or log on to www.juneteenthsanantonio. com. June 19.

July

Contemporary Art Month, various venues. More than 400 exhibitions at more than 50 venues make this month contemporary art lover's heaven (especially inside the air-conditioned galleries). To find out what's showing where, call ℂ **210/212-7082** or log on to www.cam sanantonio.org.

September

Diez y Seis. Mexican independence from Spain is feted at several different downtown venues, including La Villita, the Arneson River Theatre, and Guadalupe Plaza. Music and dance, a parade, and a *charreada* (rodeo) are part of the fun. ② 210/223-3151; www.agatx.org. Weekend nearest September 16.

Jazz'SAlive, Travis Park. Bands from New Orleans and San Antonio come together for a weekend of hot jazz. ② 210/212-8423; www.saparksfoundation.org. Third weekend in September.

October

Oktoberfest, Beethoven Halle and Garten. San Antonio's German roots show at this festival with food, dance, oompah bands, and beer. ② 210/222-1521; www.beethovenmaennerchor.com/oktoberfest.htm. Early October.

New World Wine and Food Festival, various venues. Celebrity chefs from around Texas help celebrate San Antonio's culinary roots with everything from tequila tastings and chocolate seminars to cooking classes. It's a taste treat, and all for charity. ② 210/930-3232; www.newworldwinefood.org. First weekend in November.

International Accordion Festival, La Villita. Inaugurated in 2001, this squeezebox fest was such a success it became an annual event.

More than a dozen ensembles play music from around the globe, from Cajun, merengue, zydeco, and conjunto to klezmer, Basque, and Irish music. There are also dancing and workshops for all ages. ② 210/865-8578; www.internationalaccordionfestival.org. Mid-October.

November

Ford Holiday River Parade and Lighting Ceremony. Trees and bridges along the river are illuminated by some 122,000 lights. Celebrities and duded-up locals and lots of bands participate in this floating river parade, which kicks off the Paseo del Rio Holiday Festival. ② 210/227-4262; www.thesanantonioriverwalk.com. Friday following Thanksgiving.

December

Fiestas Navideñas, Market Square. The Mexican market hosts piñata parties, a blessing of the animals, and surprise visits from Pancho Claus. ② 210/207-8600; www.sanantonio.gov/sapar. First 3 weekends in December.

La Gran Posada, Milam Park to San Fernando Cathedral. Dating back to the 1800s, when it was staged in the same area, this candlelit procession reenacts Mary and Joseph's search for shelter in a moving rendition of the Christmas story. ② 210/227-1297; www.sanantonio.gov/sapar. Third Sunday in December.

4 Insurance

There are three kinds of travel insurance: trip cancellation, medical, and lost luggage. Trip cancellation insurance is a good idea if you have paid a large portion of your vacation expenses up front.

But the other two types of insurance don't make sense for most travelers. Your existing health insurance should cover you if you get sick while on vacation (although if you belong to an HMO, you should check to see whether you are fully covered when away from home). And your homeowner's insurance should cover stolen luggage if you have off-premises theft. Check your existing policies before you buy any additional coverage. The airlines are responsible for $2,500 on domestic flights if they lose your luggage; if you plan to carry anything more valuable than that, keep it in your carry-on bag.

Some credit cards (American Express and certain gold and platinum Visas and MasterCards, for example) offer automatic flight insurance against death or dismemberment in case of an airplane crash. If you still feel you need more insurance, try one of the companies listed below. But don't pay for more insurance than you need. For example, if you need only

trip cancellation insurance, don't purchase coverage for lost or stolen property. Trip cancellation insurance costs approximately 6% to 8% of the total value of your vacation. Reputable issuers of travel insurance include **Access America** (© 866/807-3982; www.accessamerica.com); **Travel Guard International** (© 800/826-4919; www.travelguard.com); **Travel Insured International** (© 800/243-3174; www.travelinsured.com); and **Travelex Insurance Services** (© 888/457-4602; www.travelex-insurance.com).

5 Specialized Travel Resources

FOR TRAVELERS WITH DISABILITIES

Lots of work has been done in recent years to make San Antonio friendlier to those who use wheelchairs. The Riverwalk Trolley Station, for example, was built with a large elevator to transport people down to the water. Contact the **San Antonio Planning Department** (© 210/207-7245, voice and TTY) for additional information (including a map of River Walk access), or log on to the disability access section of the department's website (www.sanantonio.gov/planning/disability_access.asp). Several taxis have also been equipped with lifts and ramps; **Yellow-Checker** (© 210/222-2222) has most of them. And two downtown trolleys and about 85% of the public buses are now accessible. For **VIA Trans Disabled Accessibility Information,** phone © 210/362-2140 (voice) or 362-2217 (TTY) or click on the "Accessible Service" section of www.viainfo.net. In addition, the Weekender section of the *San Antonio Express-News* includes accessibility symbols for restaurants, theaters, galleries, and other venues.

Many travel agencies offer customized tours and itineraries for travelers with disabilities. **Flying Wheels Travel**

(© 507/451-5005; www.flyingwheels travel.com) offers escorted tours and cruises that emphasize sports and private tours in minivans with lifts. **Access-Able Travel Source** (© 303/232-2979; www.access-able.com) offers extensive access information and advice for traveling around the world with disabilities. **Accessible Journeys** (© 800/846-4537 or 610/521-0339; www.disabilitytravel.com) caters specifically to slow walkers and wheelchair travelers and their families and friends.

Avis Rent A Car has an "Avis Access" program that offers such services as a dedicated 24-hour toll-free number (© 888/879-4273) for customers with special travel needs; special car features such as swivel seats, spinner knobs, and hand controls; and accessible bus service.

Organizations that offer assistance to disabled travelers include **Moss-Rehab** (www.mossresourcenet.org), which provides a library of accessible-travel resources online; **SATH (Society for Accessible Travel & Hospitality)** (© 212/447-7284; www.sath.org; annual membership fees: $45 adults, $30 seniors and students), which offers a wealth of travel resources for people with all types of disabilities and informed recommendations on destinations, access guides, travel agents, tour operators, vehicle rentals, and companion services; and the **American Foundation for the Blind (AFB)** (© **800/232-5463;** www.afb.org), a referral resource for travelers who are blind or visually impaired that includes information on traveling with Seeing Eye dogs.

For more information specifically targeted to travelers with disabilities, the community website **iCan** (www.icanonline.net/channels/travel/index.cfm) has destination guides and several regular columns on accessible travel. Also check out the quarterly magazine **Emerging Horizons** ($14.95 per year, $19.95 outside the U.S.; www.emerginghorizons.com) and *Open World* magazine, published by SATH (see above; subscription: $13 per year, $21 outside the U.S.).

FOR GAY & LESBIAN TRAVELERS

San Antonio has a fairly large, but not exceedingly visible, gay and lesbian population. The website of the **Diversity Center of San Antonio,** 531 San Pedro Ave., second level (© **210/223-6106;** www.diversitycentersa.org), includes a calendar of events—many of which are held at **The Esperanza Peace & Justice Center,** 922 San Pedro (© **210/228-0201;** www.esperanzacenter.org), which often screens films or has lectures on topics of interest to gay, lesbian, and transgender travelers. If you stay at the **Painted Lady Inn,** a lesbian-owned bed-and-breakfast at 620 Broadway (© **210/220-1092;** www.thepaintedladyinn.com), you can also find out all you want to know about the local scene. See also chapter 8 for information about gay bars.

The **International Gay and Lesbian Travel Association (IGLTA)** (© **800/448-8550** or 954/776-2626; www.iglta.org) is the trade association

for the gay and lesbian travel industry, and offers an online directory of gay- and lesbian-friendly travel businesses; go to their website and click on "Members."

FOR SENIORS

If you're like many people these days, getting older doesn't necessarily mean slowing down. And, if you're savvy, you can even make those gray hairs pay off. Mention the fact that you're a senior citizen when you make your travel reservations. Although all of the major U.S. airlines except America West have cancelled their senior discount and coupon book programs, many hotels still offer discounts for seniors. In San Antonio, people over the age of 65—or in some cases, as low as 55—qualify for reduced admission to theaters, museums, and other attractions, as well as discounted fares on public transportation. (See the "One-Day Ticket, Yeah" sidebar in chapter 3.)

Members of **AARP** (formerly known as the American Association of Retired Persons), 601 E St. NW, Washington, DC 20049 (© **888/687-2277;** www.aarp.org), get discounts on hotels, airfares, and car rentals. AARP offers members a wide range of benefits, including *AARP: The Magazine* and a monthly newsletter. Anyone over 50 can join.

Many reliable agencies and organizations target the 50-plus market. **Elderhostel** (© **877/426-8056;** www.elderhostel.org) arranges study programs for those age 55 and over (and a spouse or companion of any age) in the U.S. and in more than 80 countries around the world. Most courses last 5 to 7 days in the U.S. (2–4 weeks abroad), and many include airfare, accommodations in university dormitories or modest inns, meals, and tuition.

Recommended publications offering travel resources and discounts for seniors include the quarterly magazine *Travel 50 & Beyond* (www.travel50 andbeyond.com); *Travel Unlimited: Uncommon Adventures for the Mature Traveler* (Avalon); *101 Tips for Mature Travelers,* available from Grand Circle Travel (𝄐 **800/221-2610** or 617/350-7500; www.gct. com); and *Unbelievably Good Deals and Great Adventures That You Absolutely Can't Get Unless You're Over 50* (McGraw-Hill), by Joann Rattner Heilman.

FOR FAMILIES

The family vacation is a rite of passage for many households. As any veteran family vacationer will assure you, a family trip can be among the most pleasurable and rewarding times of your life; it can also quickly devolve into a farce worthy of a *National Lampoon* movie. Good advance travel planning is essential.

The San Antonio edition of the free monthly *Our Kids* magazine includes a calendar that lists daily local activities oriented toward children. You can read it online at http://sanantonio. parenthood.com/aboutus.html; order it in advance from 8400 Blanco, Suite 201, San Antonio, TX 78216 (𝄐 **210/ 349-6667**); or find it in San Antonio at HEB supermarkets, Wal-Mart stores, Hollywood Video, and most major bookstores. Call to find out about other locations where it's available.

The **Family Travel Times** newsletter, *Travel with Your Children,* 40 Fifth Ave., New York, NY 10011 (𝄐 **212/ 477-5524**; www.familytraveltimes. com), published six times a year, offers good general information, as well as destination-specific articles. Subscriptions cost $39, and you can get one online, by phone, or by snail mail.

Recommended Internet-only sites include **Family Travel Network** (www.familytravelnetwork.com), which offers travel tips and reviews of family-friendly destinations, vacation

deals, and thoughtful features such as "What to Do When Your Kids Are Afraid to Travel" and "Kid-Style Camping"; **Family Travel Forum** (www.familytravelforum.com), a comprehensive site that offers customized trip planning; and **Family Travel Files** (www.thefamilytravelfiles.com), with features including a vacation-ideas directory and destination-specific (including San Antonio) articles about traveling with kids.

FOR STUDENTS

STA Travel (𝄐 **800/781-4040;** www. statravel.com) caters especially to young travelers, although their bargain-basement prices are available to people of all ages. **Travel CUTS** (𝄐 **800/667-2887** or 416/614-2887; www.travelcuts.com) offers similar services for both Canadians and U.S. residents.

Although San Antonio has 12 2- and 4-year institutions of higher education, it's not really a college town, and there's no general gathering place for college-age folk (though they tend to gravitate toward the entertainment strip on N. St. Mary's St. during weekends). The local branch of the state system, the **University of Texas at San Antonio** (www.utsa.edu), has three campuses: one north of town at 6900 N. Loop 1604 West (𝄐 **210/ 458-4011**); a newer one on the western side of downtown, at 501 W. Durango Blvd. (𝄐 **210/458-2400**); and the Institute of Texan Cultures (see chapter 6). The city's other major universities, **Trinity,** 1 Trinity Place (𝄐 **210/999-7011;** www.trinity.edu); **St. Mary's,** 1 Camino Santa Maria (𝄐 **210/436-3011;** www.stmarytx. edu); and **University of the Incarnate Word,** 4301 Broadway (𝄐 **210/829-6005;** www.uiw.edu), are all private. The best source of local information for student visitors is probably **Hostelling International–San Antonio** (see chapter 4).

6 Planning Your Trip Online

SURFING FOR AIRFARES

The "big three" online travel agencies, **Expedia.com, Travelocity.com,** and **Orbitz.com,** sell most of the air tickets bought on the Internet. (Canadian travelers should try expedia.ca and Travelocity.ca; U.K. residents can go for expedia.co.uk and opodo.co.uk.) Each has different business deals with the airlines and may offer different fares on the same flights, so it's wise to shop around. Expedia and Travelocity will also send you e-mail notification when a cheap fare becomes available to your favorite destination. Of the smaller travel agency websites, **Side-Step** (www.sidestep.com) has gotten the best reviews from Frommer's authors. It's a browser add-on that purports to "search 140 sites at once," but in reality only beats competitors' fares as often as other sites do.

Also remember to check **airline websites,** especially those for low-fare carriers such as Southwest, JetBlue, AirTran, WestJet, or Ryanair, whose fares are often misreported or simply missing from travel-agency websites. Even with major airlines, you can often shave a few bucks from a fare by booking directly through the airline and avoiding a travel agency's transaction fee. But you'll get these discounts only by **booking online:** Most airlines now offer online-only fares that even their phone agents know nothing about. For the websites of airlines that fly to and from your destination, go to "Getting There," p. 25.

Great **last-minute deals** are available through free weekly e-mail services provided directly by the airlines. Most of these are announced on Tuesday or Wednesday and must be purchased online. Most are valid only for travel that weekend, but some (such as Southwest's) can be booked weeks or months in advance. Sign up for weekly e-mail alerts at airline websites or check megasites that compile comprehensive lists of last-minute specials, such as **Smarter Living** (smarter living.com). For last-minute trips, **site59.com** and **lastminutetravel. com** in the U.S. and **lastminute.com** in Europe often have better air-and-hotel package deals than the major-label sites. A website listing numerous bargain sites and airlines around the world is **www.itravelnet.com**.

If you're willing to give up some control over your flight details, use what is called an **"opaque" fare service** like **Priceline** (www.priceline.com; www.priceline.co.uk for Europeans) or its smaller competitor **Hotwire** (www.hotwire.com). Both offer rock-bottom prices in exchange for travel on a "mystery airline" at a mysterious time of day, often with a mysterious change of planes en route. The mystery airlines are all major, well-known carriers—and the possibility of being sent from Philadelphia to Chicago via Tampa is remote; the airlines' routing computers have gotten a lot better than they used to be. But your chances of getting a 6am or 11pm flight are pretty high. Hotwire tells you flight prices before you buy; Priceline usually has better deals than Hotwire, but you have to play their "name our price" game. If you're new at this, the helpful folks at **BiddingForTravel** (www.biddingfortravel.com) do a good job of demystifying Priceline's prices and strategies. Priceline and Hotwire are great for flights within North America and between the U.S. and Europe. But for flights to other parts of the world, consolidators will almost always beat their fares. *Note:* In 2004 Priceline added non-opaque service to its roster. You now have the option to pick exact flights, times, and airlines from a list of offers—or opt to bid on opaque fares as before.

For much more about airfares and savvy air-travel tips and advice, pick up a copy of *Frommer's Fly Safe, Fly Smart* (Wiley Publishing, Inc.).

SURFING FOR HOTELS

Shopping online for hotels is generally done one of two ways: by booking through the hotel's own website or through an independent booking agency (or a fare-service agency like Priceline; see below). These Internet hotel agencies have multiplied in mind-boggling numbers of late, competing for the business of millions of consumers surfing for accommodations around the world. This competitiveness can be a boon to consumers who have the patience and time to shop and compare the online sites for good deals—but shop they must, for prices can vary considerably from site to site. And keep in mind that hotels at the top of a site's listing may be there for no other reason than that they paid money to get the placement.

Of the "big three" sites, **Expedia** offers a long list of special deals and "virtual tours" or photos of available rooms so you can see what you're paying for (a feature that helps counter the claims that the best rooms are often held back from bargain booking websites). **Travelocity** posts unvarnished customer reviews and ranks its properties according to the AAA rating system. Also reliable are **Hotels. com** and **Quikbook.com.** An excellent free program, **Travelaxe** (www. travelaxe.net), can help you search multiple hotel sites at once, even ones you may never have heard of—and conveniently lists the total price of the room, including the taxes and service charges. Another booking site, **Travelweb** (www.travelweb.com), is partly owned by the hotels it represents (including the Hilton, Hyatt, and Starwood chains) and is therefore plugged directly into the hotels' reservations systems—unlike independent online agencies, which have to fax or e-mail reservation requests to the hotel, a good portion of which get misplaced in the shuffle. More than once, travelers have arrived at the hotel, only to be told that they have no reservation. To be fair, many of the major sites are undergoing improvements in service and ease of use, and Expedia will soon be able to plug directly into the reservations systems of many hotel chains—none of which can be bad news for consumers. In the meantime, it's a good idea to **get a confirmation number** and **make a printout** of any online booking transaction.

In the opaque website category, **Priceline** and **Hotwire** are even better for hotels than for airfares; with both, you're allowed to pick the neighborhood and quality level of your hotel before offering up your money. Priceline's hotel product even covers Europe and Asia, though it's much better at getting five-star lodging for three-star prices than at finding anything at the bottom of the scale. On the downside, many hotels stick Priceline guests in their least desirable rooms. Be sure to go to the Bidding-ForTravel website (see above) before bidding on a hotel room on Priceline; it features a fairly up-to-date list of hotels that Priceline uses in major cities. For both Priceline and Hotwire, you pay upfront, and the fee is nonrefundable. *Note:* Some hotels do not provide loyalty program credits or points or other frequent-stay amenities when you book a room through opaque online services.

SURFING FOR RENTAL CARS

For booking rental cars online, the best deals are usually found at rental-car company websites, although all the major online travel agencies also offer rental-car reservations services. Priceline and Hotwire work well for rental cars, too. The only "mystery" is which major rental company you get, and for most travelers the difference between Hertz, Avis, and Budget is negligible.

Frommers.com: The Complete Travel Resource

For an excellent travel-planning resource, we highly recommend **Frommers.com** (www.frommers.com), voted Best Travel Site by *PC Magazine*. We're a little biased, of course, but we guarantee that you'll find the travel tips, reviews, monthly vacation giveaways, bookstore, and online-booking capabilities thoroughly indispensable. Among the special features are our popular **Destinations** section, where you'll get expert travel tips, hotel and dining recommendations, and advice on the sights to see for more than 3,500 destinations around the globe; the **Frommers.com Newsletter,** with the latest deals, travel trends, and money-saving secrets; our **Community** area featuring **Message Boards,** where Frommer's readers post queries and share advice (sometimes even our authors show up to answer questions); and our **Photo Center,** where you can post and share vacation tips. When your research is done, the **Online Reservations System** (www.frommers.com/book_a_trip) takes you to Frommer's preferred online partners for booking your vacation at affordable prices.

7 The 21st-Century Traveler

INTERNET ACCESS AWAY FROM HOME

Travelers have any number of ways to check their e-mail and access the Internet on the road. Of course, using your own laptop—or even a PDA (personal digital assistant) or an electronic organizer with a modem—gives you the most flexibility. But even if you don't have a computer, you can still access your e-mail and even your office computer from cybercafes.

WITHOUT YOUR OWN COMPUTER

It's hard nowadays to find a city that *doesn't* have a few cybercafes. Although there's no definitive directory for cybercafes—these are independent businesses, after all—two places to start looking are at **www.cybercaptive.com** and **www.cybercafe.com**.

Aside from formal cybercafes, most **youth hostels** nowadays have at least one computer you can get to the Internet on. And most **public libraries** across the world offer Internet access free or for a small charge. Avoid **hotel business centers** unless you're willing to pay exorbitant rates.

Most major airports now have **Internet kiosks** scattered throughout their gates. These kiosks, which you'll also see in shopping malls, hotel lobbies, and tourist information offices around the world, give you basic Web access for a per-minute fee that's usually higher than cybercafe prices. The kiosks' clunkiness and high price mean they should be avoided whenever possible.

To retrieve your e-mail, ask your **Internet Service Provider (ISP)** if it has a Web-based interface tied to your existing e-mail account. If your ISP doesn't have such an interface, you can use the free **mail2web** service (www.mail2web.com) to view and reply to your home e-mail. For more flexibility, you may want to open a free, Web-based e-mail account with **Yahoo! Mail** (http://mail.yahoo.com). (Microsoft's Hotmail is another popular option, but Hotmail has severe spam problems.) Your home ISP may be able to forward your e-mail to the Web-based account automatically.

If you need to access files on your office computer, look into a service called **GoToMyPC** (www.gotomypc. com). The service provides a Web-based interface for you to access and manipulate a distant PC from any-where—even a cybercafe—provided your "target" PC is on and has an always-on connection to the Internet (such as with Road Runner cable). The service offers top-quality security, but if you're worried about hackers, use your own laptop rather than a cybercafe computer to access the GoToMyPC system.

WITH YOUR OWN COMPUTER

Wi-fi (wireless fidelity) is the buzz-word in computer access, and more and more hotels, cafes, and retailers are signing on as wireless "hot spots" from where you can get high-speed connection without cable wires, net-working hardware, or a phone line (see below). You can get wi-fi connec-tion one of several ways. Many laptops sold in the last year have built-in wi-fi capability (an 802.11b wireless Ether-net connection). Mac owners have their own networking technology, Apple AirPort. For those with older computers, an 802.11b/wi-fi **card** (around $50) can be plugged into your laptop. You sign up for wireless access service much as you do cell-phone service, through a plan offered by one of several commercial compa-nies that have made wireless service available in airports, hotel lobbies, and coffee shops, primarily in the U.S. (followed by the U.K. and Japan). **T-Mobile HotSpot** (www.t-mobile. com/hotspot) serves up wireless con-nections at more than 1,000 Starbucks coffee shops nationwide. **Boingo** (www.boingo.com) and **Wayport** (www.wayport.com) have set up net-works in airports and high-class hotel lobbies. IPass providers (see below) also give you access to a few hundred wireless hotel lobby setups. Best of all, you don't need to be staying at the Four Seasons to use the hotel's net-work; just set yourself up on a nice couch in the lobby. The companies' pricing policies can be Byzantine, with a variety of monthly, per-connection, and per-minute plans, but in general you pay around $30 a month for lim-ited access—and as more and more companies jump on the wireless band-wagon, prices are likely to get even more competitive.

There are also places that provide **free wireless networks** in cities around the world. To locate these free hot spots, go to **www.wiki.personal telco.net/index.cgi/Wireless Communities**.

If wi-fi is not available at your des-tination, most business-class hotels throughout the world offer dataports for laptop modems, and a few thou-sand hotels in the U.S. and Europe now offer free high-speed Internet access using an Ethernet network cable. You can bring your own cables, but most hotels rent them for around $10. **Call your hotel in advance** to see what your options are.

In addition, major Internet Service Providers (ISPs) have **local access numbers** around the world, allowing you to go online by simply placing a local call. Check your ISP's website or call its toll-free number and ask how you can use your current account away from home, and how much it will cost.

If you're traveling outside the reach of your ISP, the **iPass** network has dial-up numbers in most of the world's countries. You'll have to sign up with an iPass provider, who will then tell you how to set up your com-puter for your destination(s). For a list of iPass providers, go to www.ipass. com and click on "Individuals Buy Now." One solid provider is **i2Roam** (www.i2roam.com; ✆ **866/811-6209** or 920/235-0475).

Online Traveler's Toolbox

- **www.mysanantonio.com**. The website of the city's only mainstream newspaper, the *San Antonio Express-News,* is a one-stop e-shop for the city: In addition to providing the daily news, it also links to local business such as dry cleaners and florists and to movie, nightlife, and restaurant listings and reviews. A couple of caveats: You have to register to use the site (a one-time annoyance, and no fee is involved) and many of the searches require zip codes, so be sure to know the one you'll be traveling from when you log on.
- **www.sanantonio.gov**. The City of San Antonio's website offers timely information on such topics as traffic and street closures. Most of the other sections that would be of interest to visitors, such as the city-sponsored arts events and public parks, can be found in the "Recreation" section.
- **www.sanantoniovisit.com**. You're not going to get honest critiques of hotels and attractions on the San Antonio Convention and Visitors Bureau's website; you are, however, going to get useful links to many of them. The "Discounts" section is especially good if you're looking for discounts on everything from accommodations to theme parks. This is not the easiest site to navigate, but once you click on "Visitors" you should find what you need.
- **http://sanantonio.citysearch.com**. I don't always agree with this site's reviews, but it's always good to have a variety of opinions about dining, nightlife, and shopping (even if mine are ultimately right). And there are a few things I can't do—like provide you with an up-to-date weather report or Yellow Pages information—that this site can.
- **www.texasmonthly.com**. You won't necessarily find San Antonio stories on the *Texas Monthly* site, but the state's best magazine offers in-depth treatments of lots of interesting topics, so you'll be keyed into a Texas mindset. And the site sometimes highlights hot new San Antonio dining spots.
- **www.mapquest.com**. This best of the mapping sites lets you choose a specific address or destination, and in seconds, it will return a map and detailed directions.
- **Airplane Seating and Food.** Find out which seats to reserve and which to avoid (and more) on all major domestic airlines at www.seatguru.com. And check out the type of meal (with photos) you'll likely be served on airlines around the world at www.airlinemeals.com.

USING A CELLPHONE ACROSS THE U.S.

Just because your cellphone works at home doesn't mean it'll work elsewhere in the country (thanks to our nation's fragmented cellphone system). It's a good bet that your phone will work in major cities. But take a look at your wireless company's coverage map on its website before heading out—T-Mobile, Sprint, and Nextel are particularly weak in rural areas. If you need to stay in touch at a destination where you know your phone won't work, **rent** a phone that does from **InTouch Global** (☎ **800/872-7626;** www.intouchglobal.com) or a rental-car location, but beware that you'll pay $1 a minute or more for airtime.

If you're venturing deep into national parks, you may want to consider renting a **satellite phone ("satphone"),** which is different from a cellphone in that it connects to satellites rather than ground-based towers. A satphone is more costly than a cellphone but works where there are no cellular signal and no towers. Unfortunately, you'll pay at least $2 per minute to use the phone, and it works only where you can see the horizon (that is, usually not indoors). In North America, you can rent iridium satellite phones from **Roadpost** (www.road post.com; ☎ **888/290-1606** or 905/272-5665). InTouch USA (see above) offers a wider range of satphones but at higher rates. As of this writing, satphones were very expensive to buy.

If you're not from the U.S., you'll be appalled at the poor reach of our **GSM (Global System for Mobiles) wireless network,** which is used by much of the rest of the world (see below). Your phone will probably work in most major U.S. cities; it definitely won't work in many rural areas. (To see where GSM phones work in the U.S., check out www.t-mobile. com/coverage/national_popup.asp.) And you may or may not be able to send SMS (text messaging) home—something Americans tend not to do anyway, for various cultural and technological reasons. (International budget travelers like to send text messages home because it's much cheaper than making international calls.) Assume nothing—call your wireless provider and get the full scoop. In a worst-case scenario, you can always rent a phone; InTouch USA delivers to hotels.

BY PLANE
THE MAJOR AIRLINES
The major domestic carriers serving San Antonio are **America West** (☎ 800/235-9292; www.americawest. com), **American** (☎ 800/433-7300; www.aa.com), **Continental** (☎ 800/525-0280; www.continental.com), **Delta** (☎ 800/221-1212; www.delta. com); **Midwest Airlines** (☎ 800/452-2022; www.midwestairlines.com),

---

Tips **Don't Stow It—Ship It**

If ease of travel is your main concern and money is no object, you can ship your luggage and sports equipment with one of the growing number of luggage-service companies that pick up, track, and deliver your luggage (often through couriers such as Federal Express) with minimum hassle for you. Traveling luggage-free may be ultraconvenient, but it's not cheap. One-way overnight shipping can cost from $100 to $200, depending on what you're sending. Still, for some people, especially the elderly or the infirm, it's a sensible solution to lugging heavy baggage. Specialists in door-to-door luggage delivery are **Virtual Bellhop** (www.virtualbellhop. com), **SkyCap International** (wwww.skycapinternational.com), **Luggage Express** (www.usxpluggageexpress.com), and **Sports Express** (www.sports express.com).

Travel in the Age of Bankruptcy

Airlines go bankrupt, so protect yourself by **buying your tickets with a credit card,** as the Fair Credit Billing Act guarantees that you can get your money back from the credit card company if a travel supplier goes under (and if you request the refund within 60 days of the bankruptcy). **Travel insurance** can also help, but make sure it covers against "carrier default" for your specific travel provider. And be aware that if a U.S. airline goes bust midtrip, a 2001 federal law requires other carriers to take you to your destination (albeit on a space-available basis) for a fee of no more than $25, provided you rebook within 60 days of the cancellation.

Northwest (© 800/225-2525; www. nwa.com), **Southwest** (© 800/435-9792; www.iflyswa.com), and **United** (© 800/241-6522; www.united.com). **Aerolitoral** (© 800/237-6639; www. aerolitoral.com), **Aeromar** (© 888/627-0207; www.aeromarairlines.com), **Continental,** and **Mexicana** (© 800/531-7921; www.mexicana.com) offer service to and from Mexico.

For the most current information on who jets into town, call 210/207-3411. Because San Antonio isn't a hub, service to the city has been circuitous in the past, but airlines servicing San Antonio currently provide nonstop flights to such major U.S. cities as Atlanta, Austin, Baltimore, Chicago, Cincinnati, Dallas–Fort Worth, Denver, El Paso, Houston, Kansas City, Las Vegas, Los Angeles, Memphis, Minneapolis/St. Paul, Nashville, Newark, Orlando, Phoenix, Salt Lake City, St. Louis, and Tampa.

FLYING FOR LESS: TIPS FOR GETTING THE BEST AIRFARE

Passengers sharing the same airplane cabin rarely pay the same fare. Travelers who need to purchase tickets at the last minute, change their itinerary at a moment's notice, or fly one-way often get stuck paying the premium rate. Here are some ways to keep your airfare costs down:

- Passengers who can book their ticket **long in advance,** who can **stay over Saturday night,** or who fly **midweek** or **at less-trafficked hours** may pay a fraction of the full fare. If your schedule is flexible, say so, and ask if you can secure a cheaper fare by changing your flight plans.
- You can also save on airfares by keeping an eye out in local newspapers for **promotional specials** or **fare wars,** when airlines lower prices on their most popular routes. You rarely see fare wars offered for peak travel times, but if you can travel in the off-months, you may snag a bargain.
- Search the **Internet** for cheap fares (see "Planning Your Trip Online," earlier in this chapter).
- Join **frequent-flier clubs.** Accrue enough miles, and you'll be rewarded with free flights and elite status. It's free, and you'll get the best choice of seats, faster response to phone inquiries, and prompter service if your luggage is stolen, if your flight is canceled or delayed, or if you want to change your seat. You don't need to fly to build frequent-flier miles—**frequent-flier credit cards** can provide thousands of miles for doing your everyday shopping.
- For many more tips about air travel, including a rundown of the major frequent-flier credit cards, pick up a copy of *Frommer's Fly Safe, Fly Smart* (Wiley Publishing, Inc.).

BY CAR

As has been said of Rome, all roads lead to San Antonio. The city is fed by four interstates (I-35, I-10, I-37, and I-410), three U.S. highways (U.S. 281, U.S. 90, and U.S. 87), four state highways (Tex. 16, Tex. 211, Tex. 151, and Tex. 1604), and several Farm-to-Market (FM) roads. In San Antonio, I-410 and Hwy. 1604, which circle the city, are referred to as Loop 410 and Loop 1604. All freeways lead into the central business district; U.S. 281 and Loop 410 are closest to the airport.

San Antonio is 975 miles from Atlanta, 1,979 miles from Boston, 1,187 miles from Chicago, 1,342 miles from Los Angeles, 1,360 miles from Miami, 527 miles from New Orleans, 1,781 miles from New York, 1,724 miles from San Francisco, and 2,149 miles from Seattle. The distance to Dallas is 282 miles, to Houston 199 miles, and to Austin 80 miles.

BY TRAIN

Amtrak provides service three times a week, going east to Orlando (via Houston, Lafayette, and New Orleans), and west to Los Angeles (via El Paso and Tucson). Trains leave from the depot at 350 Hoefden St. (© **210/ 223-3226**). There is also daily service between San Antonio and Chicago via Austin, Dallas, Forth Worth, Little Rock, and St. Louis. Call © **800/ USA-RAIL** or log on to www.amtrak. com for current fares, schedules, and reservations.

Flying with Film & Video

Never pack film—developed or undeveloped—in checked bags, as the new, more powerful scanners in U.S. airports can fog film. Scanners can damage the film you carry with you as well. X-ray damage is cumulative; the faster the film, and the more times you put it through a scanner, the more likely the damage. Film under 800 ASA is usually safe for up to five scans. If you're taking your film through additional scans, U.S. regulations permit you to demand hand inspections. In international airports, you're at the mercy of airport officials. Keep in mind that airports are not the only places where your camera may be scanned: Highly trafficked attractions are X-raying visitors' bags with increasing frequency.

Most photo supply stores sell protective pouches designed to block damaging X-rays. The pouches fit both film and loaded cameras. They should protect your film in checked baggage, but they also may raise alarms and result in a hand inspection.

You'll have little to worry about if you are traveling with **digital cameras.** Unlike film, which is sensitive to light, the digital camera and storage cards are not affected by airport X-rays, according to Nikon. Still, if you plan to travel extensively, you may want to play it safe and hand-carry your digital equipment or ask that it be inspected by hand.

Carry-on scanners will not damage **videotape** in video cameras, but the magnetic fields emitted by the walk-through security gateways and hand-held inspection wands will. Always place your loaded camcorder on the screening conveyor belt or have it hand-inspected. Be sure your batteries are charged because you may be required to turn the device on to ensure that it's what it appears to be.

BY BUS

San Antonio's **Greyhound** station, 500 N. St. Mary's St. (© **210/270-5834**), is located downtown about 2 blocks from the River Walk. This bustling station, which is open 24 hours, is within walking distance of a number of hotels, and many public streetcar and bus lines run nearby. Look for Greyhound's advance purchase specials, companion specials (if you book a full-fare ticket for either round-trip or one-way travel, a companion rides at half-price), and other promotional discounts. For all current price and schedule information, call © **800/231-2222** (© 800/345-3109 TTY; 800/752-4841 for assistance for customers with disabilities), or log on to www.greyhound.com.

9 Tips on Accommodations

SAVING ON YOUR HOTEL ROOM

The **rack rate** is the maximum rate that a hotel charges for a room. Hardly anybody pays this price, however, except in high season or on holidays. To lower the cost of your room:

- **Ask about special rates or other discounts.** Always ask whether a room less expensive than the first one quoted is available, or whether any special rates apply to you. You may qualify for corporate, student, military, senior, or other discounts. Mention membership in AAA, AARP, frequent-flier programs, or trade unions, which may entitle you to special deals as well. Find out the hotel policy on children—do kids stay free in the room or is there a special rate?
- **Dial direct.** When booking a room in a chain hotel, you'll often get a better deal by calling the individual hotel's reservation desk rather than the chain's main number.
- **Book online.** Many hotels offer Internet-only discounts, or supply rooms to Priceline, Hotwire, or Expedia at rates much lower than the ones you can get through the hotel itself. Shop around. And if you have special needs—a quiet room, a room with a view—call the hotel directly and make your needs known after you've booked online.
- **Remember the law of supply and demand.** Resort hotels are most crowded and therefore most expensive on weekends, so discounts are usually available for midweek stays. Business hotels in downtown locations are busiest during the week, so you can expect big discounts over the weekend. Many hotels have high-season and low-season prices, and booking the day after high season ends can mean big discounts.
- **Look into group or long-stay discounts.** If you come as part of a large group, you should be able to negotiate a bargain rate, since the hotel can then guarantee occupancy in a number of rooms. Likewise, if you're planning a long stay (at least 5 days), you might qualify for a discount. As a general rule, expect 1 night free after a 7-night stay.
- **Avoid excess charges and hidden costs.** When you book a room, ask whether the hotel charges for parking. Use your own cellphone, pay phones, or prepaid phone cards instead of dialing direct from hotel phones, which usually have exorbitant rates. And don't be tempted by the room's minibar offerings: Most hotels charge through the nose for water, soda, and snacks. Finally, ask about

local taxes and service charges, which can increase the cost of a room by 15% or more. If a hotel insists upon tacking on a surprise "energy surcharge" that wasn't mentioned at check-in or a "resort fee" for amenities you didn't use, you can often make a case for getting it removed.

- Consider the pros and cons of **all-inclusive** resorts and hotels. The term "all-inclusive" means different things at different hotels. Many all-inclusive hotels will include three meals daily, sports equipment, spa entry, and other amenities; others may include all or most drinks. In general, you'll save money going the "all-inclusive" way—as long as you use the facilities provided. The downside is that your choices are limited and you're stuck eating and playing in one place for the duration of your vacation.

- Carefully consider your hotel's meal plan. If you enjoy eating out and sampling the local cuisine, it makes sense to choose a **Continental Plan (CP),** which includes breakfast only, or a **European Plan (EP),** which doesn't include any meals and allows you maximum flexibility. If you're more interested in saving money, opt for a **Modified American Plan (MAP),** which includes breakfast and one meal, or the **American Plan (AP),** which includes three meals. If you must choose a MAP, see if you can get a free lunch at your hotel if you decide to do dinner out.

- **Book an efficiency.** A room with a kitchenette allows you to shop for groceries and cook your own meals. This is a big money saver, especially for families on long stays.

- **Consider enrolling in hotel "frequent stay" programs,** which reward repeat customers who accumulate enough points or credits to earn free hotel nights, airline miles, complimentary in-room amenities, or even merchandise. These are offered not only by many chain hotels and motels (Hilton HHonors, Marriott Rewards, Wyndham ByRequest, to name a few), but also by individual inns and B&Bs. Many chain hotels partner with other hotel chains, car-rental firms, airlines, and credit card companies to give consumers additional ways to accumulate points in the program.

LANDING THE BEST ROOM

Somebody has to get the best room in the house. It might as well be you. You can start by joining the hotel's frequent-guest program, which may make you eligible for upgrades. A hotel-branded credit card usually gives it owner "silver" or "gold" status in frequent-guest programs for free. Always ask about a corner room. They're often larger and quieter, with more windows and light, and they often cost the same as standard rooms. When you make your reservation, ask if the hotel is renovating; if it is, request a room away from the construction. Ask about nonsmoking rooms, rooms with views, rooms with twin, queen- or king-size beds. If you're a light sleeper, request a quiet room away from vending machines, elevators, restaurants, bars, and discos. Ask for a room that has been most recently renovated or redecorated.

If you aren't happy with your room when you arrive, ask for another one. Most lodgings will be willing to accommodate you.

In resort areas, particularly in warm climates, ask the following questions before you book a room:

- What's the view like? Cost-conscious travelers may be willing to pay less for a back room facing the parking lot, especially if they don't plan to spend much time in their room.

- Does the room have air-conditioning or ceiling fans? Do the windows open? If they do, and the nighttime entertainment takes place alfresco, you may want to find out when show time is over.
- What's included in the price? Your room may be moderately priced, but if you're charged for beach chairs, towels, sports equipment, and other amenities, you could end up spending more than you bargained for.
- How far is the room from hotel amenities, such as pools, tennis courts, or golf courses? If it's far, is there transportation to and from the amenities, and is it free?

10 Recommended Reading

Before Frederick Law Olmsted became a landscape architect—New York's Central Park is among his famous creations—he was a successful journalist, and his 1853 *A Journey Through Texas* includes a delightful section on his impressions of early San Antonio. William Sidney Porter, better known as O. Henry, had a newspaper office in San Antonio for a while. Two collections of his short stories, *Texas Stories* and *Time to Write,* include a number of pieces set in the city, among them "A Fog in Santone," "The Higher Abdication," "Hygeia at the Solito," "Seats of the Haughty," and "The Missing Chord."

O. Henry wasn't very successful at selling his newspaper *Rolling Stone* (no, not *that* one) in San Antonio during the 1890s, but there's a lively literary scene in town today. Resident writers include Sandra Cisneros, whose powerful, critically acclaimed short stories in *Women Hollering Creek* are often set in the city; and mystery writer Jay Brandon, whose excellent *Loose Among the Lambs* kept San Antonians busy trying to guess the identities of the local figures they (erroneously) thought had been fictionalized therein. Rick Riordan, whose hard-boiled detective novels such as *Tequila Red* and *Southtown* take place in an appropriately seamy San Antonio, is also a resident.

Two Austin writers use San Antonio settings: Novelist Sarah Bird's humorous *The Mommy Club* pokes fun at the yuppies of the King William district, while Stephen Harrigan's *The Gates of the Alamo* is a gripping, fictionalized version of Texas's most famous battle.

3

Getting to Know San Antonio

For visitors, San Antonio is really two cities. Downtown, site of the original Spanish settlements, is the compact, eminently strollable tourist hub. The River Walk and its waterside development have revitalized a once-decaying urban center that now buzzes with hotels, restaurants, and shops. And thanks in large part to the San Antonio Conservation Society, many of downtown's beautiful old buildings are still intact. Some house popular tourist attractions and hotels, while others are occupied by the large businesses that are increasingly trickling back to where it all began. Public transportation is cheap and plentiful downtown, and as a result a car tends to be more of a hindrance than a help.

The other San Antonio is spread out, mostly low-rise, and connected by more than its fair share of freeways.

The city's most recent growth has been toward the northwest, where you'll find the sprawling South Texas Medical Center complex and, farther out, the ritzy Dominion Country Club and housing development, the Six Flags Fiesta Texas theme park, and the Westin La Cantera Resort. The old southeast section, home to four of the five historic missions, remains largely Hispanic, while much of the southwest is taken up by Kelly and Lackland Air Force Bases. Whether you fly or drive in, you're likely to find yourself in the northeastern reaches of the city at some point: Along with the airport, this section hosts the Brackenridge Park attractions and some of the best restaurants and shops in town. You'll probably want your own wheels if you're staying in this second San Antonio.

1 Orientation

ARRIVING

BY PLANE   The two-terminal **San Antonio International Airport** (℘ 210/207-3411; www.sanantonio.gov/airport), about 13 miles north of downtown, is compact, clean, well marked—even cheerful. Among its various amenities are a postal center, ATM, foreign-currency exchange, game room, and well-stocked gift shops. Advantage, Alamo, Avis, Budget, Dollar, Enterprise, Hertz, National, and Thrifty all have desks at both of the airport terminals.

Loop 410 and U.S. 281 south intersect just outside the airport. If you're renting a car here (see "By Car" in "Getting Around," later in this chapter), it should take about 15 to 20 minutes to drive downtown via U.S. 281 south.

Most of the hotels within a radius of a mile or two offer **free shuttle service** to and from the airport (be sure to check when you make your reservation). If you're staying downtown, you'll most likely have to pay your own way.

VIA Metropolitan Transit's bus no. 2 is the cheapest (80¢) way to get downtown but also the slowest, stopping first at the North Star shopping center. Unless you've come without luggage and want to stop off at the mall to buy a few things, the trip should take from 40 to 45 minutes. You need exact change.

Impressions

We were already almost out of America and yet definitely in it and in the middle of where it's maddest. Hotrods blew by. San Antonio, ah-haa!
                                                   —Jack Kerouac, *On the Road* (1955)

SATRANS (© **800/868-7707** or 210/281-9900, www.saairportshuttle.com), with a booth outside each of the terminals, offers shared van service from the airport to the downtown hotels for $12 per person one-way, $22 round-trip. Check the website for prices to other destinations. Vans run from about 7am until 1am; phone 24 hours in advance for van pickup from your hotel.

There's a **taxi** queue in front of each terminal. The base charge on a taxi is $1.70; add $1.80 for each mile. It should cost you about $18 to $20 to get downtown.

BY TRAIN   San Antonio's train station is located in St. Paul's Square, on the east side of downtown near the Alamodome and adjacent to the Sunset Station entertainment complex. Cabs are readily available from here. Drink and snack machines are available inside the station, and there's an ATM at the Alamodome. Lockers are not available, but Amtrak will hold passengers' bags in a secure location for $2 per bag. Information about the city is available at the main counter.

VISITOR INFORMATION

The main office of the **City of San Antonio Visitor Information Center** is across the street from the Alamo, at 317 Alamo Plaza (© **210/207-6748**). Hours are daily 9am to 5pm, except Thanksgiving, Christmas, and New Year's, when the center is closed.

Publications such as the free *Fiesta,* a glossy magazine with interesting articles about the city, and *Rio,* a tabloid focusing on the River Walk, are available at the Visitor Information Center, as well as at most downtown hotels and many shops and tourist sights. Both of these advertising-heavy publications list sights, restaurants, shops, cultural events, and some nightlife, though there's an obvious bias toward advertisers. Also free—but more objective—is San Antonio's alternative paper, the *Current.* Though skimpy, it is a good source for nightlife listings; just don't depend on it for movie schedules, however. The *San Antonio Express-News* is the local newspaper. It's got a good arts/entertainment section called "The Weekender," which comes out on Friday, though not free, and it's available around town.

Arguably the best state-oriented magazine in the country, *Texas Monthly* contains excellent short reviews of restaurants in San Antonio, among other cities, and its incisive articles about local politics, people, and events are a great way to get acquainted with Lone Star territory in general. You can buy a copy at almost any city bookstore, grocery, or newsstand.

CITY LAYOUT

Although it lies at the southern edge of the Texas Hill Country, San Antonio itself is basically flat. As I noted earlier, the city divides into two distinct districts: a compact central downtown surrounded by a Western-style, freeway-laced sprawl. Neither section is laid out in a neat grid system; many of downtown's streets trace the meandering course of the San Antonio River, while a number of the thoroughfares in the rest of town follow old conquistador routes or 19th-century wagon trails.

MAIN ARTERIES & STREETS   Welcome to loop land. Most of the major roads in Texas meet in San Antonio, where they form a rough wheel-and-spoke pattern: I-410 traces a 53-mile circumference around the city, and Highway 1604 forms an even larger circle around them both. I-35, I-10, I-37, U.S. 281, U.S. 90, and U.S. 87, along with many smaller thoroughfares, run diagonally, but not always separately, across these two loops to form its main spokes. For example, U.S. 90, U.S. 87, and I-10 converge for a while in an east–west direction just south of downtown, while U.S. 281, I-35, and I-37 run together on a north–south route to the east; I-10, I-35, and U.S. 87 bond for a bit going north–south to the west of downtown. As a result, you may hear locals referring to something as being "in the loop." That doesn't mean it's privy to insider information, but rather, that it lies within the circumference of I-410. True, this covers a pretty large area, but with the spreading of the city north and west, it's come to mean central.

Among the most major of the minor spokes are Broadway, McCullough, San Pedro, and Blanco, all of which lead north from the city center into the most popular shopping and restaurant areas of town. Fredericksburg goes out to the Medical Center from just northwest of downtown.

Downtown is bounded by I-37 to the east, I-35 to the north and west, and U.S. 90 (which merges with I-10) to the south. Within this area, Durango, Commerce, Market, and Houston are the important east–west thoroughfares. Alamo on the east side and Santa Rosa (which turns into South Laredo) on the west side are the major north–south streets. ***Note:*** A lot of the north–south streets change names midstream (or should I say mid-macadam). That's another reason, besides the confusing one-way streets, to consult a map carefully before attempting to steer your way around downtown.

FINDING AN ADDRESS   Few locals are aware that there's any method to the madness of finding downtown addresses, but in fact directions are actually based on the layout of the first Spanish settlements—back when the San Fernando cathedral was at the center of town. Market is the north–south street divider, and Flores separates east from west. Thus, South St. Mary's becomes North St. Mary's when it crosses Market, with addresses starting from zero at Market going in both directions. North of downtown, San Pedro is the east–west dividing line, although not every street sign reflects this fact.

There are few clear-cut rules like this in loop land, but on its northernmost stretch, Loop 410 divides into east and west at Broadway, and at Bandera Road, it splits into Loop 410 north and south. Keep going far enough south, and I-35 marks yet another boundary between east and west. Knowing this will help you a little in locating an address, and explains why, when you go in a circle around town—you probably won't do this on purpose, unless you're trying to put a baby to sleep (as one friend of mine successfully did)—you'll notice that the directions marked on overhead signs have suddenly completely shifted.

STREET MAPS   The Visitor Information Center (see "Visitor Information," above) and most hotels distribute the free street maps published by the **San Antonio Convention and Visitors Bureau (SACVB).** They mark the main attractions in town and are useful enough as a general reference, especially if you're on foot. They even indicate which downtown streets are one-way—a bonus for drivers. But if you're going to do much navigating around town, you'll need something better. Both **Rand McNally** and **Gousha**'s maps of San Antonio are reliable; you'll find one or the other at most gas stations, convenience stores, drugstores, bookstores, and newsstands.

San Antonio at a Glance

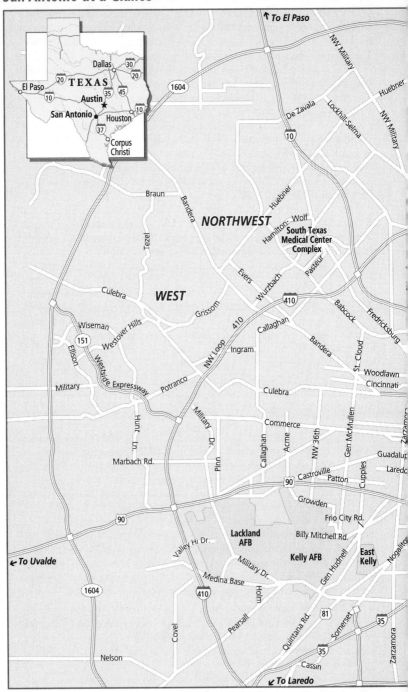

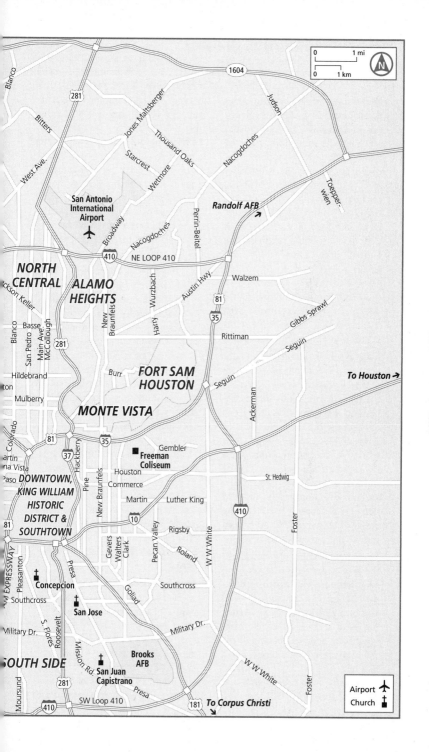

THE NEIGHBORHOODS IN BRIEF

The older areas described here, from downtown through Alamo Heights, are all "in the loop" (410). The Medical Center area in the Northwest lies just outside it, but the rest of the Northwest, as well as North Central and the West, are expanding beyond even Loop 1604.

Downtown Site of San Antonio's three oldest Spanish settlements, this area includes the Alamo and other historic sites, along with the River Walk, the Alamodome, the convention center, the Rivercenter Mall, and many high-rise hotels, restaurants, and shops. It's also the center of commerce and government, so many banks and offices, as well as most city buildings, are located here. Once seedy and largely deserted at night, it has rebounded with a vengeance—a proliferation of bars and clubs catering to younger crowds even resulted in a city ordinance restraining the volume of outdoor noise.

King William The city's first suburb, this historic district directly south of downtown was settled in the mid- to late 1800s by wealthy German merchants who built some of the most beautiful mansions in town. It began to be yuppified in the 1970s, and, at this point, you'd never guess it had ever been allowed to deteriorate. Only two of the area's many impeccably restored homes are generally open to the public, but a number have been turned into bed-and-breakfasts.

Southtown Alamo Street marks the border between King William and Southtown, an adjoining commercial district. Long a depressed area, it's slowly becoming trendy thanks to a Main Street refurbishing project and the opening of the Blue Star arts complex. You'll find a nice mix of Hispanic neighborhood shops and funky coffeehouses and galleries here.

South Side The old, largely Hispanic southeast section of town that begins where Southtown ends (there's no agreed-upon boundary, but I'd say it lies a few blocks beyond the Blue Star arts complex) is home to four of the city's five historic missions. Thus far, it hasn't been experiencing the same gentrification and redevelopment as much of the rest of the city—but that could change when the hike-and-bike trail along a stretch of the San Antonio River here is completed.

Monte Vista Area Immediately northwest of downtown, Monte Vista was established soon after King William by a conglomeration of wealthy cattlemen, politicos, and generals who moved "on to the hill" at the turn of the century. A number of the area's large houses have been split into apartments for students of nearby Trinity University and San Antonio Community College, but many lovely old homes have been restored in the past 30 years. It hasn't reached King William status yet, but this is already a highly desirable (read: pricey) place to live. Monte Vista is close to the once thriving, but now less lively, restaurant and entertainment district along North St. Mary's Street between Josephine and Magnolia known locally as **The Strip.**

Fort Sam Houston Built in 1876 to the northeast of downtown, Fort Sam Houston boasts a number of stunning officers' homes. Much of the working-class neighborhood surrounding Fort Sam is now rundown, but renewed interest in restoring San Antonio's older areas is beginning to have some impact here, too.

Alamo Heights Area In the 1890s, when construction in the area began, Alamo Heights was at the far northern reaches of San Antonio. It has slowly evolved into one of the city's most exclusive neighborhoods, and is now home to wealthy families, expensive shops, and trendy restaurants. **Terrell Hills** to the east, **Olmos Park** to the west, and **Lincoln Heights** to the north are all offshoots of this moneyed area. The latter is home to the Quarry, once just that, but now a ritzy golf course and huge shopping mall. Shops and restaurants are concentrated along two main drags: Broadway and, to a lesser degree, New Braunfels. Most of these neighborhoods share a single zip code ending in the numbers "09"—thus the local term "09ers," referring to the area's affluent residents. The Witte Museum, San Antonio Botanical Gardens, and Brackenridge Park are all in this part of town.

Northwest The mostly characterless neighborhood surrounding the South Texas Medical Center (always just referred to as **Medical Center**), which hosts the majority of San Antonio's hospitals and healthcare facilities, is one of the city's more recently established areas. Many of the homes occupied by the young professionals who have been moving here are condominiums and apartments, and much of the shopping and dining is in strip malls (the trendy, still-expanding Heubner Oaks retail center is an exception). The farther north you go, the nicer the housing

complexes get. The high-end Westin La Cantera resort, the exclusive La Cantera and Dominion residential enclave, several tony golf courses, and the Shops at La Cantera, San Antonio's fanciest new retail center, mark the direction that development is taking in the far northwest part of town, just beyond Six Flags Fiesta Texas and near the public Friedrich Park. It's becoming one of San Antonio's prime growth areas.

North Central San Antonio is inching toward Bulverde and other Hill Country towns via this major corridor of development clustered from Loop 410 north to Loop 1604, east of I-10 and west of I-35, and bisected by U.S. 281. The airport and many developed industrial strips line U.S. 281 in the southern section, but the farther north you go, the more you see the natural beauty of this area, hilly and dotted with small canyons. Recent city codes have motivated developers to retain trees and native plants in their residential communities.

West Although SeaWorld has been out here since the late 1980s, and the Hyatt Regency Hill Country Resort settled here in the early 1990s, other development was comparatively slow in coming. Now the West is booming with new midprice housing developments, strip malls, schools, and businesses. Road building hasn't kept pace with growth, however, so traffic can be a bear.

2 Getting Around

BY PUBLIC TRANSPORTATION

BY BUS San Antonio's public transportation system is visitor-friendly and prices to ride are very reasonable. The 74 **VIA Metropolitan Transit Service** bus routes cost 80¢ for regular lines, with an additional 15¢ charge for transfers, and $1.60 for express buses (15¢ for transfers). You'll need exact change. Call

ⓒ **210/362-2020** for transit information, check the website at **www.viainfo. net**, or stop in one of VIA's many service centers, which you can find by checking the website. The most convenient for visitors is the downtown center, 260 E. Houston St., open Monday to Friday 7am to 6pm, Saturday 9am to 2pm. The new bus no. 7, which travels from downtown to the San Antonio Museum of Art, Japanese Tea Garden, San Antonio Zoo, Witte Museum, Brackenridge Park, and the Botanical Garden, is particularly geared toward tourists. *Tip:* During large festivals such as Fiesta and the Texas Folklife Festival, VIA offers many Park & Ride lots that allow you to leave your car and bus it downtown.

BY STREETCAR   In addition to its bus lines, VIA offers four convenient downtown streetcar routes that cover all the most popular tourist stops. Designed to look like the turn-of-the-century trolleys used in San Antonio until 1933, the streetcars cost 80¢ (exact change required, drivers carry none). The trolleys, which have signs color-coded by route, display their destinations.

BY CAR

If you can avoid driving downtown, by all means do so. The pattern of one-way streets is confusing and parking is extremely limited. It's not that the streets in downtown San Antonio are narrower or more crowded than those in most old city centers, but it's that there's no need to bother when public transportation is so convenient. There's also the matter of the 3-second traffic light (I'm not making this up) many downtown streets have. The continuous stop-and-go can get old pretty fast.

As for highway driving, pay attention. Because of the many convergences of major freeways in the area—described in the "Main Arteries & Streets" section, above—you could suddenly find yourself in an express lane headed somewhere you really don't want to go. Don't let your mind wander; watch signs carefully, and be prepared to make lots of quick lane changes.

Rush hour lasts from about 7:45 to 9am and 4:30 to 6pm Monday through Friday. The crush may not be bad compared with that of Houston or Dallas, but it's getting worse all the time. Because of San Antonio's rapid growth, you can also expect to find major highway construction or repairs going on somewhere in the city at any given time. Feeder roads into Loop 410 will be particularly hard hit in the next few years, especially the Loop 410/U.S. 281 interchanges,

---

One-Day Ticket, Yeah!

A $3 day-tripper pass, good for an entire day of travel on all VIA transportation except express buses, can be purchased at any of the VIA Information Centers (see the "By Bus" section, above). Seniors (62 and over) can also get a discount card there and at several other locations (if downtown isn't convenient, phone the downtown office or check the website to locate the office closest to you). You have to go in person, with proof of age and knowledge of your Social Security number; the picture ID that you receive on the spot will entitle you to ride for 20¢ Monday to Friday from 9am to 3pm and all day Saturday and Sunday, and for 40¢ before 9am and after 3pm, with a 7¢ transfer fee at all times.

where construction starts in spring 2005 and is not scheduled to be completed until 2008. For the gory details, log on to the Texas Department of Transportation's website at **www.dot.state.tx.us**.

RENTALS   **Advantage** (ⓒ 800/777-5500; www.advantagerentacar.com), **Alamo** (ⓒ 800/327-9633; www.alamo.com), **Avis** (ⓒ 800/331-1212; www.avis.com), **Budget** (ⓒ 800/527-0700; www.budget.com), **Dollar** (ⓒ 800/800-4000; www.dollarcar.com), **Enterprise** (ⓒ 800/325-8007; www.enterprise.com), **Hertz** (ⓒ 800/654-3131; www.hertz.com), **National** (ⓒ 800/CAR-RENT; www.nationalcar.com), and **Thrifty** (ⓒ 800/367-2277; www.thrifty.com) all have desks at both of the airport terminals. **Hertz** is also represented downtown at the Marriott Rivercenter at Bowie and Commerce (ⓒ 210/225-3676). And in case you were wondering, yes, the Alamo car-rental company got its start right here in San Antonio.

Almost all the major car-rental companies have their own discount programs. Your rate will often depend on the organizations to which you belong, the dates of travel, and the length of your stay. Some companies give discounts to AAA members, for example, and some have special deals in conjunction with various airlines or telephone companies. Off-season rates are likely to be lower, and prices are sometimes reduced on weekends (or midweek). Call as far in advance as possible to book a car, and always ask about specials.

On top of the standard rental prices, other optional charges apply to most car rentals. The Collision Damage Waiver (CDW), which requires you to pay for damage to the car in a collision, is illegal in some states but not Texas. It is, however, covered by many credit card companies. Check with yours before you go so you can avoid paying this hefty fee (as much as $20 a day).

The car-rental companies also offer additional liability insurance (if you harm others in an accident), personal accident insurance (if you harm yourself or your passengers), and personal effects insurance (if your luggage is stolen from your car). If you have insurance on your car at home, you are probably covered for most of these "unlikelihoods." If your own insurance doesn't cover rentals, or if you don't have auto insurance, you should consider the additional coverage (keeping in mind that the car-rental companies are liable for certain base amounts).

As with other aspects of planning your trip, using the Internet can make comparison shopping for a car rental much easier. You can check rates at most of the major agencies' Web sites. Plus, all the major travel sites—**Travelocity** (www.travelocity.com), **Expedia** (www.expedia.com), **Orbitz** (www.orbitz.com), and **Smarter Living** (www.smarterliving.com), for example—have search engines that can dig up discounted car-rental rates. Just enter the car size you want, the pickup and return dates, and the location, and the server returns a price. You can even make the reservation through any of these sites.

PARKING   Parking meters are not plentiful in the heart of downtown, but you can find some on the streets near the River Walk and on Broadway. The cost is $1 per hour (which is also the time limit) in San Fernando Plaza and near the courthouse, 75¢ in other locations. There are some very inexpensive (2 hr. for $1) meters at the outskirts of town but the real trick is to find one. If you don't observe the laws, you'll be quickly ticketed. Note that, although very few signs inform you of this fact, parking at meters is free after 6pm Monday through Saturday and free all day Sunday except during special events.

Tips **Free Parking**

If you're staying for only a short time, consider leaving your car in the Rivercenter Mall garage and getting your ticket validated at one of the shops. You don't have to buy anything, and you'll have 2 hours of free parking. This is only a good idea, however, if you have an iron will or are allergic to shopping; otherwise, you could end up spending a lot more than at a parking garage.

Except during Fiesta or other major events, you shouldn't have a problem finding a parking lot or garage for your car. Rates run from $6 to $8 per day, though the closer you get to the Alamo and the River Walk, the more expensive they become. Prices tend to go up during special events and summer weekends, so a parking lot that ordinarily charges $6 a day is likely to charge $9 or more.

DRIVING RULES   Right turns on red are permitted after a full stop. Left turns on red are also allowed, but only if you're going from a one-way street onto another one-way street. Seat belts and child restraint seats are mandatory.

BY RIVER TAXI

Yanaguana Cruises (see "Organized Tours," in chapter 6) runs the **Rio Trans Taxi Service** (© **800/417-4139** or 210/244-5700; www.sarivercruise.com/rio trans.htm), which operates daily from 9am to 9pm. Its 39 pickup locations are marked by Rio Trans signs with black-and-yellow checker flags. You buy your tickets once you board. At $3.50 one-way, $10 for an all-day pass, or $25 for a 3-day pass, it's more expensive than ground transport, but it's a treat.

BY TAXI

Cabs are available outside the airport, near the Greyhound and Amtrak terminals (only when a train is due, however), and at most major downtown hotels, but they're next to impossible to hail on the street; most of the time, you'll need to phone for one in advance. The best of the taxi companies in town (and also the largest, since it represents the consolidation of two of the majors) is **Yellow-Checker Cab** (© **210/222-2222**), which has an excellent record of turning up when promised. See "By Plane," in the "Arriving" section earlier in this chapter, for rates. Most cabbies impose a minimum of $8 for trips from the airport, $3 for rides downtown.

ON FOOT

Downtown San Antonio is a treat for walkers, who can perambulate from one tourist attraction to another or stroll along a beautifully landscaped river. Traffic lights even have buttons to push to make sure the lights stay green long enough for pedestrians to cross without putting their lives in peril. Jaywalking is a ticketable offense, but it's rarely enforced.

FAST FACTS: **San Antonio**

Airport See "Arriving," earlier in this chapter.

Area Code The telephone area code in San Antonio is **210**.

Business Hours Banks are open Monday to Friday 9am to 4pm, Saturday 9am to 1pm. Drive-up windows are open 7am to 6pm Monday to Friday, and 9am to noon on Saturday. Office hours are generally weekdays from 9am to 5pm. Shops tend to be open from 9 or 10am until 5:30 or 6pm Monday to Saturday, with shorter hours on Sunday. Most malls are open Monday to Saturday from 10am to 9pm, Sunday from noon to 6pm.

Car Rentals See "Getting Around," above.

Climate See "When to Go," in chapter 2.

Dentist To find a dentist near you in town, contact the San Antonio District Dental Society, 3355 Cherry Ridge, Suite 214 (© **210/732-1264**).

Doctor For a referral, contact the Bexar County Medical Society at 6243 W. Ih 10, Suite 600 (© **210/301-4368**; www.bcms.org), Monday through Friday from 8am to 5pm.

Driving Rules See "Getting Around," above.

Drugstores Most branches of CVS (formerly Eckerd) and Walgreens, the major chain pharmacies in San Antonio, are open late Monday through Saturday. There's a CVS downtown at 211 Losoya/River Walk (© **210/224-9293**). Call © **800/925-4733** to find the Walgreens nearest you; punch in the area code and the first three digits of the number you're phoning from and you'll be directed to the closest branch.

Embassies/Consulates See "Fast Facts: For the International Traveler," in Appendix B.

Emergencies For police, fire, or medical emergencies, dial © **911.**

Holidays See "Calendar of Events" in chapter 2.

Hospitals The main downtown hospital is Baptist Medical Center, 111 Dallas St. (© **210/297-7000**). Christus Santa Rosa Health Care Corp., 333 N. Santa Rosa St. (© **210/704-2011**), is also downtown. Contact the San Antonio Medical Foundation (© **210/614-3724**) for information about other medical facilities in the city.

Hot Lines Contact the National Youth Crisis Hot Line at © **800/448-4663**; Rape Crisis Hot Line at © **210/349-7273**; Child Abuse Hot Line at © **800/252-5400**; Mental Illness Crisis Hot Line at © **210/227-4357**; Bexar County Adult Abuse Hot Line at © **800/252-5400**; and Poison Control Center at © **800/764-7661.**

Information See "Visitor Information," earlier in this chapter.

Internet You can check your e-mail at the various FedEx Kinko's around town. Check the Yellow Pages for the location nearest you. All the Starbucks in San Antonio have wireless connectivity with T-Mobile.

Libraries San Antonio's magnificent main library is located downtown at 600 Soledad Plaza (© **210/207-2500**). See "More Attractions," in chapter 6, for details.

Liquor Laws The legal drinking age in Texas is 21. Under-age drinkers can legally imbibe as long as they stay within sight of their legal-age parents or spouses, but they need to be prepared to show proof of the relationship. Open containers are prohibited in public and in vehicles. Liquor laws are strictly enforced; if you're concerned, check www.tabc.state.tx.us for the entire Texas alcoholic beverage code. Bars close at 2am.

Lost Property Be sure to tell all of your credit card companies the minute you discover your wallet has been lost or stolen, and file a report at the nearest police precinct. Your credit card company or insurer may require a police report number or record of the loss. Most credit card companies have an emergency toll-free number to call if your card is lost or stolen. They may be able to wire you a cash advance immediately or deliver an emergency credit card in a day or two. Visa's U.S. emergency number is © 800/847-2911 or 410/581-9994. American Express cardholders and traveler's check holders should call © 800/221-7282. MasterCard holders should call © 800/307-7309 or 636/722-7111. For other credit cards, call the toll-free number directory at © 800/555-1212.

If you need emergency cash over the weekend when all banks and American Express offices are closed, you can have money wired to you via **Western Union** (© 800/325-6000; www.westernunion.com).

Identity theft or fraud are potential complications of losing your wallet, especially if you've lost your driver's license along with your cash and credit cards. Notify the major credit-reporting bureaus immediately. Placing a fraud alert on your records may protect you against liability for criminal activity. The three major U.S. credit-reporting agencies are **Equifax** (© 800/766-0008; www.equifax.com), **Experian** (© 888/397-3742; www. experian.com), and **TransUnion** (© 800/680-7289; www.transunion.com). Finally, if you've lost all forms of photo ID call your airline and explain the situation; they might allow you to board the plane if you have a copy of your passport or birth certificate and a copy of the police report you've filed.

Maps See "City Layout," earlier in this chapter.

Newspapers & Magazines The *San Antonio Express-News* is the only mainstream source of news in town. See "Visitor Information," earlier in this chapter, for magazine recommendations.

Police Call © 911 in an emergency. The Sheriff Department's 24-hour nonemergency number is © 210/335-6000, and the Texas Highway Patrol can be reached at © 210/531-2220.

Safety The crime rate in San Antonio has gone down in recent years, and there's a strong police presence downtown (in fact, both the transit authority and the police department have bicycle patrols); as a result, muggings, pickpocketings, and purse snatchings in the area are rare. Still, use common sense as you would anywhere else: Walk only in well-lit, well-populated streets. Also, it's generally not a good idea to stroll south of Durango Avenue after dark.

Smoking Smoking is prohibited in all public buildings and common public areas (that includes hotel lobbies, museums, enclosed malls, and so on). It's permitted in bars or enclosed bar areas of restaurants, on designated restaurant patios, and in smoking sections of restaurants that comply with city codes.

Taxes The sales tax here is 8%, and the city surcharge on hotel rooms increases to a whopping 16.75%.

Taxis See "Getting Around," earlier in this chapter.

Time Zone San Antonio is on Central Standard Time, 1 hour behind New York and 2 hours ahead of Los Angeles. Texas observes daylight saving time.

Useful Phone Numbers For transit information, call © **210/362-2020**; call © **210/226-3232** for time and temperature.

4

Where to Stay in San Antonio

You don't have to leave your lodgings to go sightseeing in San Antonio: This city has the highest concentration of historic hotels in Texas. Even low-end hotel chains are reclaiming old buildings—many examples are covered in this chapter—so don't judge a place by its affiliation. Most of these, as well as other more recently built luxury accommodations, are in the downtown area, which is where you'll likely want to be whether you're here on pleasure or business. Prices in this prime location tend to be high, especially for hotels on the river, but you'll generally get your money's worth. And if you're willing to forgo your own wheels for a bit, you'll economize by eliminating car-rental and parking fees. Most of the city's tourist attractions are within walking distance or are accessible by efficient and inexpensive public transportation, and many restaurants favored by locals are within an inexpensive cab ride from downtown.

The good news for visitors, though not for the local economy, is that there's likely to be a glut of downtown hotel rooms soon. New lodgings seem to be cropping up everywhere you look. As a result, rates are likely to get more and more competitive.

In recent years, a number of the old mansions in the King William and Monte Vista historic districts—both close to downtown—have been converted into bed-and-breakfasts; several of them are reviewed in this chapter. For information about additional bed-and-breakfasts in these areas and in other neighborhoods around the city,

check out www.sanantoniobb.org, the website of the **San Antonio Bed & Breakfast Association.** Several of San Antonio's inns can also be booked via **Historic Accommodations of Texas,** P.O. Box 203, Vanderpool, TX 78885 (© **800/HAT-0368;** www.hat.org).

San Antonio also has two top-notch destination resorts on the outskirts of town, the Hyatt Regency Hill Country Resort and the Westin La Cantera Resort. They're great places to hole up and relax and maybe play some golf, with sightseeing as a secondary potential goal.

Expect most downtown hotels to fall into the Very Expensive or Expensive range, especially if they sit right on the river. With a few notable exceptions, detailed below, only chain hotels on the outskirts of downtown tend to be Moderate or Inexpensive. Pricewise, you'll do better if you stay in a B&B in a historic area near downtown (the Monte Vista neighborhood gives especially good value), so you won't have to give up many amenities. Although they're not formally called concierges, B&B owners and innkeepers also do far more to guide their guests around town than employees given that title in many large city hotels. You can also expect B&Bs to be able to provide fax and other business services, and these days most offer high-speed and/or wireless Internet connection.

With a few other exceptions, detailed here, the vast majority of the other lodgings around town are low-priced chains. The most convenient

Deal Well, Sleep Well

Don't eliminate a choice because of its price category alone. The prices listed here are the hotel's "rack rates"—the room rate charged without any discount—and you can almost always do better. The San Antonio Convention and Visitors Bureau's annual SAVE (San Antonio Vacation Experience) promotion features discounts on hotel rooms (more than 50 properties participate) as well as on dining and entertainment. Some bed-and-breakfasts and hotels offer better rates to those who book for at least 4 days, although a week is usually the minimum. Even though most leisure travelers visit in summer, rooms tend to be less expensive then; in general, rates are highest from November through April, when conventions converge on the town. Rates also are at their highest when the city's many festivals cause a run on rooms.

But even during peak times, hotel rates vary widely. Some hotels in San Antonio host business clients during the week, whereas others cater to tourists who come on the weekend, so you never know when a property is not fully booked and willing to give you a good deal. In addition, ask about any discounts you can think of—corporate, senior citizen, military, Internet, AAA, entertainment/hotel coupon books, your Uncle Morty's high-school friendship with the manager—and about packages such as family, romance, or deals that include meals or sightseeing tours. *Bottom line: Always ask for the lowest-priced room with the most perks available.* Reservation agents are eager to sell rooms, so you shouldn't have a problem getting a good deal. See also chapter 2 for information about booking rooms online, p. 21.

are clustered in the northwest near the Medical Center and in the north central area, around the airport. For a full alphabetical listing of the accommodations in the city, mapped by area and including rate ranges as well as basic amenities, phone the **San Antonio Convention and Visitors Bureau** (© **800/447-3372**) and request a lodging guide. The "Accommodations" section of www.SanAntonioVisit.com is a good resource too.

Wherever you decide to stay, try to book as far in advance as possible—especially if the property is located downtown. And don't even think about coming to town during Fiesta (the third week in Apr) if you haven't reserved a room 6 months in advance.

In the following reviews, price categories are based on rates for a double room in peak season, and don't factor in the 16.75% room tax.

1 Downtown

VERY EXPENSIVE

Hotel Valencia Riverwalk   It's easy to see why the Valencia is considered the hottest new lodging in town. The rooms are super chic—lots of white, retro lamps, and such tongue-in-cheek touches as the faux mink throw on the bed—and very techie-friendly. The on-site **Vbar and Citrus** restaurant, serving excellent Mediterranean-inspired food, are übertrendy. And, in the abstract, the panoply of colors and sounds (a splashing waterfall, music wafting through the halls) that you encounter as you enter the hotel is stimulating. But the entryway, on a busy street with a limited area for luggage (or vehicle) drop-off, is a tad *too* stimulating (as in chaotic), whether or not the remote Palm Pilot check-in is in operation. The hallways leading to the guest quarters—the priciest offering river views from narrow balconies—are narrow and dark, and the rooms themselves have too many individual dimmer switches and lighting devices, and not enough space. If you're looking for style tips, the Valencia is a great lab. But if you're regular folk seeking a stress-free getaway, this may not be your place.

150 E. Houston St. (at St. Mary's), San Antonio, TX 78205. ✆ **866/842-0100** or 210/227-9700. Fax 210/227-9701. www.hotelvalencia.com. 213 units. $299–$389 double, suites from $559. Leisure, corporate, and Internet rates available. AE, DC, DISC, MC, V. Valet parking $25. **Amenities:** Restaurant; bar; exercise room; spa; concierge; business center; wi-fi throughout public areas; 24-hr room service; same-day laundry/dry cleaning. *In room:* A/C, TV w/pay movies, dataport, high-speed Internet access, minibar, hair dryer, iron.

Hyatt Regency San Antonio on the River Walk ✿ There's something stimulating about all that glass and steel rising from this hotel's lobby, where the Hyatt's signature cage elevators ascend and descend the sky-lit atrium. Maybe it's airiness that determines the difference between a hotel that's bustling and one that just feels overcrowded? This one's definitely bustling, with both business travelers and families who enjoy its convenience to all the downtown attractions. You couldn't be closer to the river's hopping South Bank section, and having a bit of said river running through the lobby adds to the dramatic effect. A $16 million makeover, completed in late 2004, gave the rooms a distinctly Texan, earthy, elegant look (the Texas part comes in with the tooled leather accents), and added super-comfortable bedding. And you've got easy access to the New Orleans–oriented bar **The Landing,** longtime home to the Dixieland jazz of Jim Cullum and his band (see chapter 8).

123 Losoya St. (at College St.), San Antonio, TX 78205. ✆ **800/233-1234** or 210/222-1234. Fax 210/227-4925. www.sanantonioregency.hyatt.com. 632 units. $269–$349 double; $328–$768 suite. AE, DC, DISC, MC, V. Self-parking $15; valet parking $21. **Amenities:** Restaurant; 2 bars; outdoor pool; health club; concierge; business center; wi-fi in lobby; shopping arcade; limited room service; dry cleaning; club-level rooms. *In room:* A/C, TV w/pay movies, dataport, high-speed Internet access ($11 per day), minibar, coffeemaker, hair dryer, iron.

La Mansión del Río ✿✿ This lushly landscaped Spanish hacienda–style hotel—converted from a 19th-century seminary in 1968—not only oozes character, but is also convenient. It sits right on the Paseo del Río, just a block from the Majestic Theater. Moorish arches, Mexican tile, a central patio, wrought-iron balconies, and antique pieces in every nook and cranny combine to create a low-glitz, high-tone Mediterranean atmosphere. The layout is a bit mazelike—the directionally challenged, like me, may find themselves wandering in circles—but staff discretion and a willingness to cater to special requests make this hotel the pick for many of San Antonio's high-profile visitors (their entourages no doubt steer them in the right direction).

Guest rooms are equally low profile and high-toned, with rich green, gold, and burgundy draperies and bedspreads complementing the rough-hewn beamed ceilings, and brick walls. The more expensive quarters boast balconies overlooking the River Walk, but the interior courtyard views are fine, too. The hotel's dining room, **Las Canarias,** serves up a terrific river view with its excellent American regional cuisine (see chapter 5 for the full review). The opening of a sister property, the Watermark Hotel (see below), just across the river means easy access to that hotel's excellent spa. Guests at La Mansión can also pay an

Downtown San Antonio Accommodations

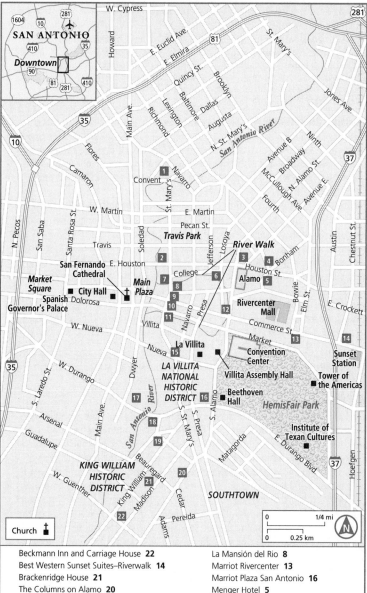

Beckmann Inn and Carriage House **22**	La Mansión del Rio **8**
Best Western Sunset Suites–Riverwalk **14**	Marriot Rivercenter **13**
Brackenridge House **21**	Marriot Plaza San Antonio **16**
The Columns on Alamo **20**	Menger Hotel **5**
Crockett Hotel **4**	Noble Inns **19**
Drury Inn & Suites San Antonio Riverwalk **9**	The O'Brien Historic Hotel **14**
Emily Morgan **3**	Ogé House Inn on the River Walk **18**
Havana Riverwalk Inn **1**	Riverwalk Inn **17**
Homewood Suites by Hilton **10**	Riverwalk Vista **12**
Hotel Valencia Riverwalk **2**	The Watermark Hotel **7**
Hyatt Regency San Antonio on the River Walk **6**	Westin Riverwalk Inn **11**

extra $15 for privileges at the Watermark's gym, whirlpool, and pool (or free with a spa treatment).

112 College St. (between St. Mary's and Navarro), San Antonio, TX 78205. (C) **800/292-7300** or 210/518-1000. Fax 210/226-0389. www.lamansion.com. 337 units. $249–$329 double; $575–$1,949 suite. AE, DC, DISC, MC, V. Valet parking $25. Pets under 20 lb. accepted for $25 per pet per day. **Amenities:** Restaurant; outdoor pool; fitness room; concierge; business center; 24-hr. room service; dry cleaning; complimentary transportation around downtown business district. *In room:* A/C, TV w/pay movies, dataport, high-speed Internet access, minibar, coffeemaker, hair dryer, iron.

Marriott Rivercenter 🐾   Serious retail hounds will find heaven in this glitzy conventioneer high-rise, where they can shop more than 100 Rivercenter emporiums until they're ready to drop, and then collapse back into their hotel rooms without ever leaving the mall. Sightseers will be happy here, too, with a cruise along the River Walk departing from the mall's downstairs "dock," and the Alamo and HemisFair Park are just a few blocks away.

Convenience is definitely the goal here—free washers and dryers on the same floor as the health club let you bicycle while your clothes cycle. Guest rooms have an earth-toned, simple elegance, and many afford spectacular River Walk or city views. If you find all this convenience—and the bustle that goes along with it—a bit overwhelming, an option is to stay at the smaller Marriott Riverwalk across the street. This slightly older and less expensive sister hotel has equally comfortable Southwest-style rooms, and its guests have access to all the facilities of the Rivercenter.

101 Bowie St. (at Commerce St.), San Antonio, TX 78205. (C) **800/228-9290** or 210/223-1000. Fax 210/223-6239. www.marriotthotels.com. 1,001 units. $314 double; suites from $450. AE, DC, DISC, MC, V. Self-parking $12; valet parking $17. Pets under 20 lb. permitted; $25 deposit required. **Amenities:** 3 restaurants; indoor pool; outdoor pool; health club; Jacuzzi; sauna; concierge; car-rental desk; business center; wi-fi; 24-hr. room service; babysitting; dry cleaning; shoeshine stand; club-level rooms; ATM. *In room:* A/C, TV/w pay movies, dataport, high-speed Internet access; coffeemaker, hair dryer, iron.

The Watermark Hotel 🐾🐾🐾   The latest entry into the River Walk luxury hotel sweepstakes, the Watermark is a big-time winner. The Western-style lobby, which pays tribute to the historic L. Frank Saddlery Building, which once occupied this site, is high-toned yet welcoming. And the rooms are some of the nicest in downtown (make that the city). Bright, with high ceilings, they've got a Texas-meets-Tokyo elegance, their leather and wrought-iron accents balanced by a Zen-like sea-foam green and off-white color scheme; the marble bathrooms offer jetted tubs. And, outside of the resorts on the outskirts of town, this hotel has the city's best spa and beauty salon—not to mention **Pesca,** arguably San Antonio's premiere seafood restaurant (see chapter 5 for the full review).

And that's not even getting into the service. No stressful encounters with the front desk when you arrive. Instead, you're escorted to your room—where your minifridge has been stocked with goodies that you requested in advance—to complete the check-in process. What with the spa, the soothing guest quarters, and the staff attentiveness, you'd have to have the personality of Woody Allen not to relax in this place.

212 W. Crockett St. (at St. Mary's), San Antonio, TX 78205. (C) **866/605-1212** or 210/396-5800. Fax 210/226-0389. www.watermarkhotel.com. 99 units. $300–$400 double; $650–$1,250 suite. AE, DC, DISC, MC, V. Valet parking $25. **Amenities:** Restaurant; cafe; outdoor pool; whirlpool; health club; spa; concierge; business center; salon; 24-hr. room service; dry cleaning. *In room:* A/C, TV w/pay movies, dataport, high-speed Internet access, minifridge, coffeemaker, hair dryer, iron, safe.

Westin Riverwalk Inn 🐾🐾 *Kids*   The recycling of downtown historic buildings into hotels is an admirable trend, but there's also something to be said for new construction—at least when it's done right. Opened at the very end of the last century, this ultraluxe property was designed to blend in architecturally with the older structures that flank it on this (relatively) quiet section of the river bend, but its clean, elegant lines are attuned to 21st-century sensibilities.

From the lobby to the rooms, earth tones balance with Spanish colonial accents to create an atmosphere that's soothing without being bland. Built-from-scratch also means incorporating the latest amenities, including Westin's signature "Heavenly Beds." Perhaps in a nod to its many high-end Latin American business visitors, the hotel has recently introduced two tasty traditions: a large bowl of Venezuelan chocolate at the check-in desk and, on Tuesday through Saturday afternoons, Le Marienda—a kind of Mexican high tea, featuring hot chocolate, cookies, and other light refreshments (it's free to hotel guests). This Westin has also nicely incorporated several kid-friendly features (see "Family-Friendly Hotels" on p. 55).

420 W. Market St. (at Navarro), San Antonio, TX 78205. ⓒ 800/WESTIN-1 or 210/224-6500. Fax 210/444-6000. www.westin.com/riverwalk. 473 units. $359–$389 double; $419–$479 suite. AE, DC, DISC, MC, V. Self-parking $15; valet parking $23. **Amenities:** Restaurant; lounge; outdoor pool; health club; sauna; concierge; business center; 24-hr. room service; dry cleaning. *In room:* A/C, TV w/pay movies, dataport, high-speed Internet access, minibar, coffeemaker, hair dryer, iron, safe.

EXPENSIVE

Emily Morgan ★★ *Value*   You know what they say about judging a book by its cover? Located just a musket shot from the Alamo, the Emily Morgan was named after the mulatto slave mistress of Mexican general Santa Anna, who was reputed to have spied on him for the Texas independence fighters. And it resides in a 1926 Gothic Revival–style medical arts center, replete with gargoyles, said to have been placed there to help the doctors ward off diseases. But there's little to suggest either battlefields or things medicinal inside. As a result of an extreme makeover in the early 2000s, the rooms have a light, contemporary feel, designed to appeal to a young and affluent crowd who go for the pared-down look popularized by the W chain. Any industrial chic coldness is offset by lots of dark, burnished wood and such touches as a lit votive candle at turndown. For all its perks—250-count sheets, Aveda bath products, CD players, 27-inch TVs, and (in 115 of the rooms) jetted tubs—this place is considerably less expensive than many comparable hotels on the river, and its combination of hipness, luxury, and history is hard to beat.

705 E. Houston St. (at Ave. E), San Antonio, TX 78205. ⓒ 800/824-6674 or 210/225-8486. Fax 210/225-5100. www.emilymorganhotel.com. 177 units. $189–$229 double; $259–$289 suite. Corporate, promotional rates available. AE, DC, DISC, MC, V. Valet parking $16. **Amenities:** Restaurant; outdoor pool; exercise room; Jacuzzi; sauna; concierge; wi-fi throughout public areas; 24-hr. room service; dry cleaning. *In room:* A/C, TV w/pay movies, dataport, high-speed Internet access, minifridge, coffeemaker, hair dryer, iron.

Marriott Plaza San Antonio ★   Pheasants and peacocks stroll the beautifully landscaped grounds of this gracious hotel, located across from HemisFair Park, close to La Villita, and just north of the King William district. Four 19th-century buildings that were saved from HemisFair's bulldozer in 1968 were later incorporated into the Plaza complex. Three are used for intimate conference centers—the initialing ceremony for the North American Free Trade Agreement was held in one of them—and the fourth houses a health club and spa. This is also one of the few hotels in town that has lit tennis courts—not to mention a croquet lawn.

The service is old-world style, too. The staff is efficient and friendly, and you're pampered with such touches as a complimentary shoeshine and evening turndowns with bottled water and filled ice buckets. And while the old-world-style facilities had begun to look just plain old in recent years, a $6-million revamp of the public areas and rooms was completed in March 2005.

555 S. Alamo St. (at Durango), San Antonio, TX 78205. © 800/228-9290 or 210/229-1000. Fax 210/229-1418. www.plazasa.com. 251 units. $169–$274 double, suites from $420. AE, DC, DISC, MC, V. Self-parking $15; valet parking $21. Pets up to 20 lb. accepted with $25 deposit. **Amenities:** Restaurant; lounge; outdoor pool; tennis courts; croquet garden; health club; spa; Jacuzzi; bikes (free); concierge; business center; wi-fi throughout; limited room service; massage; babysitting; dry cleaning; complimentary shoeshine. *In room:* A/C, TV w/pay movies, dataport, high-speed Internet access, coffeemaker, hair dryer, iron.

Menger Hotel 🌟 In the late 19th century, no one who was anyone would consider staying anywhere but the Menger, which opened its doors in 1859 and has never closed them. Ulysses S. Grant, Sarah Bernhardt, and Oscar Wilde were among those who walked—or, rumor has it, in the case of Robert E. Lee, rode a horse—through the halls, ballrooms, and gardens. Successfully combining the original, restored building with myriad additions, the Menger now takes up an entire city block. The hotel's location is terrific—smack between the Alamo and the Rivercenter Mall, a block from the River Walk, with the tourist information office on the ground floor. And its public areas, particularly the Victorian Lobby, are gorgeous. The **Menger Bar** (see chapter 8) is one of San Antonio's great historic taverns, and while nearly every historic hotel in town promotes a ghost, this one claims to have no fewer than 32. The Menger also has a small spa, still a relative rarity in San Antonio hotels.

Ask for one of the recently refurbished rooms, as those that haven't been redone are somewhat tired. Decor ranges from ornate 19th-century to modern. If you want one of the antiques-filled Victorian rooms, be sure to request it when you book.

204 Alamo Plaza (at Crockett St.), San Antonio, TX 78205. © 800/345-9285 or 210/223-4361. Fax 210/228-0022. www.historicmenger.com. 316 units. $195 double; $275–$495 suite. AE, DC, DISC, MC, V. Valet parking $19. **Amenities:** Restaurant; bar; outdoor pool; fitness room; spa; Jacuzzi; shopping arcade; limited room service; dry cleaning. *In room:* A/C, TV w/pay movies, dataport, high-speed Internet access, fridge rental ($25), hair dryer, iron.

Riverwalk Vista 🌟 *Value* Intimacy, history, amenities—and a teddy bear to sleep with. That's a tough combination to beat. The 17 high-ceiling rooms in the 1883 Dullnig building are extremely attractive, with polished pine floors, large windows, and clean-lined reproduction antiques. They come with all the modern fittings—flatscreen TVs with DVD players, to name just one—as well as such posh touches as plush robes, makeup mirrors, and umbrellas. The great location, near the River Walk, Alamo, and other top downtown sights, is also this place's drawback, since you have to fend for yourself when it comes to parking, and it's not exactly serene at night around here. But you're far better off without wheels in this area anyway, and each room comes equipped with a noise machine. If you're a really light sleeper, this hotel's charm, combined with amenities that you usually get only in pricier spots, makes it well worth an investment in earplugs.

262 Losoya (at Commerce St.), San Antonio, TX 78205. © 866/898-4782 or 210/223-3200. www.riverwalk vista.com. 17 units. $150–$190 double; $180–$250 suite; midweek convention discounts often available. Rates include Continental breakfast. AE, DC, DISC, MC, V. **Amenities:** Passes to nearby fitness center, business center. *In room:* A/C, TV/DVD player, dataport, high-speed Internet access, minifridge, coffeemaker, hair dryer, iron, safe.

MODERATE

Crockett Hotel 🌟 *Value* This hotel comes by its name honestly, unlike many of the places that bank on Davy Crockett's moniker. The famed Alamo hero definitely walked the land on which the hotel rose in 1909, as it—the land, that is—served as the Alamo's battleground. The property is a bit of a hybrid, consisting of the original historical landmark building (expanded in 1927) and several low-slung, motel-style units that surround what may be downtown's nicest swimming pool and a tropical landscaped courtyard. Rooms in both sections of the hotel are consistently attractive, with lots of vibrant Southwest colors and allusions to Texas history (regional artwork, pine beds with Lone Star headboards, and the like). And the rates—discounted for every imaginable reason—are quite good for this prime location between the Alamo and the Rivercenter Mall, and right near several River Walk entrances.

320 Bonham St. (at Crockett St.), San Antonio, TX 78205. © 800/292-1050 or 210/225-6500. Fax 210/225-7418. www.crocketthotel.com. 204 units. Rooms $135–$145; suites from $175. Various discounts (including Internet booking) and specials. AE, DC, DISC, MC, V. Valet parking $19. Pets accepted; $100 deposit required ($50 refundable). **Amenities:** Restaurant; lounge; unheated outdoor pool and hot tub; limited room service; coin-op laundry; same-day dry cleaning (weekdays). *In room:* A/C, TV w/pay movies, dataport, high-speed Internet access, coffeemaker, hair dryer, iron.

Drury Inn & Suites San Antonio Riverwalk (Value)

One of San Antonio's more recent River Walk conversions, the one-time Petroleum Commerce Building is now a comfortable modern lodging. The polished marble floors and chandeliers in the lobby and the high ceilings and ornate window treatments in the guest rooms hearken back to a grander era, also evoked in business-traveler perks such as free hot breakfasts, free evening cocktails and snacks, free local phone calls, and 1 hour of free long distance per day. Guests also appreciate the on-premises **Texas Land & Cattle Co.** steakhouse, located on the River Walk level—it's a reasonably priced place to schmooze clients—as well as the 24-hour business center. Anyone who wants to economize on meals will also like the fact that many of these attractive Southwest-style rooms are equipped with refrigerators and microwaves.

201 N. St. Mary's St. (at Commerce St.), San Antonio, TX 78205. © 800/DRURY-INN or 210/212-5200. Fax 210/352-9939. www.druryinn.com. 150 units. $129–$154 double; $159–$185 suite. AE, DC, DISC, MC, V. Self-parking $10. Small pets accepted. **Amenities:** Restaurant; outdoor pool; exercise room; Jacuzzi; wi-fi in lobby; dry cleaning. *In room:* A/C, TV, dataport, high-speed Internet access, fridge and microwave (in king rooms and suites), coffeemaker, hair dryer, iron.

Havana Riverwalk Inn ★

Though no longer the River Walk's newest new thing, this is still a pretty hot bed stop. Decked out to suggest travelers' lodgings from the 1920s, this intimate inn—built in 1914 in Mediterranean Revival style—oozes character. All the guest quarters are delightfully different, with a safari hat covering a temperature control gauge here, an old photograph perched over a toilet paper roll there, gauzy curtains draped on a canopy bed, wooden louvers on the windows, and so on. Touches like fresh flowers and bottled water add to the charm, and modern amenities such as irons have not been ignored. Not all rooms have closets, however, so be prepared to have your clothes (ironed or not) hanging in public view if you plan to invite anyone to your room. Singles will absolutely want to hit the hotel's happening cigar bar, **Club Cohiba.**

1015 Navarro (between St. Mary's and Martin sts.), San Antonio, TX 78205. © 888/224-2008 or 210/222-2008. Fax 210/222-2717. www.havanariverwalkinn.com. 28 units. $109–$209 double; $249–$599 suite. AE, DC, DISC, MC, V. Self-parking $10. Children ages 15 and over only accepted. **Amenities:** Restaurant; bar; concierge; business center; secretarial services; limited room service; dry cleaning. *In room:* A/C, TV, dataport, hair dryer, iron.

Homewood Suites by Hilton ★ (Kids)

Occupying the former San Antonio Drug Company building (built in 1919), this all-suites hotel is a good downtown deal. Located on a quiet stretch of the river, it's convenient to west-side attractions such as Market Square and located only a few more blocks away from the Alamo. In-room amenities such as microwave ovens, refrigerators with ice makers, and dishwashers appeal to business travelers and families alike; the dining area can double as a work space, and there's a sleeper sofa in each suite as well as two TVs with VCRs—that means fewer squabbles over TV shows and movies. The decor is a cut above that of most chains, with Lone Star–design headboards, wood desks and bureaus, and attractive Southwestern bedspreads and drapes. Some suites even have river views.

432 W. Market St. (at St. Mary's St.), San Antonio, TX 78205. (C) **800/CALL-HOME** or 210/222-1515. Fax 210/222-1575. www.homewood-suites.com. 146 units. $149–$249 suite. Rates include breakfast, and (Mon–Fri) afternoon drinks and snacks. AE, DC, DISC, MC, V. Valet parking $20. **Amenities:** Outdoor pool; fitness center; Jacuzzi; concierge; business center; wi-fi in lobby; coin-op washer/dryers; dry cleaning. In room: A/C, TV/VCR w/pay movies, dataport, high-speed Internet access, full kitchens, coffeemaker, hair dryer, iron.

O'Brien Historic Hotel 𝒢 (Value)   This hotel is not all that historic—the 1904 building it occupies was gutted, so only the facade is old—but who cares when you've got attractive rooms with luxury appointments for very reasonable prices? Rich greens, gold, and gilt touches—as well as nice carpeting—lend a richness to the guest quarters, as do the upscale bed and bath linens, robes, CD players, and such perks as a free overnight shoeshine. Some rooms offer balconies and/or whirlpool tubs. And the savings afforded by moderate room rates are supplemented by such things as free bottled water and local phone calls. Opened in 2003, this small property became an instant hit with conventioneers, who like the location—some 4 blocks from the convention center—and in-room business perks. It's great for leisure travelers, too, as it's right near La Villita and a quiet part of the River Walk, and close to both the heart of downtown and the King William district. **Note:** This is a totally nonsmoking hotel.

116 Navarro St. (at St. Mary's), San Antonio, TX 78205. (C) **800/257-6058** or 210/527-1111. Fax 210/527-1112. www.obrienhotel.com. 39 units. $109–$149 double. Rates include continental breakfast. AE, DC, DISC, MC, V. Self-parking $10. Pets (up to 50 lb.) accepted for $25 one-time fee. **Amenities:** Exercise room; coin-op washer/dryers; dry cleaning. In room: A/C, TV w/HBO, dataport, high-speed Internet access, coffeemaker, hair dryer, iron.

Riverwalk Inn (Finds)   If you've ever had a hankering to stay in an old log cabin but don't really care to go rustic, consider this unusual bed-and-breakfast. Native Texans Jan and Tracy Hammer had eight 1840s Tennessee cabins taken apart log by log and put back together again near the banks of the San Antonio River, a few blocks south of HemisFair Park and north of the King William area.

Except for a few anachronistic (but welcome) details such as indoor plumbing, wi-fi, refrigerators, and phones with voice mail and dataports, everything else in the cabins is authentic. Each room has a fireplace, quilt, braided rug, and fascinating primitive antiques; most also possess balconies or porches fronting the river. Freshly made desserts are served in the parlor each evening. The wooden-plank breakfast table can get a bit crowded on weekend mornings, but that's in keeping with the inn's pioneer spirit. (Note that a maximum of two guests are permitted in each room, which means it's not for families.)

329 Old Guilbeau (off Durango, near Dwyer St.), San Antonio, TX 78204. (C) **800/254-4440** or 210/212-8300. Fax 210/229-9422. www.riverwalkinn.com. 11 units. $130–$145 nonriverview double; $145–$175 river view. Rates include continental breakfast. 2-night minimum required for Fri–Sun stays, 3-night stay required for some holiday weekends. AE, DISC, MC, V. Free off-street parking. **Amenities:** Complimentary passes to downtown fitness studio; wi-fi in common area. In room: A/C, TV, dataport, fridge, coffeemaker.

INEXPENSIVE

Best Western Sunset Suites–Riverwalk ★★ *Value*   Don't be put off by the brand name or the fact that this all-suites hotel is located on the wrong side of the tracks, er, highway. In a converted turn-of-the-century building you'll find some of the nicest rooms in downtown San Antonio—large, with custom-made Arts and Crafts–style furnishings, including comfy, clean-lined lounge chairs and faux Tiffany lamps. They're also some of the best-equipped rooms around: All offer sleeper sofas, microwaves, minifridges, and 27-inch TVs. And talk about deals: You get a bargain ($2) hot buffet breakfast, free afternoon cocktails, and free local calls. If you don't want to move your car from its free parking spot or take a 10-minute walk to the heart of downtown, you can take advantage of the free trolley passes that'll get you there. With all the money you've saved on perks and on the room, you just might be able to afford dinner at Ruth's Chris Steak House, a few blocks away in the Sunset Station complex.

1103 E. Commerce St. (at Hwy. 281), San Antonio, TX 78205. © **866/560-6000** or 210/223-4400. Fax 210/223-4402. www.bestwesternsunsetsuites.com. 64 units. $89–$119 double. Rates include evening snacks and drinks and trolley pass. AE, DC, DISC, MC, V. Free parking. **Amenities:** Health club; business center. *In room:* A/C, TV w/pay movies, dataport, high-speed Internet access, kitchenette, coffeemaker, hair dryer, iron.

2 King William Historic District

EXPENSIVE

Noble Inns ★   It's hard to imagine that Donald and Liesl Noble, both descended from King William founding families, grew up in the neighborhood when it was run-down. The area has undergone an amazing metamorphosis in the short span of the young couple's life. Indeed, their gracious lodgings—the 1894 Jackson House, a traditional-style B&B, and, a few blocks away, the 1896 Aaron Pancoast Carriage House, offering three suites with full kitchens—are a tribute to just how far it has come. The decor in both houses hearkens back to the period in which they were built, and manages to do so without being overly fussy. Rooms, individually decorated with fine antiques, are ideal for both business and leisure travelers. All have gas fireplaces, while three in the Jackson House and one in the Carriage House feature two-person Jacuzzi tubs. Other luxurious touches include Godiva chocolate at turndown, and fresh flowers. A silver-gray classic Rolls Royce is available for airport transportation or downtown drop-off.

107 Madison St. (off St. Mary's St.), San Antonio, TX 78204. © **800/221-4045** or 210/225-4045. Fax 210/227-0877. www.nobleinns.com. 9 units. $130–$225 double; $185–$295 suite. Rates at Jackson House include full breakfast, afternoon snacks, and beverages; rates at Carriage House include continental breakfast. Corporate, weekday discounts available. AE, DC, DISC, MC, V. Free off-street parking. **Amenities:** Outdoor pool; Jacuzzi; wi-fi throughout. *In room:* A/C, TV, dataport, high-speed Internet access, kitchen (carriage house suites only), hair dryer, iron.

Ogé House Inn on the River Walk ★★   One of the most glorious of the mansions that grace the King William district, this 1857 Greek revival–style property is more of a boutique inn than a bed-and-breakfast. You'll still get the personalized attention you would expect from a host home, but it's combined here with the luxury of a sophisticated small hotel. All rooms are impeccably decorated in high Victorian style, yet feature modern conveniences such as small refrigerators; many rooms also have fireplaces and views of the manicured, pecan-shaded grounds, and one looks out on the river from its own balcony. The units downstairs aren't as light as those on the upper two floors, but they're less expensive and offer private entrances.

A bountiful gourmet breakfast is served on individual white-clothed tables set with the finest crystal and china. Travelers can also bury themselves in daily newspapers laid out on the bureau just beyond the dining room. In late 2004, the Nobles (see Noble Inns listing, above) acquired the inn and added such modern touches as wi-fi throughout and high-speed Internet access in the rooms, and are in the process of freshening and upgrading the place.

209 Washington St. (at Turner St.), San Antonio, TX 78204. ℂ **800/242-2770** or 210/223-2353. Fax 210/ 226-5812. www.ogeinn.com. 10 units. $155–$250 double; $185–$295 suite. Rates include breakfast. Corporate rates available for single business travelers. 2-night minimum stay on weekends; 3 nights during holidays and special events. AE, DC, DISC, MC, V. Free off-street parking. **Amenities:** Wi-fi throughout. *In room:* A/C, TV, dataport, high-speed Internet access, fridge, hair dryer, iron.

MODERATE

Beckmann Inn and Carriage House   Sitting on the lovely wraparound porch of this 1886 Queen Anne home, surrounded by quiet, tree-lined streets on an underdeveloped stretch of the San Antonio River, you can easily imagine yourself in a kinder, gentler era. In fact, you can still see the flour mill on whose property the Beckmann Inn was originally built. Nor will the illusion of time travel be dispelled when you step through the rare Texas red-pine door into the high-ceilinged parlor.

The house is filled with antique pieces that do justice to the setting, such as the ornately carved Victorian beds in each of the guest rooms. Two of the rooms have private entrances, as does the separate Carriage House, decorated in a somewhat lighter fashion. A full breakfast—perhaps cranberry French toast topped with orange twist—is served in the formal dining room, but you can also enjoy your coffee on a flower-filled sun porch.

Note: New owners bought the house in late 2004 and plan several upgrades, possibly a hot tub by the end of 2005.

222 E. Guenther St. (at Madison St.), San Antonio, TX 78204. ℂ **800/945-1449** or 210/229-1449. Fax 210/ 229-1061. www.beckmanninn.com. 5 units. $110–$169. Rates include breakfast. AE, DC, DISC, MC, V. Free off-street parking. **Amenities:** Wi-fi throughout main house. *In room:* A/C, TV, dataport, fridge, hair dryer, iron.

Brackenridge House *Finds*   These days many B&Bs are beginning to resemble boutique hotels, with an almost hands-off approach on the part of the hosts. If you seek out B&Bs because you prefer warmer, more traditional treatment, this King William abode is likely to suit you.

It's not just that the house is homey rather than fancy—although it's got its fair share of antiques, you don't feel as though they're too priceless to approach—but that owners Sue and Bennie (aka the King of King William) Blansett instantly make you feel welcome. They also help you find whatever you need, and even provide free trolley passes to get you there. But that's not to say you have to be communal constantly. All rooms have TVs with HBO and Showtime, as well as minifridges, microwaves, and coffeemakers. And if you're really antisocial (or traveling with kids and/or a pet), you can always book the separate carriage house, a few doors down from the main house.

230 Madison St. (off Beauregard St.), San Antonio, TX 78204. ℂ **800/221-1412** or 210/271-3442. www. brackenridgehouse.com. 6 units. $110–$130 double, $125–$145 suites and carriage house. Rates include breakfast (full in main house, continental in carriage house). Corporate, state, and federal rates, discounts for weekdays during slow times; extended stay plans available for the carriage house. 2-night minimum stay

Kids Family-Friendly Hotels

Homewood Suites (p. 51)   This reasonably priced all-suites hotel near the River Walk, with in-room kitchen facilities and two TVs per suite (each with its own VCR)—not to mention a guest laundry—is extremely convenient for families.

Hyatt Regency Hill Country Resort (p. 61)   In addition to its many great play areas (including a beach with a shallow swimming area), and its proximity to SeaWorld, this hotel offers Camp Hyatt—a program of excursions, sports, and social activities for children 3 to 12. The program fills up fast during school breaks and other holidays, when reservations are mandatory.

O'Casey's Bed & Breakfast (p. 57)   Usually B&Bs and family vacations are a contradiction in terms, but O'Casey's is happy to host well-behaved kids. *Best bet:* Stay in the separate guesthouse with the fold-out bed, and then join the main-house guests for breakfast in the morning.

Omni San Antonio (p. 61)   This hotel's proximity to the theme parks as well as in-room Nintendo and various other Omni Kids features makes the Omni appealing to families.

Radisson Hill Country Resort (p. 62)   Seasonal specials such as the Ultimate SeaWorld Adventure package provide passes, transportation, and complimentary souvenirs for both you and the kids.

Terrell Castle (p. 57)   Those with relatives stationed at nearby Fort Sam Houston who'd rather stay at a B&B than a chain hotel will enjoy this unique lodging. It's very welcoming to children.

Westin La Cantera (p. 60)   It's close to Six Flags Fiesta Texas, it's got two pools just for children, and it offers the Enchanted Rock Kids Club—an activities program for ages 5 through 12—from May through Labor Day.

Westin Riverwalk Inn (p. 48)   Though not as family-friendly as the Westin La Cantera, this Westin on the River Walk still offers such amenities as free in-room movies, a kids' treat pack upon check-in, and bedtime stories told over the phone.

required on weekend. AE, DISC, MC, V. Free off-street parking. Small pets accepted in carriage house. **Amenities:** Hot tub; wi-fi throughout house. *In room:* A/C, TV, dataport, fridge, microwave, coffeemaker, hair dryer, iron.

The Columns on Alamo ⭐   You're spoiled for choice at this gracious B&B. You can stay in the 1892 Greek revival mansion from which the inn derives its name; in an adjacent guesthouse, built 9 years later; or in a separate limestone cottage that's new, yet built in a rustic, early-1880s style. The mansion, where the innkeepers live, is the most opulent and offers unusual walk-through windows leading to a veranda, while the guesthouse—which houses most of the lodgings—affords more privacy if you're uncomfortable with the idea of staying in someone else's home. Those who really want to hole up should book the Honeymoon and Anniversary cottage, attached to the guesthouse, or the separate Rock House cottage in the back; it's large enough for four.

All the rooms are light, airy, and very pretty, although this is not the place for those allergic to pastels and frills; pink dominates many of the accommodations, and even the darker-toned Imari Room has lace curtains. (The Rock House, done in more casual country style, is the exception.) Several of the units boast two-person Jacuzzis and gas-log fireplaces. Hosts Ellenor and Arthur Link are extremely helpful, and their breakfasts are all you could ask for in morning indulgence.

1037 S. Alamo (at Sheridan, 5 blocks south of Durango), San Antonio, TX 78210. ✆ **800/233-3364** or 210/271-3245. www.columnssanantonio.com. 13 units. $92–$162 double; $162–$230 cottage. Rates include breakfast. Extended stay discounts. 2-day minimum stay required for Fri or Sat. AE, MC, V. Free off-street parking. **Amenities:** Wi-fi throughout. *In room:* A/C, TV, dataport, fridge, hair dryer, iron.

3 Monte Vista Historic District

MODERATE

The Inn at Craig Place ✿   This 1891 mansion-turned-B&B appeals to history, art, and architecture buffs alike. It was built by one of Texas's preeminent architects, Alfred Giles, for H. E. Hildebrand, one of San Antonio's movers and shakers; the living room boasts a mural by Julian Onderdonk, an influential Texas landscape artist.

But that's all academic. More to the point, this place is gorgeous, with forests of gleaming wood and clean Arts and Crafts lines, as well as cushy couches and a wraparound porch. Rooms are at once luxurious—all have working fireplaces and hardwood floors, and come with robes, slippers, feather pillows, and down comforters—and equipped for modern needs. Just to gild the lily, one of the innkeepers, Tamra Black, worked as a professional chef, so you can expect the three-course breakfasts here to be outstanding.

117 W. Craig Place (off N. Main Ave.), San Antonio, TX 78212. ✆ **877/427-2447** or 210/736-1017. Fax 210/737-1562. www.craigplace.com. 4 units. $115–$200. Corporate rates available. Rates include breakfast. AE, DC, DISC, MC, V. Free off-street parking. *In room:* A/C, TV, dataport (but no telephone), high-speed Internet access, hair dryer, iron.

INEXPENSIVE

Bonner Garden ✿ *Value*   Those who like the intimacy of the bed-and-breakfast experience but aren't keen on Victorian froufrou should consider the Bonner Garden, located in the Monte Vista Historic District, about a mile north of downtown. Built in 1910 for Louisiana artist Mary Bonner, this large, Italianate villa has a beautiful, classical simplicity and lots of gorgeous antiques—not to mention a 45-foot sunken swimming pool.

The Portico Room, in which guests can gaze up at a painted blue sky with billowing clouds, offers a private poolside entrance. You don't have to be honeymooners to enjoy the large Jacuzzi tub in the Bridal Suite, perhaps the prettiest room, with its blue porcelain fireplace. Most of the rooms feature European-style decor, but Mary Bonner's former studio, separate from the main house, is done in tasteful Santa Fe style. A rooftop deck affords a sparkling nighttime view of downtown.

145 E. Agarita (at McCullough), San Antonio, TX 78212. ✆ **800/396-4222** or 210/733-4222. Fax 210/733-6129. www.bonnergarden.com. 5 units. $95–$125 double. Rates include full breakfast. Extended stay (minimum 3 nights) and corporate rates available. AE, DISC, MC, V. Free off-street parking. **Amenities:** Outdoor

pool; Jacuzzi; high-speed Internet access. *In room:* A/C, TV/VCR, dataport, high-speed Internet access (in some), hair dryer, iron.

O'Casey's Bed & Breakfast *(Kids (Value*   If there's a twinkle in John Casey's eye when he puts on a brogue, it's because he was born on U.S. soil, not the auld sod. But his and his wife Linda Fay's down-home friendliness is no blarney. This Irish-themed B&B is one of the few around that welcomes families, and it's well equipped to handle them. One suite in the main house has a sitting area with a futon large enough for a couple of youngsters; another has a trundle bed for two kids in a separate bedroom. Studio apartments in the carriage house both offer full kitchens.

Which is not to suggest that accommodations are utilitarian—far from it. Rooms in the main house, a gracious structure built in 1904, feature hardwood floors and fine antiques, and many bathrooms also sport claw-foot tubs. There's a wraparound balcony upstairs, too. For a treat, ask Linda (a professional pianist) and John (a choir director and singer) to perform a few numbers for you.

225 W. Craig Place (between San Pedro Ave. and Main St.), San Antonio, TX 78212. (*C*) **800/738-1378** or 210/738-1378. www.ocaseybnb.com. 7 units. $79–$99 double; $89–$109 suite (single-night stays on weekends may be slightly higher). Rates include breakfast. Weekday and extended-stay discounts. AE, DISC, MC, V. Street parking. Pets allowed in apartments only; $10 for up to a week. **Amenities:** Wi-fi in public areas. *In room:* A/C, TV, kitchen (some).

Ruckman Haus   The accommodations in this pretty turn-of-the-century stucco home, just a block from San Pedro Springs Park, are comfy but elegant, with lots of nice antiques and plenty of light. Two offer showers with three body jets—almost as good as an in-room massage (which is also available). One unit, the Highlands, is large enough to sleep four, should you decide to bring the kids. Breakfasts are generous and, if you haven't already encountered them in the morning, you can bond with fellow guests over afternoon drinks on either the covered deck or the fern-shaded side patio. The in-room refrigerators come stocked with water, soft drinks, and beer. Hey, it can get toasty in San Antonio and your friendly hosts don't want you to dehydrate!

629 W. French St. (at Breeden, 1 block west of San Pedro Ave.), San Antonio, TX 78212. (*C*) **866/736-1468** or 210/736-1468. Fax 210/736-1468. www.ruckmanhaus.com. 5 units. $85–$100 double; $120 suite. Rates include breakfast. Corporate rates for single travelers, summer specials. AE, DISC, MC, V. Free off-street parking. Pets accepted (inquire when making reservations). **Amenities:** Wi-fi in public areas. *In room:* A/C, TV, dataport, fridge, coffeemaker, hair dryer.

4 Fort Sam Houston Area

MODERATE

Terrell Castle *(Kids*   Unless a trip to Scotland is in the cards, this could be your best chance to spend a night in a castle. Built in 1894 by English-born architect Alfred Giles, this massive limestone structure was commissioned by Edwin Terrell, a statesman who fell in love with the European grand style while serving as U.S. ambassador to Belgium. Turned into a bed-and-breakfast in 1986, it's an anomaly in the working-class area near the Fort Sam Houston quadrangle—and a nice alternative to the many faceless chain lodgings around here. Guest rooms don't feature as many antiques as you'll see in the public areas, but they're comfortable and clean; several offer fireplaces. A variety of suites, as well as free lodging for children under 6 and the free use of a crib, make this B&B uncharacteristically family-friendly. Business travelers, on the other hand, have to make do with a single dataport that shares a line with the fax in the public area.

Greater San Antonio Accommodations & Dining

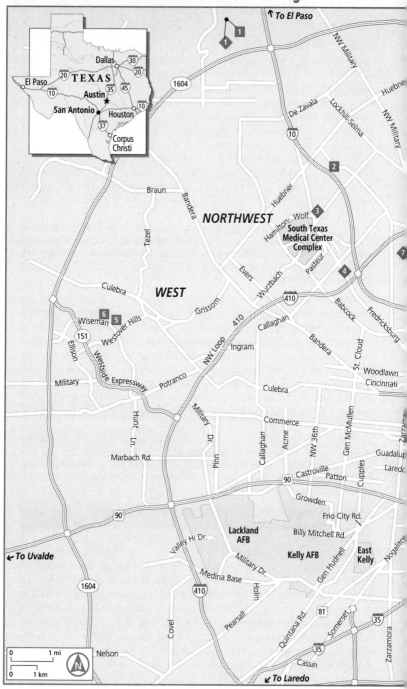

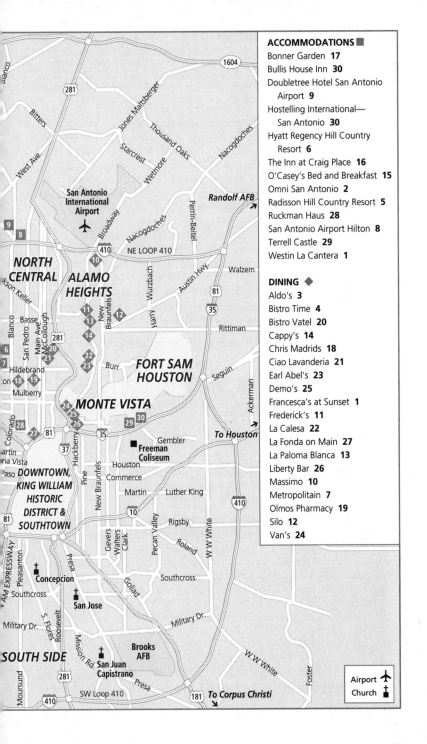

Map labels: 1604, 281, Blanco, Bitters, Jones Maltsberger, Thousand Oaks, Starcrest, Wetmore, Nacogdoches, West Ave., San Antonio International Airport, Broadway, Nacogdoches, Perrin-Beitel, Randolf AFB, NE LOOP 410, Walzem, 81, 35, Rittiman, NORTH CENTRAL, ALAMO HEIGHTS, Wurzbach, Austin Hwy., kson Keller, New Braunfels, Harry, FORT SAM HOUSTON, Seguin, Ackerman, Bianco, Basse, Main Ave., McCollough, San Pedro, 281, Hildebrand, Mulberry, Burr, MONTE VISTA, To Houston, Colorado, 81, artin, na Vista, Gembler, Freeman Coliseum, Paso, DOWNTOWN, KING WILLIAM HISTORIC DISTRICT & SOUTHTOWN, Hackberry, Houston, Commerce, Martin, Luther King, 10, Rigsby, 410, Pine, New Braunfels, Pecan Valley, Roland, Gevers, Walters, Clark, W W White, AM EXPRESSWAY, Pleasanton, Presa, Concepcion, Southcross, San Jose, Goliad, Southcross, Military Dr., Military Dr., S. Flores, Roosevelt, Mission Rd., SOUTH SIDE, 281, Brooks AFB, San Juan Capistrano, Presa, Moursund, 410, SW Loop 410, 181, To Corpus Christi, Foster, W W White

Airport ✈
Church ⊞

950 E. Grayson St., San Antonio, TX 78208. © **800/481-9732** or 210/271-9145. Fax 210/527-1455. www. terrellcastle.net. 8 units. $105–$120 double; $140 suite. Rates include full breakfast. Single and midweek discounts often available; corporate, military, and government per diem rates available. Most rooms require 2-night minimum stay on weekends. AE, DISC, MC, V. Free off-street parking. Take Exit 159A off I-35, turn right to gate at Fort Sam Houston; take left on Grayson St., go approximately 4½ blocks. *In room:* A/C, TV, no phone.

INEXPENSIVE

Bullis House Inn *(Value)*   This graceful neoclassical mansion, just down the street from the Fort Sam Houston quadrangle and easily accessible from the airport and downtown by car, is an excellent bed-and-breakfast bargain, especially for those who don't mind sharing bathrooms. Beautifully restored in the 1980s, it was built from 1906 to 1909 for Gen. John Lapham Bullis, a frontier Indian fighter who played a key role in capturing Geronimo (some claim the Apache chief's spirit still roams the mansion). More concerned with creature comforts when he retired, the general had oak paneling, parquet floors, crystal chandeliers, and marble fireplaces installed in his home, which is now often used for wedding receptions. Guest rooms all have 14-foot ceilings and are furnished with some period antiques along with good reproductions; three of them feature fireplaces, and one offers a private bathroom. The family room, which sleeps up to six, also has a refrigerator. VCR and video rentals are among the other perks.

621 Pierce St. (at Grayson, directly across from Fort Sam Houston), San Antonio, TX 78208. © **877/477-4100** or 210/223-9426. Fax 210/299-1479. www.bullishouseinn.com. 5 units. $59–$89 double with shared bathroom; $99 double with private bathroom. Weekly rates available; rates reduced by $8 if you opt out of breakfast. Rates include continental breakfast. AE, MC, V. Free off-street parking. **Amenities:** Outdoor pool. *In room:* A/C, TV, no phone (except 1 room).

Hostelling International–San Antonio   Right next door to the Bullis House Inn (see above), this youth hostel has a reading room, small kitchen, dining area, lockers, and picnic tables, in addition to male and female dorms and three private rooms. Hostelers are welcome at the Bullis House Inn, and the two lodgings share a pool. A continental breakfast, served at the inn, is available for an additional $5.

621 Pierce St. (at Grayson, directly across from Fort Sam Houston), San Antonio, TX 78208. © **210/223-9426.** Fax 210/299-1479. HISanAnton@aol.com. 38 beds, 3 units. Dorm beds: $20 (members), $23 (nonmembers); private rooms $39 double. AE, MC, V. **Amenities:** Outdoor pool. *In room:* A/C, TV (in private rooms), no phone.

5 Northwest

VERY EXPENSIVE

Westin La Cantera *★★★ (Kids)*   This lovely retreat gives the (slightly) older Hyatt Regency Hill Country Resort (see under "West," below) a run for the high-end-visitor money. They're similar in many ways, with knockout facilities, sprawling, gorgeous grounds, and loads of Texas character. Both are family-friendly, with theme parks in their backyards (here it's Six Flags Fiesta Texas) and excellent children's programs. But the Westin has the edge when it comes to golf, boasting two championship courses (in addition to the much-praised La Cantera, there's a newer Arnold Palmer–designed course) plus a professional golf school. It's a tad more romantic, too, with dramatic rocky outcroppings and drop-dead gorgeous views from its perch on one of the highest points in San Antonio. And with the opening of The Shops at La Cantera in September 2005, guests will have easy access to the city's only Neiman Marcus and Nordstrom, as well as lots of other upscale retail.

The resort is elaborately designed around state historical motifs. The Texas colonial architecture is impressive, and the tales and legends detailed in plaques in the various rooms are interesting; but you'll probably be too busy having fun to pay them much mind. Likewise, the casual-elegant rooms—beautifully decorated in muted earth tones and subtle florals and equipped with all the business amenities conference attendees need—are likely to be abandoned for the resort's myriad recreational areas, or at least for the balconies that many of the guest quarters offer. Remnants of the limestone quarry on which the resort was built were incorporated into the five swimming pools interconnected with bridges and channels and a dramatic waterfall. And the indigenous plant life and animal life—deer, rabbits, and wild turkeys come out at dusk—should have you oohing and cooing. So will the Southwest cuisine—speaking of game—and the sundown vistas of **Francesca's at Sunset** (see chapter 5).

16641 La Cantera Pkwy. (take the La Cantera Pkwy. exit off I-10 and turn left; resort entrance is ¾ mile ahead, on the right), San Antonio, TX 78256. ℭ 800/WESTIN-1 or 210/558-6500. Fax 210/641-0721. www.westin lacantera.com. 508 units. $259–$349 double; suites from $380; casitas from $350. AE, DC, DISC, MC, V. Free self-parking; valet parking $12. **Amenities:** 3 restaurants; 2 bars; outdoor pool; 2 golf courses; 2 tennis courts; health club; spa; Jacuzzi; children's center; video arcade; concierge; car-rental desk; business center; 24-hr. room service; massage; dry cleaning. In room: A/C, TV w/pay movies, dataport, high-speed Internet access, minibar, coffeemaker, hair dryer, iron, safe.

EXPENSIVE

Omni San Antonio 🐿 (Kids) This polished granite high-rise off I-10 west is convenient to SeaWorld, Six Flags Fiesta Texas, the airport, and the Hill Country, and the shops and restaurants of the 66-acre Colonnade complex are within easy walking distance. The lobby is soaring and luxurious, and guest rooms are well-appointed in a traditional but cheery Continental style. The proximity to the theme parks as well as in-room Nintendo and various other Omni Kids features makes this hotel as appealing to families as it is to business travelers, who appreciate its exercise facilities, better than most in San Antonio and definitely the best in this part of town, dominated by inexpensive chains (guests can also get treadmills brought into their rooms as part of the Omni "Get Fit" program). Although the hotel sees a lot of tourist and Medical Center traffic, service here is always prompt and courteous.

9821 Colonnade Blvd. (at Wurzbach), San Antonio, TX 78230. ℭ 800/843-6664 or 210/691-8888. Fax 210/691-1128. www.omnihotels.com. 326 units. $169 double; suites from $300. A variety of discount packages available. AE, DC, DISC, MC, V. Free self-parking; valet parking $7. Pets 25 lb. or under permitted; $50 nonrefundable fee. **Amenities:** Restaurant; bar; indoor pool; outdoor pool; health club; Jacuzzi; sauna; game room; concierge; courtesy car; business center; wi-fi in public areas; limited room service; babysitting; same-day dry cleaning; club-level rooms. In room: TV w/pay movies, dataport, high-speed Internet access, minibar, coffeemaker, hair dryer, iron.

6 West

VERY EXPENSIVE

Hyatt Regency Hill Country Resort 🐿🐿🐿 (Kids) If I were feeling flush and didn't want to spend a lot of time downtown, this would be my favorite place to settle in for a week. The setting, on 200 acres of former ranch land on the far-west side of San Antonio, is idyllic. The resort's low-slung native limestone buildings, inspired by the architecture of the nearby Hill Country, showcase the best of Texas design. The on-site activities, ranging from golf to tubing on the 950-foot-long Ramblin' River, seem to be endless.

And it just keeps getting better. A spa, added with the new millennium. Low-key and relaxing, it boasts all the latest treatments, and is one of the best pampering palaces in this part of Texas. And the rooms underwent a major revamp in 2004–05, morphing from country cute to haute Dallas: neutral-toned rugs, dark wood furnishing, silks and brocades in shades of mocha and taupe, and cushy new bedding. Many offer French doors that open out onto wood-trimmed porches. And 9 more Arthur Hill–designed holes of golf are in the offing (bringing the total up to 27 holes).

The resort is also extremely family-friendly. SeaWorld sits at your doorstep, there are free laundry facilities and a country store for supplies, and every room has a refrigerator (not stocked with goodies, alas). When you're tired of all that family bonding, the Hyatt Kids Club will keep the youngsters happily occupied while you spend some quality time relaxing on Ramblin' River.

9800 Hyatt Resort Dr. (off Hwy. 151, between Westover Hills Blvd. and Potranco Rd.), San Antonio, TX 78251. © **800/233-1234** or 210/647-1234. Fax 210/681-9681. http://hillcountry.hyatt.com. 500 units. $285–$400 double; $450–$1,550 suite. Rates lower late Nov to early Mar; packages available. AE, DC, DISC, MC, V. Free self-parking; valet parking $10. **Amenities:** 4 restaurants; 2 bars; outdoor pool; golf course; 3 tennis courts; health club; spa; Jacuzzi; bike rentals; children's programs; game room; concierge; car-rental desk; business center; wi-fi in public areas; limited room service; laundry service; dry cleaning; club-level rooms. *In room:* A/C, TV w/pay movies, dataport, high-speed Internet access; fridge, hair dryer, iron.

EXPENSIVE

Radisson Hill Country Resort ★ *Kids* The name of this property is a bit misleading as a spa and proximity to a golf course do not a resort make. And the Radisson, opened in 2002, is a pretty blatant knockoff of its ritzier next-door neighbor, the Hyatt Regency Hill Country Resort (see above), down to the Ralph Lauren-does-Texas lobby and the on-site ATM and upscale convenience store. But you're also not paying resort prices, and comparisons aside, this is a very pleasant place to stay. Vacationers and conventioneers alike will enjoy the generous menu of spa treatments and products, as well as guest privileges at two good golf courses. Rooms are attractive in a dark, masculine way. Suites offer jetted tubs and rainforest shower heads, and all accommodations feature cushy "seven-layer beds." It's got plenty of family appeal: Seasonal specials such as the Ultimate SeaWorld Adventure package provide passes, transportation, and complimentary souvenirs for both you and the kids.

9800 Westover Hills Blvd. (off Hwy. 151), San Antonio, TX 78251. © **800/333-3333** or 210/509-9800. Fax 210/509-9814. www.radisson.com/sanantoniotx_resort. 227 units. $159–$179 double; $239–$289 suite. AE, DC, DISC, MC, V. Free parking. **Amenities:** 2 restaurants; bar; 3 outdoor pools; health club; spa; Jacuzzi; business center; limited room service; dry cleaning. *In room:* A/C, TV w/pay movies, dataport, high-speed Internet access, fridge (suites only), coffeemaker, hair dryer, iron.

7 North Central (Near the Airport)

EXPENSIVE

San Antonio Airport Hilton ★ You'll go straight from the airport to the heart of Texas if you stay at this friendly hotel, where the cheerful lobby has a bull-rider mural and **Tex's Grill** (see chapter 8) is loaded with Lone Star sports memorabilia—and serves some mean Texas barbecue. Such nongeneric features as an outdoor putting green also help make your stay enjoyable. But while this hotel may be playful, it also knows how to get down to business. A $5-million renovation, completed in February 2005, added high-speed wireless Internet access to all the rooms and public areas. It also added comfy pillow-top beds to the guest quarters, and gave them a more elegant, understated look than they had before. Pretty spiffy—but I for one am going to miss the cowboy lamps and Lone Star–pattern chairs. Don't mess with Texas.

611 NW Loop 410 (San Pedro exit), San Antonio, TX 78216. ℭ **800/HILTONS** or 210/340-6060. Fax 210/377-4674. www.hilton.com. 386 units. $169–$199 double; suites from $175. Romance, weekend packages available. AE, DC, DISC, MC, V. Free covered parking. **Amenities:** Restaurant; bar; outdoor pool; putting green; Jacuzzi; sauna; video arcade; courtesy car; business center; wi-fi in public areas, 24-hour room service; same-day dry cleaning; club-level rooms. *In room:* TV w/pay movies, dataport, wi-fi, high-speed Internet access, coffeemaker, hair dryer, iron.

MODERATE

Doubletree Hotel San Antonio Airport   For an airport hotel, the Doubletree is surprisingly serene. The same developer who converted a downtown seminary into the posh La Mansión del Río hotel (see "Downtown," earlier in the chapter) was responsible for this hotel's design. Moorish arches, potted plants, stone fountains, and colorful Mexican tile create a Mediterranean mood in the public areas. Intricate wrought-iron elevators descend from the guest floors to the lushly landscaped pool patio, eliminating the need to tromp through the lobby in a swimsuit. Guest rooms are equally appealing, with brick walls painted in peach or beige, wood-beamed ceilings, draped French doors, and colorful contemporary art. A small spa, added recently, is another perk. And because this hotel gets a large business clientele from Mexico, most of the staff is bilingual.

37 NE Loop 410 (McCullough exit), San Antonio, TX 78216. ℭ **800/535-1980** or 210/366-2424. Fax 210/341-0410. www.doubletree.com. 290 units. $130–$170 double; $230–$300 suite. Packages available. AE, DC, DISC, MC, V. Free self-parking. **Amenities:** Restaurant; 2 bars; outdoor pool; exercise room; spa; Jacuzzi; sauna; concierge; courtesy car; business center; limited room service; dry cleaning; club-level rooms; ATM. *In room:* A/C, TV w/pay movies, dataport, high-speed Internet access, coffeemaker, hair dryer, iron, safe.

5

Where to Dine in San Antonio

It's easy to eat very well indeed in San Antonio, especially if you enjoy Mexican food—or are at least willing to give it a try. But that's hardly all you'll find to eat in town. New American cuisine, emphasizing fresh regional ingredients and spices combined in creative ways, is served in some of the most chic dining rooms in town, as well as in some unlikely dives. Then there are high-class French, old-fashioned Italian, Asian anything, chicken-fried steak, burgers, barbecue . . . in short, something to satisfy every taste and budget. The national chains are well represented here, naturally—everything from McDonald's to Morton's—but I've concentrated on eateries that are unique to San Antonio, or at least to Texas.

The downtown dining scene, especially that found along the River Walk, is the one most visitors will become familiar with, and because most out-of-towners either stay in downtown or visit it at least once, I've devoted a good deal of space to restaurants in this area. Keep in mind, however, that many restaurants that overlook the water—and even those that don't but are nearby—can be overpriced and overcrowded. And parking is either tough to find or expensive (on busy weekend nights, when garage space may sell out, it can be both). In short, even if you're willing to pass up a river view, downtown may not be the best place for economical or serene fine dining. (To locate restaurants in Downtown, see the map on p. 67.)

You'll find some good restaurants in Southtown, the aptly named area just below downtown, but most prime places to chow down are scattered throughout the north. By far the most fertile ground for outstanding San Antonio dining is on and around Broadway, starting a few blocks south of Hildebrand, extending north to Loop 410, and comprising much of the posh area known as Alamo Heights. Brackenridge Park, the zoo, the botanical gardens, and the Witte and McNay museums are all situated in this part of town, so you can combine your sightseeing with some serious eating.

Although I've pretty much stuck to areas that out-of-towners are likely to visit, I've also included a few restaurants worth driving out of your way to find. One in particular I recommend to those hankering for down-home, Southern-style cooking in a venue that's not especially near anywhere you'd be likely to go. Check out **Hoover's Cooking,** 6868 San Pedro Ave., in North Central (C **210/828-2300;** www.hooverscooking.com), a recent venture by the owner of the Austin original (it's reviewed in chapter 13)—and just as good as its Austin counterpart. You can sample barbecued pork ribs, chicken-fried steak, fried okra, Cajun-style muffulettas, and Caribbean specialties like jerk chicken. (To locate restaurants outside of Downtown, see the map on p. 58.)

> **Tips** **The Early Bird**
>
> If you're budget-conscious, consider eating early, when some restaurants have early-bird specials, or hitting the expensive restaurants at lunch, since some of the most upscale eateries in town have good lunch specials.

RESTAURANT CATEGORIES

Rather than trying to make sharp distinctions between Regional American, New Texan, and American Fusion cuisine, as some chefs insist on categorizing their creations, I defined any menu likely to include things like mashed potatoes, feta cheese, pesto, and chorizo (not necessarily all in the same dish) as **New American. Southwestern,** on the other hand, is a contemporary cooking style that tends to emphasize ingredients from the American Southwest, such as blue corn and jicama. I've merged Tex-Mex and northern Mexican cuisine, which are inextricably intertwined, into a single **Mexican** category. **Regional Mexican** cooking encompasses cuisine from other parts of Mexico. This year I've also added **Nuevo Latino,** with its creatively updated dishes from all over Latin America.

The price categories into which the restaurants have been divided are only rough approximations, based on the average costs of the appetizers and entrees. By ordering carefully or splurging, you can eat more or less expensively at almost any place you choose.

1 Restaurants by Cuisine

AMERICAN
Cappy's ⭐ (Alamo Heights Area, $$$, p. 77)

Chris Madrids (Monte Vista Area, $, p. 75)

Earl Abel's (Alamo Heights Area, $, p. 79)

Guenther House ⭐ (Southtown, $, p. 74)

Little Rhein Steak House (Downtown, $$$$, p. 68)

Olmos Pharmacy (Alamo Heights Area, $, p. 80)

Pesca on the River ⭐⭐ (Downtown, $$$$, p. 69)

ASIAN FUSION
Frederick's ⭐⭐ (Alamo Heights Area, $$$, p. 77)

BAKERY
Metropolitain (Alamo Heights Area, $$, p. 78)

BURGERS
Chris Madrids (Monte Vista Area, $, p. 75)

CHINESE
Van's (Alamo Heights Area, $$, p. 79)

CONTINENTAL
Bistro Time ⭐⭐ (Northwest, $$$, p. 80)

DELI
Madhatters (Southtown, $, p. 74)

Schilo's (Downtown, $, p. 73)

Twin Sisters (Downtown and Alamo Heights Area, $, p. 73)

ECLECTIC
Madhatters (Southtown, $, p. 74)

FRENCH
Bistro Vatel ⭐⭐ (Alamo Heights Area, $$$, p. 76)

Frederick's ⭐⭐ (Alamo Heights Area, $$$, p. 77)

Key to Abbreviations: $$$$ = Very Expensive $$$ = Expensive $$ = Moderate $ = Inexpensive

Metropolitain (Alamo Heights
Area, $$, p. 78)
Le Rêve ✹✹✹ (Downtown, $$$$,
p. 68)

GERMAN
Schilo's (Downtown, $, p. 73)

GREEK
Demo's (Monte Vista Area, $,
p. 75)

HEALTH FOOD
Twin Sisters (Downtown and
Alamo Heights Area, $, p. 73)

ITALIAN
Aldo's (Northwest, $$$, p. 80)
Ciao Lavanderia ✹✹ (Alamo
Heights Area, $$, p. 78)
Massimo ✹✹ (Alamo Heights
Area, $$$, p. 77)
Paesano's Riverwalk ✹ (Down-
town, $$$, p. 69)

JAPANESE
Sushi Zushi (Downtown, $$,
p. 71)
Van's (Alamo Heights Area, $$,
p. 79)

MEXICAN (NORTHERN & TEX-MEX)
Acenar ✹✹ (Downtown, $$, p. 71)
Aldaco's ✹ (Downtown, $$, p. 71)
La Fonda on Main ✹ (Monte
Vista Area, $$, p. 74)
Mi Tierra (Downtown, $, p. 72)
Rosario's ✹ (Southtown, $$,
p. 73)

NEW AMERICAN
Biga on the Banks ✹✹ (Down-
town, $$$$, p. 66)
Boudro's ✹ (Downtown, $$$,
p. 69)
Las Canarias ✹✹ (Downtown,
$$$$, p. 68)
Liberty Bar ✹ (Monte Vista Area,
$$, p. 75)
Silo ✹✹ (Alamo Heights Area,
$$$, p. 77)

NUEVO LATINO
Azuca ✹(Southtown, $$$, p. 73)

REGIONAL MEXICAN
La Calesa ✹ (Alamo Heights Area,
$$, p. 78)
La Fonda on Main ✹ (Monte
Vista Area, $$, p. 74)
Paloma Blanca (Alamo Height
Area, $$, p. 79)

SEAFOOD
Pesca on the River ✹✹ (Downtown, $$$$, p. 69)

SOUTHWESTERN
Francesca's at Sunset ✹✹✹
(Northwest, $$$$, p. 80)
Zuni Grill ✹ (Downtown, $$$,
p. 70)

STEAKS
Little Rhein Steak House (Down-
town, $$$$, p. 68)

VIETNAMESE
Van's (Alamo Heights Area, $$,
p. 79)

2 Downtown

VERY EXPENSIVE

Biga on the Banks ✹✹ NEW AMERICAN   With its new millennium move
to the River Walk, one of San Antonio's earliest culinary innovators found an
elegant, bold, and contemporary venue to match its menu. Clean lines, high
ceilings, gleaming wood floors, and lots of harem-like draperies—plus a balcony
with dramatic river views—set the scene for chef/owner Bruce Auden's consistently interesting cuisine. The starters, for example, cross a few continents, combining Texas and Asia in spring-style rolls filled with minced venison, buffalo,

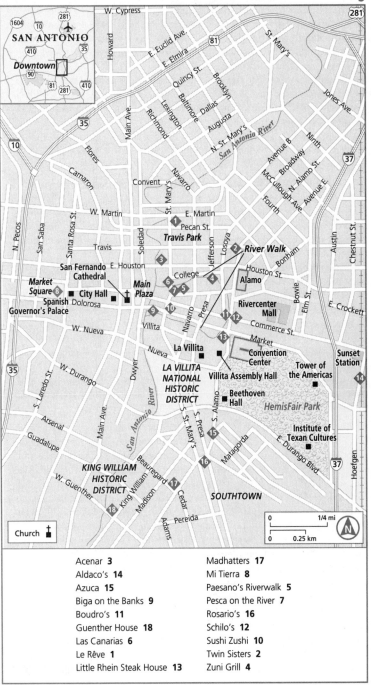

Acenar **3**
Aldaco's **14**
Azuca **15**
Biga on the Banks **9**
Boudro's **11**
Guenther House **18**
Las Canarias **6**
Le Rêve **1**
Little Rhein Steak House **13**

Madhatters **17**
Mi Tierra **8**
Paesano's Riverwalk **5**
Pesca on the River **7**
Rosario's **16**
Schilo's **12**
Sushi Zushi **10**
Twin Sisters **2**
Zuni Grill **4**

ostrich, and pheasant accompanied by two spicy dipping sauces. The bone-on ten-derloin steak with beer-battered onion rings and habanero ketchup raises comfort-cum-bar cuisine to new heights, and the variations on a theme in the Paseo de Chocolate dessert will send you happily into sugar shock, international-style.

Perhaps because he's reached celebrity-chef status, Auden seems to be spend-ing less time in the kitchen, and the food is not nearly as dazzling as it was when the setting was more low-key. Still, it's way above average, and if you're willing to eat before 6:30pm or after 9pm, you can sample a three-course meal for $35 per person, or four courses for $43.

International Center, 203 S. St. Mary's St./River Walk. ⓒ 210/225-0722. www.biga.com. Reservations rec-ommended. Main courses $19–$36; brunch $32 adults, $17 ages 12 and under. AE, DC, DISC, MC, V. Mon–Thurs 5:30–10pm; Fri–Sat 5:30–11pm; Sun 11am–2:30pm (brunch) and 5:30–10pm.

Las Canarias ★★ NEW AMERICAN   The fine dining room at La Mansión del Río has a couple of things going for it, namely the setting and food. You have a choice of dining on inventive and beautifully presented cuisine on a lovely riverside veranda, a palm-decked, Mexican-tiled patio, or inside in one of sev-eral cozy, antiques-filled interior rooms where you can listen to the soft music of a grand piano or a classical guitar.

Menus change seasonally, but such dishes as seared ahi tuna with saffron jas-mine rice, or pepper-crusted venison loin with sweet potato crisps demonstrate the chef's ability to balance unusual textures and flavors. Appetizers are equally exciting, but you'll want to share to leave room for dazzling desserts like the mas-carpone cheesecake with warm cinnamon curry apples. The $12 lunchtime "Two Courses in 40 Minutes" special nabs you a choice of soup or salad, an entree such as oregano-crusted chicken breast with mashed potatoes, and homemade bread and coffee.

La Mansión del Río, 112 College St./River Walk. ⓒ 210/518-1063. Reservations recommended. Main courses $19–$32; 5-course tasting menu $42 ($60 paired with wine); champagne brunch $32. AE, DC, DISC, MC, V. Sun–Thurs 6:30am–10:30pm; Fri–Sat 6:30am–11pm; Sun brunch 10:30am–2:30pm.

Le Rêve ★★★ FRENCH   Chef/owner Andrew Weissman, a local boy who studied in France and did a stint at New York's famed Le Cirque, is very serious about his food—and it shows (and tastes). Presentations are gorgeous, and everything's made from scratch with the freshest of ingredients, so such dishes as the caramelized onion tart appetizer, the duck breast with foie gras and calvados apples, or the light but rich sour cream cheesecakes are sensual delights.

But Weissman expects patrons to take the dining experience as seriously as he does. Nothing is available a la carte, so you've got to invest time—and money—on one of the fixed-price menus. And this is the only place in San Antonio that requires men to wear jackets. Still, for foodies of all stripes, this tiny, chic din-ing room with a peek-a-boo view of the river is *the* place to eat in town. Come on Wednesday, and you can bring your own wine without a corking fee.

152 E. Pecan St. at St. Mary's. ⓒ 210/212-2221. www.restaurantlereve.com. Reservations required. Jacket required for men. Tasting menu $95, $135 with wine; prix fixe 3 courses $70, 4 courses $80, 5 courses $90. AE, DC, DISC, MC, V. Tues–Sat 5:30–11pm (last reservation taken for 8:30pm seating).

Little Rhein Steak House AMERICAN/STEAKS   Built in 1847 in what was then the Rhein district, the oldest two-story structure in San Antonio has hosted an elegant steakhouse abutting the river and La Villita since 1967. Antique memorabilia decks the indoor main dining room, and a miniature train surrounded by historic replicas runs overhead. Leafy branches overhanging the

River Walk patio—elevated slightly and railed off for privacy—are draped in little sparkling lights.

The setting is pretty as ever, and the choice USDA Prime steaks from the restaurant's own meat plant are tasty, but recent competition from chains such as The Palm and Morton's nearby have resulted in a price hike. Now everything here is a la carte, which means you'll shell out $4.75 for a baked potato, another $6.95 for creamed spinach (you do still get a loaf of fresh wheat bread, gratis). The restaurant can also get quite noisy. That said, this is still one of the few family-owned steakhouses around, and it offers a unique River Walk dining experience.

231 S. Alamo at Market. ℂ **210/225-2111.** www.littlerheinsteakhouse.com. Reservations recommended. Main courses $20–$38. AE, DC, DISC, MC, V. Daily 5–10pm.

Pesca on the River ✿✿ AMERICAN/SEAFOOD   For terrific fish in a swank nautical setting, it's tough to beat the new riverside restaurant at the Watermark Hotel. Except for the oyster bar that centers the dining room, the marine touches are more subliminal than overt: sea-blue table settings, hardwood floors, smooth glass surfaces, sleek, vaguely boat-shaped water pitchers. But once you tuck into the "catches" of the day, you'll have no doubt about this restaurant's deep devotion to things Piscean.

The creamy smooth cool asparagus soup with a mound of crab at the bottom was one of the best things I've tasted, ever. The oyster sampler, the seared rare tuna crusted with coriander and fennel seed . . . nothing disappointed. The only thing a bit off was the inexperienced, obsequious ("excellent choice, ma'am") staff. But that was a minor glitch; all the choices were, in fact, excellent. *Note:* Meat eaters and even vegetarians won't go hungry here—but they won't find a vast sea of selections, either.

212 W. Crockett St. (Watermark Hotel). ℂ **210/396-5817.** www.watermarkhotel.com. Reservations recommended on weekends. Main courses $18–$29. AE, DC, DISC, MC, V. Daily 6:30am–11pm.

EXPENSIVE

Boudro's ✿ NEW AMERICAN   Locals tend to look down their noses at River Walk restaurants—with the long-running exception of Boudro's—and with good reason. The kitchen uses fresh local ingredients—Gulf Coast seafood, Texas beef, Hill Country produce—and the preparations and presentations do them justice. The setting is also out of the ordinary, boasting a turn-of-the-century limestone building with hardwood floors and a handmade mesquite bar.

You might start with the guacamole, prepared tableside and served with tostadas, or the pan-fried Texas crab cakes. The prime rib, blackened on a pecan-wood grill, is deservedly popular, as is the pork chop with sun-dried cherry and chili marmalade. The food may be innovative, but portions are hearty nevertheless. Lighter alternatives include the coconut shrimp with orange horseradish and the rosemary-grilled yellowfin tuna. For dessert, the whisky-soaked bread pudding is fine, and the lime chess pie with a butter pastry crust is divine. Service is very good despite the volume of business and the time the servers spend mixing up guacamole.

421 E. Commerce St./River Walk. ℂ **210/224-8484.** www.boudros.com. Reservations strongly recommended. Main courses $15–$28. AE, DC, DISC, MC, V. Sun–Thurs 11am–11pm; Fri–Sat 11am–midnight.

Paesano's Riverwalk ✿ ITALIAN   This River Walk incarnation of a long-time San Antonio favorite relinquished its old Chianti bottle–kitsch decor for a soaring ceiling, lots of inscrutable contemporary art, and a more up-to-date

San Antonio's Movable Feasts

Not satisfied to dine with an immobile river view? Three of the River Walk restaurants recommended in this chapter—Paesano's, Boudro's, and Zuni Grill—offer communal river-barge dinners, which let you book a place (or two or three or four) on one of the restaurant's regular river runs. It's a terrific sightseeing-while-snacking experience, but not especially romantic, as you'll be sitting with a bunch of strangers around a long table. Another caveat is the boats don't have kitchens, so the menu is more limited than it would be if you were dining in the restaurant itself (you get only a few appetizers, entrees, and desserts to select from). And if you don't like the way something is cooked, you can't send it back.

Prices and schedules vary. Call the restaurants, all listed in the "Downtown" section, for details. Not enough choices? Check with **Yanaguana Cruises** (© **800/417-4139** or 210/244-5700; www.sariver cruise.com/charters_restaurants.htm), which operates the barges, for information on other eateries that'll let you sit in on their splashy foodfests.

menu. But the one thing the restaurant couldn't give up, at the risk of a local insurrection, was the signature shrimp Paesano's. The crispy crustaceans are as good as their devotees claim, as are the reasonably priced pizzas, including the one topped with grilled chicken, artichokes, basil pesto, and feta cheese. Other good values are the hearty southern Italian staples such as lasagna with meat sauce. Standouts among the pricier entrees include the grilled pork chops with potato gnocchi, and the veal Francesa. Locals tend to go to the newer—and somewhat quieter—Paesano's, across from the Quarry Golf Club at 555 Basse Rd., Suite 100 (© **210/828-5191**).

111 W. Crockett, Suite 101/River Walk. © **210/227-4102**. www.paesanosriverwalk.com. Reservations accepted for 10 or more only. Pizzas $14; pastas $8.95–$19; main courses $20–$29. AE, DISC, MC, V. Sun–Thurs 11am–10pm; Fri–Sat 11am–11pm.

Zuni Grill ⚓ SOUTHWESTERN With its chile strings, stylized steers, and chic Southwestern menu, this popular River Walk cafe is a little bit of Santa-Fe-on-the-San-Antonio. If you've never had a prickly pear margarita, this is the place to try one: Puréed cactus fruit, marinated overnight in tequila and cactus-juice schnapps, turns the potent, delicious drink a shade ranging from pink to startling purple, depending on the ripeness of the fruit.

This is a good place to come from morning 'til dark. You can kick-start your day with a breakfast taco, or take a midafternoon break with an upgraded BLT (the turkey is apple smoked and the bread has ancho chilies in it). At night, vegetarians will appreciate the gardener and gatherer platter (grilled vegetables accompanied by roasted garlic mashed potatoes and wilted spinach). For something more substantial, try the honey-coriander pork loin with adobo sauce or salmon with a creamed corn tart. While the food is as good as ever, the service seems to be slacking lately. Be aware that your visit might be more leisurely than you'd like.

223 Losoya St./River Walk. © 210/227-0864. www.zunigrill.com. Reservations suggested on weekends. Main courses $15–$26. AE, DISC, MC, V. Daily 7:30am–11pm.

MODERATE

Acenar ☆/☆ *Value* MEXICAN   When Lisa Wong (Rosario) and Bruce Auden (Biga), two longtime darlings of the San Antonio dining scene, collaborate on a restaurant, you figure the food and the atmosphere are going to be creative. Their "modern Tex-Mex" fare and the seemingly endless series of wildly colorful dining rooms (one on the river) in which it's served don't disappoint. In fact, both the food and the service exceed expectations, given the (over) size of this place and the crowds that immediately began to throng to it.

It's hard to go wrong with any of the dishes, but standouts include the buttermilk-fried oysters, served on yucca chips with jalapeño honey mayo; the *entomatadas,* tacos filled with chicken and sweet potatoes and topped with roasted chiles and Mexican cheese; and the duck chorizo chalupas with cabbage lime slaw. My adventurous friends tell me the *cabrito* (goat) with arbol chiles is delicious, but I wanted to try the incredibly rich Mexican chocolate mousse. You can eat well and leave very solvent if you go for anything except the more expensive specialty dishes, but they're definitely worth a splurge.

146 E. Houston St. (next to the Hotel Valencia). © 210/222-CENA. www.acenar.com. Reservations not accepted (priority seating for large parties). Lunch $6.75–$10 (specialties $9.25–$16); dinner $9–$15 (specialties $14–$21). AE, DC, MC, V. Mon–Thurs 11am–10pm, Fri–Sat 11am–11pm; bar Mon–Wed 4–10pm, Thurs–Sat 11am–2am.

Aldaco's ☆ MEXICAN   Yes, this restaurant is in a converted train station–cum–entertainment complex and has been known to host large convention groups, but there's nothing transient or impersonal about either the setting or the food. With its original wood beams, murals of Mexican scenes, wrought-iron room dividers, and large plants, the high-ceiling room feels very festive, and an outdoor patio adds charm. The menu, created by chef/owner Blanca Aldaco, includes several dishes from her hometown near Guadalajara—for example, tostadas made with shrimp ceviche, and *pozole rojo,* a pork and cabbage soup. But there are also plenty of standard Tex-Mex dishes, from chicken fajitas and nachos to grilled sirloin served with white rice, black beans, and guacamole. And no one can (or should) resist the chef's justifiably renowned traditional *tres leches* (three-milk) cake.

100 Hoefgen St. in Sunset Station. © 210/222-0561. www.aldacos.net. AE, MC, V. Lunch $6–$17; dinner $9–$15. Mon–Thurs 11am–9pm; Fri–Sat 11am–10pm.

Sushi Zushi *Value* JAPANESE   For a Japanese food fix in a congenial atmosphere, you can't beat this clean, well-lighted place. You'll find sushi in all its incarnations here, including a My Spurs roll—yellowtail, cilantro, avocado, chives, and *serro* chiles—but far more is on the menu. There are rice bowls, soba noodle bowls, soups, teppanyakis, tempuras—in fact, a mind-boggling array of food choices, not to mention a long list of sakes. The need to make all those decisions notwithstanding, this spot is popular with downtown office workers who know that, in this case, they'll be rewarded for whatever bold initiatives they take.

Two more branches of Sushi Zushi are both open for lunch on Sunday (in addition to the downtown store's hours): in the Northwest at the Colonnade Shopping Center, 9901 W I-10 (© **210/691-3332**); and in the Northeast at Stone Oak Plaza II, 18720 Stone Oak Pkwy. at Loop 1604 (© **210/545-6100**).

203 S. Saint Mary's St. (The International Center). ✆ **210/472-2900.** www.sushizushi.com. Reservations suggested on weekends. Sushi rolls and sashimi $4–$15; bowls, tempuras, and other hot entrees $8–$17. DISC, MC, V. Mon–Thurs 11:30am–10pm; Fri 11:30am–11pm; Sat 12:30–11pm; Sun 5–9pm.

INEXPENSIVE

Mi Tierra MEXICAN   Almost anyone who's ever been within striking distance of San Antonio has heard of this Market Square restaurant, open since 1941. Much expanded and gussied up since then, it still draws a faithful clientele of Latino families and businesspeople—along with busloads of tourists. Perhaps its prime asset is its round-the-clock schedule, so if you're looking for chorizo and eggs or a 10-ounce charbroiled rib-eye at 2am, this is the place to come. Not that hungry? Mi Tierra has a *panadería* (bakery), and you can get all kinds of good *pan dulces* (sweet rolls) to go along with a cup of coffee or Mexican hot chocolate.

It's Always Chili in San Antonio

It ranks up there with apple pie in the American culinary pantheon, but nobody's mom invented chili. The iconic stew of meat, chilies, onions, and a variety of spices was likely conceived around the 1840s by Texas cowboys who needed to make tough meat palatable—while also covering up its taste as it began to go bad. The name is a Texas corruption of the Spanish *chile* (*chee*-leh), after the peppers—which are not really peppers at all, but that's another story—most conventionally used in the stew.

The appellation chili *con carne* is really redundant in Texas, where chili without meat isn't considered chili at all, and indeed, most Texans think that adding beans is only for wimps. Beef is the most common base, but everything from armadillo to venison is acceptable.

No one really knows exactly where chili originated, but San Antonio is the prime candidate for the distinction: In the mid–19th century, accounts were widespread of the town's "chili queens," women who ladled steaming bowls of the concoction in open-air markets and on street corners. It wasn't until the 1940s that they stopped dishing out chili in front of the Alamo.

William Gebhardt helped strengthen San Antonio's claim to chili fame when he began producing chili powder in the city in 1896. His Original Mexican Dinner package, which came out around 20 years later, included a can each of chili con carne, beans, and tamales, among other things, and fed five for $1. This precursor of the TV dinner proved so popular that it earned San Antonio the nickname "Tamaleville."

Oddly enough, chili isn't generally found on San Antonio restaurant menus. But modern-day chili queens come out in force for special events at Market Square, as well as for Nights in Old San Antonio, one of the most popular bashes of the city's huge Fiesta celebration. And there's not a weekend that goes by without a chili cook-off somewhere in the city.

218 Produce Row (Market Sq.). ℭ 210/225-1262. www.mitierracafe.com. Reservations accepted for large groups only. Breakfast $6.25–$9.25; lunch and dinner plates $8.25–$17. AE, MC, V. Open 24 hr.

Schilo's *(Value* *(Kids* GERMAN/DELI   You can't leave town without stopping in at this San Antonio institution, if only for a hearty bowl of split-pea soup or a piece of the signature cherry cheesecake. The large, open room with its worn wooden booths is a door into the city's German past. The waitresses—definitely not "servers"—wear dirndl-type outfits, and live German bands play on Saturday from 5 to 8pm. It's a great refueling station near Alamo Plaza for the entire family, with a large kid-friendly selection and retro low prices. For around $5, a good, greasy Reuben or a kielbasa plate should keep you going the rest of the day. Come Friday or Saturday evening if you want your food accompanied by accordion music.

424 E. Commerce St. ℭ 210/223-6692. Reservations for large groups for breakfast and dinner only. Sandwiches $3.25–$4.75; hot or cold plates $4.75–$5.45; main dishes (served after 5pm) $7–$8.95. AE, DC, DISC, MC, V. Mon–Sat 7am–8:30pm.

Twin Sisters *(Finds* HEALTH FOOD/DELI   If you want to avoid overpriced sandwiches and junk food while sightseeing, join the downtown working crowd at this bakery and health-food cafe just a few blocks from the Alamo. Eggless and meatless doesn't mean tasteless here—you can get great Greek salads, spicy tofu scrambles, and salsa-topped veggie burgers—but carnivores can also indulge in the likes of ham, pastrami, and salami sandwiches on the excellent bread made on the premises.

Tip: This popular place fills up by 11:30am but empties after 12:45pm, so gauge your visit accordingly. A branch in Alamo Heights, 6322 N. New Braunfels (ℭ 210/822-2265), has longer hours (Mon–Fri 7am–9pm; Sat 7am–3pm; Sun 9am–2pm).

124 Broadway at Travis. ℭ 210/354-1559. http://hotx.com/twinsister/. Reservations not accepted. $2–$6 breakfast; $4–$9 lunch. MC, V. Mon–Fri 8am–3pm.

3 King William/Southtown

EXPENSIVE

Azuca *✦* NUEVO LATINO   Anyone familiar with the late, great Latina singer Celia Cruz knows that her signature shout was "Azuca!"—roughly, "Sweetie!" This Southtown restaurant pays tribute to the Cuban-born salsa queen in ways other than its name and the pop images of her that hang in one of the dining rooms (the one with the stage and the bar, naturally).

For one, there's the ability to cross over cultures. Just as Celia appealed to a wide array of Latin American (and American) tastes, so too do such well-prepared, creatively updated dishes as Bolivian empanadas, Caribbean *carrucho* (conch meat with olives, onion, and lime), and Peruvian-style rabbit stew with Inca corn. The glass art pieces from the studio next door and brightly hued walls create visual excitement—as Celia's performances did. And the live tango shows, the merengue and Latin bands (Wed–Sat), the warm, friendly service . . . well, come on by, sugar, you'll have a blast.

713 S. Alamo. ℭ 210/225-5550. www.azuca.net. Reservations recommended. Lunch (salads and sandwiches) $6.50–$9; main courses $16–$20. AE, DC, DISC, MC, V. Mon–Thurs 11am–9:30pm (bar until 11pm); Fri–Sat 11am–10:30pm (bar until 2am).

MODERATE

Rosario's *✦* MEXICAN   This longtime Southtown favorite, one of the first restaurants to establish a hip culinary presence in the area, has toned its menu down a bit; maybe owner Lisa Wong's adventurous urges have found an outlet in Acenar (see "Downtown," earlier in this chapter). But the room, with its Frida Kahlo and Botero knockoffs and abundant neon, seems as witty as ever. And if there are fewer regional dishes, the updated Tex-Mex fare, prepared with super-fresh ingredients, is still mighty tasty. You might start with the shrimp nachos with all the fixin's or the more restrained *ceviche fina* (white fish, onions, and jalapeños marinated in lime juice), and then go on to the delicious chile relleno, with raisins and potatoes added to the chopped beef stuffing. The large size of the room means that you generally don't have to wait for a table, but it also means that the noise level can make conversation difficult.

A branch of Rosario's at the airport (Terminal 2, near Gate 34) has a more limited menu, but there's still a full bar and cool waitstaff.

910 S. Alamo. © 210/223-1806. Reservations not accepted. Main courses $7.25–$13. AE, DC, DISC, MC, V. Mon 11am–3pm; Tues–Thurs 11am–10pm; Fri–Sat 11am–11pm (bar until 2am on Fri).

INEXPENSIVE

Guenther House ★ *Value* AMERICAN   If you're not staying in a King William B&B, this is your chance to chow down in one of the neighborhood's historic homes. And it's a winner. Hearty breakfasts and light lunches are served both indoors—in a pretty Art Nouveau–style dining room added on to the Guenther family residence (built in 1860)—and outdoors on a trellised patio. The biscuits and gravy are a morning specialty, and the chicken salad (made with black olives) at lunch is excellent, but you can't go wrong with any of the wonderful baked goods made on the premises, either. Adjoining the restaurant are a small museum, a Victorian parlor, and a mill store featuring baking-related items, including mixes for lots of the Guenther House goodies. The house fronts a lovely stretch of the San Antonio River.

205 E. Guenther St. © 210/227-1061. www.guentherhouse.com. Reservations not accepted. Breakfast $3.95–$7.50; lunch $6.50–$7.25. AE, DC, DISC, MC, V. Daily 7am–3pm (house and mill store Mon–Sat 8am–4pm; Sun 8am–3pm).

Madhatters *Finds* *Kids* DELI/ECLECTIC   This colorful, sprawling storefront attracts everyone from nouveau hippies to buttoned-down refugees from the convention center 5 minutes away. They come for Age-of-Aquarius-meets-south-of-the-border food: granola bowls and breakfast burritos in the morning, veggie sandwiches and pork tamales in the evening. After work (or protests), there are cold cases full of reasonably priced wines and beers. Anglophiles won't be disappointed, either, since among the various tea parties offered, there's one for kids that includes peanut-butter-and-jelly sandwiches (crusts cut off, naturally). The NO CELLPHONES sign seems to be taking effect, so you no longer have to retreat from the bustling front room to have a conversation without hearing ringing in your ears (though the back room is very pleasant and still considerably quieter).

320 Beauregard St. © 210/212-4832. www.madhatterstea.com. Reservations not accepted. Breakfast $4–$10, sandwiches and salad plates $5.95–$9.95. AE, DISC, MC, V. Mon–Fri 7am–9pm; Sat 9am–9pm; Sun 9am–6pm.

4 Monte Vista Area

MODERATE

La Fonda on Main ★ *Value* *Kids* MEXICAN/REGIONAL MEXICAN   One of San Antonio's oldest continually operating restaurants, established in 1932, never went the way of most culinary institutions thanks to Cappy Lawton of Cappy's fame (see "Alamo Heights Area," below), who acquired it and spiffed up both menu and premises in the late 1990s. The lovely red-tile-roof residence is cheerful and bright—almost as inviting as the garden-fringed outdoor patio. The menu is divided between classic Tex-Mex, featuring giant combination plates such as the La Fonda Special (two cheese enchiladas, a beef taco, a chicken tamale, guacamole, Mexican rice, refried beans) and a "Cuisines of Mexico" section, including such traditional dishes as *mojo de ajo* (Gulf shrimp with garlic butter served with squash). Many celebrities dined here in the old days—including Franklin Roosevelt, John Wayne, and Yul Brenner, among others—and the fresh, tasty, generous specialties dished up here daily still attract power-lunch types and local families alike.

2415 N. Main. ℭ 210/733-0621. www.lafondaonmain.com. Reservations recommended for 6 or more. Main courses $10–$15. AE, DC, MC, V. Sun–Thurs 11am–3pm and 5–9:30pm; Fri–Sat 11am–3pm and 5–10:30pm; Sun brunch 11am–3pm.

Liberty Bar ⭐ *Finds* NEW AMERICAN You'd be hard-pressed to guess that this ramshackle former brothel (which opened in 1890, in case you were wondering) near the Hwy. 281 underpass hosts one of the hippest haunts in San Antonio. But, as every foodie in town can tell you, it's bright and inviting inside, and you'll find everything from comfort food (pot roast, say, or a ham-and-Swiss sandwich) to regional Mexican cuisine (the *chiles rellenos en nogada*—in a walnut cream sauce—are super). The toasted English bread with roast garlic spread or eggplant purée goes great with many of the fine—and generally affordable—wines available by the glass; there's a good beer selection, too. And don't worry—even if you've had a few too many, you're not imagining it. The house really *is* leaning.

328 E. Josephine St. ℭ 210/227-1187. Reservations recommended. Main courses $6.95–$19. AE, DISC, MC, V. Sun–Thurs 11:30am–10:30pm; Fri–Sat 11:30am–midnight; Sun brunch 10:30am–2pm (bar until midnight Sun–Thurs, 2am Fri–Sat).

INEXPENSIVE

Chris Madrids *Kids* AMERICAN/BURGERS It's hard to drop much money at this funky gas-station-turned-burger-joint, but you might lose your shirt—over the years, folks have taken to signing their tees and hanging them on the walls. An even more popular tradition is trying to eat the macho burger, as huge as its name and topped with cheese and jalapeños. The kid-friendly menu is pretty much limited to burgers, nachos, fries, and various combinations thereof, but the casual atmosphere and down-home cooking keep the large outdoor patio filled.

1900 Blanco. ℭ 210/735-3552. www.chrismadrids.com. Reservations not accepted. Main courses $3.75–$6.50. AE, DC, DISC, MC, V. Mon–Sat 11am–10pm.

Demo's *Value* GREEK Demo's is a little bit of Greece in San Antonio, across from a Greek Orthodox church. Either on the airy patio or in a two-tiered dining room with lots of murals of Greek island scenes, you can enjoy gyros, Greek burgers, dolmas, spanakopita, and other Mediterranean specialties. If you go for Dieter's Special—a Greek salad with your choice of gyros or souvlaki (beef or chicken)—you might be able to justify the baklava. In addition to this location, there's the original (but more characterless) restaurant at 7115 Blanco Rd. (ℭ 210/342-2772) near Loop 10 across from what used to be Central Park Mall. A belly dancer gyrates at the Blanco Road store on Monday nights, and at the North St. Mary's Street location on Wednesdays.

(Kids) Family-Friendly Restaurants

Chris Madrids (p. 75)   The kid-friendly menu includes burgers, nachos, fries, and various combinations thereof, and the casual atmosphere and down-home cooking make it popular with families.

Earl Abel's (p. 79)   The menu's so large—and the prices so low—at this bustling diner-type restaurant that everyone's bound to find something they like at a price that won't break the budget.

La Calesa (p. 78) and **La Fonda on Main** (p. 74)   With their friendly staff and inexpensive children's plates, both of these restaurants are great places to introduce your kids to Mexican food (Anglo options are available as well).

Madhatters (p. 74)   Even if your kids aren't up for an entire children's tea, they'll be happy to find their faves on the menu, from PB&J to plain turkey or cheese sandwiches. The chocolate chip cookies and brownies won't be sneezed at, either.

Olmos Pharmacy (p. 80)   Kids entertain themselves by swiveling in the seats at this classic soda fountain, where the food is as reasonable as it comes. They won't even mind too much when you go on and on about how this is ice cream the way it's *supposed* to be.

Schilo's (p. 73)   A high noise level, a convenient location near the River Walk (but with prices far lower than anything you'll find there), and a wide selection of familiar food make this German deli a good choice for the family.

2501 N. St. Mary's St. Ⓒ **210/732-7777**. Reservations accepted for parties of 10 or more only. Main courses $7–$9. AE, DC, DISC, MC, V. Mon–Thurs 11am–9pm; Fri–Sat 11am–midnight.

5 Alamo Heights Area

EXPENSIVE

See also Paesano's, in the "Downtown" section, p. 69.

Bistro Vatel ★★ *Value* FRENCH   Talk about a pressure cooker: In 1671, the great French chef Vatel killed himself out of shame because the fish for a banquet he was preparing for Louis XIV wasn't delivered on time. Fortunately, his descendant, Damian Watel, has less stress to contend with in San Antonio, where diners are very appreciative of the chef's efforts to bring them classic French cooking at comparatively reasonable prices. In fact, despite its strip-mall location, the place became so popular that it recently expanded into the store next door.

You can't go wrong with the rich escallop of veal with foie gras and mushrooms, and fans of sweetbreads will be pleased to find them here beautifully prepared in truffle crème fraîche sauce. Your best bet is the bargain prix-fixe dinner, where you can choose one each from four appetizers (perhaps shrimp *vol au vent*) and entrees like roasted quail and enjoy the dessert of the day.

218 E. Olmos Dr. at McCullough. Ⓒ **210/828-3141**. www.bistrovatel.com. Reservations recommended on weekends. Main courses $15–$27; prix-fixe dinner $27. AE, MC, V. Tues–Fri 11:30am–1:30pm; Tues 5:30–9pm; Wed–Fri 5:30–10pm.

Cappy's ⍟ AMERICAN   One of the earliest businesses to open in the now-burgeoning Alamo Heights neighborhood, Cappy's is set in an unusual broken-brick structure dating back to the late 1930s. But there's nothing outdated about this cheerful, light-filled place—high, wood-beam ceilings, hanging plants, colorful work by local artists—or its romantic, tree-shaded outdoor patio. The enticing smell of a wood-burning grill (not mesquite, but the somewhat milder live oak) gives a hint of some of the house specialties: the peppercorn-crusted prime tenderloin or slow-roasted Italian chicken with porcini mushrooms. Lighter fare includes honey-glazed salmon on polenta with sautéed spinach. A chef's prix fixe lets you choose an appetizer, salad, and entree. See chapter 8 for **Cappyccino's** ⍟, an offshoot of Cappy's down the block with a great by-the-glass wine list and a more casual Southwest menu.

5011 Broadway (behind Twig Book Store). ✆ **210/828-9669**. www.sawhost.com/cappy. Main courses $15–$28; prix fixe $30 (add $3 for steak entrees). AE, DC, MC, V. Mon–Fri 11am–2:30pm and 5:30–10pm; Sat 11am–3pm and 5:30–11pm; Sun 10:30am–3pm (for brunch) and 5–10pm.

Frederick's ⍟⍟ *Finds* FRENCH/ASIAN FUSION   Not as well-known as many of San Antonio's glitzier culinary stars, this restaurant—in the back of a Broadway strip mall—can match them any day (or night). The setting is nothing special, although white draperies and sunny antiqued walls have prettified the low-ceiling, darkish room. But once the food arrives at the table, you won't care if you're dining inside a concrete bunker.

For starters, consider tempura-battered sushi, strange in the abstract but wonderful in the tasting; the oh-so-crispy spring rolls of shrimp, pork, and mushrooms; or a delicate crab salad with avocado. Stellar entrees might include baked sea bass in truffle oil with artichoke hearts (yes, the restaurant's specialty is seafood). Call the cuisine Indochine—it's a mix of French and Vietnamese—or call it French fusion, as the menu does. I call it delicious.

7701 Broadway, Suite 20 (in the back of Dijon Plaza). ✆ **210/828-9050**. Reservations recommended on weekends. Main courses $17–$33. AE, DC, MC, V. Mon–Thurs 11:30am–2pm and 5:30–10pm; Fri 11:30am–2pm and 5:30–10:30pm; Sat 5:30–10:30pm.

Massimo ⍟⍟ ITALIAN   There's lots of good Americanized Italian fare in San Antonio, but for authentic *cucina italiana,* prepared by a chef from Rome (by way of New York), this is the place. The kitchen is particularly strong in pastas and risotto, all made fresh on the premises, and the potato gnocchi are a special treat. The Tuscan yellow dining rooms are airy, even if some of the tables are a bit too close together, and the romantic Red Room Bar is a popular place to listen to live music on the weekends.

Tip: If you want to economize, share a generous salad (such as the primavera with artichokes, asparagus, hearts of palm, and pecorino cheese) followed by a house-made pasta (the bowtie with salmon, say). Of course, then you'd miss such excellent *secondi* (main courses) as the veal Marsala, with a touch of cream in the delicate sauce, or the saltimbocca, a Roman specialty.

1896 Nacogdoches Rd. ✆ **210/342-8556**. www.massimo-sa.com. Reservations recommended on weekends. Pastas $13–$18; main courses $18–$29. AE, DC, DISC, MC, V. Mon–Fri 11am–2:30pm and 5–10:30pm; Sat–Sun 5–10:30pm (bar Mon–Sat 5pm–2am).

Silo ⍟⍟ NEW AMERICAN   Although it's gone through a series of chefs in recent years, Silo is regularly top-listed by San Antonio foodies, and deservedly so. More than the other chic restaurants in town, it has concentrated on food rather than on attitude, consistently presenting a small but well-balanced menu using fresh ingredients in fresh combinations. Starters such as the spicy Angus beef tenderloin lettuce wrap with chili and mint or a salad of roasted figs, spicy pecans, and goat cheese get the mix of textures and tastes just right, as do entrees like seared yellowfin tuna au poivre with soba noodle salad or chipotle marinated pork tenderloin on white cheddar andouille grits. Desserts, which change nightly, are divine too. The industrial-chic perch (the "Elevated Cuisine" alluded to in the restaurant's logo) makes for a somewhat cold setting, but service is warm and super-efficient to boot.

1133 Austin Hwy. (© 210/824-8686. www.siloelevatedcuisine.com. Reservations recommended. Main courses $17–$35; prix fixe (salad, entree, dessert) $18 (5:30–6:45pm nightly). AE, DC, DISC, MC, V. Sun 11am–2:30pm (lunch and brunch menu available) and 5:30–9pm; Tues–Thurs 11am–2:30pm and 5:30–10pm; Fri–Sat 11am–2:30pm and 5:30–11pm.

MODERATE

Ciao Lavanderia 𝑘𝑘 𝒱𝑎𝑙𝑢𝑒 ITALIAN   Goodbye laundromat, hello great dining deal. When the owner of Bistro Vatel (see above) opened a casual Italian eatery just a few doors down from his French restaurant, he stuck with his winning good-food-at-good-prices formula—and then some. In this open, cheery storefront, with its tongue-in-cheek tributes to the business that used to reside here (exposed ductwork, an old washing machine), you select from dishes in three price categories. For $6 you can opt for a salad or sandwich (perhaps a tomato, mozzarella, and pesto panini); $9 nabs you one of the pastas, thin-crust pizzas, or lighter seafood and chicken dishes; while for $12 you might enjoy such hearty entrees as a quail and mushroom risotto or pork loin scaloppine parmigiana. Daily specials such as osso buco tend to fall into these price categories, too, although a few dishes go for $15. Everything's fresh and delicious, and the portions are geared toward a normal human appetite, not supersize. A nice selection of (mostly) Italian wines enhances an already optimal experience.

226 E. Olmos Dr. (© 210/822-3990. www.ciaolavanderia.com. Reservations accepted for large parties only. Sandwiches and pizzas $6–$9; main courses $9–$15. AE, DC, DISC, MC, V. Mon 11am–2pm and 5–9pm; Tues–Thurs 11am–2pm and 5–9:30pm; Fri 11am–2pm and 5–10pm; Sat 5–10pm.

La Calesa 𝑘 𝒦𝑖𝑑𝑠 REGIONAL MEXICAN   Tucked away in a small house just off Broadway—look for Earl Abel's large sign across the street—this family-run restaurant features several dishes from the southern Yucatán region, as well as the more familiar ones from northern Mexico. The difference is mainly in the sauces, and they're done to perfection here. The mole poblano, for example, strikes a fine balance between its rich chocolate base and its fresh spices, and the *achiote* (musky-flavored seed) marinade lends a distinctive taste to the *conchinita pibil*, a classic Yucatan pork dish. Rice and black beans (more flavorful than the usual pintos) accompany many of the meals. You can eat indoors in one of three cozy dining rooms, decorated with Mexican art prints and tile work, or outside on the small flower-decked wooden porch.

2103 E. Hildebrand (just off Broadway). (© 210/822-4475. www.lacalesa.com. Reservations required for 6 or more. Main courses $5.95–$16. AE, DC, DISC, MC, V. Mon–Thurs 11am–9:30pm; Fri 11am–10:30pm; Sat 11:30am–10:30pm; Sun 11:30am–8pm.

Metropolitain 𝐹𝑖𝑛𝑑𝑠 FRENCH/BAKERY   Who'd expect to find a slice of Paris in a sprawling outdoor San Antonio mall? This bistro looks and smells authentic, from the typeface on the sign (the same used for the Paris Metro), etched glass, magazine-and-newspaper rack, and black-and-white-tiled floor to the pastry case filled with croissants, eclairs, tarts—the usual yummy French suspects. The salads and quiches and croques are also on target and well accompanied with good coffee or a nice selection of wines by the glass. This is a perfect place to take a shopping break, and it's extremely popular with locals for Sunday break-fast (the brioche French toast, served with powdered sugar, cinnamon, and Chantilly cream, is a dream). Don't bother to stick around for the overpriced dinners, though.

255 E. Basse, #940 (Alamo Quarry Market). ✆ 210/822-8227. Reservations recommended on weekends. Breakfast $6.95–$8.50; sandwiches, crepes, quiches, salads, pizzas $7.25–$13. AE, DISC, MC, V. Mon–Thurs 7am–10pm; Fri–Sat 7am–midnight, Sun 8am–10pm.

Paloma Blanca REGIONAL MEXICAN   This long-standing San Antonio favorite recently underwent a location—and personality—change. The wide-ranging menu that inspired local devotion is essentially the same, but the venue is now more upscale Mexico City than low-key San Antonio. Favorites include the enchiladas *verdes* in a tangy green tomatillo sauce, the Veracruz-style red snapper, and the vegetable chiles rellenos, a light, delicious version of the popu-lar dish. And even though it rarely gets so cold in San Antonio that you're likely to crave warmer-uppers, this restaurant has a nice selection of soups, including a comforting cream of chile poblano with corn, and *caldo tlapeño,* a spicy ver-sion of the classic tortilla soup. Sit out on the patio on a winter evening (when the temperature might drop below 60 degrees) to enjoy a bowl.

5600 Broadway. ✆ 210/822-6151. www.palomablanca.net. Reservations suggested for large groups only. Main courses $7–$15. AE, MC, V. Sun–Tues 11am–9pm; Wed–Sat 11am–10pm..

Van's CHINESE/JAPANESE/VIETNAMESE   Talk about pan-Asian. The sign outside announces that Van's is a "Chinese Seafood Restaurant and Sushi Bar," but you'll also find Vietnamese dishes on the huge menu. The dining room is low-key but appealing, with crisp green and white cloth table coverings. If you like seafood, go for the shrimp in a creamy curry sauce or the fresh crab with black-bean sauce. Alternatively, consider one of the meal-size soups—beef brisket with rice noodles, say, or a vegetable clay pot preparation—or tasty ver-sions of such Szechwan standards as spicy kung pao chicken with carrots and peanuts. Van's also has a surprisingly large wine list, so scour the shelves and cold cases for a bottle.

3214 Broadway. ✆ 210/828-8449. Reservations for large parties only. Main courses $8.95–$20. AE, DC, DISC, MC, V. Daily 11am–10pm.

INEXPENSIVE

Earl Abel's (Kids) AMERICAN   Earl Abel opened his first restaurant on Main Street in 1933. An organist for silent-film theaters in the 1920s, he had to find something else to do when the talkies took over. But his old Hollywood pals didn't forget him, and Bing Crosby and Gloria Swanson always dropped into Earl's place when they blew through San Antone.

Earl's granddaughter now runs the restaurant, which moved to Broadway in 1940, and the menu is much like it was more than 50 years ago, when what is now called comfort food was simply chow. The restaurant is no longer open 24 hours, but you can still come in after midnight for a cup of coffee and a thick slice of lemon meringue pie. The bargain daily specials and fried chicken remain the all-time favorites, but lots of folks come around for a hearty breakfast of eggs, biscuits and gravy, and grits.

4210 Broadway. ✆ 210/822-3358. Reservations not accepted. Sandwiches $5.50–$6.75; main courses $5.25–$20 (daily specials $7–$8). AE, DC, DISC, MC, V. Daily 6:30am–1am.

Olmos Pharmacy *Finds* *Kids* AMERICAN   When was the last time you drank a rich chocolate malt served in a large metal container—with a glass of whipped cream on the side? Grab a stool at Olmos's Formica counter and reclaim your childhood. Olmos Pharmacy, opened in 1938, also scoops up old-fashioned ice-cream sodas, Coke or root beer floats, sundaes, banana splits . . . if it's cold, sweet, and nostalgia-inducing, they've got it. This is also the place to come for filling American and Mexican breakfasts, a vast array of tacos, and classic burgers and sandwiches, all at seriously retro prices.

3902 McCullough. ⓒ 210/822-3361. Main courses $1.50–$5.50. AE, MC, V. Mon–Fri 7am–5pm (fountain until 6pm); Sat 8am–4pm (fountain until 5pm).

6 Northwest
VERY EXPENSIVE

Francesca's at Sunset ★★★ SOUTHWESTERN   A menu created by chef Mark Miller of Coyote Café fame, an excellent wine list (about 150 bottles, including some 30 by the glass), fine service, and idyllic Hill Country views from an ultraromantic terrace—what's not to like about Francesca's at Sunset? Starters on the seasonally changing menu might include a jumbo crab cake on spicy slaw or quail on corn basil grits. For entrees, you might find loin of antelope rubbed with mole and served with blue corn griddlecakes, or free-range chicken spiced with *pasilla chiles* sided by a piquant squash stew. I haven't tasted anything here that was too hot to handle—or less than wonderful—but if you're spice intolerant it might be best to ask about the heat of whatever you're contemplating ordering. Of course, you can always placate your palate with excellent house-made sorbets or a Jack Daniels pecan tart.

Westin La Cantera, 16641 La Cantera Pkwy. ⓒ 210/558-6500. www.westinlacantera.com/san_antonio/francesca.htm. Reservations strongly recommended. Main courses $24–$36. AE, DC, DISC, MC, V. Tues–Sat 6–10pm.

EXPENSIVE

Aldo's ITALIAN   A northwest San Antonio favorite, Aldo's offers good, old-fashioned Italian food in a pretty, old-fashioned setting. You can enjoy your meal outside, on a tree-shaded patio, or inside a 100-year-old former ranch house in one of a series of Victorian-style dining rooms. The scampi Valentino—sautéed shrimp with a basil cream sauce—is a nice starter, as are the lighter steamed mussels in marinara sauce, available seasonally. A house specialty, sautéed snapper di Aldo, comes topped with fresh lump crabmeat, artichoke hearts, mushrooms, and tomatoes in a white-wine sauce. A recent *San Antonio-Express News* review reported abysmal service—as a result, expect to be treated like royalty these days.

8539 Fredericksburg Rd. ⓒ 210/696-2536. Reservations recommended, especially on weekends. Pastas $12–$18; main courses $19–$32. AE, DC, DISC, MC, V. Mon–Thurs 11am–10pm; Fri 11am–11pm; Sat 5–11pm; Sun 5–10pm.

Bistro Time ★★ *Finds* CONTINENTAL   Hidden within a nondescript mall, which is itself buried in a nondescript northwest neighborhood, is one gem of a restaurant. This elegant eatery, with a central fountain and candlelit tables, features a series of weekly alternating menus highlighting French, Asian, American, and northern European dishes. Whichever part of the globe you visit, expect to be satisfied; when in doubt, you can't go wrong with the signature rack of lamb with blackberry peppercorn sauce. And, although I don't generally like buffets,

Frozen Assets

Austin has long had Amy's ice cream, but when it comes to home-grown frozen desserts, San Antonio has been, well, left out in the cold. But that's all changed with the new century and the introduction of **Brindles Awesome Ice Cream,** 11255 Huebner Rd. (© **210/641-5222**). Brindles features more than 200 varieties of creative ice creams, gelati, and sorbets. About 45 to 50 flavors are available on any given day. You might find such unique creations as spice apple brandy or bananas Foster ice cream; white chocolate Frangelico or candied ginger gelato; and champagne or cranberry sorbet—as well as, in every category, far more traditional flavors for ice-cream purists. Among the best-selling ice creams is the signature Brindles, a butterscotch fudge crunch inspired, like the store's name, by the multicolored coat of the owners' pet boxer. And don't miss "The Kick" ice cream whenever it's available. This mixture of pineapple, coconut, mint, and habanero chile doesn't taste hot initially, but it packs a bit of a wallop afterward.

If you don't want to have to trek all the way to Brindles' mother ship, the espresso and ice-cream parlor in the Strand shopping center on San Antonio's northwest side, you can also sample Brindles products at several of San Antonio's finest restaurants, including Acenar, Biga on the Banks, Bistro Vatel, Boudros, and Ciao Lavanderia, all covered elsewhere in this chapter.

---

the one served here (Tues–Fri 11:15am–1:45pm) is a gourmet treat as well as a bargain (it's just $12). This is not a place to watch your weight, however, as portions are huge, and rich sauces are a specialty. Desserts are particularly hard to resist; if you're lucky, a supremely chocolaty Sacher torte might be in your stars.

Tip: The early-bird specials (Mon–Fri) add soup or salad and dessert to an entree ordered before 6pm for no additional charge.

5137 Fredericksburg Rd. at Callaghan. © **210/344-6626**. www.bistro-time.com. Reservations recommended. Main courses $17–$28. AE, DC, DISC, MC, V. Mon–Thurs 11am–2pm and 5–9pm; Fri 11am–2pm and 5–10pm; Sat 5–10pm.

MODERATE

See also Sushi Zushi, in the "Downtown" section, p. 71 .

7 Only in San Antonio

Some of San Antonio's best and most popular places to eat have been reviewed in this chapter, but you can be sure you'll run into San Antonians who are passionate about other eateries I haven't covered in detail.

TACQUERIAS

Everyone has a favorite tacqueria. A couple of high-ranking ones near downtown are **Estela's,** 2200 W. Martin St. (© **210/226-2979**), which has musical (salsa, mariachi) breakfasts on Saturday and Sunday from 10am to noon, as well as a great conjunto/Tejano jukebox; and **Taco Haven,** 1032 S. Presa St. (© **210/533-2171**), where the breakfast *migas* (hearty egg and tortilla dish) or *chilaquiles* (tortillas layered with meats, beans, and cheese) will kick-start your day. In Olmos Park, **Panchito's,** 4100 McCullough (© **210/821-5338**), has hungry San Antonians lining up on weekend mornings for *barbacoa* (Mexican-style barbecue) plates, heaped with two eggs, potatoes, beans, and homemade tortillas.

BARBECUE

You'll also find emotions rising when the talk runs to barbecue, with many locals insisting that their favorite is the best and most authentic joint in town. Maybe it's because the meat has been smoked the longest, or because the place uses the best smoking technique, or its sauce is the tangiest—the criteria are endless and often completely arcane to outsiders.

Of San Antonio's more than 90 barbecue joints, a longtime local favorite that's spawned a Texas chain is **Rudy's,** 24152 I-10 West at the Leon Springs/ Boerne Stage Road exit (© **210/698-2141**). Cowboys, bicyclists, and other city folk come from miles around for what they insist are the best pork ribs, brisket, and turkey legs in town. A newer Rudy's is located near SeaWorld at 10623 Westover Hills, corner of Hwy. 151 (© **210/520-5552**).

County Line, 111 W. Crockett St., Suite 104 (© **210/229-1941**), brings the menu and the signature 1940s Texas decor of a popular Austin-based restaurant to the River Walk, although its smoker is not actually on the premises. Locals liked the brisket, sausage—and sweet ice tea—at the homegrown **Bill Miller Bar-B-Q** so much that it spread to 49 San Antonio locations (Austin and Corpus Christi are the only other two cities where Bill has ventured). To find the one nearest to you, log on to www.billmillerbbq.com.

San Antonians have been coming to **Bun 'N' Barrel,** 1150 Austin Hwy. (© **210/828-2829**), since 1950 to chaw barbecue and to check out each other's cool Chevys. Hang around on a Friday night and you might even see the occasional drag race down Austin Hwy.; winner gets the other guy's car! This joint is in a featureless area, but it's not far from the McNay Museum and the botanical gardens. ***Note to film buffs:*** If you're short on time, catch shots of this retro classic eatery in the film *Selena*.

6

Exploring San Antonio

San Antonio's dogged preservation of its past and avid development of its future guarantee that there's something in town to suit every visitor's taste. The biggest problem with sightseeing here is figuring out how to get it all in; you can spend days in the downtown area alone and still not cover everything. The itineraries below give some suggestions on how to organize your time. Walkers will love being able to hoof it from one downtown attraction to another, but the sedentary needn't despair—or drive. One of the most visitor-friendly cities imaginable, San Antonio has excellent and inexpensive tourist transportation lines, extending to such far-flung sights as SeaWorld San Antonio and Six Flags Fiesta Texas and including a "Sightseer Special" line, with stops at the Alamo, the San Antonio Museum of Art, the Witte Museum, and the San Antonio Botanical Gardens, among other attractions. See chapter 3, p. 67, for details.

Before you visit any of the paid attractions, stop in at the **San Antonio Visitor Information Center,** 317 Alamo Plaza (© **210/207-6748**), across the street from the Alamo, and ask for their *SAVE San Antonio* discount book, including everything from the large theme parks to some city tours and museums. Many hotels also have a stash of discount coupons for their guests.

SUGGESTED ITINERARIES

If You Have 1 Day

If your time is very limited, it makes sense to stay downtown, where most of the prime attractions are concentrated. Start your day at the **Alamo,** which tends to get more crowded as the day goes on. When you finish touring the complex, take a streetcar from Alamo Square to **HemisFair Park;** from the observation deck at the Tower of the Americas, you can see everything there is to see in town from a bird's-eye view. You'll easily spot **La Villita,** just across the road, a good place to do some picturesque—and historic—crafts shopping. Then board the streetcar again and head to the nearby **King William Historic District,** where you can pick up a self-guided walking tour at the office of the San Antonio Conservation Society. Have lunch at the historic Guenther House or, if you're up for Mexican, at Rosario's, in nearby Southtown. Trolley back to downtown, do a quick tour of the **San Fernando Cathedral,** the **Spanish Governor's Palace,** and **Market Square,** and then head over to the **River Walk,** where you might catch a riverboat tour before eating at one of the riverside restaurants (Boudro's or Acenar would be my top picks). Alternatively, if you can manage to get tickets to anything at either the Majestic or the Arneson River theaters, eat early (again, you'll have beaten the crowds) and enjoy the show.

If You Have 2 Days

Day 1 Follow the itinerary outlined above.

Day 2 See the San Antonio **missions** in the morning (at the least, Mission San José). In the afternoon, go to **San Antonio Museum of Art** or the **McNay** or **Witte museums.** If you're traveling with kids, you might want to visit the **Children's Museum** first thing in the morning, then go to **SeaWorld** or **Six Flags Fiesta Texas** in the afternoon (although the Witte is terrific for kids, too).

If You Have 3 Days

Day 1 Start at the **Alamo** and then tour the rest of the **missions;** that way, you'll see the military shrine in its historic context. Spend the late afternoon at one of the **theme parks** or at one of the **museums** (the San Antonio Museum of Art, the McNay, or the Witte).

Day 2 Go to **HemisFair Park** and visit the Tower of the Americas and the Institute of Texan Cultures, then stroll around nearby **La Villita.** Afterward, head down to the **King William Historic District** and take the tour of the **Steves Homestead.** (Those looking for a more contemporary experience might add—or substitute—**Southtown** and the **Blue Star Arts Complex.**) In the afternoon, enjoy a **riverboat tour** and visit the **Southwest School of Art and Craft** and, if you like cutting-edge work, **ArtPace.**

Day 3 See the **Spanish Governor's Palace** and the **San Fernando Cathedral,** then shop and have lunch at **Market Square** (if it's open, add the **Museo Americano Smithsonian [MAS]** at Market Square's entryway). In the afternoon, go to one of the **museums** you haven't yet visited or to the **San Antonio Botanical Gardens.**

If You Have 4 Days

Days 1 to 3 Follow the itinerary outlined in "If You Have 3 Days," but eliminate the attractions in the Brackenridge Park area (the Witte and the McNay museums), substituting another downtown sight or a theme park.

Day 4 Visit the attractions in the **Brackenridge Park area,** including the Japanese Tea Garden, the Witte Museum, the McNay Museum, the zoo, and the San Antonio Botanical Gardens. Some of the best restaurants in San Antonio are in this part of town.

If You Have 5 Days or More

Days 1 to 4 Follow the above 4-day itinerary.

Day 5 A day trip through scenic ranch country to **Bandera,** a cowboy town that will remind you you're in the Wild West. An afternoon trail ride is great, but if you have more time, book a room at one of Bandera's many dude ranches (a 2-night minimum stay is usually required).

1 The Top Attractions

DOWNTOWN AREA

The Alamo 🎦🎦   Visiting San Antonio without going to the Alamo is like visiting New York and not going to the Statue of Liberty. You can do it, but it would be wrong. Don't expect something dramatic, however. If you've never been to the Alamo before, you'll likely be surprised to discover that Texas's most visited site—and the symbol of its turmoil-filled history—not only is rather small, but also sits smack in the heart of downtown San Antonio. Still, you'll immediately recognize the graceful mission church, if only from having seen

Downtown San Antonio Attractions

The Alamo **11**

Artpace **4**

Blue Star Arts Complex **18**

Buckhorn Saloon & Museum **10**

Casa Navarro State Historical Park **7**

Institute of Texan Cultures **16**

Museo Americano Smithsonian **5**

Plaza Wax Museum &
Ripley's Believe It or Not **12**

Ripley's Haunted Adventure, Guinness World Records
Museum, and Davy Crockett's Tall Tales Ride **13**

San Antonio Children's Museum **9**

San Antonio Central Library **3**

San Antonio IMAX Theatre Rivercenter **14**

San Antonio Museum of Art **1**

San Fernando Cathedral **8**

Southwest School of Art & Craft **2**

Spanish Governor's Palace **6**

Steves Homestead Museum **17**

Tower of the Americas **15**

Greater San Antonio Attractions

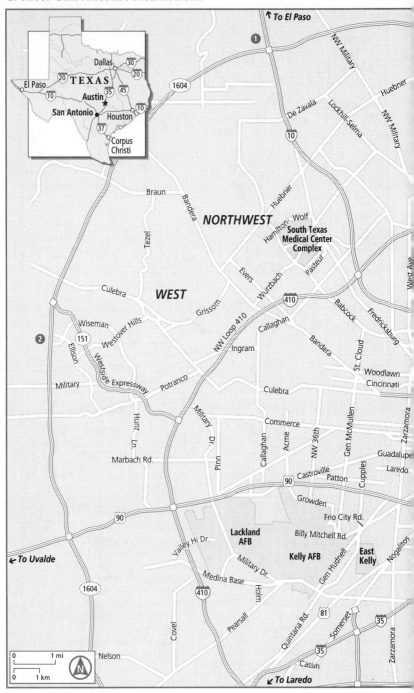

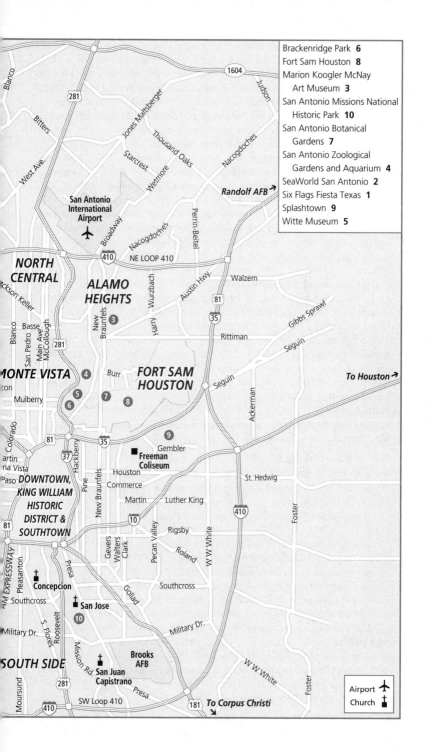

Brackenridge Park **6**
Fort Sam Houston **8**
Marion Koogler McNay
Art Museum **3**
San Antonio Missions National
Historic Park **10**
San Antonio Botanical
Gardens **7**
San Antonio Zoological
Gardens and Aquarium **4**
SeaWorld San Antonio **2**
Six Flags Fiesta Texas **1**
Splashtown **9**
Witte Museum **5**

Randolf AFB →

To Houston →

NORTH
CENTRAL

ALAMO
HEIGHTS

FORT SAM
HOUSTON

MONTE VISTA

DOWNTOWN,
KING WILLIAM
HISTORIC
DISTRICT &
SOUTHTOWN

SOUTH SIDE

San Antonio
International
Airport

Freeman
Coliseum

Concepcion

San Jose

San Juan
Capistrano

Brooks
AFB

To Corpus Christi ↘

Airport ✈
Church ⌖

endless images of it from the moment you landed in any Texas airport. Here 188 Texas volunteers turned back a much larger army—its numbers vary depending on the Texas chauvinism of the teller—of Mexican dictator Santa Anna for 13 days in March 1836. Although all the men, including pioneers Davy Crockett and Jim Bowie, were killed, their deaths were used by Sam Houston in the cry "Remember the Alamo!" to rally his troops and defeat the Mexican army at the Battle of San Jacinto a month later, securing Texas's independence.

The Daughters of the Republic of Texas, who saved the crumbling complex from being turned into a hotel by a New York syndicate in 1905, have long maintained it as a shrine to these fighters. More recently, however, additional emphasis has been placed on the Alamo's other historic roles, including as a Native American burial ground: The Alamo was actually founded on a nearby site in 1718 as the Mission San Antonio de Valero, and many converted Indians from a variety of tribes lived and died there. The complex was secularized by the end of the 18th century and leased out to a Spanish cavalry unit; however, by the time the famous battle took place, it had been abandoned. **A Wall of History,** erected in the late 1990s, provides a good chronology of these events.

Little remains of the original mission today: Only the **Long Barrack** (formerly the *convento,* or living quarters for the missionaries) and the **mission church** are still here. The former houses a museum detailing the history of Texas in general and the battle in particular, and the latter includes artifacts of the Alamo fighters, along with an information desk and a small gift shop. A larger **museum** and gift shop are at the back of the complex. There are also a peaceful **garden** and an excellent **research library** (closed Sun) on the grounds. All in all, though, the complex is fairly small. You won't need to spend more than an hour here. Interesting historical presentations are given every half-hour by Alamo staffers; for private, after-hour tours, phone ℂ **210/225-1391,** ext. 34.

300 Alamo Plaza. ℂ **210/225-1391.** www.thealamo.org. Free admission (donations welcome). Mon–Sat 9am–5:30pm; Sun 10am–5:30pm. Closed Dec 24–25. Streetcar: Red or Blue lines.

King William Historic District ⊛   San Antonio's first suburb, King William was settled in the late 19th century by prosperous German merchants who displayed their wealth through extravagant homes and named the 25-block area after Kaiser Wilhelm of Prussia. (The other residents of San Antonio were rather less complimentary about this German area, which they dubbed "Sauerkraut Bend.")

The neighborhood fell into disrepair for a few decades, but you'd never know it from the pristine condition of most of the houses here today. The area has gotten so popular that tour buses have been restricted after certain hours. Anyway, it's much more pleasant to stroll up and down tree-shaded King William Street, gawking at the beautifully landscaped, magnificent mansions. Stop at the headquarters of the San Antonio Conservation Society, 107 King William St. (ℂ **210/224-6163;** www.saconservation.org), and pick up a self-guided walking tour booklet outside the gate. If you go at a leisurely pace, the stroll should take about an hour. Only the Steves Homestead Museum (see "More Attractions," later in this chapter) and the Guenther House (see chapter 5) are open to the public; figure 2 more hours if you plan to visit both.

East bank of the river just south of downtown. Streetcar: Blue line.

La Villita National Historic District ⊛   Developed by European settlers along the higher east bank of the San Antonio River in the late 18th and early

19th centuries, La Villita (the Little Village) was on the proverbial wrong side of the tracks until natural flooding of the west-bank settlements made it the fashionable place to live. It fell back into poverty by the beginning of the 20th century, only to be revitalized in the late 1930s by artists and craftspeople and the San Antonio Conservation Society. Now boutiques, crafts shops, and restaurants occupy this historic district, which resembles a Spanish/Mexican village, replete with shaded patios, plazas, brick-and-tile streets, and some of the settlement's original adobe structures. You can see (but not enter, unless you rent it for an event) the house of General Cós, the Mexican military leader who surrendered to the Texas revolutionary army in 1835, or attend a performance at the Arneson River Theatre (see "The Performing Arts," chapter 8). Walking tour maps of these and other historical structures are available throughout the site. It'll take you only about 20 minutes to do a quick walk-through, unless you're an inveterate shopper—in which case, all bets are off.

Bounded by Durango, Navarro, and Alamo sts. and the River Walk. ⓒ 210/207-8610. www.lavillita.com. Free admission. Shops daily 10am–6pm. Closed Thanksgiving, Dec 25, and Jan 1. Streetcar: Red, Purple, or Blue lines.

Market Square ⓡ   It may not be quite as colorful as it was when live chickens squawked around overflowing, makeshift vegetable stands, but Market Square will still transport you south of the border. Stalls in the indoor El Mercado sell everything from onyx paperweights and manufactured serapes to high-quality crafts from the interior of Mexico. Across the street, the Farmer's Market, which formerly housed the produce market, has carts with more modern goods. If you can tear yourself away from the merchandise, take a look around at the buildings in the complex; some date back to the late 1800s.

Bring your appetite along with your wallet: In addition to two Mexican restaurants (see chapter 5 for the Mi Tierra), almost every weekend sees the emergence of food stalls selling specialties such as *gorditas* (chubby corn cakes topped with a variety of goodies) or funnel cakes (fried dough sprinkled with powdered sugar). Most of the city's Hispanic festivals are held here, and mariachis usually stroll the square. The Museo Americano Smithsonian (MAS), scheduled to open on July 4, 2005 (see "More Attractions," later in this chapter), should provide a historic context to an area that can seem pretty touristy—though no more so than any Mexican border town.

Bounded by Commerce, Santa Rosa, Dolorosa, and I-35. ⓒ 210/207-8600. http://tavernini.com/mercado. Free admission. El Mercado and Farmer's Market Plaza summer daily 10am–8pm; winter daily 10am–6pm; restaurants and some shops open later. Closed Thanksgiving, Dec 25, Jan 1, and Easter. Streetcar: Red, Purple, or Yellow lines.

The River Walk (Paseo del Río) ⓡⓡⓡ   Just a few steps below the streets of downtown San Antonio is another world, alternately soothing and exhilarating, depending on where you venture. The quieter areas of the 2½ paved miles of winding riverbank, shaded by cypresses, oaks, and willows, exude a tropical, exotic aura. The River Square and South Bank sections, chockablock with sidewalk cafes, tony restaurants, bustling bars, high-rise hotels, and even a huge shopping mall, have a festive, sometimes frenetic feel. Tour boats, water taxis, and floating picnic barges regularly ply the river, and local parades and festivals fill its banks with revelers.

Although plans to cement over the river after a disastrous flood in 1921 were stymied, it wasn't until the late 1930s that the federal Works Project Administration

The Alamo: The Movie(s)

At least one weighty tome, Frank Thompson's *Alamo Movies,* has been devoted to the plethora of films featuring the events that occurred at San Antonio's most famous site. Some outtakes:

Most famous movie about the Alamo not actually shot at the Alamo: *The Alamo* (1959), starring John Wayne as Davy Crockett. Although it has no San Antonio presence, it was shot in Texas. Wayne had considered shooting the film in Mexico, but was told it wouldn't be distributed in Texas if he did.

Latest controversy-ridden attempt to tell the story of the Alamo: A 2004 Disney version that was originally supposed to be directed by Ron Howard but was eventually only coproduced by him. Directed by John Lee Hancock and starring Dennis Quaid, Billy Bob Thornton, and Jason Patric, among others, it was not as big a flop as the battle, perhaps, but not a winner, either.

Most accurate celluloid depiction of the Alamo story (and also the largest): *Alamo—The Price of Freedom,* showing at the San Antonio IMAX Theater Rivercenter. According to writer and historian Stephen Harrigan in an interview on National Public Radio, it's "90% accurate."

Least controversial film featuring the Alamo: *Miss Congeniality,* starring Sandra Bullock and Benjamin Bratt. A beauty pageant presided over by William Shatner takes place in front of the shrine to the Texas martyrs.

(WPA) carried out architect Robert Hugman's designs for the waterway, installing cobblestone walks, arched bridges, and entrance steps from various street-level locations. And it wasn't until the late 1960s, when the River Walk proved to be one of the most popular attractions of the HemisFair exposition, that its commercial development began in earnest.

There's a real danger of the River Walk becoming overdeveloped—new restaurants, hotels, and entertainment complexes continue to open at an alarming pace, and the crush of bodies along the busiest sections can be claustrophobic in the summer heat—but plenty of quieter spots still exist. And if you're caught up in the sparkling lights reflected on the water on a breeze-swept night, you might forget there was anyone else around.

All the streetcars stop somewhere along the river's route. The River Walk Streetcar Station at Commerce and Losoya is accessible to travelers with disabilities.

San Antonio Museum of Art ⭐⭐ This attraction may not be top-listed by everyone, but I enjoy doable (read: not overwhelmingly large) museums with interesting architecture and collections related to the cities in which they're located—and this one definitely fits the bill on all those counts. Several castle-like buildings of the 1904 Lone Star Brewery were gutted, connected, and transformed into a visually exciting exhibition space in 1981, which also offers terrific views of downtown from the multiwindowed crosswalk between the structures. Although holdings range from early Egyptian, Greek, Oceanic, and Asian (see note, below) to 19th- and 20th-century American, for me the prime reason to come is the $11 million Nelson A. Rockefeller Center for Latin American Art, opened in 1998. This 30,000-square-foot wing hosts the most comprehensive collection of Latin American art in the United States, with pre-Columbian, folk, Spanish colonial, and contemporary works. You'll see everything here from magnificently ornate altarpieces to a whimsical Day of the Dead tableau. Computer stations add historical perspective to the collection, which is a nationwide resource for Latino culture. If any of this sounds appealing to you, allot at least 2 hours for your visit.

Note: The Lenora and Walter F. Brown Asian Art Wing will debut in the spring of 2005, giving the museum the largest Asian art collection in Texas and one of the largest in the Southwest. Some galleries are currently closed due to the wing's construction. If you're visiting before spring and want to make sure the section you're interested in will be open, phone ahead or check the museum's website.

200 W. Jones Ave. ⓒ 210/978-8100. www.sa-museum.org. Admission $8 adults, $7 seniors, $5 students with ID, $3 children 4–11, free for children under 4. Free general admission Tues 4–9pm (fee for some special exhibits). Tues 10am–8pm; Wed–Sat 10am–5pm; Sun noon–6pm. Closed Thanksgiving Day, Dec 25, Jan 1, Easter Sunday, and Fiesta Friday. Bus: 7, 8, 9, or 14.

ALAMO HEIGHTS AREA

Marion Koogler McNay Art Museum ★★   Well worth a detour from downtown, this museum is one of my favorite spots. It's got a knockout setting on a hill north of Brackenridge Park with a forever view of the city, and it's in a sprawling Spanish Mediterranean–style mansion (built 1929) so picturesque that it's constantly used as a backdrop for weddings and photo shoots. The McNay doesn't have a world-class art collection, but it has a good one, with at least one work by most American and European masters of the past 2 centuries. And the Tobin Collection of Theatre Arts, including costumes, set designs, and rare books, is outstanding. The McNay also hosts major traveling shows. It'll take you at least an hour to go through this place at a leisurely pace, longer if it's cool enough for you to stroll the beautiful 23-acre grounds dotted with sculpture and stunning landscaping. It's also well worth taking the time to view the 15-minute orientation film about oil heiress and artist Marion Koogler McNay, who established the museum. And, of course, there's a gift shop.

6000 N. New Braunfels Ave. ⓒ 210/824-5368. www.mcnayart.org. Free admission ($5 suggested donation; fee for special exhibits). Tues–Sat 10am–5pm; Sun noon–5pm. Docent tours Sun at 2pm Oct–May. Closed Jan 1, July 4, Thanksgiving, and Dec 25. Bus: 14.

Witte Museum ★ *Kids*   A family museum that adults will enjoy as much as kids, the Witte focuses on Texas history, natural science, and anthropology, with occasional forays as far afield as the Berlin Wall. Your senses will be engaged along with your intellect: You might hear bird calls as you stroll through the Texas Wild exhibits, or feel rough-hewn stone carved with Native American pictographs beneath your feet. Children especially like exhibits devoted to mummies and dinosaurs, as well as the EcoLab, where live Texas critters range from tarantulas to tortoises. But the biggest draw for kids is the terrific HEB Science Treehouse, a four-level, 15,000-square-foot science center that sits behind the museum on the banks of the San Antonio River; its hands-on activities are geared to all ages. Also on the grounds are a butterfly and hummingbird garden and three restored historic homes. *Note:* The museum recently acquired the wonderful Herzberg Circus Collection, and parts of it are regularly incorporated into the museum's exhibits.

3801 Broadway (adjacent to Brackenridge Park). € 210/357-1900. www.wittemuseum.org. Admission $7 adults, $6 seniors, $5 children 4–11, free for children under 4. Free Tues 3–8pm. Tues 10am–8pm; Mon and Wed–Sat 10am–5pm; Sun noon–5pm. Closed 3rd Mon in Oct, Thanksgiving, and Dec 24–25. Bus: 7, 9, or 14.

SOUTH SIDE

San Antonio Missions National Historical Park ★★   Remember the Alamo? Well, it was originally just the first of five missions established by the Franciscans along the San Antonio River to Christianize the native population. The four other missions, which now fall under the aegis of the National Park Service, are still active parishes, run in cooperation with the Archdiocese of San Antonio. But the missions were more than churches: They were complex communities. The Park Service has assigned each of them an interpretive theme to educate visitors about the roles they played in early San Antonio society. You can visit them separately, but if you have the time, see them all; they were built uncharacteristically close together and—now that you don't have to walk there or ride a horse—it shouldn't take you more than 2 or 3 hours to see them. Currently, you have to follow the brown signs that direct you from the Alamo to the 5½-mile mission trail that begins at Mission Concepción and winds its way south through the city streets to Mission Espada, but in the late 1990s ground was broken for the $17.7 million Mission Trails Project, designed to create a 12-mile hike-and-bike route along the San Antonio River and improve signage along the driving route. Parts of it—especially the biking trails—are already operational, but the entire project won't be completed until late 2006 and the signage is currently still rather confusing.

The first of the missions you'll come to as you head south, **Concepción,** 807 Mission Rd. at Felisa, was built in 1731. The oldest unrestored Texas mission, Concepción looks much as it did 200 years ago. We tend to think of religious sites as somber and austere, but traces of color on the facade and restored wall paintings inside show how cheerful this one originally was.

San José ★★, 6701 San José Dr. at Mission Road, established in 1720, was the largest, best known, and most beautiful of the Texas missions. It was reconstructed to give visitors a complete picture of life in a mission community—right down to the granary, mill, and Indian quarters. The beautiful Rose Window is a big attraction, and popular mariachi masses are held here every Sunday at noon (come early if you want a seat). This is also the site of the missions' excellent visitor center. If you're going to visit only one of the missions, this is it.

Moved from an earlier site in east Texas to its present location in 1731, **San Juan Capistrano,** 9101 Graf at Ashley, doesn't have the grandeur of the missions to the north—the larger church intended for it was never completed—but the original simple chapel and the wilder setting give it a peaceful, spiritual aura. A short (.3-mile) interpretive trail, with a number of overlook platforms, winds through the woods to the banks of the old river channel.

The southernmost mission in the San Antonio chain, **San Francisco de la Espada** ★, 10040 Espada Rd., also has an ancient, isolated feel, although the beautifully maintained church shows just how vital it still is to the local community. Be sure to visit the Espada Aqueduct, part of the mission's original *acequia* (irrigation ditch) system, about 1 mile north of the mission. Dating from 1740, it's one of the oldest Spanish aqueducts in the United States.

Headquarters: 2202 Roosevelt Ave. Visitors Center: 6701 San José Dr. at Mission Rd. € 210/932-1001. www.nps.gov/saan. Free admission (donations accepted). All the missions open daily 9am–5pm. Closed

Thanksgiving, Dec 25, and Jan 1. National Park Ranger tours daily. Bus: 42 stops at Mission San José (and near Concepción).

FAR NORTHWEST

Six Flags Fiesta Texas *Kids*   Every year brings another thrill ride to this theme park, set on 200 acres in an abandoned limestone quarry and surrounded by 100-foot cliffs. In 2004, Tornado, an extremely wet and wild tunnel and funnel tubing experience, joined the Superman Krypton Coaster, nearly a mile of twisted steel with six inversions; the Rattler, one of the world's highest and fastest wooden roller coasters; the 60-mph-plus Poltergeist roller coaster; and Scream!, a 20-story space shot and turbo drop, to name just a few. Laser games and virtual reality simulators complete the technophile picture. Feeling more primal? Wet 'n' wild attractions include the Lone Star Lagoon, the state's largest wave pool; the Texas Treehouse, a five-story drenchfest whose surprises include a 1,000-gallon cowboy hat that tips over periodically to soak the unsuspecting; and Bugs' White Water Rapids.

If you want to avoid both sogginess and adrenaline overload, there is a vast variety of food booths, shops, crafts demonstrations, and live shows—everything from 1950s musical revues to the laser-fireworks shows (held each summer evening). This theme park still has some local character, dating back to the days when it was plain old Fiesta Texas: Themed areas include a Hispanic village, a western town, and a German town. But when it came under the aegis of Six Flags—a Time Warner company—Looney Tunes cartoon characters such as Tweety Bird became ubiquitous, especially in the endless souvenir shops.

17000 I-10W (corner of I-10W and Loop 1604). ✆ **800/473-4378** or 210/697-5050. www.sixflags.com/parks/fiestatexas. Admission $42 adults, $29 seniors 55 and over, $27 children under 48 in., free for children under 3. Discounted 2-day and season passes available. Parking $8 per day. The park opens at 10am; closing times vary depending on the season, as late as 10pm in summer. The park is generally open daily late May to mid-Aug; Sat–Sun Mar–May and Sept–Oct; closed Nov–Feb. Call ahead or visit website for current information. Bus: 94 (summer only). Take exit 555 (La Cantera Pkwy.) on I-10W.

WEST SIDE

SeaWorld San Antonio *Kids*   Leave it to Texas to provide Shamu, the performing killer whale, with his most spacious digs: At 250 acres, this SeaWorld is the largest of the Anheuser-Busch–owned parks, which also makes it the largest marine theme park in the world. If you're a theme park fan, you're likely to find the walk-through habitats where you can watch penguins, sea lions, sharks, tropical fish, and flamingos do their thing fascinating, but the aquatic acrobatics at such stadium shows as Shamu Adventure, combining live action and video close-ups, and Viva, where divers and synchronized swimmers frolic with whales and dolphins, might be even more fun.

You needn't get frustrated just looking at all that water because there are loads of places here to get wet. The Lost Lagoon has a huge wave pool and water slides aplenty, and the Texas Splashdown flume ride and the Rio Loco river-rapids ride also offer splashy fun. Younger children can cavort in Shamu's Happy Harbor and the "L'il Gators" section of the Lost Lagoon or take a ride on the Shamu Express kiddie coaster.

Nonaquatic activities abound, too. You can ride the Steel Eel, a huge "hyper-coaster" that starts out with a 150-foot dive at 65 mph, followed by several bouts of weightlessness, or Great White, the Southwest's first inverted coaster—which means riders will go head-over-heels during 2,500 feet of loops (don't eat before either of them). It's well worth sticking around for the shows offered in the evening during the peak summer season or the Halloween activities held on October weekends—if you're not too tuckered from the rides.

10500 SeaWorld Dr., 16 miles northwest of downtown San Antonio at Ellison Dr. and Westover Hills Blvd. ⓒ 800/700-7786. www.seaworld.com. 1-day pass $43 adults, $3 off adult price for seniors (55 and over), $33 children 3–9, free for children under 3. Discounted 2-day and season passes available. Parking $8 per day. Open early Mar to late Nov. Days of operation vary. Open at 10am on operating days, closing times vary. Call ahead or check website for current information. Bus: 64. From Loop 410 or from Hwy. 90W, exit Hwy. 151W to the park.

2 More Attractions

DOWNTOWN AREA

ArtPace   San Antonio's cutting-edge contemporary art gallery features rotating shows displaying the work of artists selected by a guest curator for 2-month residencies at the facility. One artist must be from Texas, one from anywhere else in the United States, and one from anywhere else in the world. The result has been a fascinating mélange, including everything from twists on the traditional—such as a monumental drawing of a winter landscape populated by men in black tracksuits, a lenticular print (an image that shows depth and motion when the viewing angle changes) in which the Alamo vanishes before one's eyes—to the more cutting edge: an installation of 5,500 pounds of airplane parts or rooftop speakers that sing until the sun sets. Lecture series by the artists as well as public forums to discuss the work have also helped make this a very stimulating art space.

445 N. Main Ave. ⓒ 210/212-4900. www.artpace.org. Free admission. Wed and Fri–Sun noon–5pm; Thurs noon–8pm. Check local listings or call for lectures and other special events. Bus: 2, 82, or 88.

Blue Star Arts Complex ⭐   This huge former warehouse in Southtown hosts a collection of working studios and galleries, along with a performance space for the Jump-Start theater company. The 11,000-square-foot artist-run Contemporary Art Center is its anchor. The style of work varies from gallery to gallery—you'll see everything from primitive-style folk art to feminist photography—but the level of professionalism is generally high. One of the most interesting spaces is SAY Si, featuring exhibitions by talented neighborhood high-school students that might include collages or book art. A number of galleries are devoted to (or have sections purveying) arty gift items such as jewelry, picture frames, and crafts.

116 Blue Star (bordered by Probandt, Blue Star, and South Alamo sts. and the San Antonio River). ⓒ 210/ 227-6960. www.bluestarartspace.org. Free admission ($2 suggested donation for art center). Hours vary from gallery to gallery; most are open Wed–Sun noon–6pm, with some opening at 10am. Streetcar: Blue line.

Buckhorn Saloon & Museum *(Overrated*   If you like your educational experiences accompanied by a tall cold brew, this is the place for you. With its huge stuffed animals, mounted fish, and wax museum version of history, this collection fulfills every out-of-stater's stereotype of what a Texas museum might be like. It's not nearly as funky as it was when it was in the old Lone Star brewery—all those dead animals seem out of place in this modern space—but it's still got exhibits like the church made out of 50,000 matchsticks and pictures designed from rattlesnake rattles. The facility includes a re-creation of the turn-of-the-century Buckhorn saloon, a curio shop, and a transported historic bar. Lots of people seem to like this place, but others think it's a bit pricey for what you get.

318 E. Houston St. ⓒ 210/247-4000. www.buckhornmuseum.com. Admission $10 adults, $9 seniors (55 and up), $7.50 children 3–11. Labor Day to Memorial Day daily 10am–5pm; rest of year daily 10am–6pm (later hours in summer). Closed Thanksgiving and Dec 25. Streetcar: Red or Blue lines.

Casa Navarro State Historic Site   A key player in Texas's transition from Spanish territory to American state, José Antonio Navarro was the Mexican mayor of San Antonio in 1821, a signer of the 1836 declaration of Texas independence, and the only native Texan to take part in the convention that ratified the annexation of Texas to the United States in 1845. His former living quarters, built around 1850, are an interesting amalgam of the architectural fashions of his time: The restored office, house, and separate kitchen, constructed of adobe and limestone, blend elements from Mexican, French, German, and pioneer styles. Guided tours and demonstrations are available; call ahead to inquire.

228 S. Laredo St. ⓒ 210/226-4801. www.tpwd.state.tx.us/park/jose. Admission $2 adults, $1 children 6–12, free for children under 6. Wed–Sun 10am–4pm. Streetcar: Purple line.

Institute of Texan Cultures *Kids*   It's the rare visitor who won't discover here that his or her ethnic group has contributed to the history of Texas: 26 different ethnic and cultural groups are represented in the imaginative, hands-on displays of this educational center, which is one of three campuses of the University of Texas at San Antonio. Outbuildings include a one-room schoolhouse, an adobe home, a windmill, and the multimedia Dome Theater, which presents images of Texas on 36 screens. There are always a variety of heritage festivals and kid-friendly shows and events such as pioneer life reenactments, holography exhibits, ghost-tale storytellers at Halloween, and the like; phone or check the institute's website for a current schedule. An excellent photo archive here, open to the public by appointment, holds more than 3 million images. Call ⓒ **210/458-2298** for information on using it.

801 S. Bowie St. (at Durango St. in HemisFair Park). ⓒ 210/458-2300. www.texancultures.utsa.edu. Admission $7 adults; $4 seniors, military (with ID), and children 3–12. Tues–Wed 10am–6pm; Thurs–Sat 10am–8pm; Sun noon–5pm. Dome shows presented at 11am, 12:30, 2, and 4pm (Thurs–Sat 6pm shows also, Sun no 11am show). Closed Thanksgiving, Dec 24–25, Jan 1, and for 3 days during the Texas Folklife Festival (held in June). Streetcar: Yellow or Purple lines.

Museo Americano Smithsonian   Anyone who's visited Market Square in the past few years has seen the bland white structure at its entryway, the Centro des Artes, turn vivid shades of raspberry and lime. The building is slated to open on July 4, 2005, as a showcase of Hispanic arts and culture in Texas. It's appropriate that among the first exhibits of this Smithsonian affiliate is "Our Journeys/Our Stories: Portraits of Latino Achievements," a traveling show created by the Smithsonian. Using photographs and biographical profiles of 24 individuals (from Nobel Laureate Mario Molina to singer Celia Cruz) and one family, the exhibit traces Latino experiences, traditions, and ideals in the U.S. Check the website or phone closer to the opening date to find out what else there is to see—and what the museum's hours are.

101 S. Santa Rosa Blvd. (at Commerce, in Market Square). ⓒ 210/458-2300. www.thealameda.org. Admission $6 adults, $3 children. Call for hours. Streetcar: Red, Purple, or Yellow lines.

San Antonio Central Library   San Antonio's main library, opened in the mid-1990s at a cost of $38 million, has a number of important holdings (including part of the Hertzberg Circus Collection, scattered when it lost its museum home in 2001) but it is most notable for its architecture. Ricardo Legorreta, renowned for his buildings throughout Mexico, created a wildly colorful and whimsical public space that people apparently love to enter—by the second month after the library opened, circulation had gone up 95%. The boxy building, painted what has been called "enchilada red," is designed like a hacienda around an internal courtyard. A variety of skylights, windows, and wall colors (including bright purples and yellows) afford a different perspective from each of the six floors. A gallery offers monthly exhibits of paintings, photography, textiles, and more.

600 Soledad. (C) 210/207-2500. www.santantonio.gov/library. Free admission. Mon–Thurs 9am–9pm; Fri–Sat 9am–5pm; Sun 11am–5pm. Bus: 3, 4, 90, 91, or 92.

San Fernando Cathedral ⭐   Construction of a church on this site, overlooking what was once the town's central plaza, was begun in 1738 by San Antonio's original Canary Island settlers and completed in 1749. Part of the early structure—the oldest cathedral sanctuary in the United States and the oldest parish church in Texas—is incorporated into the magnificent Gothic revival–style cathedral built in 1868. Jim Bowie got married here, and General Santa Anna raised the flag of "no quarter" from the roof during the siege of the Alamo in 1836. The cathedral underwent major interior and exterior renovations in 2002; its most impressive new addition, a 24-foot-high gilded *retablo* (gradine), was unveiled in 2003.

115 Main Plaza. (C) 210/227-1297. www.sfcathedral.org. Free admission. Daily 6am–7pm; gift shop Mon–Fri 9am–4:30pm, Sat until 5pm. Streetcar: Purple or Yellow lines.

Southwest School of Art and Craft ⭐   A stroll along the River Walk to the northern corner of downtown will lead you into another world: a rare French-designed cloister where contemporary crafts are now being created. An exhibition gallery and artist studios–cum–classrooms (not open to visitors) occupy the garden-filled grounds of the first girl's school in San Antonio, established by the Ursuline order in the mid–19th century. Learn about both the school and the historic site at the Visitors Center Museum in the First Academy Building. The Ursuline Sales Gallery carries unique crafts items, most made by the school's artists. You can enjoy a nice, light lunch in the Copper Kitchen Restaurant (weekdays 11:30am–2pm, closed national holidays). The adjacent Navarro Campus, built in the late 1990s, is not as architecturally interesting, but it's worth stopping there for its large contemporary art gallery—and for the Art*O*Mat [sic], a converted vending machine selling local artists' work for $5 a pop. What a steal!

300 Augusta. (C) 210/224-1848. www.swschool.org. Free admission. Mon–Sat 9am–5pm (galleries on both campuses), Sun 11am–4pm (Navarro Campus gallery only); Mon–Sat 10am–5pm (gift shop); Mon–Sat 10am–5pm, Sun 11am–4pm (museum). Streetcar: Blue line.

Spanish Governor's Palace ⭐ *Finds*   Never actually a palace, this 1749 adobe structure formerly served as the residence and headquarters for the captain of the Spanish presidio. It became the seat of Texas government in 1772, when San Antonio was made capital of the Spanish province of Texas and, by the time it was purchased by the city in 1928, it had served as a tailor's shop, barroom, and schoolhouse. The building, with high ceilings crossed by protruding viga beams, is beautiful in its simplicity, and the 10 rooms crowded with period furnishings paint a vivid portrait of upper-class life in a rough-hewn society. It's interesting to see how the other half lived in an earlier era, and I love to sit out on the tree-shaded, cobblestone patio, listening to the burbling of the stone fountain. Be sure to ask a staff member to explain the symbols carved in the grand wooden entryway to the complex.

105 Plaza de Armas. (C) 210/224-0601. www.sanantonio.gov/sapar/spanishgovernorspalace.asp. Admission $1.50 adults, 75¢ children 7–13, free for children under 7. Mon–Sat 9am–5pm; Sun 10am–5pm. Closed, Jan 1, San Jacinto Day, Thanksgiving, andDec 25(during Fiesta week). Streetcar: Purple line.

Impressions

We have no city, except, perhaps, New Orleans, that can vie, in point of picturesque interest that attaches to odd and antiquated foreignness, with San Antonio.

—Frederick Law Olmsted, *A Journey Through Texas* (1853)

Steves Homestead Museum   Built in 1876 for lumber magnate Edward Steves, this Victorian mansion was restored by the San Antonio Conservation Society, to whom it was willed by Steves's granddaughter. Believed to have been built by prominent San Antonio architect Alfred Giles, and one of the only houses in the King William Historic District open to the public, it gives a fascinating glimpse into the lifestyles of the rich and locally famous of the late 19th century. You can't enter without taking a 30- to 45-minute-long docent-led tour, which is fine, as you don't want to miss the great gossip about the Steves family that the Society's very knowledgeable volunteers pass along.

509 King William St. ✆ 210/225-5924. www.saconservation.org. Admission $5 adults, $4 seniors, $3 students with ID and active military, free for children under 12. Daily 10am–4:15pm (last tour at 3:30pm). Closed major holidays. Streetcar: Blue line.

Tower of the Americas ⊛   For a quick take on the lay of the land, just circle the eight panoramic panels on the observation level of the Tower of the Americas. The 750-foot-high tower was built for the HemisFair in 1968. The deck sits at the equivalent of 59 stories and is lit for spectacular night viewing. The tower also hosts a rotating restaurant with surprisingly decent food (for the revolving genre) as well as a thankfully stationary cocktail lounge.

Note: As of press time, due to an unresolved contractual dispute, there is a possibility that the Tower will be closed for up to a year.

600 HemisFair Park. ✆ 210/207-8615. Admission $4 adults, $2.50 seniors 55 and up, $1.50 children 4–11, free for children under 4. Sun–Thurs 9am–10pm; Fri–Sat 9am–11pm. Streetcar: Yellow or Purple lines.

ALAMO HEIGHTS AREA

San Antonio Zoological Gardens and Aquarium (Kids   I want to like this zoo, considered one of the top facilities in the country because of its conservation efforts and its successful breeding programs (it produced the first white rhino in the U.S.). Home to more than 700 species, it has one of the largest animal collections in the United States. But, although the zoo has expanded and upgraded its exhibits many times since it opened in 1914, the cages are small, the landscaping looks droopy, and some of the animals seem depressed. Still, kids who haven't recently been to SeaWorld or the San Diego Zoo will get a kick out of many critters (the Lory Encounter is especially popular), and parents will appreciate the fact that they won't run into an expensive gift shop around every corner.

3903 N. St. Mary's St. in Brackenridge Park. ✆ 210/734-7183. www.sazoo-aq.org. Admission $8 adults, $6 seniors 62 and over and children 3–11, free for children under 3. Daily 9am–5pm (until 6pm in summer). Bus: 7 or 8.

FORT SAM HOUSTON AREA

Fort Sam Houston   Since 1718, when the armed Presidio de Béxar was established to defend the Spanish missions, the military has played a key role in San Antonio's development, and it remains one of the largest employers in town today. The 3,434-acre Fort Sam Houston affords visitors an unusual opportunity to view the city's military past (the first military flight in history took off from the fort's spacious parade grounds) in the context of its military present—the fort currently hosts the Army Medical Command and the headquarters of the Fifth Army. Most of its historic buildings are still in use and thus off-limits, but three are open to the public. The **Fort Sam Houston Museum,** 1210 Stanley Rd., Bldg. 123 (© **210/221-1886;** www.cs.amedd.army.mil/rlbc; free admission; open Wed–Sun 10am–4pm), details the history of the armed forces in Texas with a special focus on San Antonio. The **U.S. Army Medical Department Museum,** 2310 Stanley Rd., Bldg. 1046 (© **210/221-6277** or 221-6358; www.ameddgiftshop.com/museum.htm; free admission; open Tues–Sat 10am–4pm), displays army medical equipment and American prisoner-of-war memorabilia. The oldest building on the base, the **Quadrangle** ⭐, 1400 E. Grayson St. (no ©; free admission; open Mon–Fri 8am–5pm, Sat–Sun noon–5pm), an impressive 1876 limestone structure, is centered on a brick clock tower and encloses a grassy square where peacocks and deer roam freely. The Apache chief Geronimo was held captive here for 40 days in 1886. Free self-guided tour maps of the historic sites are available in all three buildings. Anyone wishing to visit the fort must enter through the Walters Gate (take the Walters St. exit off I-35) and present a driver's license.

Grayson St. and New Braunfels Ave., about 2½ miles northeast of downtown. © **210/221-1151** (public affairs). There is no longer public transportation to the Quadrangle.

3 Parks & Gardens

Brackenridge Park ⭐   With its rustic stone bridges and winding walkways, the city's main park, opened in 1899, has a charming, old-fashioned feel, and serves as a popular center for such recreational activities as golf, polo, biking, and picnicking. I especially like the **Japanese Tea Garden** ⭐ (also known as the Japanese Sunken Garden), created in 1917 by prison labor to beautify an abandoned cement quarry, one of the largest in the world in the 1880s and 1890s. (The same quarry furnished cement rock for the state capitol in Austin.) You can still see a brick smokestack and a number of the old lime kilns among the beautiful flower arrangements, lusher than those in most Japanese gardens. After Pearl Harbor, the site was officially renamed the Chinese Sunken Garden, and a Chinese-style entryway was added on. Not until 1983 was the original name restored. Just to the southwest, a bowl of limestone cliffs found to have natural acoustic properties was turned into the **Sunken Garden Theater** (see "The Performing Arts" in chapter 8). A 60-foot-high waterfall and water lily–laced ponds are among its lures. Across from the entrance to the **San Antonio Zoological Gardens** (see above), you can buy tickets for the **Brackenridge Eagle** (© **210/ 734-7183**), a miniature train that replicates an 1863 model. The pleasant 2-mile ride through the park takes about 20 minutes (tickets $2.50 for adults, $2 for children 3–11; opens 9:30am daily, weather permitting, closes generally when zoo gate closes).

Main entrance 2800 block of N. Broadway. © **210/207-3000.** www.sanantonio.gov/sapar. Daily dawn–dusk. Bus: 7, 8, or 9.

HemisFair Park   Built for the 1968 HemisFair, an exposition celebrating the 250th anniversary of the founding of San Antonio, this urban oasis boasts **water gardens** and a **wood-and-sand playground** constructed by children (near the

---

Fun Fact Did You Know?

- Elmer Doolin, the original manufacturer of Fritos corn chips, bought the original recipe from a San Antonio restaurant in 1932 for $100. He sold the first batch from the back of his Model-T Ford.
- *Wings,* a silent World War I epic that won the first Academy Award for best picture in 1927, was filmed in San Antonio. The film marked the debut of Gary Cooper, who was on screen for a total of 102 seconds.
- Lyndon and Lady Bird Johnson were married in San Antonio's St. Mark's Episcopal Church.

Alamo St. entrance). Among its indoor diversions are the **Institute of Texan Cultures** and the **Tower of the Americas** (both detailed above). Be sure to walk over to the Henry B. Gonzales Convention Center and take a look at the striking mosaic **mural** by Mexican artist Juan O'Gorman. **The Schultze House Cottage Garden** *✿*, 514 HemisFair Park (*✆* 210/229-9161), created and maintained by Master Gardeners of Bexar County, is also worth checking out for its heirloom plants, varietals, tropicals, and xeriscape area. Look for it behind the Federal Building.

Bounded by Alamo, Bowie, Market, and Durango sts. No phone. www.sanantonio.gov/sapar/hemisfair.asp. Streetcar: Blue, Yellow, or Purple lines.

San Antonio Botanical Gardens *✿*   Take a horticultural tour of Texas at this gracious 38-acre garden, encompassing everything from south Texas scrub to Hill Country wildflowers. Fountains, pools, paved paths, and examples of Texas architecture provide visual contrast to the flora. The formal gardens include a garden for the blind, a Japanese garden, an herb garden, a biblical garden, and a children's garden. Perhaps most outstanding is the $6.9 million Lucile Halsell Conservatory complex, a series of greenhouses replicating a variety of tropical and desert environments. The 1896 Sullivan Carriage House, built by Alfred Giles and moved stone-by-stone from its original downtown site, serves as the entryway to the gardens. It houses a gift shop (*✆* **210/829-1227**) and a restaurant (*✆* **210/821-6447**) offering salads, quiches, sandwiches, and outrageously rich desserts, open Tues to Sun from 11am to 2pm.

555 Funston. *✆* 210/207-3250. www.sabot.org. Admission $6 adults; $4 seniors, students, and military; $3 children 3–13; free for children under 3. Daily 9am–5pm. Closed Dec 25 and Jan 1. Bus: 7, 9, or 14.

4 Especially for Kids

Without a doubt, the prime spots for kids in San Antonio are **SeaWorld** and **Six Flags Fiesta Texas.** They'll also like the hands-on, interactive **Witte Museum** and the various ethnic-pride kids' programs at the **Institute of Texas Cultures.** There's a children's area in the **zoo,** which vends food packets so kids can feed the fish and the ducks. The third floor of the main branch of the **San Antonio Public Library** is devoted to children, who get to use their own catalogs and search tools. Story hours are offered regularly, and there are occasional puppet shows.

In addition to these sights, detailed in "The Top Attractions" and "More Attractions" sections, earlier in this chapter, and the **Magik Theatre** (p. 123) the following should also appeal to the sandbox set and up.

Plaza Wax Museum & Ripley's Believe It or Not ⍟ Adults may get the bigger charge out of the waxy stars—Dustin Hoffman and Dallas Cowboy coach Tom Landry are among the latest to be added to an impressive array—and some of the oddities collected by the globe-trotting Mr. Ripley, but there's plenty for kids to enjoy at this twofer attraction. The walk-through wax Theater of Horrors, although tame compared to *Friday the 13th*–type adventures, usually elicits some shudders. At Believe It or Not, youngsters generally get a kick out of learning about people around the world whose habits—such as sticking nails through their noses—are even weirder than their own.

301 Alamo Plaza. ℂ 210/224-9299. www.plazawaxmuseum.com. Either attraction $14 adults, $7 children 4–12; both attractions $18 adults, $10 children 4–12. Memorial Day to Labor Day daily 9am–10pm; remainder of the year Sun 9am–8pm, Mon–Thurs 9:30am–8pm, Fri–Sat 9am–10pm (ticket office closes 1 hr. before listed closing times). Streetcar: Red or Blue lines.

Ripley's Haunted Adventure, Guinness World Records Museum, and Davy Crockett's Tall Tales Ride ⍟ San Antonio's newest attraction, this multimillion-dollar downtown entertainment complex just keeps growing—and getting better. Ripley's Haunted Adventure, which debuted in 2002, is a 10,000-square-foot, state-of-the-art haunted house (if that's not a contradiction in terms), combining live actors, animatronics, and lots of special effects. The Guinness Museum, opened in 2003, brings the famed record book to life with such hands-on exhibits as a drum set that lets you see how hard it is to best the most-drum-beats-per-minute record and a multiple-choice quiz room where you can guess at the actual world record. Davy Crockett's Tall Tales Ride, opened in March 2005, combines a theme park–style ride through Davy's life and times with an interactive outpost where, among other things, you can wrestle with a bear (the real history's left to the Alamo, across the street, while this stuff is based on Crockett's colorful self-fictions). There are other Ripley's Haunted Adventure and Guinness World Records Museums in the country, but only here are the two combined, and the Davy Crockett adventure is unique to San Antonio. All in all, this a great place for the family to come for a little education and a lot of fun.

329 Alamo Plaza. ℂ 210/226-2828. www.hauntedadventure.com. Admission $15 for any 1 attraction, $18 for 2, $21 for all 3 for adults; $7.95 for 1, $11 for 2, $14 for 3 for children 4–12; $1 off any rate for seniors. Labor Day to Memorial Day Sun–Thurs 10am–10pm, Fri–Sat 10am–midnight; off season Sun–Thurs 10am–7pm, Fri–Sat 10am–10pm. Call ahead to verify hours and prices.

San Antonio Children's Museum ⍟⍟ San Antonio's children's museum offers a terrific, creative introduction to the city for the pint-sized and grown-up alike. San Antonio history, population, and geography are all explored through such features as a miniature River Walk, a multicultural grocery store, a bank where kids can use their own ATM, and even a miniature dentist's office (more fun than you'd imagine). Activities range from crawl spaces and corn-grinding rocks to a weather station and radar room. Don't miss this place if you're traveling with children up to age 10.

305 E. Houston St. ℂ 210/21-CHILD. www.sakids.org. Admission $5.95, free for children under 2. Memorial Day to Labor Day Mon–Fri 9am–5pm, Sat 9am to 6pm, Sun noon–4pm; rest of the year Mon 9am–noon, Tues–Fri 9am–3:30pm, Sat 9am–6pm, Sun noon–4pm. Bus: 7 or 40. Streetcar: Red line.

San Antonio IMAX Theater Rivercenter ⍟ Having kids view this theater's main attraction, *Alamo—The Price of Freedom,* on a six-story-high screen with a stereo sound system is a sure-fire way of getting them psyched for the historical battle site (which, although it's just across the street, can't be reached without wending your way past lots and lots of Rivercenter shops). It's a reasonably accurate rendition of the historical events, to boot. The first commercial IMAX venue to double its viewing pleasures by introducing a second megascreen (this one with 3-D capability and a state-of-the-art sound system) at the beginning of the 21st century, this theater also shows thrilling—and educational—nature and scientific adventure movies produced especially for the large screen.

849 E. Commerce St., in the Rivercenter Mall. ✆ 800/354-4629 or 210/247-4629. www.imax-sa.com. Admission $8.95 adults, $7.95 seniors and youth 12–17, $5.50 children 3–11. Times of daily shows vary, but generally the 1st show is screened at 8:30 or 9am, the last at 9:45pm. Streetcar: All lines.

Splashtown   Cool off at this 20-acre water park, which includes a huge wave pool, hydro tubes nearly 300 feet long, a Texas-size water bobsled ride, more than a dozen water slides, and a two-story playhouse for the smaller children. A variety of concerts, contests, and special events are held here.

3600 N. I-35 (exit 160, Splashtown Dr.). ✆ 210/227-1100 (recorded info) or 227-1400. www.splashtown sa.com. Admission $22 adults, $17 children under 48 in. (after 5pm, $14 for any age), free for seniors over 65 and children under 2. Call ahead or check website for exact dates and closing times.

5 Special-Interest Sightseeing

FOR MILITARY HISTORY BUFFS

San Antonio's military installations are crucial to the city's economy, and testaments to their past abound. Those who aren't satisfied with touring Fort Sam Houston (see "More Attractions," earlier in this chapter) can also visit the **Hangar 9/Edward H. White Museum** at Brooks Air Force Base, Southeast Military Drive at the junction of I-37 (✆ **210/536-2203;** www.brooks.af.mil). The history of flight medicine, among other things, is detailed via exhibits in the oldest aircraft hangar in the Air Force. Admission is free, and it's open Monday to Friday 8am to 3pm, except the last 2 weeks of December. Lackland Air Force Base (12 miles southwest of downtown off U.S. 90 at Southwest Military Dr. exit; www.lackland.af.mil) is home to the **Air Force History and Traditions Museum,** 2051 George Ave., Bldg. 5206 (✆ **210/671-3055**), which hosts a collection of rare aircraft and components dating back to World War II. Admission is free; it's open Monday to Friday 8am to 4:30pm. At the **Security Police Museum,** about 3 blocks away at Bldg. 10501 (on Femoyer St., corner of Carswell Ave., ✆ **210/671-2615**), weapons, uniforms, and combat gear dating up to Desert Storm days are among the security police artifacts on display. Admission is free; it's open Mon to Fri 8am to 3pm. Inquire at either museum about the 41 static aircraft on view throughout the base. With current security measures in place, the bases are sometimes restricted to retired military, their families, and those sponsored by someone who works at the base. But it's worth phoning the museums or the Public Affairs Office at Brooks (✆**210/536-3234**) or the visitor center at Lackland (✆**210/671-6174**) to inquire about visitation status. In any case, phone ahead to find out if anyone is permitted on the base on the day you're planning to visit. As may be expected, the museums are closed all national holidays.

FOR THOSE INTERESTED IN HISPANIC HERITAGE

A Hispanic heritage tour is almost redundant in San Antonio, which is a living testament to the role Hispanics have played in shaping the city. **Casa Navarro State Historic Site, La Villita, Market Square, San Antonio Missions National Historical Park,** and the **Spanish Governor's Palace,** all detailed earlier in this chapter, give visitors a feel for the city's Spanish colonial past, while the Nelson A. Rockefeller wing of the **San Antonio Museum of Art,** also discussed earlier, hosts this country's largest collection of Latin American art. The sixth floor of the main branch of the **San Antonio Public Library** (see above) hosts an excellent noncirculating Latino collection, featuring books about the Mexican-American experience in Texas and the rest of the Southwest. It's also the place to come to do genealogical research into your family's Hispanic roots.

The city's exploration of its own Hispanic roots is ongoing. The **Centro Alameda cultural zone** on downtown's west side includes the **Museo Americano Smithsonian** at the entryway to Market Square (see "More Attractions," earlier in this chapter). In addition, at 310 W. Houston St., you can see the spectacular 86-foot-high sign (lit by rare cold cathode technology, not neon) of the **Alameda Theater,** opened in 1949 as one of the last of the grand movie palaces, and the largest ever dedicated to Spanish-language entertainment. Among its many impressive features were private nursemaids for the patrons' children and gorgeous "Deco tropical" tile work hand-created in San Antonio. Described as being "to U.S. Latinos what Harlem's Apollo Theater is to African Americans," the Alameda is scheduled to reopen as a multivenue performance hall—affiliated with the prestigious Kennedy Center—and teaching facility for Latino arts and culture by the end of this decade, when its multimillion restoration will be complete. Clearly Latino culture is coming into its own in the U.S. The Alameda National Center of Latino Arts and Culture, as the project is officially known, is the only arts complex to be linked with both the Smithsonian and the Kennedy Center. For additional information and progress reports, log on to www.thealameda.org or call © **210/299-4300.**

Cultural events and blowout festivals, many of them held at Market Square, abound. The **Guadalupe Cultural Arts Center,** which organizes many of them, is detailed in chapter 8. In HemisFair Park, the **Instituto Cultural Mexicano/Casa Mexicana,** 600 HemisFair Plaza Way (© **210/227-0123**), sponsored by the Mexican Ministry of Foreign Affairs, hosts Latin American film series, concerts, conferences, performances, contests, and workshops—including ones on language, literature, and folklore as well as art. The institute also hosts shifting displays of art and artifacts relating to Mexican history and culture, from pre-Columbian to contemporary (Tues–Fri 10am–5pm; Sat–Sun noon–5; free admission).

For information on the various festivals and events, contact the **San Antonio Hispanic Chamber of Commerce** (© **210/225-0462;** www.sahcc.org). Another roundup resource for Latin *cultura* is the **"Guide to Puro San Antonio,"** available from the San Antonio Convention and Visitors Bureau (© **800/447-3372**).

6 Strolling Around Downtown San Antonio

One of downtown San Antonio's great gifts to visitors on foot is its wonderfully meandering early pathways—not laid out by drunken cattle drivers as has been wryly suggested, but formed by the course of the San Antonio River and the various settlements that grew up around it. Turn any corner in this area and you'll come across some fascinating testament to the city's historically rich past.

Note: Stops 1, 5, 6, 7, 9, 11, 13, and 14 are described earlier in this chapter. Entrance hours and admission fees (if applicable) are listed there. See chapter 4 for additional information on stop no. 2 and chapter 7 for additional information on stop no. 3.

Walking Tour: Downtown San Antonio

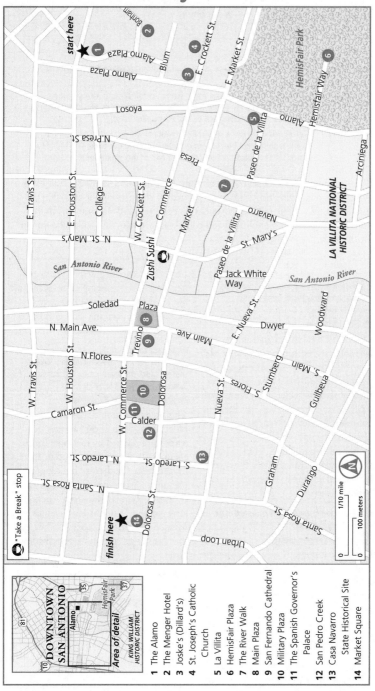

"Take a Break" stop

start here

finish here

LA VILLITA NATIONAL HISTORIC DISTRICT

HemisFair Park

San Antonio River

Zushi Sushi

Jack White Way

Urban Loop

1/10 mile
100 meters

DOWNTOWN SAN ANTONIO

Area of detail

KING WILLIAM HISTORIC DISTRICT

Alamo

HemisFair Park

WALKING TOUR	DOWNTOWN

Start: The Alamo.

Finish: Market Square.

Time: Approximately 1½ hours, not including stops at shops, restaurants, or attractions.

Best Times: Early morning during the week, when the streets and attractions are less crowded. If you're willing to tour the Alamo museums and shrine another time, consider starting out before they open (9am).

Worst Times: Weekend afternoons, especially in summer, when the crowds and the heat render this long stroll uncomfortable. (If you do get tired, you can always pick up a streetcar within a block or two of most parts of this route.)

Built to be within easy reach of each other, San Antonio's earliest military, religious, and civil settlements are concentrated in the downtown area. The city spread out quite a bit in the subsequent 2½ centuries, but downtown still functions as the seat of the municipal and county government, as well as the hub of tourist activities.

Start your tour at Alamo Plaza (bounded by E. Houston St. on the north); at the plaza's northeast corner, you'll come to the entrance for:

❶ The Alamo

Originally established in 1718 as the Mission San Antonio de Valero, the first of the city's five missions, the Alamo was moved twice before settling at this site. The heavy limestone walls of the church and its adjacent compound later proved to make an excellent fortress. In 1836, fighters for Texas's independence from Mexico took a heroic, if ultimately unsuccessful, stand against Mexican general Santa Anna here.

When you leave the walled complex, walk south along the plaza to:

❷ The Menger Hotel

German immigrant William Menger built this hotel in 1859 on the site of Texas's first brewery, which he had opened with partner Charles Deegan in 1855. Legend has it that Menger wanted a place to lodge hard-drinking friends who used to spend the night sleeping on his long bar. Far more prestigious guests—presidents, Civil War generals, writers, stage actors, you name it—stayed here over the years, and the hotel turns up in several short

stories by frequent guest William Sidney Porter (O. Henry). The Menger has been much expanded since it first opened, but retains its gorgeous, three-tiered Victorian lobby.

On the south side of the hotel, Alamo Plaza turns back into North Alamo Street. Take it south 1 block until you reach Commerce Street, where you'll spot:

❸ Joske's (now Dillard's)

This is San Antonio's oldest department store. The more modest retail emporium opened by the Joske Brothers in 1889 was swallowed up in 1939 by the huge modernist building you see now, distinctive for its intricate Spanish Renaissance–style details; look for the miniaturized versions of Mission San José's sacristy window on the building's ground-floor shadow boxes.

Walk a short way along the Commerce Street side of the building to:

❹ St. Joseph's Catholic Church

This church was built for San Antonio's German community in 1876. The Gothic revival–style house of worship is as notable for the intransigence of its congregation as it is for its beautiful stained-glass windows. The worshipers' refusal to move from the site when Joske's department store was rising up all around it earned the church the affectionate moniker "St. Joske's."

Head back to Alamo Street and continue south 2 blocks past the San Antonio Convention Center to reach:

⑤ La Villita

Once the site of a Coahuiltecan Indian village, La Villita was settled over the centuries by Spanish, Germans, and, in the 1930s and '40s, a community of artists. A number of the buildings have been continuously occupied for more than 200 years. The "Little Village" on the river was restored by a joint effort of the city and the San Antonio Conservation Society, and now hosts a number of crafts shops and two upscale restaurants in addition to the historic General Cós House and the Arneson River Theatre.

Just south of La Villita, you'll see HemisFair Way and the large iron gates of:

⑥ HemisFair Park

This park was built for the 1968 exposition held to celebrate the 250th anniversary of San Antonio's founding. The expansive former fairgrounds are home to two museums, a German heritage park, and an observation tower—the tallest structure in the city and a great reference point if you get lost downtown. The plaza is too large to explore even superficially on this tour, so come back another time.

Retrace your steps to Paseo de la Villita and walk 1 block west to Presa Street. Take it north for about half a block until you see the Presa Street Bridge, and descend from it to:

⑦ The River Walk

You'll find yourself on a quiet section of the 2.6-mile paved walkway that lines the banks of the San Antonio River through a large part of downtown and the King William Historic District. The bustling cafe, restaurant,

and hotel action is just behind you, on the stretch of the river that winds north of La Villita.

Stroll down this tree-shaded thoroughfare until you reach the St. Mary's Street Bridge (you'll pass only one other bridge, the Navarro St. Bridge, along the way) and ascend here. Then walk north half a block until you come to Market Street. Take it west 1 long block, where you'll find:

⑧ Main Plaza (Plaza de Las Islas)

This is the heart of the city established in 1731 by 15 Canary Island families sent by King Philip V of Spain to settle his remote New World outpost. Much of the history of San Antonio—and of Texas—unfolded on this modest square. A peace treaty with the Apaches was signed (and later broken) on the plaza in 1749. In 1835, freedom fighters battled Santa Anna's troops here before barricading themselves in the Alamo across the river. Much calmer these days, the plaza still sees some action as home to the Romanesque-style Bexar County Courthouse, built out of native Texas granite and sandstone in 1892.

TAKE A BREAK
I know, it's not strictly in keeping with the Hispanic history of this area, but multiculturalism is San Antonio's trademark. And if you like Japanese food as much as I do, you'll enjoy cooling your heels at **Sushi Zushi** in the International Center, 203 S. St. Mary's St. at Market (✆ 210/ 472-2900). You can get a quick raw fish fix at the sleek sushi bar (they've got lots of cooked and vegetarian rolls, too), or settle in at one of the tables for a bowl of soba noodles or some teppan grilled beef.

Walk along the south side of Main Plaza to the corner of Main Avenue. Across the street and just to the north you'll encounter:

⑨ San Fernando Cathedral

This is the oldest parish church building in Texas and site of the earliest marked graves in San Antonio. Three walls of the original church started by the Canary Island settlers in 1738 can still be seen in the rear of the 1868 Gothic revival cathedral, which recently underwent a massive renovation. Among those buried within the sanctuary walls are Eugenio Navarro, brother of José Antonio Navarro (see stop no. 13, below), and Don Manuel Muñoz, first governor of Texas when it was a province of a newly independent Mexico.

On the north side of the cathedral is Trevino Street; take it west to the next corner and cross the street to reach:

⑩ Military Plaza (Plaza de Armas)

Once the drill ground for the Presidio San Antonio de Béxar, this garrison— established in 1718 to protect the Mission San Antonio de Valero—was moved to this nearby site 4 years later. Military Plaza was one of the liveliest spots in Texas for the 50 years after Texas won its independence. In the 1860s, it was the site of vigilante lynchings, and after the Civil War it hosted a bustling outdoor market. At night, the townsfolk would come to its open-air booths to buy chili con carne from their favorite chili queen. The plaza remained completely open until 1889, when the ornate City Hall was built at its center.

The one-story white building you'll see directly across the street from the west side of the plaza is the:

⑪ Spanish Governor's Palace

This was the former residence and headquarters of the captain of the Presidio de Béxar (but not of any Spanish governors). From here, the commander could watch his troops drilling across the street. The source of the house's misnomer is not entirely clear; as the home of the highest local authority and thus the nicest digs in the area, the "palace" probably hosted important Spanish officials who came through town.

From the front of the Governor's Palace, walk south until you come to the crosswalk; just west across Dolorosa Street is a drainage ditch, the sad remains of:

⑫ San Pedro Creek

The west bank of this body of water, once lovely and flowing and now usually dry, was the original site of both Mission San Antonio de Valero and the Presidio de Béxar. At the creek's former headwaters, approximately 2 miles north of here, San Pedro Park was established in 1729 by a grant from the king of Spain; it's the second-oldest municipal park in the United States (the oldest being the Boston Common).

Continue west along Dolorosa Street to Laredo Street and take it south about three-quarters of a block until you come to:

⑬ Casa Navarro State Historic Site

The life of José Antonio Navarro, for whom the park is named, traces the history of Texas itself: He was born in Spanish territory, fought for Mexico's independence from Spain, and then worked to achieve Texas's freedom from Mexico. (He was one of only two Texas-born signatories to the 1836 Declaration of Independence.) In 1845, Navarro voted for Texas's annexation to the United States, and a year later, he became a senator in the new Texas State Legislature. He died here in 1871, at the age of 76.

Trace your steps back to Laredo and Dolorosa, and go west on Dolorosa Street; when you reach Santa Rosa, you'll be facing:

⑭ Market Square

This square was home to the city's Market House at the turn of the century. When the low, arcaded structure was converted to El Mercado in 1973, it switched from selling household goods and personal items to crafts, clothing, and other more tourist-oriented Mexican wares. Directly behind and west of this lively square, the former Haymarket Plaza has become the

Farmer's Market, and now sells souvenirs instead of produce. If you haven't already stopped for sushi, you can enjoy a well-deserved lunch here at Mi Tierra, reviewed in chapter 5. At the entryway to Market Square is the new Museo Americano Smithsonian. Even if it's not open yet, look at the stainless steel screen that fronts it. Inspired by Mexican *hojalata* (punched tin) crafts, the 30-foot-high screen consists of a series of panels that incorporate Hispanic cultural symbols, from the Pre-Columbian headdress of the Aztec god Quetzalcoatl to the Smithsonian sun logo.

7 Organized Tours

BUS TOURS

San Antonio City Tours   This company serves up a large menu of guided bus tours, covering everything from San Antonio's missions and museums to shopping forays south of the border and Hill Country excursions.

1331 N. Pine. ℂ 800/868-7707 or 210/228-9776. www.sacitytours.net. Tours range from $18 adults, $12 children 4–10, free for children under 4 (3½ hr.) to $45 adults, $23 children 4–10 (full day). Earliest tours depart at 9am, latest return is 6pm daily (including holidays).

TROLLEY TOURS

Alamo Trolley Tour   This is a good way to sightsee without a car. The trolley tour touches on all the downtown highlights, plus two of the missions in the south. If you want to get off at any of these sights, you can pick up another trolley (they run every 45 min.) after you're finished. At the least, you get oriented and learn some of the city's history.

216 Alamo Plaza (next to the Alamo). ℂ 210/228-9776. www.sacitytours.net. Tickets for 60-min. tour are $17 adults, $20 for "hop" pass (good for 2 days), $7.50 children 3–11, $9 for the pass. Daily 9:30am–4:15pm.

RIVER CRUISES

Yanaguana Cruises ℱ   Maybe you've sat in a River Walk cafe looking out at people riding back and forth in open, flat-bottom barges. Go ahead—give in and join 'em. An amusing, informative tour, lasting from 35 to 40 minutes, will take you more than 2 miles down the most built-up sections of the Paseo del Río, with interesting sights pointed out along the way. You'll learn a lot about the river—and find out what all those folks you watched were laughing about. The company also runs a non-narrated shuttle (see "By River Taxi" in the "Getting Around" section of chapter 3 for details).

Ticket offices: Rivercenter Mall and River Walk, across the street from the Hilton Palacio del Rio Hotel. ℂ 210/244-5700. www.sarivercruise.com. Tickets $6.50 adults, $4.50 seniors and active military, $1.50 children under 6. Boats depart daily every 15–20 min. Nov to mid-Mar Sun–Thurs 10am–8pm, Fri–Sat 10am–9pm; extended hours rest of the year.

8 Staying Active

Most San Antonians head for the hills—that is, nearby Hill Country—for outdoor recreation. Some suggestions of sports in or around town follow; see chapter 17 for more.

BIKING   With the creation and continuing improvements of the biking paths along the San Antonio River, part of the larger **Mission Trails** project (see the San Antonio Missions National Historical Park listing earlier in this chapter), local and visiting cyclists will finally have a good place within the city to spin their wheels (it's not quite there yet, but soon . . .). Other options within San

Antonio itself include **Brackenridge Park; McAllister Park** on the city's north side, 13102 Jones-Maltsberger (☎ 210/207-PARK or 207-3120); and around the area near **SeaWorld of Texas.** If you didn't bring your own, **Charles A. James Bicycle Company,** 329 N. Main Ave. (☎ **210/224-8717;** www.charlesa jamesbicycle.com), will deliver bikes to your door free if you're staying down-town ($10 extra charge for delivery and pickup to other parts of the city). Rates run up to $30 for 24 hours. Perhaps the best resource in town is the website of the San Antonio Wheelmen, **www.sawheelmen.com,** with details on local organized rides, links to bicycle shops in the area, and more (it's even got an essay on history of bicycling).

FISHING   Closest to town for good angling are **Braunig Lake,** a 1,350-acre, city-owned reservoir, a few miles southeast of San Antonio off I-37, and **Calaveras Lake,** one of Texas's great bass lakes, a few miles southeast of San Antonio off U.S. 181 South and Loop 1604. A bit farther afield but still easy to reach from San Antonio are **Canyon Lake,** about 20 miles north of New Braunfels, and **Medina Lake,** just south of Bandera. Fishing licenses—sold at most sport-ing-goods and tackle stores and sporting-goods departments of large discount stores such as Wal-Mart or Kmart, as well as county courthouses and Parks and Wildlife Department offices—are required for all nonresidents; for current information, call ☎ **512/389-4800,** ext. 3, or go to www.tpwd.state.tx.us/ publications/annual/fish/fishlicense.phtml. **Tackle Box Outfitters,** 6330 N. New Braunfels (☎ **210/821-5806;** www.tackleboxoutfitters.com), offers referrals to private guides for fishing trips to area rivers and to the Gulf coast ($250–$400 per person).

GOLF   Golf has become a big deal in San Antonio, with more and more visi-tors coming to town expressly to tee off. Of the city's six municipal golf courses, two of the most notable are **Brackenridge,** 2315 Ave. B (☎ 210/226-5612), the oldest (1916) public course in Texas, featuring oak- and pecan-shaded fair-ways; and northwest San Antonio's $4.3 million **Cedar Creek,** 8250 Vista Col-ina (☎ **210/695-5050**), repeatedly ranked as South Texas's best municipal course in golfing surveys. For details on both and other municipal courses, log on to www.sanantonio.gov/sapar/golf.asp. Other options for unaffiliated golfers include the 200-acre **Pecan Valley,** 4700 Pecan Valley Dr. (☎ **210/333-9018;** www.pecanvalleygc.com), which crosses the Salado Creek seven times and has an 800-year-old oak near its 13th hole; the high-end **Quarry,** 444 E. Basse Rd. (☎ **800/347-7759** or 210/824-4500; www.quarrygolf.com), on the site of a for-mer quarry and one of San Antonio's newest public courses; and **Canyon Springs,** 24405 Wilderness Oak Rd. (☎ **888/800-1511** or 210/497-1770; www. canyonspringsgc.com), at the north edge of town in the Texas Hill Country, lush with live oaks and dotted with historic rock formations. There aren't too many resort courses in San Antonio because there aren't too many resorts, but the two at the **Westin La Cantera,** 16401 La Cantera Pkwy. (☎ **800/446-5387** or 210/ 558-4653; www.lacanteragolfclub.com)—one designed by Jay Morish and Tom Weiskopf, the other by Arnold Palmer—have knockout designs and dramatic hill-and-rock outcroppings to recommend them. Expect to pay $37 to $53 per person for an 18-hole round at a municipal course with a cart, from $70 to as much as $130 (on weekends) per person at a private resort's course. Twilight (afternoon) rates are often cheaper. To get a copy of the free *San Antonio Golfing Guide,* call ☎ **800/447-3372** or log on to www.sanantoniovisit.com/ visitors/things_golfhome.asp.

HIKING The 240-acre **Friedrich Wilderness Park,** 21480 Milsa (© 210/698-1057; wildtexas.com/parks/fwp.php), operated by the city of San Antonio as its only nature preserve, is crisscrossed by 5.5 miles of trails that attract bird-watchers as well as hikers; a 2-mile stretch is accessible to people with disabilities. **Enchanted Rock State Natural Area,** near Fredericksburg, is the most popular spot for trekking out of town (see chapter 17).

RIVER SPORTS For tubing, rafting, or canoeing along a cypress-lined river, San Antonio river rats head 35 miles northwest of downtown to the 2,000-acre **Guadalupe River State Park,** 3350 Park Rd. 31 (© 830/438-2656; www.tpwd.state.tx.us/park/guadalup), near Boerne (see chapter 17 for more details about the town). Five miles north of Highway 46, just outside the park, you can rent tubes, rafts, and canoes at the **Bergheim Campground,** FM 3351 in Bergheim (© 830/336-2235). Standard tubes run $10 per person (but the ones with a bottom for your cooler, at $12, are better), rafts are $15 per person ($10 for ages 12 and under), and canoes go for $35. The section of the Guadalupe River near Gruene is also extremely popular; see the "New Braunfels" section of chapter 17 for details.

SWIMMING/WATER PARKS Most hotels have swimming pools, but if yours doesn't, the Parks and Recreation Department (© 210/207-3113; www.sanantonio.gov/sapar/swimming.asp) can direct you to the nearest municipal pool. Both SeaWorld and Six Flags Fiesta Texas, detailed in the section "The Top Attractions," earlier in this chapter, are prime places to get wet (the latter has a pool in the shape of Texas and a waterfall that descends from a cowboy hat). Splashtown water recreation park is described in the "Especially for Kids" section, earlier in this chapter. Many San Antonians head out to New Braunfels to get wet at the Schlitterbahn, the largest water park in Texas; see the "New Braunfels" section of chapter 17 for additional information.

TENNIS You can play at the 22 lighted hard courts at the **McFarlin Tennis Center,** 1503 San Pedro Ave. (© 210/732-1223), for the very reasonable fees of $2.50 per hour per person ($1 for students and seniors), $3.50 ($2) after 5pm. Log on to www.sanantonio.gov/sapar/tennis.asp for additional information about McFarlin, which requires reservations for you to play, and for a list of other city facilities (all operate on a first-come, first-served basis).

9 Spectator Sports

AUTO RACING Texas takes its NASCAR seriously and the place to catch the local action March through October is at the **San Antonio Speedway,** 14901 S. Hwy. 16, 4 miles south of Loop 410 (© 210/628-1499; www.sanantoniospeedway.com); it's the self-proclaimed "home of the fastest half-mile NASCAR oval in Texas." Admission runs $10 for adults, $3 for ages 7 to 11, free for 6 and under.

BASEBALL From early April through early September, the minor-league **San Antonio Missions** plays at the Nelson Wolff Stadium, 5757 Hwy. 90 W. Most home games for this Seattle Mariners farm club start at 7:05pm, except Sunday games, which start at 4:05pm. Tickets range from $6 for adult general admission to $9 for seats in the lower box. Call © 210/675-7275 for schedules and tickets, or check the website at www.samissions.com.

BASKETBALL   Spur madness hits San Antonio every year from mid-October through May, when the city's only major-league franchise, the **San Antonio Spurs,** shoots hoops. At the end of 2002, the Spurs found—or should we say inspired the creation of—a new home, the state-of-the-art SBC Center near downtown. Ticket prices range from $10 for nosebleed-level seats to $100 for seats on the corners of the court. Tickets are available at the Spurs Ticket Office in the SBC Center, 1 SBC Center Pkwy. (© **210/444-5819**), or via Ticketmaster San Antonio (© **210/224-9600;** www.ticketmaster.com). Get schedules, players' stats, and promotional news—everything you might want to know or buy relating to the team—online at www.nba.com/spurs.

GOLF   The **SBC Championship,** an Official Senior PGA Tour Event, is held each October at the Oak Hills Country Club, 5403 Fredericksburg Rd. (© **210/ 698-3582**). One of the oldest professional golf tournaments, now known as the **Valero Texas Open,** showcases the sport in September at the Resort Course at La Cantera Golf Club, 16401 La Cantera Pkwy. (© **201/345-3818**). Log on to www.pgatour.com/tournaments for information about both.

HORSE RACING   **Retama Park,** some 15 minutes north of San Antonio in Selma (© **210/651-7119;** www.retamapark.com), is the hottest place to play the ponies; take exit 174-A from I-35, or the Lookout Road exit from Loop 1604. The five-level Spanish-style grandstand is impressive, and the variety of food courts, restaurants, and lounges is almost as diverting as the horses. Live racing is generally from late April through mid-October on Wednesday or Thursday through Sunday. Call or check the website for thoroughbred and quarter horse schedules. Simulcasts from top tracks around the country are shown year-round. General admission for live racing is $2.50 adults, $1.50 seniors; for clubhouse, $3.50 adults, $2.50 seniors; for simulcast, $2. Kids 15 and under and members of the military, active or retired, can enter gratis.

ICE HOCKEY   San Antonio has had professional hockey only since 1994, when the Central Hockey League's San Antonio Iguanas appeared on the scene. Disbanded after the 2001–02 season, they were replaced by the American Hockey League's **San Antonio Rampage,** who dropped their first puck at the SBC Center (1 SBC Center Pkwy.) in 2002. AHL tickets cost $7 to $55. Try © **210/227-GOAL** or www.sarampage.com for schedules and other information.

RODEO   If you're in town in early February, don't miss the chance to see 2 weeks of Wild West events like calf roping, steer wrestling, and bull riding at the annual **San Antonio Stock Show and Rodeo.** You can also hear major live country-and-western talent—Brad Paisley, Alan Jackson, Reba McEntire, and Joe Nichols were on the 2005 roster—and you're likely to find something to add to your luggage at the SBC Center's exposition hall, packed with Texas handicrafts. Call © **210/225-5851** or log on to www.sarodeo.com for information on schedules. Smaller rodeos are held throughout the year in nearby **Bandera,** the self-proclaimed "Cowboy Capital of the World." Contact the Bandera County Convention and Visitors Bureau (© **800/364-3833** or 830/796-3045; www. banderacowboycapital.com) for more information.

7

Shopping in San Antonio

San Antonio offers the retail-bound a nice balance of large malls and little enclaves of specialized shops. You'll find everything here from the utilitarian to the unusual: a huge Sears department store, a Saks Fifth Avenue fronted by a 40-foot pair of cowboy boots, a mall with a river running through it, and some lively Mexican markets.

You can count on most shops around town being open from 9 or 10am to 5:30 or 6pm Monday through Saturday, with shorter hours on Sunday. Malls are generally open Monday through Saturday 10am to 9pm and on Sunday noon to 6pm. Sales tax in San Antonio is 8%.

1 The Shopping Scene

Most out-of-town shoppers will find all they need **downtown,** between the large Rivercenter Mall, the boutiques and crafts shops of La Villita, the colorful Mexican wares of Market Square, the Southwest School of Art and Craft, and assorted retailers and galleries on and around Alamo Plaza. More avant-garde boutiques and galleries, including Blue Star, can be found in the adjacent area known as Southtown.

San Antonians tend to shop the **Loop 410 malls**—especially North Star, Heubner Oaks, and Alamo Quarry Market near the airport—and cruise the upscale strip centers along Broadway in **Alamo Heights** (the posh Collection and Lincoln Heights are particularly noteworthy). Weekends might see locals poking around a number of terrific **flea markets.** For bargains on brand labels, they head out to New Braunfels and San Marcos, home to two large **factory outlet malls** (see chapter 17 for details). After September 2005, expect upscale shoppers to migrate to the far northwest part of town, where the **Shops at La Cantera** will host the city's only Neiman Marcus and Nordstrom—among other high-end retail.

2 Shopping A to Z

ANTIQUES

In addition to the places that follow, a number of antiques shops line Hildebrand between Blanco and San Pedro, and McCullough between Hildebrand and Basse.

Center for Antiques   A great place for an antiques forage near the airport, this shop hosts more than 115 vendors with specialties from knickknacks, records, and clothing to high-quality furniture for serious collectors. Be careful not to spend too much time here and miss your flight. 8505 Broadway. © **210/804-6300.** www.centerforantiques.com.

The Land of Was   Every inch of space on the two floors of this shop is crammed with stuff—some of it strange and funky, more of it rare and pricey.

The store is especially strong on Spanish-colonial and Mexican antiques; if you're seeking an altarpiece or a treasure chest, try here first. 3119 Broadway. ℂ 210/822-5265.

ART GALLERIES

ArtPace, in the northern part of downtown, and the **Blue Star Arts Complex,** in Southtown (see "More Attractions," in chapter 6, for details on both), are the best venues for cutting-edge art, but **Finesilver Gallery,** 816 Camaron St., Suites 1 and 2, just north of downtown (ℂ 210/354-3333; www.finesilver.com), is a good alternative. Downtown is home to several galleries that show more established artists. Two of the top ones are **Galería Ortiz,** 102 Concho (in Market Sq., ℂ 210/225-0731), San Antonio's premier place to buy Southwestern art; and **Nanette Richardson Fine Art,** 513 E. Houston St. (ℂ 210/224-1550; www.nanetterichardsonfineart.com), with a wide array of oils, watercolors, bronzes, ceramics, and handcrafted wood furnishings.

For more details on these and other galleries, pick up a copy of the **San Antonio Gallery Guide,** prepared by the San Antonio Art Gallery Association, at the San Antonio Convention and Visitors Bureau, 317 Alamo Plaza (ℂ **800/447-3372** or 210/207-6000). You can also check out the art scene online at the Office of Cultural Affairs' website, **www.sanantonio.gov/art/website,** with links to several local galleries, and schedules for events held during July's Contemporary Art Month (see chapter 2, p. 15).

CRAFTS

See also Alamo Fiesta, San Angel Folk Art, and Tienda Guadalupe in "Gifts/Souvenirs," below. Another top option is the Ursuline Sales Gallery in the Southwest School of Art and Craft (see chapter 6, p. 96).

Garcia Art Glass, Inc.   If you like to see the creative process in progress, come here to see beautiful glass bowls, wall sconces, mobiles, and more come into being. Not everything is very portable, but the bracelets and other pretty baubles made out of glass beads definitely are. 715 S. Alamo St. ℂ 210/354-4681. www.garcia artglass.com.

Glassworks *Finds*   With Dale Chihuly practically a household name, you know that glass art has come of age. The goal of this Alamo Heights store is to show that, in addition to being gorgeous, blown glass can also be formed into items that are interesting—a golf putter, for example—affordable, and accessible. Everyone who walks into these stores is encouraged to touch the work ("It's all insured," owner/artist Judy Millspaugh declares cheerfully). 6350 N. New Braunfels Ave. ℂ 210/822-0146.

DEPARTMENT STORES

Dillard's   You'll find branches of this Arkansas-based chain in many Southwestern cities and in a number of San Antonio malls (North Star, Ingram, and Rolling Oaks); all offer nice mid- to upper-range clothing and housewares, but the Dillard's in the Rivercenter Mall also has a section specializing in Western fashions. Enter or exit on Alamo Plaza so you can get a look at the historic building's ornate facade (see "Walking Tour: Downtown San Antonio," in chapter 6, for details). 102 Alamo Plaza (Rivercenter Mall). ℂ 210/227-4343. www.dillards.com.

Saks Fifth Avenue   Forget low-key and unobtrusive; this is Texas. Sure, this department store has the high quality, upscale wares, and attentive service one

Downtown San Antonio Shopping

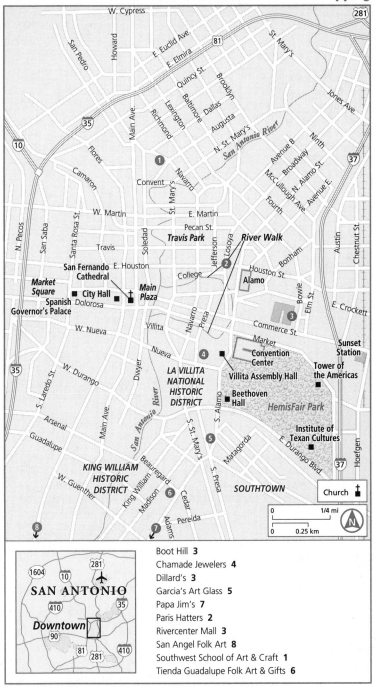

Boot Hill **3**

Chamade Jewelers **4**

Dillard's **3**

Garcia's Art Glass **5**

Papa Jim's **7**

Paris Hatters **2**

Rivercenter Mall **3**

San Angel Folk Art **8**

Southwest School of Art & Craft **1**

Tienda Guadalupe Folk Art & Gifts **6**

Greater San Antonio Shopping

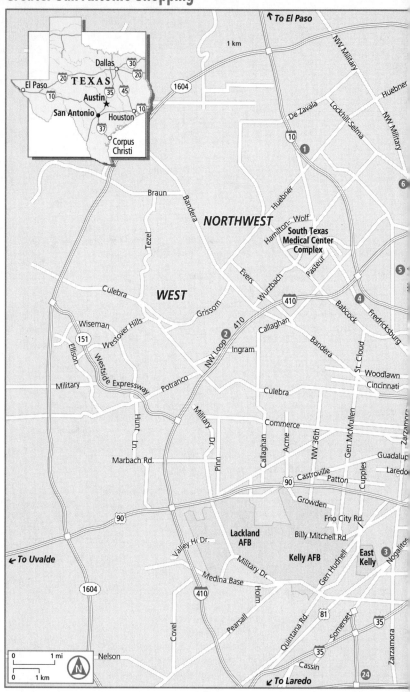

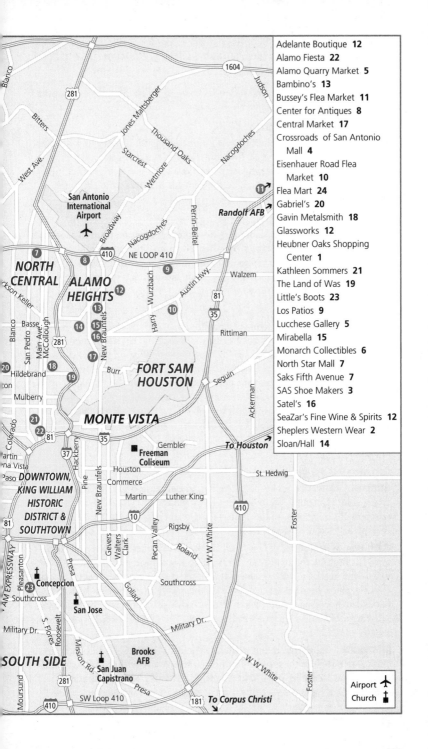

Adelante Boutique **12**
Alamo Fiesta **22**
Alamo Quarry Market **5**
Bambino's **13**
Bussey's Flea Market **11**
Center for Antiques **8**
Central Market **17**
Crossroads of San Antonio
  Mall **4**
Eisenhauer Road Flea
  Market **10**
Flea Mart **24**
Gabriel's **20**
Gavin Metalsmith **18**
Glassworks **12**
Heubner Oaks Shopping
  Center **1**
Kathleen Sommers **21**
The Land of Was **19**
Little's Boots **23**
Los Patios **9**
Lucchese Gallery **5**
Mirabella **15**
Monarch Collectibles **6**
North Star Mall **7**
Saks Fifth Avenue **7**
SAS Shoe Makers **3**
Satel's **16**
SeaZar's Fine Wine & Spirits **12**
Sheplers Western Wear **2**
Sloan/Hall **14**

would expect from a Saks Fifth Avenue, but it also has a 40-foot-high pair of cowboy boots standing out front. 650 North Star Mall. ✆ **210/341-4111.**

FASHIONS
The following stores offer clothing in a variety of styles; if you're keen on the cowpuncher look, see "Western Wear," below.

CHILDREN'S FASHION
Bambinos   Whether your child goes in for the English country look or veers more toward punk rocker, you'll find something to suit his or her (okay—your) tastes at this delightful store, which also carries a great selection of kiddie room furnishings and toys. The focus is on the younger set—infants to age 7, that is. 5934 Broadway. ✆ **210/822-9595.**

MEN'S FASHION
Satel's   This family-run Alamo Heights store has been the place to shop for menswear in San Antonio since 1950; classic, high-quality clothing and personal service make it a standout. A newer location in the Colonnade, 9801 I-10 West (✆ **210/694-0944**), offers the same fine goods and attention to customer needs. 5100 Broadway. ✆ **210/822-3376,** www.satels.com.

SHOES
SAS Shoemakers   This San Antonio footwear store is such an institution that the website for the VIA bus line lists it among the city's attractions. Men and women have been coming here to buy comfortable, sturdy, and well-made shoes and sandals since 1976. The factory store, on the south side of town, is the one to visit; you can even take one of three daily tours Monday through Thursday. Call in advance to make a reservation and to get directions. Other branches are located at Westlake Village, 1305 Loop 410 (✆ **210/673-2700**); Shoemakers Inn, 16088 San Pedro (✆ **210/494-1823**); and Garden Ridge in Shertz, 17885 I-35 N (✆ **210/651-5312**). 101 New Laredo Hwy. ✆ **210/921-7415** or 924-6507 (tour reservations).

WOMEN'S FASHION
Adelante Boutique   The focus here is on the ethnic and the handmade, with lots of colorful, natural fabrics and free-flowing lines. The store also offers a nice selection of leather belts and whimsical jewelry and gifts. 6414 N. New Braunfels Ave. (in Sunset Ridge). ✆ **210/826-6770.**

Kathleen Sommers ⭐   This small shop on the corner of Main and Wood-lawn has been setting trends for San Antonio women for years. Kathleen Sommers, who works mainly in linen and other natural fabrics, designs all the clothes, which bear her label. The store also carries great jewelry, bath items, books, fun housewares, and a selection of unusual gifts, including the San Antonio–originated Soular Therapy candles. 2417 N. Main. ✆ **210/732-8437.** www.kathleen sommers.com.

Mirabella   Super-stylish but friendly Mirabella owner Misti Riedel buys clothes according to the credo "Girls just wanna have fun." If it's sexy, colorful, creative, and wearable, you'll find it here. Good looks never come cheap, but many of the designers represented on the racks of this cozy shop are not well-known, which means costs are by no means prohibitive either. And if you're lucky, there'll be a sale on. 5910 Broadway. ✆ **210/829-4435.**

FOOD

Central Market   Free valet parking at a supermarket? On Saturday and Sunday, so many locals converge here to take advantage of the huge array of delectable samples that it's easy to understand why the store is willing to alleviate parking stress. You'll feel as though you've died and gone to food heaven as you walk amid gorgeous mounds of produce (I've never seen so many types of chiles), cheeses and other dairy products, sauces, pastas, and more. If you don't want to just graze, there are freshly prepared hot and cold gourmet foods, including a soup and salad bar, and a seating area in which to enjoy them. Wine tastings and cooking classes draw crowds in the evenings. 4821 Broadway. ℭ 210/ 368-8600. www.centralmarket.com.

GIFTS/SOUVENIRS

Alamo Fiesta *Finds*   Head just north of downtown to this two-level store near Monte Vista for a huge selection of Mexican folk art and handicrafts—everything from tinwork to colorful masks and piñatas—at extremely reasonable prices. Less touristy than most such shops, Alamo Fiesta is geared to local Hispanic families looking to celebrate special occasions. 2025 N. Main at Ashby. ℭ 210/ 738-1188. www.alamofiesta.com.

San Angel Folk Art   Combing the crafts markets of Mexico might be more fun, but exploring this large store in the Blue Star Arts Complex is a pretty good substitute. Painted animals from Oaxaca, elaborate masks from the state of Guerrero—this place is chockablock with things colorful, whimsical, and

---

Love Potion No. 9

Ask a proprietor of a **botanica**, "What kind of store is this?" and you'll hear anything from "a drugstore" to "a religious bookstore." But along with Christian artifacts (including glow-in-the-dark rosaries and dashboard icons), botanicas carry magic floor washes, candles designed to keep the law off your back, wolf skulls, amulets, herbal remedies, and, of course, love potions. The common theme is happiness enhancement, whether by self-improvement, prayer, or luck.

Many of San Antonio's countless small botanicas specialize in articles used by *curanderos*, traditional folk doctors or medicine men and women. Books directing laypersons in the use of medicinal herbs sit next to volumes that retell the lives of the saints. It's easy enough to figure out the use of the *santos* (saints), candles in tall glass jars to which are affixed such labels as "Peaceful Home," "Find Work," and "Bingo." *Milagros* (miracles) are small charms that represent parts of the body—or mind—that a person wishes to have healed. Don't worry that many of the labels are in Spanish as the person behind the counter will be happy to translate.

Papa Jim's, 5630 S. Flores (ℭ 210/922-6665; www.papajimsbotanica. com), is the best known of all the botanicas (Papa Jim, who used to bless the various artifacts he sold, died a few years ago). Can't make it to the shop? Order online or get a copy of the more comprehensive print catalog by phoning or ordering through the Papa Jim's website.

well-made. Of course, prices are better south of the border, but you're saving on airfare/gas and traveling time. 1404 S. Alamo, Suite 110, in the Blue Star Arts Complex. ✆ 210/226-6688. www.sanangelfolkart.com.

Sloan/Hall A cross between The Body Shop, Sharper Image, and Borders, only more concentrated and more upscale, this addictive boutique carries an assortment of toiletries, gadgets, books, and those uncategorizable items that you probably don't need but may find you desperately want. 5922 Broadway. ✆ 210/828-7738. www.sloanhall.com.

Tienda Guadalupe Folk Art & Gifts This incense-scented shop in the Southtown/King William area is brimming with Hispanic items: paintings and handicrafts from Latin America, Mexican antiques and religious items, and more. Come here to pick up a Day of the Dead T-shirt or anything else relating to the early November holiday celebrated with great fanfare in San Antonio. 1001 S. Alamo. ✆ 210/226-5873.

JEWELRY

See also "Crafts" and "Gifts/Souvenirs," above.

Chamade Jewelers Expect the unexpected and the beautiful at this dazzling jewelry store, representing more than 30 U.S. and international artists. You'll find everything from classically designed gold rings with precious gemstones to funny sterling silver earrings encasing beans for one ear and rice for the other. Some of the pieces are crafted by local and Southwest artisans, including Native Americans; others come from as far afield as France, Italy, China, and Indonesia. 504 Villita St. (La Villita). ✆ 210/224-7753. www.chamadejewelers.com.

Gavin Metalsmith For contemporary metal craft at its most creative, come to this small women's crafts gallery, where the exquisite original pieces range from wedding rings to salt-and-pepper shakers. The artists whose work is sold here incorporate lots of unusual stones into silver and white gold settings. They also frequently do custom work for fair prices. 4024 McCullough Ave. ✆ 210/821-5254.

MALLS/SHOPPING COMPLEXES

Alamo Quarry Market Alamo Quarry Market may be its official name, but no one ever calls this popular mall anything but "The Quarry" (from the early 1900s until 1985, the property was in fact a cement quarry). The four smokestacks, lit up dramatically at night, now signal play, not work. There are no anchoring department stores, but a series of large emporiums (Old Navy; Bed, Bath & Beyond; OfficeMax; and Borders) and smaller upscale boutiques (Laura Ashley, Aveda, and Lucchese Gallery—see "Western Wear," below) will keep you spending. A multiplex cinema and an array of refueling stations—Chili's and Starbucks, as well as the more upscale Koi Kowa, a revolving sushi bar; Piatti's, an Italian eatery well liked by locals; and Metropolitan, a French cafe (see chapter 5, p. 78)—complete this low-slung temple to self-indulgence. 255 E. Basse Rd. ✆ 210/824-8885. www.quarrymarket.com.

Crossroads of San Antonio Mall Located near the South Texas Medical Center, this is San Antonio's bargain mall, featuring Burlington Coat Factory, Super Target, and Stein Mart department stores alongside smaller discount stores. Some glitzier shops and performances at the food court are part of an effort to draw San Antonians to this low-profile shopping destination. 4522 Fredericksburg Rd. (off Loop 410 and I-10). ✆ 210/735-9137.

Travel Tip: He who finds the best hotel deal has more to spend on facials involving knobbly vegetables.

Hello, the Roaming Gnome here. I've been nabbed from the garden and taken round the world. The people who took me are so terribly clever. They find the best offerings on Travelocity. For very little cha-ching. And that means I get to be pampered and exfoliated till I'm pink as a bunny's doodah.

*** travelocity

1-888-TRAVELOCITY / travelocity.com / America Online Keyword: Travel

Plan your vacation

- flights, hotels, car rentals
- cruises & vacation packages
- destination guides
- fare alerts
- go to yahoo.com, click travel

DO YOU YAHOO!?

Huebner Oaks Shopping Center   This upscale open-air mall in the north central part of town houses a variety of yuppie favorites, including Old Navy, The Gap, Banana Republic, Victoria's Secret, and Eddie Bauer. When your energy flags, retreat to one of several casual dining spots like La Madeleine, serving good fast French food, or head straight to Starbucks for a caffeine boost. 11745 I-10. (C) 210/697-8444.

Los Patios   The self-proclaimed "other River Walk" features about a dozen upscale specialty shops in a lovely 18-acre wooded setting. You'll find shops carrying imported clothing, crafts, jewelry, and antique furniture among other offerings here. 2015 NE Loop 410, at the Starcrest exit. (C) 210/655-6171. www.lospatios.com.

North Star Mall   Starring Saks Fifth Avenue and upscale boutiques like Abercrombie & Fitch, J. Crew, Aveda, Sharper Image, and Williams-Sonoma, this is the crème de la crème of the San Antonio indoor malls. But there are many sensible shops here, too, including a Mervyn's department store. Food choices also climb up and down the scale, ranging from a Godiva Chocolatier to a Luby's Cafeteria. Loop 410, between McCullough and San Pedro. (C) 210/340-6627. www.northstarmall.com.

Rivercenter Mall   There's a festive atmosphere at this bustling, light-filled mall, fostered, among other things, by its location on an extension of the San Antonio River. You can pick up a ferry from a downstairs dock or listen to bands play on a stage surrounded by water. Other entertainment options include the IMAX theater, the multiple-screen AMC, the Cyber Zone video arcade, and the Rivercenter Comedy Club. The shops—more than 130 of them, anchored by Dillard's and Foleys—run the price gamut, but tend toward upscale casual. Food picks similarly range from Dairy Queen and A&W Hot Dogs to Morton's of Chicago. This can be a great place to shop, but remember that it's thronged with teeny-boppers Friday and Saturday nights. 849 E. Commerce, between S. Alamo and Bowie. (C) 210/225-0000. www.shoprivercenter.com.

MARKETS

Market Square   Two large indoor markets, El Mercado and the Farmer's Market—often just called, collectively, the Mexican market—occupy adjacent blocks on Market Square. Competing for your attention are more than 100 shops and pushcarts and an abundance of food stalls. The majority of the shopping booths are of the border-town sort, filled with onyx chess sets, cheap sombreros, and the like, but you can also find a few higher quality boutiques, including Galería Ortiz (see above). Come here for a bit of local color, good people-watching, and food—in addition to the sit-down Mi Tierra, detailed in chapter 5, and La Margarita, there are loads of primo places for street snacking. You'll often find yourself shopping to the beat of a mariachi band. 514 W. Commerce St. (near Dolorosa). (C) 210/207-8600.

FLEA MARKETS

Bussey's Flea Market   Unless you're heading to New Braunfels or Austin, Bussey's is a bit out of the way. But these 20 acres of vendors selling goods from as far afield as Asia and Africa are definitely worth the drive (about a half-hour north of downtown). Crafts, jewelry, antiques, incense—besides perishables, it's hard to imagine anything you couldn't find at this market. And who could resist coming to a spot with a giant armadillo in the parking lot? 18738 I-35 N. (C) 210/651-6830.

Eisenhauer Road Flea Market   The all-indoors, all air-conditioned Eisenhauer, complete with snack bar, is a good flea market to hit at the height of summer. You'll see lots of new stuff here—purses, jewelry, furniture, toys, shoes—and everything from houseplants to kinky leather wear. Closed Monday and Tuesday. 3903 Eisenhauer Rd. ☏ 210/653-7592.

Flea Mart On weekends, Mexican-American families make a day of this huge market, bringing the entire family to exchange gossip, listen to live bands, and eat freshly made tacos. There are always fruits and vegetables, electronics, crafts, and new and used clothing—and you never know what else. 12280 Hwy. 16 S. (about 1 mile south of Loop 410). ☏ 210/624-2666.

TOYS

The following stores (along with Bambinos—see "Fashions," above) carry unusual, but often pricey, toys. If your child is especially hard on playthings or your cash supply is running low, consider buying used toys at **Kids Junction Resale Shop,** 2267 NW Military Hwy. (☏ **210/340-5532**), or **Too Good to Be Threw,** 7115 Blanco (☏ **210/340-2422**).

Monarch Collectibles *(Kids* Welcome to doll heaven. Many of the models that fill Monarch's four rooms—about 3,000 dolls in all—are collectible and made from delicate materials like porcelain and baked clay, but others are cute and cuddly. Some come with real hair and eyelashes, and some are one of a kind. Doll furniture is also sold here—with a 6,000-square-foot dollhouse to showcase it—along with plates and a few stuffed animals. An entire room is devoted to Barbies. (Maybe the other dolls don't want to play with them.) 2012 NW Military Hwy. ☏ 210/341-3655. www.dollsdolls.com.

WESTERN WEAR

Boot Hill This one-stop shopping center for all duds Western, from Tony Lama boots to Stetson hats and everything in between, is one of the few left in town that's locally owned. Arnold Schwarzenegger and Ashley Judd are among the stars who have been outfitted here. This is a great store with terrific goods, but as an Arizonan, I feel compelled to mention that the *real* Boot Hill is in Tombstone, in my home state. Rivercenter Mall, 849 E. Commerce, Suite 213. ☏ 210/223-6634.

Little's Boots *(Finds* Lucchese (see below) is better known but this place— established in 1915—uses as many esoteric leathers and creates fancier footwear designs. You can get anything you like bespoke if you're willing to wait a while— possibly in line behind Reba McEntire and Tommy Lee Jones, who have had boots handcrafted here. Purchase some just so you can tell your friends back home, "Oh, Lucchese is so commercial. Little's is still the real thing." 110 Division Ave. ☏ 210/923-2221. www.davelittleboots.com.

Lucchese Gallery The name says it all: Footwear is raised to the level of art at Lucchese. If it ever crawled, ran, hopped, or swam, these folks can probably put it on your feet. The store carries boots made of alligator, elephant, ostrich, kangaroo, stingray, and lizard. Come here for everything from executive to spe-cial-occasion boots, all handmade and expensive and all still serious Texas status symbols. Lucchese also carries jackets, belts, and sterling silver belt buckles. 255 E. Basse, Suite 800. ☏ 210/828-9419. www.lucchese.com.

Paris Hatters What do Pope John Paul II, Prince Charles, Jimmy Smits, and Dwight Yoakam have in common? They've all had headgear made for them by Paris Hatters, in business since 1917 and still owned by the same family. About half of the sales are special orders, but the shelves are stocked with high-quality ready-to-wear hats, including Kangol caps from Britain, Panama hats from

Ecuador, Borsolina hats from Italy, and, of course, Stetson, Resistol, Dobbs, and other Western brands. A lot of them can be adjusted to your liking while you wait. Check out the pictures and newspaper articles in the back of the store to see which other famous heads have been covered here. 119 Broadway. © 210/223-3453. www.parishatters.com.

Sheplers Western Wear   If you want instant (as in trying on the clothes) gratification rather than waiting to get your duds in the mail from what has turned into the world's largest online western store (www.sheplers.com), come to this Ingram Mall Super Store branch of the national chain founded in Wichita, Kansas, during the 1950s. 6201 NW Loop 410. © 210/681-8230. www.sheplers.com.

WINES

See also Central Market under "Food," above.

Gabriel's   A large, warehouse-style store, Gabriel's combines good selection with good prices. You never know what oenological bargains you'll find on any given day. The Hildebrand store is slightly north of downtown; there's also another location near the airport at 7233 Blanco (© **210/349-7472**). 837 Hildebrand. © **210/735-8329**.

SeaZar's Fine Wine & Spirits   A temperature-controlled wine cellar, a large selection of beer and spirits, a cigar humidor, and a knowledgeable staff all make this a good choice for aficionados of the various legal vices. 6422 N. New Braunfels, in the Sunset Ridge Shopping Center. © **210/822-6094**.

8

San Antonio After Dark

San Antonio has its symphony and its Broadway shows, and you can see both at one of the most beautiful old movie palaces in the country. But much of what the city has to offer is not quite so mainstream. Latin influences lend spice to some of the best local nightlife. Don't forget San Antonio is America's capital for Tejano music, a unique blend of German polka and northern Mexico ranchero sounds (with a dose of pop added for good measure). You can sit on one side of the San Antonio River and watch colorful dance troupes like **Ballet Folklórico** perform on the other. And Southtown, with its many Hispanic-oriented shops and galleries, celebrates its art scene with the monthly First Friday, a kind of extended block party.

Keep in mind, too, that the Fiesta City throws big public parties year-round: Fiestas Navideñas and Las Posadas around Christmastime, Fiesta San Antonio and Cinco de Mayo

events in spring, the Texas Folklife Festival in summer, and Oktoberfest and the International Accordion Festival in autumn (see also "San Antonio Calendar of Events," in chapter 2).

For the most complete listings of what's on while you're visiting, pick up a free copy of the weekly alternative newspaper, the *Current,* or the Friday "Weekender" section of the *San Antonio Express-News.* You can also check out the website of **San Antonio Arts & Cultural Affairs:** www.sanantonio. gov/art. There's no central office in town for tickets, discounted or otherwise. You'll need to reserve seats directly through the theaters or clubs, or, for large events, through **Ticketmaster** (© 210/224-9600; www.ticketmaster. com). Generally, box office hours are Monday to Friday 10am to 5pm, and 1 to 2 hours before performance time. The **Majestic** (p. 124) and **Empire** (p. 124) also have hours on Saturday 10am to 3pm.

1 The Performing Arts

The San Antonio Symphony is the city's only resident performing arts company of national stature, but smaller, less professional groups keep the local arts scene lively, and cultural organizations draw world-renowned artists. The city provides them with some unique venues—everything from standout historic structures like the Majestic, Empire, Arneson, and Sunken Garden theaters to the state-of-the-art SBC Center. Because, in some cases, the theater is the show and, in others, a single venue offers an eclectic array of performances, I've included a category called "Major Arts Venues," below.

CLASSICAL MUSIC

San Antonio Symphony　The city's symphony is one of the finest in the United States. Founded in 1939, the orchestra celebrated its 50th anniversary by moving into the Majestic Theatre, the reopening of which was planned to coincide with the event. The symphony offers two major annual series, classical and pops. The classical series showcases the talents of music director emeritus Christopher Wilkens and a variety of guest performers, while for the pops series, you might find anyone from banjo virtuoso Buddy Wachter to nostalgia stars like The Lettermen or Three Dog Night. 222 E. Houston St. © 210/554-1000 or 554-1010 (box office). www.sasymphony.org. Tickets $16–$53 classical, $21–$61 pops.

THEATER

Most of San Antonio's major shows turn up at the Majestic or Empire theaters (see "Major Art Venues," below), but several smaller theaters are of interest too. The **Actors Theater of San Antonio,** 1920 Fredericksburg Rd. (© **210/ 738-2872**), uses local talent for its productions, which tend to be in the off-Broadway tradition. Their venue is the Woodlawn Theatre, opened as a movie house in 1945. At the King William district's **Alamo Street Restaurant & Theatre,** 1150 S. Alamo (© **210/271-7791;** www.alamostreetrestaurantandtheatre. com), interactive comedies and murder mysteries take place on Friday and Saturday nights in the Green Room Dinner Theatre—the former choir rooms of a converted 1912 church—accompanied by buffet meals; upstairs, in the former sanctuary now called The Mainstage, there are lectures, concerts, musicals, comedies, and dramas, sans food. The community-based **Josephine Street Theater,** 339 W. Josephine St. (© **210/734-4646**), puts on an average of five productions a year—mostly musicals—at the Art Deco–style Josephine Street Theater, only 5 minutes from downtown. Whether it's an original piece by a member of the company or a work by a guest artist, anything you see at the **Jump-Start Performance Company,** 108 Blue Star Arts Complex (1400 S. Alamo; © **210/227-JUMP;** www.jump-start.org), is likely to push the social and political envelope. This is the place to find the big-name performance artists like Karen Finley or Holly Hughes who tour San Antonio. The only professional family theater in town, the popular **Magik Theatre,** Beethoven Hall, 420 S. Alamo in HemisFair Park (© **210/227-2751;** www.magiktheatre.org), features a daytime series with light fare for ages 3 and up, and evening performances, recommended for those 6 and older, that may include weightier plays. About half the plays are adaptations of published scripts, while the other half are originals, created especially for the theater. San Antonio's first public theater, the **San Pedro Playhouse,** 800 W. Ashby (© **210/733-7258;** http://san_pedro_ playhouse.tripod.com), presents a wide range of plays in a neoclassical-style performance hall built in 1930. For information on other small theaters in San Antonio and links to many of those listed in this section, log on to the website of the **San Antonio Theater Coalition,** www.satheatre.com.

MAJOR ARTS VENUES

See also the "For Those Interested in Hispanic Heritage" section of chapter 6 for information on the Alameda Theater.

Arneson River Theatre   If you're visiting San Antonio in the summer, be sure to see something at the Arneson. Built by the Works Project Administration in 1939 as part of architect Robert Hugman's design for the River Walk, this unique theater stages shows on one side of the river while the audience watches from an amphitheater on the other. Most of the year, performance schedules are erratic and include everything from opera to Tejano, but the summer brings a stricter calendar: the Fandango folkloric troupe performs every Tuesday and Thursday in June and July, and the Fiesta Noche del Río takes the stage on Friday and Saturday May through July. Both offer lively music and dance with a south-of-the-border flair. La Villita. © **210/207-8610**. www.lavillita.com/arneson.

Beethoven Halle and Garten   San Antonio's German heritage is celebrated at this venue, a converted 1894 Victorian mansion in the King William area. It's open Tuesday through Saturday as a beer garden, with bands playing everything from oompah to rock. Among the regular performers are the Mannerchor (men's choir), which dates back to 1867. Lots of traditional German food, drink, and revelry make Oktoberfest an autumn high point. In December, a Kristkrindle Markt welcomes the holiday season with an old country–style arts-and-crafts fair. 422 Pereida. (𝄐 **210/222-1521**. www.beethovenmaennerchor.com.

Carver Community Cultural Center   Located near the Alamodome on the east edge of downtown, the Carver theater was built for the city's African-American community in 1929, and hosted the likes of Ella Fitzgerald, Charlie "Bird" Parker, and Dizzy Gillespie over the years. It continues to serve the community while providing a widely popular venue for an international array of performers in a variety of genres, including drama, music, and dance. In 2004, the center completed a major renovation, so performances, which had been held elsewhere, return for the 2005 season to a newly spiffy—and structurally sound—venue. 226 N. Hackberry. (𝄐 **210/207-7211** or 207-2234 (box office). www.thecarver.org. Tickets $25.

The Empire Theatre   Among the celebrities who trod the boards of the Empire Theatre before its motion picture prime were Roy Rogers and Trigger; Mae West put in an appearance, too. Fallen into disrepair and shuttered for 2 decades, this 1914 opera house made its grand re-debut in 1998 after a massive renovation. Smaller than its former rival the Majestic (see below), just down the block, the Empire hosts a similarly eclectic array of acts, including musical performances, lectures, and literary events. 226 N. St. Mary's St. (𝄐 **210/226-5700**. www.majesticempire.com.

Guadalupe Cultural Arts Center   There's always something happening at the Guadalupe Center, the heart of Latino cultural activity in San Antonio. Visiting and local directors put on six or seven plays a year; the resident Guadalupe Dance Company might collaborate with the city's symphony or invite modern masters up from Mexico City. The Xicano Music Program celebrates the popular local conjunto and Tejano sounds; an annual book fair brings in Spanish-language literature from around the world; and the CineFestival, running since 1977, is one of the town's major film events. And then there are always the parties thrown to celebrate new installations at the theater's art gallery and its annex. 1300 Guadalupe. (𝄐 **210/271-3151**. www.guadalupeculturalarts.org.

Laurie Auditorium   Some pretty high-powered people turn up at the Laurie Auditorium, on the Trinity University campus in the north-central part of town. Everyone from former weapons inspector David Kay to Fox news correspondent Brit Hume has taken part in the university's Distinguished Lecture Series, subsidized by grants and open to the public free. The 2,700-seat hall also hosts major players in the popular and performing arts: Duran Duran and the Preservation Hall Jazz Band were among those who took the stage in recent years. Dance recitals, jazz concerts, and plays, many with internationally renowned artists, are held here, too. Trinity University, 715 Stadium Dr. (𝄐 **210/999-8117** (box office information line) or 999-8119. www.trinity.edu/departments/Laurie.

Majestic Theatre   This theater introduced air-conditioning to San Antonio—the hall was billed beforehand as "an acre of cool, comfortable seats"—and society women wore fur coats to its opening, held on a warm June night in 1929. The Majestic hosts some of the best entertainment in town—the symphony, major Broadway productions, big-name solo performers—and, thanks

---

(*Fun Fact* **A Theater That Lives Up to Its Name**

Everyone from Jack Benny to Mae West played the **Majestic,** one of the last "atmospheric" theaters to be built in America. The stock market crashed 4 months after its June 1929 debut, and no one could afford to build such expensive showplaces afterward. Designed in baroque Moorish/Spanish revival style by John Eberson, this former vaudeville and film palace features an elaborate village above the sides of the stage and, overhead, a magnificent night sky dome, replete with twinkling stars and scudding clouds. Designated a National Historic Landmark, the Majestic affords a rare glimpse into a gilded era (yes, there's genuine gold leaf detailing).

---

to a wonderful restoration of this fabulous showplace, completed in 1989, coming here is still pretty cool. 230 E. Houston. ℂ **210/226-3333**. www.majesticempire.com.

Sunken Garden Theater   Built by the WPA in 1936 in a natural acoustic bowl in Brackenridge Park, the Sunken Garden Theater boasts an open-air stage set against a wooded hillside; cut-limestone buildings in Greek revival style hold the wings and the dressing rooms. This appealing outdoor arena, open from March through October, offers a little bit of everything—rock, country, hip-hop, rap, jazz, Tejano, Cajun, and sometimes even the San Antonio Symphony. Annual events include Taste of New Orleans (a Fiesta event in Apr), the Margarita Pour-Off in August, and a biannual Bob Marley Reggae Festival. Brackenridge Park, 3975 N. St. Mary's St. (Mulberry Ave. entrance). ℂ **210/207-3170** or 207-3000.

2 The Club & Music Scene

The closest San Antonio comes to having a club district is the stretch of North St. Mary's between Josephine and Magnolia—just north of downtown and south of Brackenridge Park—known as the Strip. This area was hotter about 15 years ago, but it still draws a young crowd to its restaurants and lounges on the weekend. The River Walk clubs tend to be touristy, and many of them close early because of noise restrictions. Downtown's **Sunset Station,** 1174 E. Commerce (ℂ **210/222-9481,** www.sunset-station.com), a multivenue entertainment complex in the city's original train station, has yet to take off when there are no events in the nearby Alamodome. When there are, you can get down at Club Agave, where the movement has a Latin flavor. More regular action occurs on Sunday at noon, when the House of Blues lays on a gospel brunch buffet in a covered outdoor pavilion. Call the Sunset Station office or check the website for details.

In addition to the **Alamodome,** 100 Montana St. (ℂ **210/207-3663,** www.sanantonio.gov/dome), the major concert venues in town include **Verizon Wireless Amphitheater,** 16765 Lookout Rd., north of San Antonio just beyond Loop 1604 (ℂ **210/657-8300,** www.vwatx.com), and, when the Spurs aren't playing there, downtown's **SBC Center,** 1 SBC Center Pkwy. (ℂ **210/444-5000,** www.nba.com/spurs), which opened in late 2002.

COUNTRY & WESTERN

Floores Country Store ⍟⍟   John T. Floore, the first manager of the Majestic Theatre and an unsuccessful candidate for mayor of San Antonio, opened up this country store in 1942. A couple of years later, he added a cafe and a dance floor—at half an acre, the largest in south Texas. And not much has changed since then. Boots, hats, and antique farm equipment hang from the ceiling of this typical Texas roadhouse, and the walls are lined with pictures of Willie Nelson, Hank Williams, Sr., Conway Twitty, Ernest Tubb, and other country greats who have played here. There's always live music on weekends, and Dwight Yoakum, Robert Earl Keen, and Lyle Lovett have all turned up along with Willie. The cafe still serves homemade bread, homemade tamales, old-fashioned sausage, and cold Texas beer. 14464 Old Bandera Rd./Hwy. 16, Helotes (2 miles north of Loop 1604). ℂ 210/695-8827. www.liveatfloores.com. Cover $5–$35.

Leon Springs Dancehall This lively 1880s-style dance hall can—and often does—pack some 1,200 people into its 18,000 square feet. Lots of people come with their kids when the place opens at 7pm, though the crowd turns older (but not much) as the evening wears on. Some of the best local country-and-western talent is showcased here on Friday and Saturday nights, the only 2 nights the dance hall is open. Get a group of more than 10 together and you can order BBQ from the original Rudy's, just down the road. 24135 I-10 (Boerne Stage Rd. exit). ℂ 210/698-7072. www.leonspringsdancehall.com. Cover usually $5, kids under 12 free.

ROCK

Taco Land Loud and not much to look at—think low ceilings, red vinyl booths, garage pinup calendars stapled to the ceiling—tiny Taco Land is nevertheless the hottest alternative music club in San Antonio, showcasing everything from mainstream rock to surf punk. Some of the bands that turn up may seem less than impressive, but, hey, you never know: Nirvana played here before they hit the big time (and before Taco Land actually began serving tacos). 103 W. Grayson St. ℂ 210/223-8406. Cover $3 Fri–Sat, free during the week.

White Rabbit One of the few alternative rock venues on the Strip—and one of the only ones large enough to have a raised stage—the Rabbit attracts a mostly young crowd to its black-lit recesses. Those 18 to 20 years old are allowed in for a higher cover. 2410 N. St. Mary's St. ℂ 210/737-2221. www.sawhiterabbit.com. Cover $6.

ECLECTIC

Casbeers Opened in 1932, this is the real deal, an eclectic Texas dive bar/restaurant with so much local character that the Texas Tornadoes filmed their "Anybody Goin' to San Antone" video here. The venue may be old but the sounds are new. You can hear local, regional, national, and international artists (such as Grammy Award winner Dave Alvin) in a variety of genres, including roots, rock, blues, country, folk, and gospel (for the monthly Sunday brunch to benefit the local homeless shelter). There are only beer and wine to accompany the hearty burgers and Tex-Mex chow. 1719 Blanco Rd. ℂ 210/732-3511. www.casbeers.com. No cover Tues–Wed, $5–$20 Thurs–Sat.

Kingston Tycoon Flats (Kids) This friendly music garden is a fun place to kick back and listen to blues, rock, acoustic, reggae, or jazz. The burgers and Caribbean specialties like jerk chicken are good, too. Bring the kids—an outdoor sandbox is larger than the dance floor. There's rarely any cover for the almost nightly live music. 2926 N. St. Mary's St. ℂ 210/731-9838. www.kingstontycoonflats.com. Cover $5 or under when there is one.

JAZZ & BLUES

The Landing (★★) You might have heard cornetist Jim Cullum on the airwaves. His American Public Radio program, *Riverwalk, Live from the Landing,* is now broadcast on more than 160 stations nationwide, and his band has backed some of the finest jazz players of our time. This is the best traditional jazz club in Texas, and if you like big bands and Dixieland, there's no better place to listen to this music. The Landing Cafe features a fairly basic steak and seafood menu, with a few Mexican/Southwest touches. Hyatt Regency Hotel, River Walk. ✆ 210/223-7266. www.landing.com. Cover $5 Mon–Sat, free Sun (outdoor stage only, when other bands entertain).

Salute!   Like the crowd, the music at this red-lit little wonder is eclectic, to say the least. The live jazz at this tiny club tends to have a Latin flavor, but you never know what you're going to hear—anything from synthesized '70s sounds to conjunto. 2801 N. St. Mary's St. ✆ 210/732-5307. www.saluteinternationalbar.com. Cover $1–$5 weekends, free during the week.

DANCE CLUBS

Polly Esther's   Is it just a coincidence that the last four digits in the telephone number of this lively, three-level River Walk club match the year that the disco craze started to take hold? I think not. Even if you've sworn off strobe lights forever, you just can't help yourself once you hear that funky beat. That's especially true if you have indulged in one of the club's signature liqueur drinks, which sound innocuous (Brady Bunch Punch, for example) and taste syrupy sweet but pack a major wallop. 212 College St. ✆ 210/220-1972. www.pollyesthers.com. Cover $3–$10.

COMEDY

Rivercenter Comedy Club   This club books big names in stand-up like Dennis Miller and Garry Shandling, but it also takes advantage of local talent on Mondays (Comedy Potpourri nights) and Fridays (open-mike night in the Ha!Lapeno Lounge 5–7:30pm; no cover). The late, late (12:20am) adult-oriented shows on Friday nights are also free. 849 E. Commerce St. (Rivercenter Mall, 3rd level). ✆ 210/229-1420. www.hotcomedy.com. Cover $8 Mon–Tues, $10 Wed–Thurs, $12 Fri–Sun.

THE GAY SCENE

In addition to the Bonham (see below), Main Street just north of downtown has three gay clubs in close proximity (it's been nicknamed the "gay bar mall"). **Pegasus,** 1402 N. Main (✆ 210/299-4222), is your basic cruise bar. **The Silver Dollar,** 1418 N. Main (✆ 210/227-2623), does the country-and-western thing. And **The Saint,** 1430 N. Main (✆ 210/225-7330), caters to dancing fools. Covers are low to nonexistent at all three.

Bonham Exchange   Tina Turner, Deborah Harry, and LaToya Jackson—the real ones—have all played this high-tech dance club near the Alamo. While you may find an occasional cross-dressing show here, the mixed crowd of gays and straights, young and old, come mainly to move to the beat under wildly flashing lights. All the action—five bars, three dance floors, three levels—takes place in a restored German-style building dating back to the 1880s. Roll over, Beethoven. 411 Bonham. ✆ 210/271-3811 or 224-9219. www.bonhamexchange.net. No cover for ages 21 and over before 10pm, then $5 Fri–Sat, $3 Sun.

3 The Bar Scene

Most bars close at 2am, although some alternative spots stay open until 3 or 4am. Some of the hottest bars in town are also in restaurants: see Acenar and Azuca in chapter 5.

Blue Star Brewing Company Restaurant & Bar   Preppies and gallery types don't often mingle, but the popularity of this brewpub in the Blue Star

Conjunto: An American Classic

Cruise a San Antonio radio dial or go to any major city festival, and you'll most likely hear the happy, boisterous sound of conjunto. Never heard of it? Don't worry, you're not alone. Although conjunto is one of our country's original contributions to world music, for a long time few Americans outside Texas knew much about it.

Conjunto evolved at the end of the 19th century, when South Texas was swept by a wave of German immigrants who brought with them popular polkas and waltzes. These sounds were easily incorporated into—and transformed by—Mexican folk music. The newcomer accordion, cheap and able to mimic several instruments, was happily adopted, too. With the addition at the turn of the century of the *bajo sexto,* a 12-string guitar-like instrument used for rhythmic bass accompaniment, conjunto was born.

Tejano (Spanish for "Texan") is the 20th-century offspring of conjunto. The two most prominent instruments in Tejano remain the accordion and the *bajo sexto,* but the music incorporates more modern forms, including pop, jazz, and country-and-western, into the traditional conjunto repertoire. At clubs not exclusively devoted to Latino sounds, what you're likely to hear is Tejano.

Long ignored by the mainstream, conjunto and Tejano were brought into America's consciousness by the murder of Hispanic superstar **Selena.** Before she was killed, Selena had already been slotted for crossover success—she had done the title song and put in a cameo appearance in the film *Don Juan de Marco* with Johnny Depp—and the movie based on her life boosted awareness of her music even further.

San Antonio is to conjunto music what Nashville is to country. The most famous *bajo sextos,* used nationally by everyone who is anyone in conjunto and Tejano music, were created in San Antonio by the Macías family—the late Martín and now his son, Alberto. The undisputed king of conjunto, **Flaco Jiménez**—a mild-mannered triple-Grammy winner who has recorded with the Rolling Stones, Bob Dylan, and Willie Nelson, among others—lives in the city. And San Antonio's **Tejano Conjunto Festival,** held each May (see the "San Antonio Calendar of Events," in chapter 2), is the largest of its kind, drawing aficionados from around the world—there's even a conjunto band from Japan.

Most of the places to hear conjunto and Tejano are off the beaten tourist path, and they come and go fairly quickly. Those that have been around for a while—and are visitor-friendly—include **Arturo's Sports Bar & Grill,** 3310 S. Zarzamora St. (© 210/923-0177), and **Cool Arrows,** 1025 Nogalitos St. (© 210/227-5130). For live music schedules, check the Tejano/Conjunto section under "Entertainment" and "Music" of www.mysanantonio.com, the website of the *San Antonio-Express News.* You can also phone **Salute!** (see above) to find out which night of the week they're featuring a Tejano or conjunto band. Best yet, just attend one of San Antonio's many festivals—you're bound to hear these rousing sounds.

Arts Complex with college kids demonstrates the transcendent power of good beer. (The pale ale is especially fine.) And if a few folks who wouldn't know a Picasso from a piccolo happen to wander in and see some art after dinner, then the owners have performed a useful public service. The food's good, too. 1414 S. Alamo, #105 (Blue Star Arts Complex). ✆ 210/212-5506. www.bluestarbrewing.com.

Cadillac Bar & Restaurant   During the week, lawyers and judges come to unwind at the Cadillac Bar, set in a historic stucco building near the Bexar County Courthouse and City Hall. On the weekends, singles take over the joint. A DJ spins on Saturday nights, but on Thursdays and Fridays, the sounds are live and local—anything from '70s disco to classic rock to pop. Full dinners are served on a patio out back. 212 S. Flores. ✆ 210/223-5533.

Cappyccino's   Although it's by no means deficient in the caffeine department, don't mistake Cappyccino's for a coffee bar: The name derives from neighboring Cappy's restaurant (p. 77), of which it's an offshoot. The forte here is yuppie hard stuff, including classic cocktails, tequilas, and single-malt scotches. A skinny but high-ceilinged lightwood dining room and a plant-filled patio create a relaxed setting for drinking and dining off the stylish Southwest bistro menu. 5003 Broadway. ✆ 210/828-6860. www.sawhost.com/cappy.

Durty Nellie's Irish Pub   Chug a lager and lime, toss your peanut shells on the floor, and sing along with the piano player at this wonderfully corny version of an Irish pub. You've forgotten the words to "Danny Boy"? Not to worry—18 old-time favorites are printed on the back of the menu. After a couple of Guinnesses, you'll be bellowing "H-A-double-R-I-G-A-N spells Harrigan!" as loud as the rest of 'em. 715 River Walk (Hilton Palacio del Rio Hotel). ✆ 210/222-1400.

Howl at the Moon Saloon   It's hard to avoid having a good time at this rowdy River Walk bar; if you're shy, one of the dueling piano players will inevitably embarrass you into joining the crowd belting out off-key oldies from the '60s, '70s, and '80s. Don't worry. You're probably never going to see most of these people again. 111 W. Crockett St. ✆ 210/212-4695. www.howlatthemoon.com. Cover $5 Sun–Thurs, $7 Fri–Sat until 10pm, $10 after 10pm. 21 and older only.

Menger Bar   More than 100 years ago, Teddy Roosevelt recruited men for his Rough Riders unit at this dark, wooded bar (they were outfitted for the Spanish-American War at nearby Fort Sam Houston). Constructed in 1859 on the site of William Menger's earlier successful brewery and saloon, the bar was moved from its original location in the Victorian hotel lobby in 1956, but 90% of its historic furnishings remain intact. You can still see an "X" on the bar (modeled after the bar in the House of Lords in London) put there by prohibitionist Carrie Nation, and Spanish Civil War uniforms hang on the walls. It's still one of the prime spots in town to toss back a few. Menger Hotel, 204 Alamo Plaza. ✆ 210/223-4361.

Stone Werks Cafe and Bar   At this offbeat venue—a 1920s building that used to be the Alamo Cement Company's office—a 30-something crowd moves to local cover bands from Wednesday through Saturday. A fence, hand-sculpted from cement by Mexican artist Dionicio Rodríguez, surrounds an oak-shaded patio. 7300 Jones-Maltsberger. ✆ 210/828-3508. www.stonewerks.com.

Swig Martini Bar   Craving a chocolate martini? Belly up to the bar at the River Walk's nod to retro chic. Single-barrel bourbon, single-malt scotch, and a wide selection of beer and wines fill out the drink menu, but James Bond's preferred poison is always the top seller. Nightly live jazz adds to the pizzazz. The

---

Finds **Mission Accomplished**

When it premiered in 1947, the screen of the **Mission Drive-In,** 310 Roosevelt Ave. (© **210/532-3259** or 496-2221), was framed with a neon outline of nearby Mission San Jose, replete with moving bell, burro, and cacti. San Antonio's last remaining open-air movie house, refurbished and reopened in 2001, now has four screens and features first-run films. It's as much fun to come here for a family filmfest or romantic under-the-stars evening as it ever was.

---

catch (or draw) here is those big cigars. *Note:* This place was so popular it spurred a national chain. 111 W. Crockett, #205. © **210/476-0005.** www.swigmartinibar. citysearch.com.

Tex's Grill If you want to hang with the Spurs, come to Tex's, regularly voted San Antonio's best sports bar in the *Current* readers' polls. Three satellite dishes, two large-screen TVs, and 17 smaller sets keep the bleachers happy, as do the killer margaritas and giant burgers. Among Tex's major collection of exclusively Texas sports memorabilia are a signed Nolan Ryan jersey, a football used by the Dallas Cowboys in their 1977 Super Bowl victory, and one of George Gervin's basketball shoes (the other is at the newer Tex's on the River, at the Hilton Palacio del Rio). San Antonio Airport Hilton and Conference Center, 611 NW Loop 410. © **210/ 340-6060.**

Zen Bar San Antonio's young fashionistas mingle at this LA-style watering hole near the Majestic Theatre (it even has a dress code: no sneakers on the weekends). The Buddha at the entryway and lots of intimate couches and lounges whisper Asian serenity, but the music—international, funk, salsa— shouts get your groove on. There's no smoking indoors, but the patio out back is puffer-friendly. It's worth a visit for the peekaboo bathrooms alone. 221–223 Houston St. © **210/271-7472.** www.zenbar.com.

Zinc This chic wine bar, open until 2am nightly, is perfect for a romantic after-hours glass of champagne. Hardwood floors, brick walls, and a cozy library make the indoor space appealing, but on temperate nights, head for the pretty back patio. 209 N. Presa St. © **210/224-2900.** www.zincwine.com.

4 Movies

The alternative cinemas in San Antonio are not in the most trafficked tourist areas, but if you're willing to go out of your way for an indie fix you can get one at the **Regal Fiesta Stadium 16,** 12631 Vance Jackson (© **210/641-6906**). The city also boasts a cinema that not only screens off-beat films, but also allows you to munch on more than popcorn and licorice while viewing them. At the homegrown **Bijou at Crossroads: A CaféCinema,** 4522 Fredericksburg, Crossroads Mall (© **210/737-0291** [show times] or 496-1300, ext 0; www.santikos.com/ sites/crossroads.htm), you can dine on deli sandwiches, burgers, or pizzas, accompanied by a cold one (or glass of wine) at bistro-style tables in the lobby or at your seat in the theater. An Austin import (its name notwithstanding), the **Alamo Drafthouse Westlakes,** 1255 SW Loop 410 (© **210/677-8500;** www.drafthouse.com/westlakes), shows mostly first-run films but accompanies them with seat-side food service.

The **Guadalupe Cultural Arts Center** (see "Major Arts Venues," earlier in this chapter) and the **McNay** and **Witte museums** (see chapter 6) often have interesting film series, and the **Esperanza Center,** 922 San Pedro (© 210/228-0201; www.esperanzacenter.org), usually offers an annual gay and lesbian cinema festival. In addition to *Alamo, the Price of Freedom,* the **San Antonio IMAX Theater Rivercenter,** 217 Alamo Plaza (© 210/225-4629; www.imax-sa.com), shows high-action films like *Spiderman* or *Into the Deep* suited to the big, big screen. Be on the lookout for a second large-screen theater on the River Walk, the Aztec Theater, a historic venue which was still under reconstruction in early 2005 with no definite opening date in sight; check www.aztecontheriver.com for updates.

9

The Best of Austin

Aah, Austin, laid-back city in the lake-laced hills, home to cyberpunks and environmentalists, high culture and haute cuisine. A leafy intellectual enclave lying well outside the realm of Lone Star stereotypes, Austin has been compared to Berkeley and Seattle, but it is at once its own place and entirely Texan.

The University of Texas (UT), vastly expanded beyond the 40 acres deeded to it in 1883, is a key source of the city's cultural savvy. Its assets include a presidential library; theater, dance, and concert venues; prominent literary archives (UT was the model for the wealthy American university in A.S. Byatt's novel *Possession*); and an important art collection. But UT's funding comes from oil money, and Austinites display typical Texan fervor when it comes to rooting for the Longhorns.

Despite its growing concrete nexus of business parks, many devoted to high-tech enterprises, like the one started by UT graduate Michael Dell, Austin's heart is green. It has a vast municipal system of parks and preserves, and a bustling hike-and-bike trail near downtown's Town Lake. And there isn't a species in the region, no matter how small or ugly, that isn't vociferously defended if its extinction is threatened.

When they're not exercising or espousing environmental causes—or even when they are—Austinites love music. Their obsession is large-scale: The city has gigantic record stores, a shop devoted solely to music arts, and more than 100 live music venues. One of the most appealing aspects of the local scene is the wide range of good sounds to be found at unexpected, completely original places: barbecue joints, Mexican restaurants, converted gas stations. The atmosphere almost everywhere is assiduously laid-back; legends like Bob Dylan and Joan Baez still perform at intimate spots like the **Backyard** (p. 247), and covers in the smaller clubs are still relatively low.

Many Texans who live in faster-paced cities like Dallas or Houston dream of someday escaping to Austin, which, although it grew by 41% in the 1990s and passed the half-million population mark, still has a small-town feel. Meanwhile, they smile upon the city as they would on a beloved but eccentric younger sister; whenever an especially contrary story about her is told, they shrug, shake their heads, and fondly say, "Well, that's Austin."

1 Frommer's Favorite Austin Experiences

- **Having Coffee at Mozart's:** Picture a deck overlooking Lake Austin, caffeine, and conversation (real or virtual—this is an Internet hot spot). . . . What could be bad? See chapter 13.
- **Joining the Healthy Hordes on Austin's Hike & Bike Trails:**

Head over to the shores of Town Lake to see why *Walking* magazine chose Austin as America's "Most Fit" city. Speed walkers, joggers, and in-line skaters share the turf with bicyclists and hikers on the many trails set up by the city for its urban athletes. See chapter 14.

- **Splashing around Barton Springs Pool:** The bracing waters of this natural pool have been drawing Austinites to its banks for more than 100 years. If there's one thing that everyone in town can agree on, it's that there's no better plunge pond on a hot day than this one. See chapter 14.

- **Going Batty:** From late March through November, thousands of bats emerge in smoky clouds from under the Congress Avenue Bridge, heading west for dinner. It's a mind-boggling sight, and you can thank each of the little mammals for keeping the air pest free—a single bat can eat as many as 600 mosquitoes in an hour. See chapter 14.

- **Playing in the Water at Lake Travis:** The longest of the seven Highland Lakes, Travis offers the most opportunities for watery cavorting, including jet-skiing, snorkeling, and angling. See chapter 14.

- **Touring the Capitol:** The country's largest state capitol was pretty impressive even in its run-down state, but after a massive face-lift at the end of the last century, visitors can really see that it's a legislative center fit for Texas. See p. 201.

- **Smelling the Bluebonnets at the Lady Bird Johnson Wildflower Center:** Spring is prime viewing time for the flowers, but Austin's mild winters ensure that there will always be bursts of color at Lady Bird Johnson's pet project. See p. 202.

- **Shopping at Allen's Boots in SoCo.:** In the hip South Congress district, you can find a gallery devoted to outsider art, several antiques shops, and this decades-old, family-owned Western clothing store that sells tie-dyed T-shirts emblazoned with the logo KEEP AUSTIN WEIRD. See chapter 15.

- **Ascending Mount Bonnell:** Sure, the 100-odd steps are steep, but the climb is far more rewarding than a StairMaster: When you reach the top, the view of the city will take away whatever breath you have left. See chapter 14.

- **Taking a Visitor Center Walking Tour:** I wouldn't ordinarily suggest herding activities, but these historic excursions, provided free by the city, are superb. See chapter 14.

- **Playing culture groupie at the Harry Ransom Humanities Research Center:** You never know what you'll see in the rotating displays in this newly revamped exhibit space—Ernest Hemingway's letters? Scarlett O'Hara's ball gown?—but it's guaranteed to be interesting. See chapter 14.

- **Touring the Austin City Limits Studio:** C'mon, admit it, you've always wanted to play air guitar on the stage where Lyle Lovett and Mary Chapin Carpenter performed. The logistics for getting tickets to the live taping sessions is a bit more complicated than the regular tours, but it's worth a shot to take part in PBS's longest-running show. See chapter 16.

- **Listening to Toni Price at the Continental Club:** If you're in town on a Tuesday night, this folksy blues diva is not to be missed. But it's worth turning up at this Austin classic club on any night for its rockin' roots music. See chapter 16.

- **Drinking in Some History at Scholz Garten:** The oldest biergarten in Texas has loads of atmosphere—not to mention an up-to-date sound system. Just don't come here after the University of Texas Longhorns have won (or lost) a game; the place will be packed with singing (or sulking) UT fans. See chapter 16.

2 Best Austin Hotel Bets

• **Best for Conducting Business:** Located near a lot of the high-tech companies in northwest Austin, the **Renaissance Austin Hotel,** 9721 Arboretum Blvd. (© **800/ HOTELS-1** or 512/343-2626), has top-notch meeting and schmoozing spaces, not to mention fine close-the-deal-and-party spots. See p. 170.

• **Best Hotel Lobby for Pretending You're Rich:** Settle in at the lobby lounge at the posh **Four Seasons Austin,** 98 San Jacinto Blvd. (© **800/332-3442** or 512/ 478-4500), overlooking Town Lake, and for the price of a Dubonnet, you can act like you stay here every time you fly in on your Lear jet. See p. 155.

• **Best Place to Play Cattle Baron:** If you want to imagine you've acquired your fortune in an earlier era, bed down at **The Driskill,** 604 Brazos St. (© **800/252-9367** or 512/474-5911), where big meat mogul Jesse Driskill still surveys (via stone image) the opulent 1886 hotel that bears his name. See p. 155.

• **Hippest Budget Hotel:** Look for the classic neon sign for the **Austin Motel,** 1220 S. Congress St. (© **512/441-1157**), in Austin's cool SoCo district. The rooms have been individually furnished, many in fun and funky styles, but the place retains its 1950s character and its retro prices. See p. 164.

• **Best New (Old) Arrival:** The **Mansion at Judges Hill,** 1900 Rio Grande (© **800/311-1619** or 512/495-1800), has a great location near the University of Texas (it was built by one of UT's founders,

so why shouldn't it?) and rooms in both the original mansion and its 1980s complement that are timeless and elegant. The gardens are gorgeous too. See p. 165.

• **Best View of Town Lake:** Lots of downtown properties have nice water views, but the **Hyatt Regency's** location, 208 Barton Springs Rd. (© **800/233-1234** or 512/477-1234), on the lake's south shore, gives it the edge. You get a panoramic spread of the city with the capitol as a backdrop. See p. 160.

• **Best Place to Tee Off:** Austin isn't a major destination for duffers, but you'd never know it if you stay at **Barton Creek Resort,** 8212 Barton Club Dr. (© **800/336-6158** or 512/329-4000), featuring courses designed by a pantheon of golf greats—two by Tom Fazio, one by Ben Crenshaw, and one by Arnold Palmer—plus a golf school run by Austinite Chuck Cook. See p. 171.

• **Greenest Hotel:** Several hotels in Austin take eco-consciousness beyond the old "we won't wash your towels" option, but no one takes it nearly as far as **Habitat Suites,** 500 E. Highland Mall Blvd. (© **800/535-4663** or 512/467-6000). Almost everything here is eco-friendly. See p. 167.

• **Best for Forgetting Your Troubles:** Stress? That's a dirty word at the **Lake Austin Spa Resort,** 1705 S. Quinlan Park Rd. (© **800/ 847-5637,** or 512/372-7300). After a few days at this lovely, ultra-relaxing spot, you'll be ready to face the world again, even if you don't especially want to. See p. 171.

3 Best Austin Dining Bets

• **Best New Arrival on the Austin Dining Scene:** Don't think of **Uchi,** 801 S. Lamar (© **512/**

916-4808), as just a great place for sushi and Japanese cuisine. It's a great restaurant, period, with

Netting the Best of the Austin Web

Austin is such a plugged-in city that it's tough to select just a few web-sites. However, some do stand out for their depth and breadth:

www.austin360.com: Movie times, traffic reports, restaurant picks, homes, jobs, cars . . . this site, sponsored in part by the *Austin-American Statesman,* the city's daily newspaper, is a one-stop clicking center for a variety of essentials. It's easy to navigate, too.

www.austinchronicle.com: The online version of Austin's excellent alternative tabloid, the *Austin Chronicle,* has everything you would expect: muckraking stories; hard-hitting book, movie, and restaurant reviews; personal ads; and above all, attitude. And it looks a lot better online than it does on paper.

www.ci.austin.tx.us: Talk about big government. **Austin City Connection** is proof positive that practically everything in Austin falls under the aegis of its municipal system, from air quality to bus schedules and parks and recreation. A surprising number of museums (including the one devoted to O. Henry) are covered on this site, too.

www.utexas.edu: After the city government, the University of Texas might have the largest network of influence in town. In addition to providing info about the many on-campus museums, entertainment venues, and sports teams, this website links to an array of visitor-oriented sites, including the *Austin Chronicle* Restaurant Guide, the City of Austin Hike and Bike Trails, and the Austin Ice Bats hockey team. Wouldn't want the students—or their visiting parents—to get hungry or bored, right?

creative cooking that transcends its humble roots. The setting, in a beautifully revamped 1930s house, is transcendent too. See p. 183.

- **Best Place to Pretend You're in Italy:** It's not only the menu—great cappuccino, delicious thin-crust pizzas, focaccia sandwiches, and the like—that makes **Cipollina,** 1213 West Lynn (© **512/477-5211**), feel European. This deli also has a cosmopolitan atmosphere that makes you want to settle in with a copy of Umberto Eco's latest book. See p. 188.

- **Best Vegetarian Cuisine:** The **West Lynn Cafe,** 1110 W. Lynn (© **512/482-0950**), has a huge meatless selection prepared in the most innovative ways. Vegetarians of all stripes leave here completely sated. See p. 187.

- **Best Place to Spot Celebrities:** You can expect to see the likes of Quentin Tarantino, Emilio Estevez, and Richard Linklater lounging in one of the back booths or hugging a bar stool up front at **Güero's,** 1412 S. Congress (© **512/447-7688**), still the preferred hipster hangout after several years of SoCo being chic. See p. 184.

- **Most Quintessentially Austin:** Its laid-back Texas menu, huge outdoor patio, and "unplugged" music series all make **Shady Grove,** 1624 Barton Springs Rd. (© **512/474-9991**), the Platonic ideal of The Austin Restaurant. See p. 182.

- **Best Brunch:** It's a tie between the Sunday buffet at **Green Pastures,** 811 W. Live Oak Rd. (✆ **512/444-4747**), where Austinites have been imbibing milk punch, liberally dosed with bourbon, rum, brandy, ice cream, and nutmeg, seemingly forever, and the one at **Fonda San Miguel,** 2330 W. North Loop (✆ **512/459-4121**), where the spread runs deliciously toward Mexico. See p. 183 and p. 187.
- **Best Melding of Old and New Worlds:** The **Driskill Grill,** 604 Brazos St. (✆ **512/391-7162**), has the grace and tone that befits the historic hotel it serves, but there's nothing dated about the New American cuisine that dazzles this era's gastronomically demanding guests. See p. 176.
- **Best if You're Game for Game:** It's a bit of a drive and more than a bit of a wallet bite, but if you want to see how tasty venison or bison can be, you can't beat **Hudson's on the Bend,** 3509 Hwy.

620 N. (✆ **512/266-1369**). See p. 192.
- **Best View:** The easy winner is **The Oasis,** 6550 Comanche Trail, near Lake Travis (✆ **512/266-2442**), whose multiple decks afford stunning views of Lake Travis and the Texas Hill Country. See p. 193.
- **Sweetest Contribution to the Dining Scene:** Austin's home-grown brand of ice cream, **Amy's,** is wonderfully rich and creamy, and watching the colorfully clad servers juggling the scoops is always a kick. Amy's has nine Austin locations, including one on the west side of downtown, 1012 W. Sixth St. at Lamar Boulevard (✆ **512/480-0673**), one in SoCo, 1301 S. Congress Ave. (✆ **512/440-7488**), and one at the Arboretum, 10000 Research Blvd. (✆ **512/345-1006**). If you don't get a chance to try it in town, hit the airport Amy's as you leave town. See p. 184.

10

Planning Your Trip to Austin

Planning a trip not only is half the fun of getting there but also helps ensure your enjoyment when you arrive. See chapter 2 for additional information about planning your trip. The "Money" section discusses ATM networks and traveler's check agencies; "Insurance" talks about trip cancellation, medical, and lost luggage insurance; and "Planning Your Trip Online" describes Internet resources.

1 Visitor Information

Austin is one of the country's most wired cities, and I'm not talking caffeine. If you're not e-oriented, call the **Austin Visitor Center,** 209 E. Sixth St., Austin, TX 78701 (© **866/GO-AUSTIN**), to receive a general information packet in the mail; otherwise, log on to www.austintexas.org. Austin City Connection, the city's municipal site, www.ci.austin.tx.us, is a good source for learning about several aspects of the city, not just the airport, roads, police, and the like; you'd be surprised how many attractions fall under the aegis of the Department of Parks and Recreation. The site also provides several useful links, for example to the University of Texas. To read the entertainment listings and reviews in *The Austin-American Statesman,* the city's mainstream newspaper, log on to www.austin360.com. You'll find the *Austin Chronicle,* the city's alternative newspaper, at www.auschron.com.

See this same section in chapter 2 for suggestions on getting information about other parts of Texas.

2 When to Go

Although Austin's supply of hotel rooms has increased, it's still important to book ahead of time. Summer season is typically busy, but legislative sessions (the first half of odd-numbered years) and University of Texas events (graduation, say, or home-team games) can also fill up the town's lodgings quickly.

CLIMATE

May showers follow April flowers in the Austin/Texas Hill Country area; by the time the late spring rains set in, the bluebonnets and most of the other wildflowers have already peaked. Mother Nature thoughtfully arranges mild, generally dry weather in which to enjoy her glorious floral arrangements in early spring—an ideal and deservedly popular time to visit. Summers can be steamy—the past several summers have seen atypically long stretches of triple-digit temperatures—but Austin offers plenty of great places to cool off, among them the Highland Lakes and Barton Springs. Fall foliage in this leafy area is another treat, and it's hard to beat a Texas evening by a cozy fireplace—admittedly more for show than for warmth in Austin, which generally enjoys mild winters.

Austin's Average Daytime Temperature (°F & °C) & Monthly Rainfall (Inches)

	Jan	Feb	Mar	Apr	May	June	July	Aug	Sept	Oct	Nov	Dec
Avg. Temp. (°F)	52	55	61	68	75	82	84	84	80	71	60	53
Avg. Temp. (°C)	11	13	16	20	24	28	29	29	26	21	15	12
Rainfall (in.)	1.7	2.1	1.5	2.5	3.1	2.8	1.7	2.4	3.7	2.8	1.8	1.5

AUSTIN CALENDAR OF EVENTS

Many of Austin's festivals capitalize on its large community of local musicians and/or on the great outdoors. The major annual events are listed here. See also chapter 16 for information on the various free concerts and other cultural events held every summer. Additional local events may also be found by logging on to www.austintexas. org, www.austin360.com, and www. auschron.com, detailed in this chapter's first section.

January

Red Eye Regatta, Austin Yacht Club, Lake Travis. The bracing lake air at this keelboat race should help cure what ails you from the night before. ℭ **512/266-1336;** www. austinyachtclub.org. New Year's Day.

February

Carnival Brasileiro, Palmer Events Center. Conga lines, elaborate costumes, samba bands, and confetti are all part of this sizzling Carnavale-style event, started in 1975 by homesick Brazilian students at the University of Texas. ℭ **512/ 452-6832;** www.sambaparty.com. First or second Saturday of February.

March

Kite Festival, Zilker Park. Colorful handmade kites fill the sky during this popular annual contest, one of the oldest of its kind in the country. ℭ **512/647-7488;** www.zilkerkite-festival.com. First Sunday in March.

South by Southwest (S×SW) Music and Media Conference & Festival. The Austin Music Awards kick off this huge conference, which organizes hundreds of concerts at more than two dozen city venues. Aspiring music-industry and high-tech professionals sign up months in advance. ℭ **512/ 467-7979;** www.sxsw.com. Usually around third week in March (during University of Texas's spring break).

Jerry Jeff Walker's Birthday Weekend, various locations. Each year, singer/songwriter Walker performs at such venues as the Broken Spoke and the Paramount Theatre; proceeds of related events—perhaps a silent auction or golf tournament—benefit a foundation to establish a music school for at-risk youth. It's a good cause—and the man knows how to throw a party. ℭ **512/ 477-0036;** www.jerryjeff.com. Late March, early April.

Statesman Capitol 10,000. Texas's largest 10K race winds its way from the state capitol through West Austin, ending up at Town Lake. ℭ **512/445-3598;** www.statesman. com/cap10k. Late March, early April.

Star of Texas Fair and Rodeo, Travis County Exposition Center. This 2-week Wild West extravaganza features rodeos, cattle auctions, a youth fair, a parade down Congress Avenue, and lots of live country music. ℭ **512/919-3000;** www.staroftexas. org. Mid- to late March.

April

Austin Fine Arts Festival, Republic Square. The major fundraiser for the Austin Museum of Art, this show features a large juried art show, local musicians, and lots of kids' activities. ℭ **512/458-6073;** www.austinfineartsfestival.org. First weekend in April.

What Things Cost in Austin	U.S.$	U.K. £
Taxi from the airport to downtown	20.00–24.00	11.00–13.00
Bus ride between any two downtown points	Free	Free
Local telephone call	0.50	0.30
Double at the Four Seasons (very expensive)	260.00–380.00	140.00–200.00
Double at the Holiday Inn Austin Town Lake (moderate)	139.00–159.00	75.00–85.00
Double at the Austin Motel (inexpensive)	80.00–122.00	40.00–65.00
Lunch for one at the Roaring Fork (expensive)	15.00	8.00
Lunch for one at Las Manitas (inexpensive)	7.00	4.00
Dinner for one, without drinks, at Jeffrey's (very expensive)	70.00	40.00
Dinner for one, without drinks, at Vivo (moderate)	15.00	8.00
Dinner for one, without drinks, at The Iron Works (inexpensive)	8.50	5.00
Pint of beer at brewpub	5.00	2.60
Coca-Cola	1.50	0.80
Cup of espresso	2.50	1.40
Admission to the Bob Bullock Texas State History Museum	5.50	3.00
Roll of ASA 100 Kodacolor film, 36 exposures	7.50	3.00
Movie ticket	8.00	4.20
Austin Symphony ticket	19.00–37.00	10.00–20.00

Saveur Texas Hill Country Wine and Food Festival (most events at the Four Seasons Hotel). Book a month in advance for the cooking demonstrations, beer, wine, and food tasting, and celebrity chef dinners. For the food fair, just turn up with an appetite. ✆ **512/542-WINE;** www.texaswineandfood.org. First weekend after Easter.

Old Settlers Music Festival, Salt Lick BBQ Pavilion. More than two dozen bluegrass bands descend on nearby Driftwood to take part in this Americana roots music fest, which also includes songwriter workshops, arts and crafts booths, and children's entertainment. ✆ **512/346-0999,** ext. 3; www.oldsettlersmusicfest.org. Mid- to late April.

May

O. Henry Museum Pun-Off, O. Henry Museum. One of the "puniest" events around, this annual battle of the wits is for a wordy cause—the upkeep of the O. Henry Museum. ✆ **512/472-1903;** www.punpunpun.com. Mid-May.

Old Pecan Street Spring Arts and Crafts Festival, Sixth Street. Eat and shop your way along Austin's restored Victorian main street while bands play in the background. ✆ **512/441-9015;** www.roadstarproductions.com. First weekend in May.

Cinco de Mayo Music Festival, Fiesta Gardens and other locations. Norteño, Tejano, and other rousing music, as well as food, arts and crafts, and competitions—for example, a jalapeño eating contest—are all part of this 4-day family-friendly event to celebrate Hispanic culture. © 512/867-1999; www.austin-cincodemayo.com. Around May 5.

June

Juneteenth, various venues, mostly in East Austin. The celebration of African-American emancipation, which became a Texas state holiday in 1980, generally includes a parade, gospel singing, and many children's events. The best source of information is the George Washington Carver Museum and Cultural Center. © 512/472-4809; www.ci.austin.tx.us/carver. June 19.

July

Austin Symphony Orchestra, Auditorium Shores. Cannons, fireworks, and of course a rousing rendition of the "1812 Overture" contribute to the fun at this noisy freedom celebration. © 888/4-MAESTRO or 512/476-6064; www.austinsymphony.org. July 4.

August

***Austin Chronicle* Hot Sauce Festival,** Waterloo Park. The largest hot-sauce contest in the world features more than 300 salsa entries, judged by celebrity chefs and food editors. The bands that play this super party are *mucho caliente,* too. © 512/454-5766; www.austinchronicle.com. Last Sunday in August.

September

Diez y Seis, Plaza Saltillo and other sites. Mariachis and folk dancers, conjunto and Tejano music, as well as fajitas, piñatas, and clowns, help celebrate Mexico's independence from Spain. The highlight is the crowning of the Fiestas Patrias Queen. © 512/974-2264 for Plaza Saltillo events; 512/476-7502 for other events. Four days usually starting around September 16.

Fall Jazz Festival, Zilker Hillside Theater. Zilker Park swings with 2 days of free concerts by top local jazz acts. © 512/442-2263. Second weekend of September.

Austin City Limits Music Festival, Zilker Park. Yet more evidence of Austin's devotion to live music, this 2-day music extravaganza kicked off in 2002 and has grown exponentially every year since. Expect a super lineup of musical talent. © 866/GO-AUSTIN; www.acl festival.com. Late September.

October

Austin Film Festival, Paramount Theatre and other venues. If you like the idea of sitting in the dark and watching 80 films in 8 days—everything from restored classics to new indie releases—or are an aspiring screenwriter or filmmaker, this one's for you. © 800/310-FEST or 512/478-4795; www.austinfilmfestival.com. Eight days in mid-October.

Texas Book Festival, State Capitol. One of the largest literary events in the Southwest, this 2-day fundraiser for Texas public libraries draws literati from all over the U.S., though Texas authors rule the roost. © 512/477-4055; www.texasbook festival.org. Late October.

Halloween, Sixth Street. Nearly 100,000 costumed revelers take over 7 blocks of historic Sixth Street. © 866/GO-AUSTIN. October 31.

November

Chuy's Christmas Parade, Congress Avenue. With giant balloons, marching bands, floats, and gifts for needy kids, what better way is there to ring in the season? © 888/439-2489 or www.chuysparade.com. Saturday after Thanksgiving.

December

Zilker Park Tree Lighting. The lighting of a magnificent 165-foot tree is followed by the Trail of Lights, a mile-long display of life-size holiday scenes. This being Austin, a 5K run is also involved. © **512/974-6700;** www.cityofaustin.org/tol. First Sunday of the month (tree lighting); second Sunday through December 23 (Trail of Lights).

Armadillo Christmas Bazaar, Austin Music Hall. Revel in Tex-Mex food, live music, and a full bar at this high-quality art, craft, and gift show. © **512/447-1605;** www.armadillo bazaar.com. Begins approximately 2 weeks before Christmas.

3 Tips for Travelers with Special Needs

FOR TRAVELERS WITH DISABILITIES

See this section in chapter 2 for details on **Mobility International USA** and on the **Access-Able Travel Source** website. There's an active **Americans with Disabilities (ADA)** office in Austin. Its website, www.ci.austin.tx.us/ada, has lots of useful links. You can also call © **512/974-3256** or 974-**1897** if you have questions about whether any of the hotels or other facilities you're curious about is in compliance with the Act.

FOR GAY & LESBIAN TRAVELERS

A university town and probably the most left-leaning enclave in Texas, Austin is generally gay-, lesbian-, bisexual-, and transgender-friendly. To find out about clubs in addition to those listed in chapter 16 (Oilcan Harry's and Rainbow Cattle Co.), log on to http://austin.about.com/cs/gaynightlife. **Book Woman,** 918 W. 12th St., at Lamar (© **512/472-2785;** www.ebookwoman.com), and **Lobo,** 3204-A Guadalupe St. (© **512/454-5406**), are the best places to find gay and lesbian books and magazines, as well as the Austin Gay and Lesbian Yellow Pages and the statewide *Texas Triangle* weekly newspaper. **TapeLenders Video,** 1114 W. Fifth St. (© **512/472-0844;** www.tapelenders.com), in addition to films, carries a huge selection of gay-oriented gifts. For more general information, see chapter 2, p. 18, for more information about

The **International Gay and Lesbian Travel Association (IGLTA).**

Established in 1987, the annual **Austin Gay and Lesbian International Film Festival,** held late August/early September, debuts work by gay, lesbian, bisexual, and transgender filmmakers across the world. The festival recently established its headquarters at the refurbished Regal Arbor Cinema at Great Hills. Log on to www.agliff.org for additional information or call © **512/302-9889.**

FOR SENIORS

The **Old Bakery and Emporium,** 1006 Congress Ave. (© **512/477-5961;** www.ci.austin.tx.us/parks/bakery1.htm), not only sells crafts and baked goods made by senior citizens, but also serves as a volunteer center for people over 50. It's a good place to find out about any senior activities in town. Another excellent resource is the monthly *Senior Advocate* newspaper, 3710 Cedar St., Box 17, Austin, TX 78705 (© **512/451-7433;** www.senioradvocatenews.com), which you can pick up, gratis, at HEB supermarkets, libraries, hospitals, and many other places. You can also call or write in advance for a subscription ($15 per year). The online version has links to many other resources for seniors.

See chapter 2 for information about the **AARP** (formerly the American Association of Retired Persons) and **Elderhostel.** Elderhostel classes in

Austin focus on everything from the tech boom to the natural beauties of the region, and occasionally hold seminars at the Lady Bird Johnson Wildflower Center.

FOR FAMILIES

Find information on things to see and do with kids in Austin—everything from family-friendly museums to community story times—in the online newsletter Parenthood.com by logging on to http://austin.parenthood.com. Not quite as up-to-date, but a good general resource, *Kidding Around Austin,* by Drew D. Johnson and Cynthia Brantley Johnson (John Muir Publications), is available at most local bookstores for $7.95. See also this section of chapter 2 for information about the **Family Travel Times** newsletter, *Travel with Your Children,* p. 19. For Internet sites recommended for travelers with children, see p. 19.

FOR STUDENTS

There are endless resources for students in this university town. Just stop by the **University of Texas Student Union Building** (see the map in chapter 14) to check out the scene. Austin's oldest institution of higher learning, **Huston-Tillotson College,** 600 Chicon St. (© **512/505-3000,** www.htc.edu), in East Austin, is especially helpful for getting African-American students oriented. The **Hostelling International–Austin** (see chapter 12) is another great repository of information for students.

One of the best sources for information and bookings of discounted airfares, rail fares, and lodgings is **STA Travel** (© **800/781-4040;** www.sta-travel.com), with offices throughout the United States. In Austin, there's an STA Travel retail office at 2116 Guadalupe St. (© **512/472-2900**). For more information on student travel, see chapter 2, p. 19.

---

4 Getting There

FOR GENERAL INFORMATION

See the section "Planning Your Trip Online," in chapter 2, for a detailed explanation of the various ways you can make your trip more enjoyable by finding airfare, hotels, and rental cars online. For the technologically savvy, "The 21st-Century Traveler" section offers useful advice on Internet and cellphone use when far from home.

BY PLANE

THE MAJOR AIRLINES   America West (© 800/235-9292; www.americawest.com), **American** (© 800/433-7300; www.aa.com), **Continental** (© 800/525-0280; www.flycontinental.com), **Delta** (© 800/221-1212; www.delta.com), **Frontier** (© 800/432-1359; www.frontierairlines.com), **Northwest** (© 800/225-2525; www.nwa.com), **Southwest** (© 800/435-9792; www.southwest.com), and

United (© 800/241-6522; www.united.com) all fly into Austin. There are currently nonstop flights from the following U.S. cities (outside of Texas): Atlanta; Baltimore; Chicago; Cincinnati; Cleveland; Denver; Detroit; Las Vegas; Los Angeles; Memphis; Minneapolis/St. Paul; Nashville; New York; Orlando; Phoenix; Raleigh-Durham; St. Louis; San Diego; San Francisco; San Jose; Tampa; and Washington, D.C.

FINDING THE BEST AIRFARE

All the airlines run seasonal specials that can lower fares considerably. If your dates of travel don't coincide with these promotions, however, the least expensive way to travel is to purchase tickets 21 days in advance, stay over Saturday night, and travel during the week. (See chapter 2 for more advice on fighting, and winning, the airfare wars.)

BY CAR

I-35 is the north–south approach to Austin; it intersects with **Hwy. 290,** a major east–west thoroughfare, and **Hwy. 183,** which also runs roughly north–south through town. If you're staying on the west side of Austin, hook up with **Loop 1,** almost always called Mo-Pac by locals.

Stay on I-35 north and you'll get to Dallas/Fort Worth in about 4 hours. Hwy. 290 leads east to Houston, approximately 2½ hours away, and west via a scenic Hill Country route to I-10, the main east–west thoroughfare. I-10 can also be picked up by heading south to San Antonio, some 80 miles away on I-35.

In case you're planning a state capital tour, it's 896 miles from Austin to Atlanta; 1,911 miles to Boston; 921 miles to Springfield, Illinois; 671 miles to Santa Fe; 963 miles to Phoenix; and 1,745 miles to Sacramento.

BY TRAIN

To get to points east or west of Austin on the Sunset Limited by **Amtrak,** 250 N. Lamar Blvd. (© **800/872-7245** or 512/476-5684; www.amtrak.com), you'll have to pass through San Antonio (see "By Train," in chapter 2). Trains depart from Austin to San Antonio nightly. The Texas Eagle runs from Austin to Chicago daily.

BY BUS

You'll also be going through San Antonio if you're traveling east or west to Austin via **Greyhound,** 916 E. Koenig Lane (© **800/231-2222** or 512/458-4463; www.greyhound.com); see chapter 2 for details. There are approximately seven buses between the two cities each day, with one-way fares running around $14.

5 Recommended Reading

The foibles of the Texas "lege"—along with those of Congress and the rest of Washington—are hilariously pilloried by Molly Ivins, Austin's resident scourge, in two collections of her syndicated newspaper columns: *Molly Ivins Can't Say That, Can She?* and *Nothin' But Good Times Ahead.* George W. Bush was a more recent target in Ivins's *Shrub: The Short but Happy Political Life of George W. Bush.* Austinite Lou Dubose and Jan Reid give more insight into the inner workings of Texas (and national) politics with *The Hammer: Tom DeLay, God, Money, and the Rise of the Republican Congress.* Serious history buffs might want to dip into Robert Caro's excellent multivolume biography of Lyndon B. Johnson, the consummate Texas politician, who had a profound effect on the Austin area.

For background into the city's unique music scene, try Jan Reid's *The Improbable Rise of Redneck Rock.* Barry Shank's *Dissonant Identities: The Rock-'n'Roll Scene in Austin, Texas,* does a more scholarly take on the same topic.

William Sydney Porter, better known as O. Henry, published a satirical newspaper in Austin in the late 19th century. Among the many short tales he wrote about the area—collected in *O. Henry's Texas Stories*—are four inspired by his stint as a draftsman in the General Land Office. Set largely in Austin, Billy Lee Brammer's *The Gay Place* is a fictional portrait of a political figure loosely based on LBJ.

The city's most famous resident scribe, the late James Michener, placed his historical epic *Texas* in the frame of a governor's task force operating out of Austin. The city is also the locus of several of Austin resident Mary Willis Walker's mysteries, including *Zero at the Bone* and *All the Dead Lie Down;* it is also the setting for *The Boyfriend*

School, a humorous novel by San Antonian Sarah Bird. Shelby Hearon, who attended the University of Texas, lovingly and humorously contrasts old and new Austin in *Ella in Bloom.* Her novel *Armadillo in the Grass* is also set in Austin.

It's only logical that the king of cyberpunk writers, Bruce Sterling, should live in Austin; he gets megabytes of fan mail each week for such books as *Islands in the Net, The Difference Engine* (with William Gibson), and *Holy Fire.* His nonfiction work, *The Hacker Crackdown,* details a failed antihacker raid in Austin. His latest, *Tomorrow Now: Envisioning the Next 50 Years,* moves him from cyberpunk to prognostication. For a unique take on Austin, check out *The Great Psychedelic Armadillo Picnic: A "Walk" in Austin,* a travel guide and music history of the city where the writer grew up, by Kinky Friedman—a mystery writer, musician (his most famous band was Kinky Friedman and the Texas Jewboys), aspiring politician (he's running for governor of Texas in 2006) and all-around curmudgeon.

11

Getting to Know Austin

With thousands of acres of parks, preserves, and lakes set aside for public enjoyment, Austin is unusually nature-friendly. It's easy to miss that, however, when you're busy negotiating the city's freeways. As soon as possible, get out of your car and smell the flowers: Just a few blocks south of downtown's office towers lie the green shores of Town Lake, where you'll begin to see the real Austin.

Central Austin is, very roughly, bounded by Town Lake to the south, Hwy. 290 to the north, I-35 to the east, and Mo-Pac (Loop 1) to the west. South Austin tends to be blue-collar

residential, although its northern sections have been gentrified, and hotels have been cropping up like mushrooms since an airport opened in this area in the late 1990s. Although the tech boom–driven development in north Austin slowed down a bit with the early millennial recession, residential growth in this part of town did not. Some of the city's most opulent mansions perch on the lakeshores and hills of west Austin. East Austin, once flat farmland and long the home for Hispanic and African-American communities, is increasingly being eyed by middle-class buyers in search of real estate bargains.

1 Orientation

ARRIVING

BY PLANE The $581 million **Austin-Bergstrom International Airport** (© 512/530-ABIA), opened in 1999 on the site of the former Bergstrom Air Force Base, just off Hwy. 71 (Ben White Blvd.) and only 8 miles southwest of the capitol, is the town's transportation darling.

Not only did the airy glass-and-granite structure replace an outdated facility with an expanded new one, but it also was designed to capture the spirit of Austin from the moment you step off the plane. The passenger terminal, named after the late Texas Congresswoman Barbara Jordan, boasts a stage area for performances by Austin musicians (see sidebar), hosts local businesses like BookPeople and an Austin City Limits gift shop, and features Austin food concessions such as Amy's Ice Cream, Matt's El Rancho, and The Salt Lick—with prices comparable to those in town. This was also the first airport in the country to go wireless, and, as of the summer of 2004, the first to get a live TV broadcast stream. Since Austin is such a hotbed of high tech, the airport's even got a geek's dream of a website, www.ci.austin.tx.us/austinairport, featuring a virtual reality tour of the terminal, flight schedules, links to airlines and car-rental companies, descriptions of concessions, the latest bulletins on noise-pollution control, and more. For those wanting nonvirtual data, there's an information booth on the lower level of the terminal open daily from 7am to 11pm.

Taxis from the major companies in town usually form a line outside the terminal, though occasionally you won't find any waiting. To ensure off-hour pickup in advance, phone **American Yellow Checker Cab** (© 512/452-9999)

> **Fun Fact** **Leaving on a Jet Plane? Tuneful Takeoffs**
>
> Who could have predicted that musicians would scramble for an airport gig? But with music lovers flying into town from all over, the Austin airport's stage has turned out to be a great place for local bands to get national exposure—who knows what record company exec might be fortuitously stranded? The music mirrors the eclecticism of Austin's scene, including R & B, honky-tonk, jazz, conjunto, world, pop, Western retro—you name it. Don't expect to be entertained every time you fly in or depart, though. Performances generally take place in the central concourse (near Gate 10) from 3:30 to 5:30pm. Check the airport's website to find out what bands might fit in with your flight plans.

---

before you leave home. The ride between the airport and downtown generally costs around $20. The flag-drop charge is $1.75, and it's $1.75 for each mile after that.

If you're not in a huge rush to get to your hotel, **SuperShuttle** (© **800-BLUE VAN** or 512/258-3826; www.supershuttle.com) is a less expensive alternative to cabs, offering comfortable minivan service to hotels and residences. Prices range from $10 one-way ($18 round-trip) for trips to a downtown hotel to $12 ($20 round-trip) for trips to a central hotel and $15 ($26) for trips to a hotel in the northwestern part of town. The drawback is that you often must share your ride with several others, who may be dropped off first—at various points around town nowhere near your destination. You don't have to book in advance for pickups at the airport, but you do need to phone 24 hours ahead of time to arrange for a pickup if you're leaving town.

For details about public transportation from the airport, phone **Capital Metro Transit** (© **512/474-1200** or TTY 512/385-5872), or click on the "Parking-Transportation" section of the airport website. See also the "By Bus" section, below, and "By Public Transportation" in "Getting Around," later in this chapter, for additional information.

Most of the major car-rental companies—Advantage, Alamo, Avis, Budget, Dollar, Hertz, National, and Thrifty—have outlets at the airport, and you can now stroll across the road from the terminal building to pick up (and drop off) your car; see "Car Rentals" in the "Getting Around" section, later in this chapter, for details. The trip from the airport to downtown by car or taxi can take anywhere from 25 minutes to an hour, depending on the time of day and the current state of highway repairs; during rush hour, there are often backups all along Hwy. 71. Be sure to slot in extra time when you need to catch a flight.

BY TRAIN The **Amtrak** station (© **512/476-5684**) is at Lamar and West First Street, in the southwest part of downtown. There are generally a few cabs waiting to meet the trains, but if you don't see one, you'll find a list of phone numbers of taxi companies posted near the pay phones. Some of the downtown hotels offer courtesy pickup from the train station. A cab ride shouldn't run more than $4 or $5 (there's a $3 minimum charge).

BY BUS The **bus terminal** is near Highland Mall, about 10 minutes north of downtown and just south of the I-35 motel zone. There are some hotels within walking distance, and many others a short cab ride away; a few taxis usually wait outside the station. If you want to go downtown, you can catch either bus no. 7

(Duval) or bus no. 15 (Red River) from the bus stop across the street. A cab ride downtown—about 10 minutes away on the freeway—should cost from $8 to $10.

VISITOR INFORMATION

The **Austin Visitor Center,** 209 E. Sixth St. (© **866/GO-AUSTIN;** www. austintexas.org), down the street from the Convention Center in the southeast section of downtown, is open daily 9am to 6pm (closed Thanksgiving, Christmas, and Easter Sunday). You can pick up tourist information pamphlets downtown at the **Old Bakery and Emporium,** 1006 Congress Ave. (© **512/477-5961**), open Monday to Friday 9am to 4pm, and the first 2 Saturdays in December 10am to 3pm. In the **Capitol Visitors Center,** 112 E. 11th St. (© **512/305-8400;** www.texascapitolvisitorscenter.com), a Texas Department of Transportation travel center, dispenses information on the entire state; it's open Monday through Saturday 9am to 5pm, Sunday noon to 5pm, closed major holidays. Other sources of local information include the **Capital City African-American Chamber of Commerce,** 5407 N. I-35, Suite 304 (© **512/459-1181**), and the **Hispanic Chamber of Commerce of Austin/Travis County,** 3000 S. I-35 (© **512/476-7502,** www.Hispanicaustin.com).

For entertainment listings, pick up the free alternative newspaper the *Austin Chronicle,* distributed to stores, hotels, and restaurants around town every Thursday. It's got a close rival in *XLent,* the free weekend entertainment guide put out by the *Austin-American Statesman,* which also turns up on Thursday at most of the same places that carry the *Chronicle.*

Inside Line (© **512/416-5700**) can clue you in about Austin information from the essential to the esoteric—everything from weather forecasts and restaurant reviews to financial news and bat facts. Dial extension 4636 for instructions on how to use the system.

CITY LAYOUT

In 1839, Austin was laid out in a grid on the northern shore of the Colorado River, bounded by Shoal Creek to the west and Waller Creek to the east. The section of the river abutting the original settlement is now known as Town Lake, and the city has spread far beyond its original borders in all directions. The land to the east is flat Texas prairie; the rolling Hill Country begins on the west side of town.

MAIN ARTERIES & STREETS   I-35, forming the border between central and east Austin (and straddling the Balcones Fault Line), is the main north–south thoroughfare; Loop 1, usually called Mo-Pac (it follows the course of the Missouri-Pacific railroad, although some people like to say it got its name because it's "mo' packed"), is the west-side equivalent. Hwy. 290, running east and west, merges with I-35 where it comes in on the north side of town, briefly reestablishing its separate identity on the south side of town before merging with

---

Tips **The Quickest Route**

If you're heading downtown from the airport, you're best off taking Riverside Drive—one of the first exits on Hwy. 71—and then Congress Avenue north rather than staying on Hwy. 71 and using I-35. If you want to get to the northwest, take Hwy. 183 all the way, again avoiding often-congested I-35.

Austin at a Glance

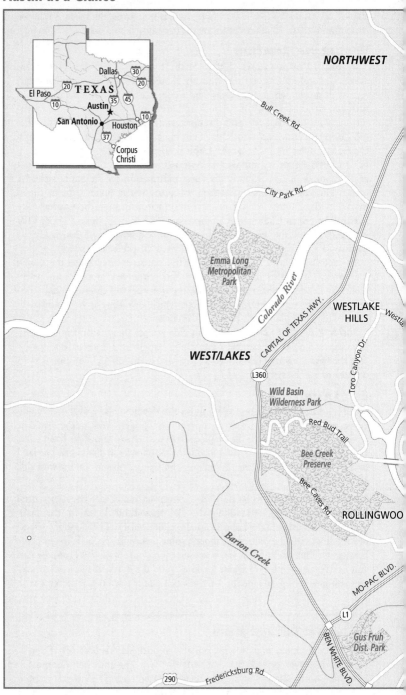

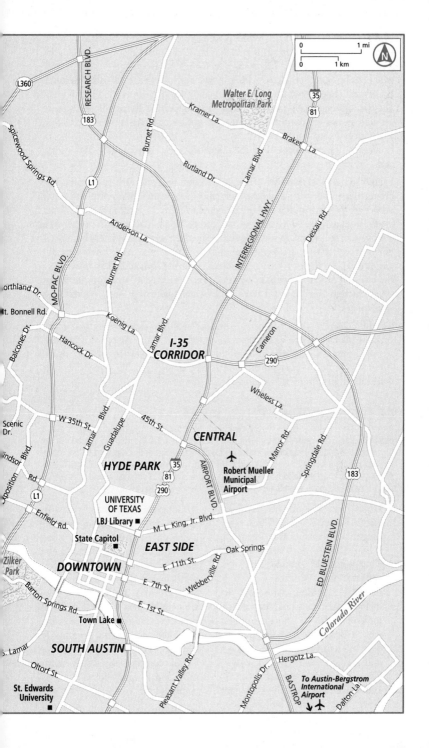

Hwy. 71 (which is called Ben White Blvd. between 183 and Lamar Blvd.). Hwy. 290 and Hwy. 71 split up again in Oak Hill, on the west side of town. Not confused enough yet? Hwy. 2222 changes its name from Koenig to Northland and, west of Loop 360, to Bullcreek, while, in the north, Hwy. 183 is called Research Boulevard. (Looking at a map should make all this clear as mud.) Important north–south city streets include Lamar, Guadalupe, and Burnet. If you want to get across town north of the river, use Cesar Chavez (once known as First St.), 15th Street (which turns into Enfield west of Lamar), Martin Luther King Jr. Boulevard (the equivalent of 19th St., and often just called MLK), 38th Street, and 45th Street.

FINDING AN ADDRESS   Congress Avenue was the earliest dividing line between east and west, while the Colorado River marked the north and south border of the city. Addresses were designed to move in increments of 100 per block, so that 1500 N. Guadalupe, say, would be 15 blocks north of the river. This system still works reasonably well in the older sections of town, but breaks down where the neat street grid does (look at a street map to see where the right angles end). All the east–west streets were originally named after trees native to the city (for example, Sixth St. was once Pecan St.); many that run north and south, such as San Jacinto, Lavaca, and Guadalupe, retain their original Texas river monikers.

STREET MAPS   The surprisingly detailed maps available for no cost at the Austin Convention and Visitors Bureau, as well as at many car-rental companies at the airport, should help you find any place you're likely to want to locate. Alternatively, I'd recommend the **Gousha** city maps, available at most convenience stores, drugstores, newsstands, and bookstores.

THE NEIGHBORHOODS IN BRIEF

Although Austin, designed to be the capital of the independent Republic of Texas, has a planned, grand city center similar to that of Washington, D.C., the city has spread out far beyond those original boundaries. These days, with a few exceptions, detailed below, locals tend to speak in terms of landmarks (the University of Texas) or geographical areas (East Austin) rather than neighborhoods. The following designations are just rough approximations. Like pretty much everything else in Austin, they're open to discussion.

Downtown   The original city, laid out by Edwin Waller in 1839, runs roughly north–south from the river (Cesar Chavez) to Martin Luther King Boulevard (around 20th St.) and east–west between I-35 and Lamar. This prime sightseeing (it includes the Capitol and several historic districts) and hotel area has seen a resurgence in the past 3 decades, with music clubs, restaurants, shops, and galleries established on and around **Sixth Street** and businesses returning to the beautiful old office buildings on and around **Congress Avenue.** The **Warehouse District,** centered on Third and Fourth streets just west of Congress, came into its own in the late 1990s as a more sophisticated entertainment arena than Sixth Street, and new restaurants and watering holes continue to pop up there, but the latest place to see and be seen is the **Red River District,** on (where else?) Red River, between 6th and 10th streets. Although downtown technically ends at Town Lake, most people would consider the lake's south shore and its hike-and-bike trail to be part of this area.

South Austin   For a long time, not a lot was happening south of Barton Springs Road/East Riverside

Drive. Then in the 1990s, **South Congress,** the once-derelict stretch of Congress Avenue that extends (presently) to Oltorf Street, started becoming gentrified—or at least "trendified." It's now lined with cutting-edge art galleries, antiques boutiques, and retro clothing shops, and has, naturally, been nicknamed "SoCo." **Fairview Park** and **Travis Heights,** adjoining neighborhoods between Congress and I-35 from Town Lake to Oltorf Street, were Austin's first settlements south of the river. At the end of the 19th century, these bluffs became desirable as Austin residents realized they were not as likely to be flooded as the lower-ground areas north of the Colorado. Many mansions in what had become a working-class district have lately been reclaimed by the newly rich kids and boomers who are helping to develop South Congress Avenue. And since the 1999 debut of the airport at Ben White Boulevard, just east of Hwy. 183, hotels and services have started cropping up in an area once dominated by faceless residential developments. It's not until you head farther south and west, toward the Lady Bird Johnson Wildflower Center and the Austin Zoo, that south Austin begins to reassert its rural roots.

Central Austin Consisting roughly of the area north of Barton Springs Road/East Riverside Drive up until 45th Street, bordered by I-35 on the east and Mo-Pac on the west, Central Austin includes **Downtown** (see above) as well as several neighborhoods on its fringes. Just north of the capitol, the original 40 acres allotted for the **University of Texas** have expanded to 357, and Guadalupe Street, along the west side of the campus, is now a popular shopping strip known as the Drag. North of the university between 38th and 45th streets, **Hyde Park** got its start in 1891 as one of Austin's first planned suburbs; renovation of its Victorian and early craftsman houses began in the 1970s, and now there's a real neighborhood feel to this pretty, tree-lined area. One of the neighborhoods that developed as downtown Austin expanded beyond Shoal Creek, **Clarksville,** just east of Mo-Pac, was founded by a former slave in 1871 as a utopian community for freed blacks; it's now an artists' enclave, but definitely not for the starving types. Directly north, from about West 15th to West 24th streets, is **Enfield,** which boasts a number of beautiful homes and upscale restaurants. Larger mansions line the northern shores of Lake Austin, in the section known as **Tarrytown;** it's just south of Mount Bonnell and a beautiful stretch of land where, some historians say, Stephen F. Austin himself planned to retire.

East Side The section east of I-35 between Cesar Chavez and Manor Road is home to many of Austin's Hispanic and African-American residents. Mexican restaurants and markets dot the area, which also hosts a number of African-American heritage sites, including Huston-Tillotson College, Metropolitan African Methodist Episcopal Church, and the George Washington Carver Museum; the French Legation Museum and state cemetery are also in this area. The quiet, tree-lined **French Place,** just east of I-35 between Manor and 38½ streets, is beginning to vie with South Congress for yuppie/artist ingress. The warehouses near MLK are increasingly being occupied by art galleries and turned into residential spaces for those likely to frequent them. Naturally, new restaurants are arriving to feed all the hungry artistes.

I-35 Corridor Austin has grown around the heavily traveled connector area between Central and the Northwest, where the airport used to be located. Lined with chain hotels and restaurants, it's as charmless as it sounds, but it's convenient to both downtown and the north. Talk of turning the unused airport acreage into mixed-use space for condos, retail, and affordable housing is still just that: talk.

West/Lakes It's been said that the higher you rise in Austin's financial ranks, the farther west you move. As you head along Lake Austin and Lake Travis into Hill Country, you'll encounter such affluent residential

developments as **Westlake Hills** (where Michael Dell lives) and **Lakeway,** as well as the more charming, low-key **Bee Cave.** But you don't have to live here to play here: This is also where those who live in Central Austin come to splash around and kick back on nice weekends.

Northwest This high-growth area, Austin's version of the suburbs, consists largely of upscale business, shopping, and residential complexes; The Arboretum is this area's retail heart. The northwest has been described as extending north from Hwy. 2222 to Dallas, but Parmer Lane is probably the real northern boundary. Farther north are such bedroom communities as Round Rock and Cedar Park.

2 Getting Around

BY PUBLIC TRANSPORTATION

Austin's public transportation system, **Capital Metropolitan Transportation Authority** (www.capmetro.org), is excellent, including more than 50 bus lines and featuring low to nonexistent fares (see the "Tourist-Friendly Transport" box, below). The regular adult one-way fare on Metro routes is 50¢; express service from various Park & Ride lots costs $1. You'll need exact change or fare tickets (see below) to board the bus; free transfers are good for 3 hours on weekdays, 4 hours on weekends. Call (✆ **800/474-1201** or 512/474-1200 (TTY 512/385-5872) from local pay phones for point-to-point routing information. You can also pick up a schedule booklet at any HEB, Fiesta, or Albertsons grocery store; at stores and hotels throughout the downtown area; or at the Capital Metro Transit Store, 106 E. Eighth St., just off Congress Avenue.

DISCOUNT FARES 'Dillos aren't the only free ride in Austin. With the exception of Special Transit Service and Public Event shuttles, passengers 65 and older or those with mobility impairments may ride all fixed bus routes free upon presenting a Capital Metro ID card to the driver. Cards are available for $3 from the Capital Metro Information Center (open Mon–Fri 7:30am–5:30pm). University of Texas students also ride free upon presentation of a UT ID card; all other students who get a Capital Metro ID card pay half-price. If you buy a Ticket Book, available at the same place as schedule booklets (see above), you can get 20 50¢ tickets for only $5—a 50% savings. Children 5 years or younger can ride free when accompanied by adults. And on ozone alert days, in order to discourage people from getting into their cars, Capital Metro lets you board all its buses gratis.

Tips **Tourist-Friendly Transport**

The seven free 'Dillo routes—Blue, Gold, Orange, Red, Silver, and the latest, Moonlight and Starlight—make it simple as well as economical for visitors to troll the tourist sights. Routes include the most popular—and most parking challenged—sections of downtown, as well as the University of Texas, the South Congress shopping district, and historic East Austin. The Orange and Silver 'Dillos are particularly geared toward sightseeing, while the Starlight and Moonlight rides, available Thursday through Saturday from 6pm to 3am, shuttle you around downtown's hottest nightspot and restaurant areas.

In addtion, Capital Metro also offers a special weekend Tour the Town route, which loops around the University of Texas, goes through downtown, and then heads for the Restaurant Row along Barton Springs Roads. Regular bus pricing applies.

BY CAR

Between its long-standing traffic oddities and the more recent—but rampant—construction, driving in Austin is, to put it mildly, a challenge. Don't fall into a driver's daze anywhere in town; you need to be as vigilant on the city streets as you are on highways. The former are rife with signs that suddenly insist LEFT LANE MUST TURN LEFT or RIGHT LANE MUST TURN RIGHT—generally positioned so they're noticeable only when it's too late to switch. A number of major downtown streets are one-way; many don't have street signs or have signs so covered with foliage they're impossible to read. Driving is particularly confusing in the university area, where streets like "32½" suddenly turn up. Multiply the difficulties at night, when you need X-ray vision to read the ill-lit street indicators.

The highways are no more pleasant. I-35—nicknamed "the NAFTA highway" because of the big rigs speeding up it from Mexico—is mined with tricky on-and-off ramps and, around downtown, a confusing complex of upper and lower levels; it's easy to miss your exit or find yourself exiting when you don't want to. The rapidly developing area to the northwest, where Hwy. 183 connects I-35 with Mo-Pac and the Capital of Texas Hwy., requires particular vigilance, as the connections occur very rapidly. There are regular lane mergers and sudden, precipitous turnoffs.

Nervous? Good. Better a bit edgy than lost or injured. Consult maps in advance and, when driving around the university or downtown, try to gauge the number of blocks before turns so you won't have to be completely dependent on street signs. You can also check the Texas Department of Transportation's (TxDOT) website, www.dot.state.tx.us, for the latest information on road conditions, including highway diversions, construction, and closures.

CAR RENTALS   If you're planning to travel at a popular time, it's a good idea to book as far in advance as you can, both to secure the quoted rates and to ensure that you get a car. Some of the companies I phoned in early October to inquire about the winter holiday season were already filled up for Christmas.

Advantage (© 800/777-5500; www.arac.com), **Alamo** (© 800/327-9633; www.alamo.com), **Avis** (© 800/831-2847; www.avis.com), **Budget** (© 800/527-0700; www.budgetrentacar.com), **Dollar** (© 800/800-4000;

www.dollarcar.com), **Hertz** (© 800/654-3131; www.hertz.com), **National** (© 800/227-7368; www.nationalcar.com), and **Thrifty** (© 800/367-2277; www.thrifty.com) all have representatives at the airport.

Lower prices are usually available for those who are flexible about dates of travel or who are members of frequent-flyer or frequent-hotel-stay programs or of organizations such as AAA or AARP. Car-rental companies are eager to get your business, so they're as likely as not to ask whether you belong to any group that will snag you a discount, but if the clerk doesn't inquire, it can't hurt to mention every travel-related program you're a member of—you'd be surprised at the bargains you might turn up. See chapter 3 for more tips about car rental.

PARKING   Unless you have congressional plates, you're likely to find the selection of parking spots downtown extremely limited during the week (construction isn't making the situation any better); as a result, lots of downtown restaurants offer valet parking (with hourly rates ranging $4–$6). There are a number of lots around the area, costing anywhere from $5 to $7 per hour, but the most convenient ones tend to fill up quickly. If you're lucky enough to find a metered spot, it'll run you 75¢ per hour, with a 2-hour limit, so bring change. Although there's virtually no street parking available near the capitol before 5pm during the week, there is a free visitor garage on 15th and San Jacinto (2-hr. time limit). *Tip:* If you're willing to forgo your own wheels for a bit, park in one of the free Park & Ride lots serviced by the Red, Gold, and Silver 'Dillo lines and take advantage of Austin's excellent free public transport (see "By Public Transportation," above).

In the university area, trying to find a spot near the shopping strip known as the Drag can be just that. However, cruise the side streets and you're eventually bound to find a pay lot that's not filled. The two most convenient on-campus parking garages are located near San Jacinto and East 26th streets and off 25th Street between San Antonio and Nueces. There's also a (free!) parking lot near the LBJ Library, but it's far from the central campus. Log on to **www.utexas.edu/ business/parking/resources** for additional places to drop off your car.

DRIVING RULES   Unless indicated, right turns are permitted on red after coming to a full stop. Seat belts and child-restraint seats are mandatory in Texas.

BY TAXI

Among the major cab companies in Austin are **Austin Cab** (© **512/478-2222**), **Roy's Taxi** (© **512/482-0000**), and **American Yellow Checker Cab** (© **512/ 452-9999**). Rides cost from $1.50 to $1.75 at the flag drop, plus $1.75 for each additional mile.

BY BIKE

Although an increase in traffic has rendered Austin's streets less bicycle-friendly than they once were, the city is still pretty good for two-wheelers. Many city streets have separate bicycle lanes, and lots of scenic areas have been set aside for hiking and biking. See the "Staying Active" section of chapter 14 for details.

⌐Fun Fact Wired? No, Wireless!

Austin has 11 wi-fi hot spots for every 100,000 residents, including 50 free ones—more places per capita to access the Internet, plug- and cash-free, than anywhere else in the country. Why? In part because of the Austin Wireless Project, an organization that coordinates the city's free networks.

ON FOOT

Downtown Austin is pedestrian-friendly, with traffic lights at nearly every intersection. The city is also dotted with lovely, tree-shaded spots for everything from strolling to in-line skating. The city's jaywalking laws are not usually enforced, except occasionally downtown.

FAST FACTS: Austin

American Express The branch at 10710 Research Blvd., Suite 328 (© 512/ 452-8166; www.americanexpress.com), is open Monday to Friday 9am to 5:30pm, Saturday 10am to 2pm.

Area Code The telephone area code in Austin is **512**.

Business Hours Banks and offices are generally open Monday to Friday 8 or 9am to 5pm. Some banks offer drive-through service on Saturday 9am to noon or 1pm. Specialty shops and malls tend to open around 9 or 10am Monday to Saturday; the former close at about 5 or 6pm, the latter at around 9 or 10pm. You can also shop at most malls and boutiques on Sunday from noon to 6pm. Bars and clubs tend to stay open until midnight during the week, 2am on weekends.

Car Rentals See "By Car," above.

Climate See "When to Go," in chapter 10.

Dentist Call the Dental Referral Service at © 800/917-6453.

Doctor The Medical Exchange (© 512/458-1121) and Seton Hospital (© 512/324-4450) both have physician referral services.

Driving Rules See "By Car," above.

Drugstores You'll find many Walgreens, Eckerd, and Randalls drugstores around the city; most HEB grocery stores also have pharmacies. Several Walgreens are open 24 hours. Have your zip code ready and call © 800/925-4733 to find the Walgreens branch nearest you.

Embassies/Consulates See "Fast Facts: For the International Traveler," in Appendix B.

Emergencies Call © 911 if you need the police, the fire department, or an ambulance.

Hospitals Brackenridge, 601 E. 15th St. (© 512/324-7000), St. David's, 919 E. 32nd St. at I-35 (© 512/397-4240), and Seton Medical Center, 1201 W. 38th St. (© 512/324-1000), have good and convenient emergency-care facilities.

Hot Lines Suicide Hot Line (© 512/472-4357); Poison Center (© 800/ 764-7661); Domestic Violence Crisis Hot Line (© 512/928-9070); Sexual Assault Crisis Hot Line (© 512/440-7273).

Information See "Visitor Information," earlier in this chapter.

Internet Most links of Schlotzsky's Deli, a chain that originated in Austin, offer free Internet access via computer stations; you're limited to 20 minutes but that should give you enough time to check your e-mail. Several Schlotzsky's also offer free wireless network access. Of the 12 Schlotzsky's in Austin, the two locations most convenient to the majority of visitors are those at 106 E. Sixth St., downtown (© 512/473-2867), and at 1915

Guadalupe (☎ **512/457-1129**), near the University of Texas. See the Austin Yellow Pages for the other locations or log on to www.cooldeli.com. The Austin Visitor Center (see the "Visitor Information" section, earlier in this chapter) offers free Internet access, and all of Austin's Starbucks and city parks are wi-fi friendly.

Laundry/Dry Cleaners Reliable dry cleaners in the downtown area include Ace Cleaners, 1117 S. Congress Ave. (☎ **512/444-2332**); Washburn's Town & Country, 1423 S. Congress Ave. (☎ **512/442-1467**); and Sweet Cleaner's, 613 Congress (☎ **512/477-4083**). The only laundromat anywhere near downtown is Kwik Wash, 1000 W. Lynn (☎ **512/473-3725**). It's not within walking distance of any city hotels, but it's a short drive away from some of them.

Libraries Downtown's Faulk Central Library, 800 Guadalupe St. (☎ **512/974-7400**), and adjoining Austin History Center, 810 Guadalupe St. (☎ **512/974-7480**), are excellent information resources. To find the closest local branch, log on to **www.ci.austin.tx.us/library**.

Liquor Laws See this section in chapter 3. Briefly, you have to be 21 to drink in Texas, it's illegal to have an open container in your car, and liquor cannot be served before noon on Sunday except at brunches (if it's billed as complimentary).

Lost Property You can check with the police to find out whether something you've lost has been turned in by calling ☎ **512/974-5000**. If you leave something on a city bus, call ☎ **512/389-7454**; on a train heading for Austin or at the Amtrak station, ☎ **512/476-5684**; on a Greyhound bus or at the station, ☎ **512/458-4463**; at the airport, ☎ **512/530-2242** (Mon–Fri 7am–5pm) or ☎ **512/530-COPS** (weekends and after-hours).

Luggage Storage/Lockers At the Greyhound station, there's only one size locker; the price is $2 per 6 hours. You can check your luggage at the Amtrak station for $1.50 per bag per 24 hours. No lockers are available at Austin's airport.

Maps See "City Layout," earlier in this chapter.

Newspapers/Magazines The daily *Austin American-Statesman* (www.austin360.com) is the only large-circulation, mainstream newspaper in town. The *Austin Chronicle* (www.auschron.com), a free alternative weekly, focuses on the arts, entertainment, and politics. Monday through Friday, the University of Texas publishes the surprisingly sophisticated *Daily Texan* (www.dailytexanonline.com) newspaper, covering everything from on-campus news to international events.

Police The nonemergency number for the Austin Police Department is ☎ **512/974-5000**.

Post Office The city's main post office is located at 8225 Cross Park Dr. (☎ **512/342-1252**); more convenient to tourist sights are the Capitol Station, 111 E. 17th St., in the LBJ Building, and the Downtown Station, 510 Guadalupe St. For information on other locations, phone ☎ **800/275-8777**. You can also find post offices online at www.mapsonus.com/db/USPS.

Radio On the FM dial, turn to KMFA (89.5) for classical music, KUT (90.5) for National Public Radio talk programming and eclectic music, KASE (100.7) for country, KUTZ (98.9) for contemporary rock, and KGSR (107.1) for folk, reggae, rock, blues, and jazz. AM stations include KVET (1300) for sports, and KJCE (1300) for soul and Motown oldies.

Safety Austin has been ranked one of the five safest cities in the United States, but that doesn't mean you can throw common sense to the wind. It's never a good idea to walk down dark streets alone at night, and major tourist areas always attract pickpockets, so keep your purse or wallet in a safe place. Although Sixth Street itself tends to be busy, use caution on the side streets in the area.

Taxes The tax on hotel rooms is 15%. Sales tax, added to restaurant bills as well as to other purchases, is 8.25%.

Taxis See "By Taxi," above.

Television You'll find CBS (KEYE) on Channel 5, ABC (KVUE) on Channel 3, NBC (KXAN) on Channel 4, Fox (KTBC) on Channel 2, and PBS (KLRU) on Channel 9. Austin cable channels include Channel 8, with nonstop local news (interspersed with updates of state and international news), and Channel 15, the city-run Austin Music Network, featuring a variety of sounds but emphasizing Austin and Texas artists.

Time Zone Austin is on Central Standard Time and observes daylight saving time.

Transit Information Call Capital Metro Transit (② **800/474-1201** or 512/474-1200 from local pay phones; TTY 512/385-5872).

Useful Telephone Numbers Get the time and temperature by dialing ② **512/476-7744.**

Weather Check the weather at ② **512/451-2424** or www.news8austin.com/content/weather.

12

Where to Stay in Austin

The room shortage that long plagued Austin has finally abated as motels have cropped up like mushrooms near Bergstrom International Airport, some excellent historic restorations have been completed in the downtown area, and several new hotels designed to serve the expanded convention center have recently opened. Still, finding a room in Austin isn't always easy.

To plan your stay, keep in mind the state legislature and the University of Texas (enrollment more than 50,000). Lawmakers and lobbyists converge on the capital for 140-day sessions at the start of odd-numbered years, so you can expect tight bookings during the first half of both 2005 and 2007. The beginning of fall term, graduation week, and weekends of important University of Texas football games— UT's football stadium seats nearly 80,000—also draw visitors en masse. During the third week of March, record label execs and aspiring artists attending the huge annual S×SW music conference take up all downtown's rooms, and the relatively new Austin City Limits Music Festival has begun to grab up a good share of lodgings in late September. Then there's the local business wild card: You never know what major microchip convention might be in town. All in all, it's always a good idea to book as far in advance as possible, and essential if your trip coincides with any major scheduled events.

Low rates and quick freeway access to both downtown and the northwest help fill the chain motels that line I-35 near the old airport; those along I-35 to the south are convenient to the new airport and downtown. But you'll get a far better feel for what makes Austin special if you stay in the verdant Town Lake area, which includes both the historic downtown area near the capitol and the resurgent South Congress area. The leafy enclaves near the University of Texas, especially the Hyde Park neighborhood, are ideal for those willing to trade some modern perks for homeyness and character. Those with a penchant for playing on the water or putting around should consider holing up near the lakes and golf courses to the west.

Austin has some glitzy high-rises but only a few historic hotels and motels, so if it's character you're after, you might opt for one of the town's bed-and-breakfasts. In addition to those listed, I'd recommend other members of the Austin Area B & B Association. Call ⓒ 866/972-2333 or 512/371-1115 or log on to www.austinareabandb.com for more info. For Austin inns that belong to Historic Accommodations of Texas, check the website at www. hat.org or contact the organization at P.O. Box 139, Fredericksburg, TX 78624 (ⓒ 800/HAT-0368).

The prices listed below are based on full rack rates, the officially established, undiscounted tariffs that you should never have to pay. Most hotels catering to business travelers offer substantially lower prices on weekends, while some bed-and-breakfasts offer reduced rates Sunday through Thursday. If you don't mind changing rooms once, you can get the best of both discount worlds. You'll find lots of Austin room deals on the Internet (see chapter 2), but don't stop there. Be sure to phone and ask about packages—which might include extras like breakfast or champagne—and reduced rates for senior citizens, families, active-duty military personnel . . . whatever you can think of. In fact, it's a good idea to call the toll-free number and the hotel itself, because sometimes the central reservation agent doesn't know about local deals.

Sure, calling is not as impersonal as the Internet, but don't be afraid of being a pain if the deal is worth it.

Speaking of which, please note that rates listed below do not include the city's 15% hotel sales tax.

Incidentally, wherever you bunk in Austin, you're likely to be in high-tech heaven. Even B&B rooms offer high-speed wireless Internet connections these days, and many hotels also offer WebTV, enabling you to retrieve e-mail and cruise the Internet via the tube.

1 Downtown

VERY EXPENSIVE

The Driskill ★★ Opened in 1886, this hotel has a history that reads like the history of the nation. Numerous Texas governors held their inaugural balls at the Driskill and Lyndon Johnson holed up here during the final days of his presidential campaign, anxiously awaiting election results. This is where the Daughters of the Republic of Texas gathered to decide the fate of the Alamo, and Texas lawmen gathered here to set an ambush for Bonnie and Clyde. Talk about historic cachet!

Of course, it's hard to stay gorgeous and up-to-date when you're more than a century old, but a $35 million renovation, celebrated with the new millennium, restored the Driskill's former sheen—and then some. The public areas, dripping with marble and crystal, are dazzling. Although you're near all the prime tourist spots (the hotel is one of them), you've got plenty of reasons to hang around. The **1886 Café** offers great breakfast selections, while the **Driskill Grill** boasts a fine dinner menu (p. 176); in addition there's a cushy piano bar (p. 250), plus a small but well-equipped spa, and—if all goes according to plan—a sound studio that will host a cooking show.

The guest rooms—100 of them in a 1929 addition, the rest in the original structure—feature beautiful reproductions of the original 19th-century furnishings, plus the latest in high-tech connectivity. Some of the king rooms are quite small, though, and so dominated by the large bed that there's little room to move about. (At least sinks and mirrors are outside the tiny bathrooms.) It's a good idea to check room size before settling in.

604 Brazos St. (at E. 6th St.), Austin, TX 78701. © 800/252-9367 or 512/474-5911. Fax 512/474-2214. www.driskillhotel.com. 188 units. $235–$270 double; suites from $350. AE, DC, DISC, MC, V. Valet parking $17. Pets under 20 lb. accepted; $50 fee per pet per stay. **Amenities:** 2 restaurants; bar; health club; spa; concierge; business center; wi-fi; 24-hr. room service; laundry service; dry cleaning. *In room:* A/C, TV with pay movies, dataport, T-1 lines, WebTV, hair dryer, safe.

Four Seasons Austin ★★ *Kids* When someone else is footing the bill, it's hard to beat this hotel. It's got a great location on Town Lake, near all the downtown tourist attractions; large, comfortable rooms; an excellent restaurant, **The Café,** which is also the toniest roost in town for watching bats stream out of the Congress Avenue Bridge; a bar, **The Lobby Lounge,** that won the first annual contest for the best Batini recipe (ask the bartender); and the best health club and spa in the downtown area. And the service . . . well, Queen Elizabeth, Prince Charles, and King Philip of Spain have all bedded down here, but even peons get the royal treatment, with attention paid to guests' tiniest needs—and the needs of the tiniest guests.

Polished sandstone floors, a cowhide sofa, horn lamps, and gallery-quality Western art in the lobby are reminders you're in Texas, but the guest rooms are European country-manse elegant, with light floral patterns, wood, and live plants. The city views are fine, but the ones of the lake are prime.

98 San Jacinto Blvd. (at 1st/Cesar Chavez St.), Austin, TX 78701. ℂ 800/332-3442 or 512/478-4500. Fax 512/478-3117. www.fourseasons.com/austin. 291 units. $260–$380 double; $435–$1525 suite. Lower rates on weekends, bed-and-breakfast and romance packages available. AE, DC, MC, V. Self-parking $12; valet parking $17. Pets no taller than 12–15 inches accepted; advance notice to reservations department required. **Amenities:** Restaurant; bar; outdoor pool; health club; spa; bike rentals; concierge; car-rental desk; secretarial services; 24-hr. room service; same-day laundry service; dry cleaning. *In room:* A/C, TV w/pay movies, dataport, hi-speed Internet access, minibar, hair dryer, iron, safe.

Hyatt Regency Austin on Town Lake ★★

Austin's Hyatt Regency brings the outdoors indoors, with a signature atrium lobby anchored by a Hill Country tableau of a limestone-banked flowing stream, waterfalls, and oak trees. It's impressive, but the genuine article outside is more striking. The hotel sits on Town Lake's south shore, so its watery vistas have stunning city backdrops. Although the Hyatt is just minutes from downtown, outdoor recreation makes this hotel tick. Bat tours and other Town Lake excursions depart from a private dock, where you can also rent paddle boats and canoes. In addition, guests can rent mountain bikes to ride on the hike-and-bike trail outside the door. All rooms are decorated in vibrant Southwest tones and rich woods; those on higher floors facing Town Lake are most coveted.

208 Barton Springs Rd. (at S. Congress), Austin, TX 78704. ℂ 800/233-1234 or 512/477-1234. Fax 512/480-2069. www.hyatt.com. 446 units. $234–$300 double; $345–$650 suite. Weekend specials, corporate and government rates available. AE, DC, DISC, MC, V. Self-parking $9; valet parking $12. **Amenities:** Restaurant; bar; outdoor pool; health club; Jacuzzi; bike rentals; business center; room service; laundry service; dry cleaning; club-level rooms. *In room:* A/C, TV, dataport, wireless Internet access, coffeemaker, hair dryer, iron.

InterContinental Stephen F. Austin ★

Built in 1924 to compete with the Driskill (see above) a block away, the Stephen F. Austin was another favorite power center for state legislators, along with celebrities like Babe Ruth and Frank Sinatra. Closed in 1987 and reopened in 2000 after being gutted and built from the ground up, the hotel is once again welcoming movers and shakers, although now they're most likely to be high-tech and music industry execs.

The public areas are elegant, if not quite as grand as those in the Driskill. The trade-off is the less fussy guest quarters, done in soothing earth tones (caveat: shell out for a deluxe as the standards are quite small). Luxe amenities include down duvets, alarm clock/CD players, in-room safes large enough to fit a laptop—and every type of in-room business perk that you could want, including ergonomic chairs. Two other assets: **Stephen F's Bar and Terrace,** with great views of Congress Avenue and the capitol, and the excellent **Roaring Fork** restaurant (see chapter 13).

701 Congress Ave. (at E. 7th St.), Austin, TX 78701. ℂ 800/327-0200 or 512/457-8800. Fax 512/457-8896. www.intercontinental.com. 189 units. $249–$299 double; $399–$2,000 suite. Weekend, Internet discounts. AE, DC, DISC, MC, V. Valet (only) parking $17. **Amenities:** 2 restaurants; bar; indoor pool; health club; spa; concierge; business center; 24-hr. room service; dry cleaning; club-level rooms. *In room:* A/C, TV w/pay movies, dataport, high-speed Internet access, minibar, hair dryer, iron, safe.

Downtown Austin Accommodations

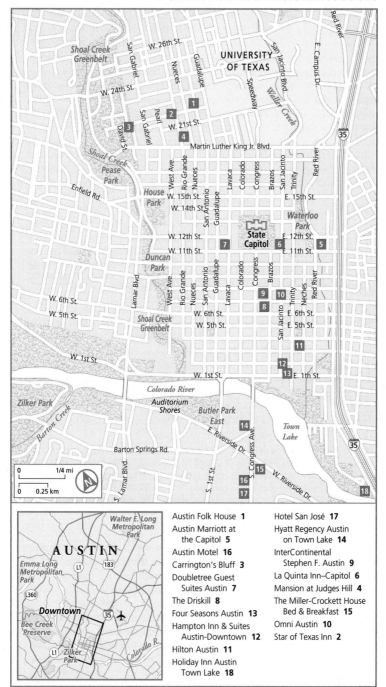

Austin Folk House **1**

Austin Marriott at
    the Capitol **5**

Austin Motel **16**

Carrington's Bluff **3**

Doubletree Guest
    Suites Austin **7**

The Driskill **8**

Four Seasons Austin **13**

Hampton Inn & Suites
    Austin-Downtown **12**

Hilton Austin **11**

Holiday Inn Austin
    Town Lake **18**

Hotel San José **17**

Hyatt Regency Austin
    on Town Lake **14**

InterContinental
    Stephen F. Austin **9**

La Quinta Inn–Capitol **6**

Mansion at Judges Hill **4**

The Miller-Crockett House
    Bed & Breakfast **15**

Omni Austin **10**

Star of Texas Inn **2**

Omni Austin Part of the posh Austin Center office and retail complex, the Omni's spectacular 200-foot rise of sun-struck glass and steel leaves you feeling simultaneously dwarfed and exhilarated. Rooms are far less overwhelming—they're not especially large, and ceilings tend to be low. But they're attractive enough, in a bland contemporary way, and well equipped. If you need to hole up for a while and your company is footing the bill, your best bet is one of the condominium rooms—studio efficiencies with full kitchens, walk-in closets, and jetted tubs. If you're here on vacation, you're not going to be spending that much time indoors, what with the hotel's proximity to all the downtown sights, but the Omni's rooftop pool, sun deck, and Jacuzzi (with terrific city views) is an inducement to lounge around. The hotel's Get Fit program gives you incentive to exercise, offering free fitness kits and healthy snacks; for $25, a treadmill will be brought to your room (inducement to leave or stay? Only you can say . . .). *Note:* The slate stone in the public areas is to be renovated in 2005, so things may be messy for a bit.

700 San Jacinto Blvd. (at E. 8th St.), Austin, TX 78701. (C) **800/THE-OMNI** or 512/476-3700. Fax 512/320-5882. www.omnihotels.com. 375 units. $239–$279 double; $299–$389 suite. AE, DC, DISC, MC, V. Self-parking $12; valet parking $16. Pets up to 50 lb. accepted with $50 nonrefundable deposit (pet menu available). **Amenities:** Restaurant; bar; heated outdoor pool; health club; Jacuzzi; sauna; car-rental desk; business center; secretarial services; wi-fi in public areas; shopping arcade; salon; room service; dry cleaning; club-level rooms. *In room:* A/C, TV w/pay movies, dataport, wi-fi, minibar, hair dryer, iron.

EXPENSIVE

Austin Marriott at the Capitol For those who want to be in the northwest part of downtown, which puts you within walking distance of the University of Texas (if you're energetic), this is a good pick. The hotel itself isn't exciting, just your basic blocky high-rise, but for a business-oriented place it's got a relaxed, comfortable atmosphere, enhanced by a nice indoor/outdoor pool complex. The walls of windows on the hotel's atrium levels give its public areas an open, airy feel, and the rooms—done in a nondescript but light style—also feel unconfined; those on the higher floors have terrific city views, and those on the west side all look out on the state capitol, 4 blocks away.

701 E. 11th St. (at Red River), Austin, TX 78701. (C) **800/228-9290** or 512/478-1111. Fax 512/478-3700. http://marriott.com. 365 units. $199 double; suites from $350. Weekend discounts, holiday rates. AE, DC, DISC, MC, V. Self-parking $10; valet parking $15. Pets under 30 lb. accepted for nonrefundable $50 fee. **Amenities:** Restaurant; bar; indoor pool; outdoor pool; exercise room; Jacuzzi; sauna; concierge; business center; secretarial services; wi-fi in public areas; 24-hr. room service; babysitting; dry cleaning; coin-op laundry. *In room:* A/C, TV w/pay movies, dataport, high-speed Internet access, coffeemaker, hair dryer, iron.

Doubletree Guest Suites Austin ★ *Kids* Lobbyists sock in for winter legislative sessions at this tony all-suites high-rise, a stone's throw from the state capitol. It would be hard to find more comfortable temporary quarters. At 625 square feet, the standard one-bedroom suites are larger than a typical New York apartment, and all are decorated in attractive Western style with Texas details, offering cushy foldout sofas and large mirrored closets, and spacious bathrooms, too. Many rooms have small balconies with capital capitol views, and—that rarity in hotels, and especially in downtown Austin—the windows open. Full-sized appliances with all the requisite cookware allow guests to prepare meals in comfort. And, unlike kitchens in many all-suite hotels, the ones here are separate—you don't have to stare at dirty dishes after you eat. (The housekeepers wash them every day, regardless.)

303 W. 15th St. (at Guadalupe), Austin, TX 78701. (C) **800/222-TREE** or 512/478-7000. Fax 512/478-3562. www.doubletree.com. 189 units. 1-bedroom suite $159–$189; 2-bedroom suite $209–$259. Corporate,

extended-stay, Internet, and other discounts available. Children under 18 stay free. AE, DC, DISC, MC, V. Self-parking $10; valet parking $15. Pets under 25 lb. accepted for $25 per day. **Amenities:** Restaurant; outdoor pool; health club; Jacuzzi; sauna; concierge; business center; secretarial services; wi-fi throughout hotel; room service; same-day dry cleaning/laundry; coin-op laundry. *In room:* A/C, TV w/pay movies, dataport, high-speed Internet access; full-size kitchen, hair dryer, iron.

Hampton Inn & Suites Austin-Downtown ☆ *Value* This convention-oriented hotel, opened in 2003, may be part of a chain but it's definitely a cut above cookie-cutter. Rooms, done in clean-lined Western style with gleaming wood headboards, polished stone floors, and wrought-iron curtain rods, are very attractive. The hot breakfast buffet, included in the room rate, is generous. And how many hotels, even upscale ones, offer room service from P.F. Chang's and Fleming's? Other perks include free local phone calls and no surcharge for using a calling card, as well as a coin-op laundry. The location, a block from the convention center and close to all of downtown's sights, restaurants, and nightlife, is hard to beat.

200 San Jacinto Blvd. (at 2nd St.), Austin, TX 78701. ✆ **800/HAMPTON** or 512/472-1500. Fax 512/472-8900. www.hamptoninn.com. 209 units. $169–$209 double. Corporate, AAA discounts available. Children under 18 stay free; rates include breakfast buffet and happy hour (Mon–Thurs). AE, DC, DISC, MC, V. Valet (only) parking $12. **Amenities:** Heated outdoor pool, fitness room, business center, room service, guest laundry. *In room:* AC, TV, dataport, high-speed Internet access, mini-fridge, coffeemaker, hair dryer, iron.

Hilton Austin Austin's major new convention high-rise has a lot to recommend it, including attractive Euro-chic meets Hill Country–homey rooms; the stylish **Finn & Porter** restaurant, serving outstanding sushi (dinner only); excellent exercise facilities, including a large pool; and a convenient downtown location. But the standard rooms aren't especially spacious, and you have to pay extra to use the fitness center. Plus, as of late 2004, the views tended to be of construction sites. Nor is the service terribly impressive. After straightening out a reservation that had been messed up twice, the desk clerk didn't deign to point the way to the guest elevator. Maybe it was just a bad day for both of us.

500 E. 4th St., Austin, TX 78701. ✆ **800//HILTONS** or 512/482-5000. Fax 512/486-0078. www.hilton.com. 447 units. $189 double. Weekend, online specials. AE, DC, DISC, MC, V. Valet parking $16, self-parking $11. **Amenities:** 2 restaurants; bar; coffee shop; heated outdoor pool; health club; business center; room service; laundry service; dry cleaning. *In room:* A/C, TV w/pay movies, dataport, high-speed Internet access, minibar, coffeemaker, hair dryer, iron.

Hotel San José ☆ Opened in the late 1990s, this revamped 1930s motor court is the epitome of SoCo cool. It's got retro appeal, with small porches and a small pool, and it's right across the street from the famed Continental Club, which means lots of musicians and their handlers stay here. There are nods to local design—red Spanish tile roofs, cowhide throw rugs, and Texas pine beds—but the dominant theme is Zen, with Japanese-style outdoor landscaping and rooms so stripped down they border on the stark, though they do have the Austin high-tech basics of high-speed Internet access plus VCRs and CD players. You'll get more amenities for your money elsewhere, but you won't get a hipper scene. Book a room in the back to avoid the Congress Avenue traffic noise.

1316 S. Congress Ave. (south of Nelly, about ½ mile south of Riverside), Austin, TX 78704. ✆ **800/574-8897** or 512/444-7322. Fax 512/444-7362. www.sanjosehotel.com. 40 units. $80 (for 3 rooms with shared bathroom); $140–$170 double; $190–$250 suite. Corporate and entertainment discounts available; lower rates during the week. AE, DC, MC, V. Free parking. Dogs accepted for $10 per dog per day. **Amenities:** Bar/lounge; coffee shop; outdoor pool; bike rentals; breakfast-only room service; dry cleaning. *In room:* TV/VCR, dataport., high-speed Internet access, CD player.

MODERATE

Holiday Inn Austin Town Lake *(Kids)*   The most upscale Holiday Inn in Austin, this high-rise is also the best situated on the north shore of Town Lake, at the edge of downtown, and just off I-35. Guest rooms, renovated in 2004, are unexpectedly stylish, with a sleek, contemporary decor; it won't cost you much more to get one that looks out on Town Lake. Many of the units have additional sofa sleepers, which can translate into real family savings, especially since kids stay free (and if they're under 12, eat free at the hotel restaurant too). Other amenities include a rooftop pool large enough to swim laps, happy-hour specials, and a big-screen TV in the lounge.

20 N. I-35 (exit 233, Riverside Dr./Town Lake), Austin, TX 78701. ✆ **800/HOLIDAY** or 512/472-8211. Fax 512/472-4636. www.holiday-inn.com./austintownlake. 320 units. $139–$179 double. Weekend and holiday rates, corporate discounts. Children under 18 stay free. AE, DC, DISC, MC, V. Free parking. Pets under 25 lb. accepted; $125 deposit plus $25 fee. **Amenities:** Restaurant; bar; outdoor pool; exercise room; unstaffed business center; secretarial services; wi-fi in some public areas; room service; laundry; coin-op laundry; dry cleaning; executive floors. *In room:* AC, TV w/pay movies, dataport, high-speed wi-fi (some rooms), coffeemaker, hair dryer, iron.

La Quinta Inn–Capitol *(Value)* *(Finds)*   Practically on the grounds of the state capitol, this is a great bargain for both business and leisure travelers. Rooms are more attractive than those in your typical motel: TVs are large, the rich-toned furnishings are far from cheesy, and perks such as free local phone calls (on dataport phones with voice mail), free high-speed Internet access, and free continental breakfasts keep annoying extras off your bill. The sole drawback is the lack of a restaurant on the premises. But there's a bus 'Dillo stop, and an increasing number of area restaurants are staying open on the weekends, so getting in a car is less necessary than it once was.

300 E. 11th St. (at San Jacinto), Austin, TX 78701. ✆ **800/NU-ROOMS** or 512/476-1166. Fax 512/476-6044. www.laquinta.com. 150 units. $92–$119 double; $119–$169 suite. Rates include continental breakfast. Children under 18 stay free with parents. AE, CB, DC, DISC, MC, V. Valet parking $10. Pets accepted (no deposit or extra fee). **Amenities:** Outdoor pool; secretarial services; laundry service; dry cleaning. *In room:* A/C, TV w/pay movies, dataport, high-speed Internet access, coffeemaker, hair dryer, iron.

The Miller-Crockett House Bed & Breakfast *(★)* *(Finds)*   Sure, it's got all the B&B accouterments, including gracious veranda-wrapped quarters dating back to 1888, 1½-acre grounds spread with ancient live oaks, the requisite generous gourmet breakfasts, and, in several rooms, lovely antiques. But don't expect ducks and gingham—or even your typical B&B guests. The cast and crew for *The Newton Boys,* including Matthew McConaughey, stayed here, as have members of several bands, including Barenaked Ladies and Blues Traveler, and depending on who's visiting, the music at breakfast could range from Jimi Hendrix to Frank Sinatra. If you want to escape the B&B experience entirely, you can hole up in one of the appealing Southwest-decor bungalows, with separate kitchens. You can't beat the location, near all the Town Lake and SoCo action but far quieter than the lodgings that sit right on Congress Avenue.

112 Academy Dr. (1 block east of Congress Ave.), Austin, TX 78704. ✆ **888/441-1641** or 512/441-1600. Fax 512/474-5910. www.millercrockett.com. 5 units. $139 double; $169 suite; $149 bungalow. Rates include full breakfast. AE, MC, V. Free off-street parking. **Amenities:** Bikes (free). *In room:* A/C, TV/VCR, dataport, kitchen (in bungalows), iron.

INEXPENSIVE

Austin Motel *(★)* *(Value)*   It's not only nostalgia that draws repeat guests to this Austin institution, established in 1938 on what used to be the old San Antonio Hwy. and in the current owner's family since the 1950s. A convenient (but not

It Pays to Stay

If you're planning to settle in for a spell, two downtown accommodations at prime locations will save you major bucks. Rooms at **Extended Stay America Downtown,** 600 Guadalupe (at Sixth), Austin, TX 78701 (✆ **800/EXT-STAY** or 512/457-9994; www.extstay.com), within easy walking distance of both the Warehouse District and the Lamar and Sixth shops, and at **Homestead Studio Suites Austin–Downtown/Town Lake,** 507 S. First St. (at Barton Springs), Austin, TX 78704 (✆ **888/ 782-9473** or 512/476-1818; www.homesteadhotels.com), near the Barton Springs restaurant row and the hike-and-bike trail, will run you from $400 to $500 per week. Full kitchens and coin-op laundries at both bring your costs down even more.

quiet) location on trendy South Congress Avenue and reasonable rates help, too. Other assets are a classic kidney-shaped pool, a great neon sign, free HBO, free coffee in the lobby, and **El Sol y La Luna,** a good Latin restaurant that's popular with Town Lake athletes on weekend mornings. It's also got one of those rarities: real single rooms, so those traveling on their own don't have to pay for a bed they're not sleeping in. All rooms are different and some are more recently renovated than others, so ask to look before settling in.

1220 S. Congress St. (south of Nelly, about ½ mile south of Riverside), Austin, TX 78704. ✆ 512/441-1157. Fax 512/441-1157. www.austinmotel.com. 41 units. $60–$90 single; $80–$122 double; $143–$153 suite. AE, DC, DISC, MC, V. Free parking. Limited number of rooms for pets; one-time $10 fee. **Amenities:** Outdoor pool. *In room:* A/C, TV, fridge (some), coffeemaker, hair dryer, iron, safe.

Hostelling International–Austin (Value) Youth-, nature-, and Internet-oriented Austin goes all out for its hostelers at this winning facility, located on the hike-and-bike trail, with views of Town Lake that many would pay through the nose to get. Amenities not only include the standard laundry room and kitchen, but also a high-speed Internet kiosk (with a meager $1 fee per stay), and in 2004, the grounds became wi-fi (un)wired, too. The building, which once served as a boathouse, is solar paneled, and other eco-friendly features include low-flow shower heads.

2200 S. Lakeshore Blvd. (east of I-35, on the southern shore of Town Lake), Austin, TX 78741. ✆ 800/ 725-2331 or 512/444-2294. Fax 512/444-2309. www.hiaustin.org. 39 beds in 4 dorms. $17 for AYH members, $3 additional for nonmembers, half price for those under 14. AE, MC, V. Free parking. **Amenities:** Kayak rentals; bike rentals; Internet kiosk; wi-fi; co-op laundry; kitchen. *In room:* A/C, no phone.

2 Central

EXPENSIVE

Mansion at Judges Hill (★★) Most hip hotels these days—think the W chain—tend to be cold and angular. So who would have guessed that an opulent mansion built at the turn of the last century near the University of Texas would be one of Austin's hottest places to bunk?

It's easy to see the appeal. Guest quarters in two separate wings, one the original residence and the other (North Wing) artfully created as its complement in 1983, are reassuringly reminiscent of a kinder, gentler era—but also conveniently outfitted with contemporary techno-gizmos. Rooms in the mansion, furnished with genuine antiques and quirkier in size and design, are the most interesting—for a special occasion, shell out for one that opens out onto the wraparound veranda—but all convey a sense of old-world grace without being overly fussy. The garden, with its rows of century-old crepe myrtles, and the opulent fine dining room, serving excellent Continental/New American cuisine, are the stuff memories are made of. Whoever said romance was dead?

1900 Rio Grande (at 19th St.), Austin, TX 78705 (✆ **800/311-1619** or 512/495-1800. www.mansionat judgeshill.com. 48 units. $129–$199 North Wing; $159–$399 Mansion. AE, DC, DISC, MC, V. Free off-street parking. Pets accepted (North Wing only) with $150 refundable deposit. **Amenities:** Restaurant; bar. *In room:* TV, dataport, high-speed Internet access, hair dryer, iron, CD player.

MODERATE

Austin Folk House ★★ (Value) You get the best of both worlds at this appealing B&B where old-time charm mixes with new plumbing. When it was transformed from a tired apartment complex at the beginning of the new millennium, this 1880s house near the University of Texas got a complete interior overhaul, but maintained such integral traditional assets as the comfy front porch. The sunny rooms have cheerfully painted walls and the wiring to accommodate megachannel cable TVs, private phone lines, broadband cable access, and radio/alarms with white noise machines. At the same time, nice antiques and such amenities as fancy bedding and towels, candles, robes, expensive lotions, and soaps make you feel like you're in a small luxury inn. The lavish breakfast buffet served in a dining room decorated with the folk art for which the B&B is named does nothing to dispel that idea. Prices are more than reasonable for all this, while the free off-street parking, near the heart of the Drag, puts this place at a premium all by itself. Local phone calls are also gratis.

506 W. 22nd St. (between San Antonio and Nueces), Austin, TX 78705. ✆ **866/472-6700** or 512/472-6700. www.austinfolkhouse.com. 9 units. $99–$145 double; discounts and packages available. Rates include breakfast. AE, DISC, MC, V. Free off-street parking. Pets accepted. **Amenities:** Bike rentals; wi-fi; video library. *In room:* TV/VCR, dataport, wi-fi, hair dryer, iron.

Carrington's Bluff ★ Plenty of places purport to be rural oases in an urban desert. In the case of this self-proclaimed "country inn in the city," the boast is justified (or, as they say in Texas, "it ain't braggin' if it's true"). Occupying a verdant acre on a rise at the end of a quiet street near the University of Texas, this 1877 house exudes country charm. But that doesn't mean it's lacking citified amenities. The antiques-filled rooms—five in the main house, three in a 1920 cottage across the street—keep business as well as leisure travelers happy. Both houses offer access to full kitchens, including refrigerators stocked with Bluebell ice cream—and porches where you can sit out with a bowl of it.

1900 David St. (at 22nd St.), Austin, TX 78705. ✆ **888/290-6090** or 512/479-0638. www.carringtons bluff.com. 8 units. $89–$149 double. Rates include breakfast. AE, DISC, MC, V. Free off-street parking. *In room:* A/C, TV/VCR, dataport, wi-fi, coffeemaker, hair dryer, iron.

Star of Texas Inn ★ Longtime visitors to Austin might remember this as the Governor's Inn, a converted 1897 neoclassical residence. Bought and refurbished by the young owner of the Austin Folk House (see above), this B&B is a bit more traditional than its sister property, less than a block away, but still has friendly perks for the business traveler as well as upscale amenities. Rooms vary quite a bit in size and layout, but most are reasonably large. The Star of Texas also harbors that hard-to-find gem, a real single bedroom that's small but not claustrophobic. Three rooms open directly onto a very appealing covered porch, and the others have access to it. All offer lovely antiques but don't have any of the fustiness you sometimes find in B&Bs—and B&B owners—that take their furniture way too seriously.

611 W. 22nd St. (at Rio Grande), Austin, TX 78705. (© **866-472-6700** or 512/472-6700. http://staroftexas-inn.com. 9 units. $80 single; $109–$155 double. Ask about discounts. Rates include breakfast. AE, DISC, MC, V. Free off-street parking. **Amenities:** Bike rentals; wi-fi; video library. *In room:* A/C, TV/VCR, dataport, wi-fi, hair dryer, iron.

INEXPENSIVE

The Adams House *Value* Monroe Shipe, the developer of Hyde Park, designed his homes to be both attractive and affordable to the middle class. This B&B, built as a single-story bungalow, expanded into a more grandiose colonial revival in 1931, and, restored in the 1990s by a preservation architect, honors Shipe's egalitarian spirit. Although the house is beautifully furnished, it has a friendly, open feel to it—in part because of its 12-foot ceilings and in part because of the hospitable Sydney Lock, who owns and runs it with her adorable cocker spaniel, Dulce. All the rooms are lovely, but the nicest is the suite with a king-size four-poster bed and a sun porch with a foldout couch. A separate house out back doesn't have as much character, but compensates with a TV/VCR and Jacuzzi.

4300 Ave. G (at 43rd St.), Austin, TX 85751. (© **512/453-7696.** Fax 512/453-2616. www.theadamshouse. com. 5 units. $80–$90 double; $125 suite and bungalow. Monthly rates available. Rates include breakfast. MC, V. Free off-street parking. No children under 12. *In room:* A/C, TV (in 1 room).

3 I-35 Corridor

MODERATE

Doubletree Hotel Austin *✦* Leisure travelers should take advantage of the plummeting weekend rates at this tony business-oriented hotel. Once you step inside, you'll feel as though you're in a private luxury property rather than a chain lodging just off the freeway. The dominant style is Spanish colonial. The reception area has polished Mexican-tile floors and carved-wood ceiling beams, and, in keeping with the hacienda theme, rooms are arranged around a lushly landscaped courtyard, dotted with umbrella-shaded tables. Guest quarters, renovated in 2004 in lighter tans and yellows, are airy and spacious. Wherever you stay, you needn't walk very far to reach your car as all the sleeping floors have direct access, via room key, to the parking garage. And although the airport is no longer nearby, the businesses that used to cater to air travelers remain, plus you're within minutes of a variety of restaurants and shops.

6505 N. I-35 (between Hwy. 290 E. and St. Johns Ave.), Austin, TX 78752. (© **800/222-TREE** or 512/454-3737. Fax 512/454-6915. www.austin.doubletree.com. 350 units. $129–$189 double; suites from $159. Corporate, weekend rates; romance package available. AE, DC, DISC, MC, V. Self-parking $7; valet parking $10. Pets under 75 lb. accepted; $50 refundable deposit. **Amenities:** Restaurant; bar; outdoor pool; health club; Jacuzzi; concierge; business center; room service; babysitting; concierge-level rooms. *In room:* A/C, TV, dataport, high-speed Internet access, coffeemaker, hair dryer, iron.

Habitat Suites *✦✦* *Kids* *Finds* Don't be put off by the generic name and nondescript location on the outskirts of Highland Mall: This detail-obsessive "ecotel" offers Kukicha twig tea, at least one vegan and macrobiotic entree at breakfast, a swimming pool that uses a salt generator (the better to avoid chlorine), solar-paneled buildings, and a book of Buddha's teaching in the bedside-table drawer. Lush gardens (tended without chemical fertilizers) and little front

Greater Austin Accommodations & Dining

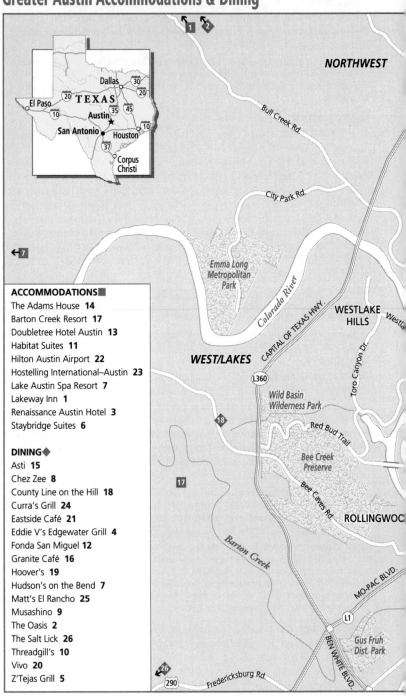

NORTHWEST

Bull Creek Rd.

City Park Rd.

Emma Long Metropolitan Park

Colorado River

WESTLAKE HILLS

Westla

WEST/LAKES

CAPITAL OF TEXAS HWY.

Toro Canyon Dr.

L360

Wild Basin Wilderness Park

Red Bud Trail

Bee Creek Preserve

Bee Caves Rd.

ROLLINGWOO

Barton Creek

MO-PAC BLVD.

L1

Gus Fruh Dist. Park

BEN WHITE BLVD.

290

Fredericksburg Rd.

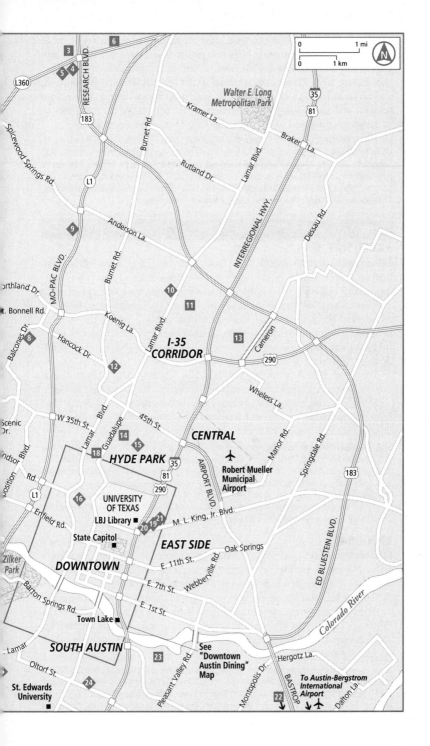

porches or decks add to the comfort. The rooms themselves don't have much character, but they're extremely large (the two-bedroom duplex suites have separate entrances) and offer full kitchens, as well as real fireplaces and windows that actually open. Chemically sensitive? Every room is cleaned with citric oil, and no other harsh chemicals are used. The "quiet hours," in effect from 9pm to 9am, and the marriage of eco-consciousness with function, make this an unusually soothing and pleasant place to stay, whether for work or play.

500 E. Highland Mall Blvd. (take exit 222 off I-35 to Airport Blvd., take a right to Highland Mall Blvd.), Austin, TX 78752. © **800/535-4663** or 512/467-6000. Fax 512/467-6000. www.habitatsuites.com. 96 units. $127 1-bedroom suite; $187 2-bedroom suite. Lower weekend rates; extended-stay rates available. Rates include full breakfast and (Mon–Sat) afternoon wine and snacks. AE, DC, DISC, MC, V. Free parking. **Amenities:** Outdoor pool; Jacuzzi; wi-fi in common areas; coin-op laundry; environmentally sound dry-cleaning. *In room:* A/C, TV, dataport, wi-fi in some suites, kitchen, fridge, coffeemaker, hair dryer, iron.

4 Northwest

EXPENSIVE

Renaissance Austin Hotel *(Value)* Anchoring the upscale Arboretum mall on Austin's northwest side, the tony Renaissance caters to executives visiting nearby high-tech firms. But on weekends, when rates are slashed, even underlings can afford to take advantage of the hotel's many amenities, including an excellent health club, a nightclub, and direct access to the myriad allures of the mall (movie theaters among them). Guests buzz around the eateries, elevator banks, and lounges in the nine-story-high atrium lobby, but the space is sufficiently large to avoid any sense of crowding.

Guest rooms, redone in 2003 with a Hill Country look—warm russets, browns, and greens, dark wood, and leather chairs—are all oversize and offer comfortable sitting areas. Suites include extras such as wet bars and electric shoe buffers. Another perk is the pet-friendly environment: Not only can you check in with Fido free, but the chef whips up some mean dog biscuits.

9721 Arboretum Blvd. (off Loop 360, near Research Blvd.), Austin, TX 78759. © **800/HOTELS-1** or 512/343-2626. Fax 512/346-7945. http://marriott.com. 478 units. $229–$239 double; suites from $249. Weekend packages available. AE, DC, DISC, MC, V. Free self-parking; valet parking $10. Pets accepted. **Amenities:** 3 restaurants; bar; nightclub; indoor pool; outdoor pool; health club; Jacuzzi; sauna; concierge; car-rental desk; business center; secretarial services; wi-fi in public areas; 24-hr. room service; babysitting; same-day laundry and dry cleaning; club-level rooms. *In room:* A/C, TV w/pay movies, dataport, high-speed Internet access, fridge (some), coffeemaker, hair dryer, iron.

MODERATE

Staybridge Suites *(Kids)(Value)* Although it's designed with business travelers in mind, this cheery Holiday Inn property is also ideal for families, who can take advantage of the kitchen in every suite, the multiple TVs (with VCR), the complimentary breakfast buffet, the pool in a leafy courtyard, and the free laundry facilities that adjoin the exercise room (the latter is small but has good cardio machines). Both types of travelers appreciate the proximity to the Arboretum and other upscale shopping complexes, as well as the many restaurants in this burgeoning area.

10201 Stonelake Blvd. (between Great Hills Trail and Braker Lane), Austin, TX 78759. © **800/238-8000** or 512/349-0888. Fax 512/349-0809. www.staybridge.com. 121 units. $129 studio suite; $149 1-bedroom suite; $189 2-bedroom suite. Rates include breakfast. Extended-stay and weekend discounts. AE, DC, DISC, MC, V. Free parking. Pets accepted; $15 fee per night. **Amenities:** Outdoor pool; tennis court; health club; business center. *In room:* A/C, TV/VCR w/pay movies, dataport, high-speed Internet access, kitchen, coffeemaker, hair dryer, iron.

5 West/Lakes

VERY EXPENSIVE

Barton Creek Resort ★★★ *Kids*   Austin's only real full-service resort—one that caters to business travelers, couples, singles, and families alike—Barton Creek would stand out even in more resort-rich cities. The facilities are top-notch, including four 18-hole championship golf courses and the Chuck Cook Golf Academy, tennis courts and a tennis clinic, and an excellent health club with an indoor track. Members of the affiliated country club, which shares the recreational facilities, include such local celebrities as über-biker Lance Armstrong, Sandra Bullock, and Michael Dell. You might even see tennis star Andy Roddick playing a few sets with friends.

Other advantages are that with 4,000 gently rolling and wooded acres and relative proximity to Lake Travis, the resort feels rural, but it's close enough to central Austin (about 15 min. away) that you can easily sightsee or party there. Rooms, in two main buildings resembling a European château and a nine-story tower connecting the spa and the conference center, are spacious and high-toned without being stuffy. The custom-made Drexel Heritage furnishings are complemented by such Texas touches as cowhide chairs and work by local artists. Some rooms have balconies, and those in the back offer superb views of the Texas Hill Country.

8212 Barton Club Dr. (1 mile west of the intersection of Loop 360 and R.R. 2244), Austin, TX 78735. ✆ 800/336-6158 or 512/329-4000. Fax 512/329-4597. www.bartoncreek.com. 300 units. $230–$300 double; suites from $450. Spa and golf packages available. AE, DC, MC, V. Free self- or valet parking. **Amenities:** 3 restaurants (1 season); bar; indoor pool; outdoor pool; 4 golf courses; 11 tennis courts; health club; spa; children's center and programs; business center; salon; room service; babysitting; laundry service; dry cleaning. *In room:* A/C, TV, dataport, high-speed Internet access, minibar, hair dryer, iron.

Lake Austin Spa Resort ★★★   If you had to create the quintessential Austin spa, it would be laid-back, be located on a serene body of water, offer lots of outdoor activities, and feature super-healthy food that lives up to the locals' high culinary standards. . . . You'll sign off on every item of that wish list here. The spa takes advantage of its proximity to the Highland Lakes and the Hill Country by offering such activities as combination canoe/hiking trips and excursions to view the wildflowers. The aromatic ingredients for soothing spa treatments like a honey-mango scrub are grown in the resort's garden, also the source for the herbs used at mealtimes. Guest rooms, many in cottages with private gardens, fireplaces, and hot tubs, are casually elegant, with all-natural fabrics and locally crafted furniture.

It would be hard to imagine an interest or activity you couldn't indulge here, from the kick-butt kind like step aerobics and spinning to the gentler yoga, tai chi, and Pilates or gardening and cooking classes. The coup de grâce is the 25,000-foot LakeHouse spa, which opened in April 2004. Will these world-class facilities, replete with hair and nail salon, separate locker and lounge areas for men and women, and the latest in trendy treatments and lectures, turn Lake Austin glitzy? And, after all that destressing, will you care?

1705 S. Quinlan Park Rd. (5 miles south of Hwy. 620), Austin, TX 78732. ✆ 800/847-5637 or 512/372-7300. Fax 512/266-1572. www.lakeaustin.com. 40 units. Packages from $1,280 per person for 3 nights minimum (double occupancy in a signature room) with spa treatments and personal training a la carte to $4,895 per person for 7 nights (single occupancy in a premier room) all-inclusive deal. Rates include all meals, classes, and activities. AE, MC, DISC, V. Free parking. Pets under 30 lb. accepted in Garden Cottage rooms; $250 pet guest fee. Children 14 and up only. **Amenities:** Restaurant; indoor pool; outdoor pool; health club; spa; kayaks; canoes; hydrobikes; room service; laundry service. *In room:* A/C, TV/VCR, dataport, wi-fi, hair dryer, CD player.

(Kids) Family-Friendly Hotels

Barton Creek Resort (p. 171)   In addition to the great recreational activities here (including a basketball court), this resort also has an activity room for ages 6 months to 8 years, open from morning 'til evening. It's $10 per hour to drop your kids off here for a maximum of 4½ hours, additional fees for longer periods.

Doubletree Guest Suites (p. 162), **Habitat Suites** (p. 167), and **Stay-bridge Suites** (p 170)   That "suites" in the name of these properties says it all. These guest quarters all offer spacious not-in-your-face quarters, plus the convenience (and economy) of kitchen facilities, so you don't have to eat out all the time.

Four Seasons Austin (p. 159)   Tell the reservations clerk that you're traveling with kids, and you'll be automatically enrolled in the free amenities program which offers age-appropriate snacks—cookies and milk for children under 10, popcorn and soda for those older—along with various toys and games which will be waiting for you when you arrive. And you don't have to travel with all your gear because the hotel will provide such items as a car seat, stroller, playpen, bedrails, disposable pacifiers, a baby bathtub, shampoo, powder and lotions, bib, bottle warmers, and disposable diapers.

Holiday Inn Austin Town Lake (p. 164)   You're near lots of the outdoor play areas at Town Lake, and kids stay and (under 12) eat free. It's hard to beat that!

Lakeway Inn (below)   There's plenty for kids to do here, and this property offers a Family Playdays Package, which includes a $100 credit toward recreational activities (such as boat rentals and tennis), plus a free meal and dessert for children 12 and under with the purchase of adult entree. Prices vary depending on the time of year.

EXPENSIVE

Lakeway Inn (Value (Kids   Not as glitzy as Barton Creek nor as New Age-y as the Lake Austin Spa, this conference resort in a planned community on Lake Travis is for those seeking traditional recreation at prices that won't require a second mortgage.

There's something for everyone in the family. At the resort's marina, you can rent pontoons, ski boats, sculls, sailboats, water-skis, WaveRunners, fishing gear and guides—just about everything but fish that promise to bite. Lakeway's excellent 32-court tennis complex, designed for indoor or outdoor, day or night games, has a pro shop with trainers and even a racket-shaped swimming pool. Duffers can tee off from 36 holes of golf on the property, get privileges at other courses nearby, or brush up on their game at the Jack Nicklaus–designed Academy of Golf.

The main lodge of this older property was razed and rebuilt at the end of the 1990s, but, oddly, the rooms were reincarnated with a rather dark and staid 1970s look. Still, they're spacious and comfortable, with all the requisite conference attendee business amenities and, in many cases, lake views.

101 Lakeway Dr., Austin, TX 78734. ✆ **800/LAKEWAY** or 512/261-6600. Fax 512/261-7322. www.lakeway inn.com. 239 units. $159–$249 double. Romance, golf, spa, B&B, and family packages available. AE, DC, DISC, MC, V. Free self-parking; valet parking $5. Pets permitted in some rooms. **Amenities:** Restaurant; bar; 2 outdoor pools; health club; spa; watersports rentals; concierge; business center; room service. *In room:* A/C, TV w/pay movies, dataport, high-speed Internet access in most rooms, coffeemaker, hair dryer, iron.

6 South (Airport)

MODERATE

Hilton Austin Airport ✈ Beam me up, Scotty. Its circular shape gives Austin's only full-service airport hotel, formerly the headquarters of Bergstrom Air Force Base, a distinctively spaceship-like look. Although the hotel retains few of the features that made it one of three bunkers where the President of the United States might be spirited in the event of a nuclear attack, the building remains rock-solid—and blissfully soundproof. (If you stay here, ask for a sheet that details the fascinating history of "The Donut," which also served as a strategic air command center during the Vietnam War, the Persian Gulf War, and Desert Storm.) These days, the dome serves as a skylight for a bright and airy lobby. The theme throughout is Texas Hill Country with lots of limestone and wood and plenty of live plants for good measure. Large, comfortable rooms are equipped with all the amenities.

9515 New Airport Dr. (½ mile from the airport, 2 miles east of the intersection of Hwy. 183 and Hwy. 71), Austin, TX 78719. ✆ **800/445-8667** or 512/385-6767. Fax 512/385-6763. www.hilton.com. 263 units. $119–$169 double; suites from $170. Weekend, online, and parking discounts. AE, DC, DISC, MC, V. Self-parking $8; valet parking $12. **Amenities:** Restaurant; lounge; outdoor pool; health club; business center; 24-hr. room service; laundry service; dry cleaning; club-level rooms. *In room:* A/C, TV w/pay movies, dataport, high-speed Internet access, minibar, coffeemaker, hair dryer, iron.

13

Where to Dine in Austin

As you would expect in a town where lawmakers schmooze power brokers, academics can be tough culinary graders, and techies and musicians require high-grade fuel, Austin's eateries don't disappoint. Chic industrial spaces vie for diners' dollars with gracious 100-year-old houses and plant-filled hippie shacks, while inside the food ranges from upscale New American to the stylish but reasonably priced cuisine once dubbed "Nouveau Grub" by *Texas Monthly* magazine to tofu burgers, barbecue, and enchiladas. Many of these dining rooms are Austin originals, but in recent years such high-end chains as Sullivan's, Fleming's, Ruth's Chris, P.F. Chang's, and Roy's have also established a local presence. (Since you're likely to be familiar with those chains, we'll skip reviews of them here.)

The two areas where the greatest number of trendy restaurants are concentrated are downtown's West End/Warehouse district, near Fourth and Colorado streets, and South Congress Avenue, less than a mile away. But there are plenty of other great places to eat in and around downtown, including the row of casual eateries on Barton Springs Road, near Zilker Park, just south of Town Lake. And the downtown dining scene is expanding its perimeters, as the Sixth and Lamar area west of the Warehouse District continues to heat up.

There's an up-and-coming restaurant row east of I-35, along Manor Road (near MLK). It's not as close to most sightseeing as the downtown dining enclaves but you can get there from the University of Texas in about 10 minutes. Many popular downtown eateries have branches in the northwest, near the Arboretum mall. Sprawling with new-growth apartment and business complexes, this area doesn't have a lot of character, but those living and doing business around here keep the top dining rooms hopping.

Fast-food joints tend to be concentrated to the north, along the I-35 corridor. If you're looking for authentic Mexican, the East Side is the place. The Enfield area around Mo-Pac, as well as Lake Austin, near the Tom Miller Dam, and the tiny town of Bee Cave to the far west are also popular dining enclaves, but there's good food to be found in almost every part of town. (To locate restaurants outside of Downtown, see the map on p. 186.) Wherever you eat, think casual. There isn't a restaurant in Austin that requires men to put on a tie and jacket, and many upscale dining rooms are far better turned out than their wealthy tech-industry clientele.

Dining out can be a competitive sport in Austin. Make reservations wherever you can or dine at off-hours. If you turn up at some of the most popular spots at around 7:30pm, you might wait an hour or more. Be aware also that many charming old houses-turned-restaurants have terrible acoustics, so if you're particularly noise sensitive, you might want to give them a pass.

Finally, if you're staying in the downtown or University of Texas area, consider taking a cab (or on the weekend, a free 'Dillo) when you go out to dinner. It's hard to find a metered spot for your car, and you won't pay much more for a taxi than you would for valet parking or an independent lot. And of course the additional bonus of not having to drive around unfamiliar, often confusing streets in the dark after having had a few cocktails is incalculable. (See chapter 5, p. 65, for an explanation of culinary categories.)

1 Restaurants by Cuisine

AMERICAN
Eastside Cafe (East Side, $$, p. 189)
Hoover's (East Side, $, p. 190)
Hut's (Downtown/Capitol, $, p. 181)
Moonshine (Downtown/Capitol, $$, p. 180)
Shady Grove ✸ (Downtown/Capitol, $, p. 182)
Threadgill's (Central and Downtown, $, p. 189)
The Oasis (West/Lakes, $$, p. 193)

ASIAN
Uchi ✸✸ (South Austin, $$$, p. 183)
Zen (South Austin, $, p. 186)

BARBECUE
County Line on the Hill ✸ (West/Lakes, $$, p. 192)
The Iron Works ✸ (Downtown/Capitol, $, p. 182)
The Salt Lick ✸ (South Austin, $$, p. 186)

CAJUN/CREOLE
Gumbo's ✸ (Downtown/Capitol, $$$, p. 178)

CONTINENTAL
Green Pastures ✸ (South Austin, $$$, p. 183)

CUBAN
Habana (South Austin, $$, p. 184)

DELI
Cipollina ✸ (Central, $, p. 188)
Katz's (Downtown/Capitol, $, p. 182)

FRENCH
Aquarelle ✸✸ (Downtown/Capitol, $$$, p. 176)
Chez Nous ✸ (Downtown/Capitol, $$$, p. 178)

INDIAN
Clay Pit ✸ (Downtown/Capitol, $$, p. 180)

ITALIAN
Asti ✸ (Central, $$, p. 188)
Cipollina ✸ (Central, $, p. 188)
Frank & Angie's (Downtown/Capitol, $, p. 181)
La Traviata ✸✸ (Downtown/Capitol, $$$, p. 179)
Vespaio ✸ (South Austin, $$$, p. 183)

JAPANESE
Musashino ✸ (Northwest, $$, p. 191)
Uchi ✸✸ (South Austin, $$$, p. 183)
Zen (South Austin, $, p. 186)

MEXICAN (NORTHERN & TEX-MEX)
Chuy's (Downtown/Capitol and Northwest, $, p. 181)
Güero's ✸✸ (South Austin, $$, p. 184)
Las Manitas ✸ (Downtown/Capitol, $, p. 182)
Manuel's (Downtown/Capitol and Northwest, $$, p. 180)
Matt's El Rancho (South Austin, $$, p. 185)
The Oasis (West/Lakes, $$, p. 193)
Vivo ✸ (East Side, $, p. 190)

NEW AMERICAN

Castle Hill Café ⋆ (Downtown/
  Capitol, $$$, p. 178)
Chez Zee ⋆ (Northwest, $$,
  p. 191)
Driskill Grill ⋆⋆ (Downtown/
  Capitol, $$$$, p. 176)
Hudson's on the Bend ⋆⋆
  (West/Lakes, $$$$, p. 192)
Jeffrey's ⋆⋆ (Central, $$$$, p. 186)
Shoreline Grill ⋆ (Downtown/
  Capitol, $$$, p. 179)
Wink ⋆⋆ (Central, $$$, p. 188)

PIZZA

Frank & Angie's (Downtown/
  Capitol, $, p. 181)

REGIONAL MEXICAN

Curra's Grill ⋆ (Downtown/South
  Austin and Northwest, $$,
  p. 184)
Güero's ⋆⋆ (South Austin, $$,
  p. 184)

Fonda San Miguel ⋆⋆ (Central,
  $$$, p. 187)
Manuel's (Downtown/Capitol and
  Northwest, $$, p. 180)

SEAFOOD

Eddie V's Edgewater Grille ⋆
  (Downtown and Northwest,
  $$$$, p. 190)
Shoreline Grill ⋆ (Downtown/
  Capitol, $$$, p. 179)

SOUTHWEST

Roaring Fork ⋆⋆
  (Downtown/Capitol, $$$, p. 179)
Ranch 616 ⋆⋆ (Downtown/
  Capitol, $$, p. 180)
Z'Tejas Southwestern Grill ⋆
  (Downtown and Northwest,
  $$$, p. 191)

STEAKS

Eddie V's Edgewater Grille ⋆
  (Northwest, $$$$, p. 190)

---

2 Downtown/Capitol

VERY EXPENSIVE

Driskill Grill ⋆⋆ NEW AMERICAN   Don't be misled by the gracious, old-world atmosphere of the Driskill Hotel's fine dining room (dim lighting, etched glass, cushy banquettes): The cuisine that emerges from the kitchen of David Bull—named one of *Food & Wine*'s Best New Chefs in 2003 and winner of Austin dining awards out the wazoo—is absolutely up-to-date. There are nods to Texas in such dishes as the hot smoked Bandera quail appetizer, perked up with cilantro, and a 22-ounce bone-in rib-eye (remember the Driskill's cattle baron roots), but it's all New American cooking at its best, as ingredients that initially seem discordant turn out to be terrifically complementary. Save room for dessert: Mark Chapman, the Driskill's pastry chef, is a culinary superstar in his own right. His chocolate silk tart, seasoned with ancho chiles and shaved ginger, is amazing. You'll also find this to be one of the quietest dining rooms in town.

604 Brazos St., The Driskill. ✆ **512/391-7162**. www.driskillgrill.com. Reservations recommended. Main courses $32–$38 (occasionally higher); prix fixe $65 per person, $90 paired with wine; chef's tasting $125 ($175 with wine). AE, DC, DISC, MC, V. Tues–Sat 5:30–10:30pm.

EXPENSIVE

Aquarelle ⋆⋆ FRENCH   Isn't it romantic? A converted neoclassical house with gilded mirrors, fresh flowers, tiny candle lamps flickering on the tables, strains of "La Vie en Rose" floating in the background—you get the picture. Aquarelle is a traditional and pretty Francophile haven. The food also stays traditionally Gallic, as Jacques Richard, the Loire-born chef, doesn't believe in messing with success. The prix-fixe menu is always a good bet, but such dishes as the warm duck foie gras with red cherry-onion compote or *loup de mer*—Mediterranean sea bass with sautéed squash and eggplant—are worth going a la

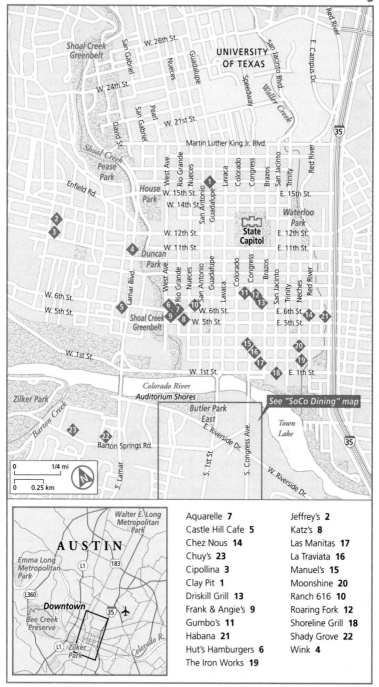

Aquarelle **7**
Castle Hill Cafe **5**
Chez Nous **14**
Chuy's **23**
Cipollina **3**
Clay Pit **1**
Driskill Grill **13**
Frank & Angie's **9**
Gumbo's **11**
Habana **21**
Hut's Hamburgers **6**
The Iron Works **19**

Jeffrey's **2**
Katz's **8**
Las Manitas **17**
La Traviata **16**
Manuel's **15**
Moonshine **20**
Ranch 616 **10**
Roaring Fork **12**
Shoreline Grill **18**
Shady Grove **22**
Wink **4**

carte. Prepare to make an evening of dinner here in classic French fashion as you're likely to spend at least 3 hours slowly savoring the experience. Cap the night off with a chocolate soufflé cake with a molten center, and you're likely to keep savoring the memory days later.

606 Rio Grande. ⓒ 512/479-8117. www.aquarellerestaurant.com. Reservations recommended. Main courses $18–$28; prix fixe $60, $80 with wine. AE, DC, DISC, MC, V. Tues–Thurs 6–9:30pm; Fri–Sat 6–10pm.

Castle Hill Café ⍟ ⟨Value⟩ NEW AMERICAN   Surrounded on three sides by trees, Castle Hill feels tucked away somewhere remote, but it's in the newly trendy Lamar and Sixth district, near those two major thoroughfares. With its dark-wood tables, rich Southwestern tones, and abundant Oaxacan folk art, this favored yuppie haunt balances comfort and creativity. The empanadas filled with curried lamb, raisins, and pecans make a superb appetizer, as do the crab-crayfish cakes with apple-rosemary vinaigrette. Imaginatively conceived and beautifully arranged dinners might include pecan-crusted pork tenderloin in Southern gravy served with grits, or *orecchiete* (ear-shaped) pasta with smoked chicken and asparagus in sage-chile pesto.

Entree prices have crept up in recent years, so at first glance this no longer appears like the dinner bargain it once was. But the low-priced starters are huge. If you really want to keep costs down, go for one of the entree salads such as the chile-lime grilled chicken with guacamole relish and two blue corn empanadas, perhaps preceded by a cup of spicy duck and sausage gumbo. You certainly won't go away hungry.

1101 W. 5th St. ⓒ 512/476-0728. Reservations accepted for parties of 5 or more only. Main courses $17–$23. AE, DISC, MC, V. Mon–Fri 11am–2:30pm; Mon–Sat 6–10pm.

Chez Nous ⍟ ⟨Value⟩ FRENCH   With its lace curtains, fresh flowers in anisette bottles, and Folies Bergère posters, this intimate restaurant feels closer to Paris, France, than to Paris, Texas. Items on the a la carte dinner menu are decently priced, but the real bargain is the menu du jour, which includes a choice of soup, salad, or pâté; one of three designated entrees; and crème caramel, chocolate mousse, or brie for dessert. The main courses might include a *poisson poivre vert* (fresh fish of the day with a green-peppercorn sauce) or a simple but delicious roast chicken.

Chez Nous's friendly French owners opened their bistro in 1982, and it hasn't gotten tired yet. When I asked an Austin foodie friend how it was doing these days, she answered, "Shhh! Quit telling people about my favorite place!"

510 Neches St. ⓒ 512/473-2413. Reservations accepted for parties of 6 or more only. Main courses $18–$27; menu du jour $24. AE, DC, DISC, MC, V. Tues–Fri 11:45am–2pm; Tues–Sun 6–10:30pm.

Gumbo's ⍟ CAJUN/CREOLE   When it comes to culinary geography, Texas is mostly associated with Mexico and the West (all that big meat, don't you know), but here's a nice reminder that the state also borders Louisiana. Come here for blackened catfish with dirty rice and sausage jambalaya, some rich crawfish étoufée, or, at lunch, a crispy oyster po'boy. The menu tends more toward casual Cajun than fancy Creole, but no matter what their level of formality, the dishes never wuss out, spice-wise. The high-ceiling dining room, with a black-and-white tiled floor, lots of gleaming wood, and piped-in jazz, successfully re-creates the atmosphere of a Louisiana cafe; it's also a treat to be able to dine in the renovated Art Deco Brown Building (1938) where LBJ used to have an office.

701 Colorado. ⓒ 512/480-8053. Reservations recommended on weekends. Main courses $13–$28. AE, DC, DISC, MC, V. Mon–Fri 11am–2pm and 5:30–10pm; Sat–Sun 5:30–10pm.

La Traviata ✿✿ ITALIAN   If you're tired of Italian restaurant clichés, you'll love this cozy, Euro-chic trattoria, with textured limestone walls complementing the hardwood floors, sleek bar, and sunny yellow walls. The food is as unfussy and fresh as the room. All the ingredients used by chef/owner Marion Gilchrist are of the highest quality, and the sauces are delicious without being overwhelming. You'll remember why classics like chicken Parmesan or spaghetti Bolognese became popular in the first place, and be dazzled by such creative dishes as scallops with couscous or crispy polenta with Gorgonzola cheese. Don't miss the tiramisu, wonderfully light with toasted hazelnuts and a dusting of espresso. The narrow room bustles with energy, especially on weekend pre-theater evenings, but the staff never seems overwhelmed. Service is both knowledgeable and friendly.

314 Congress Ave. ✆ 512/479-8131. Reservations highly recommended on weekends. Pasta $12–$17; main courses $16–$26. AE, DISC, MC, V. Mon–Thurs 11am–2pm and 5:30–10pm; Fri 11am–2pm and 5:30–10:30pm; Sat 5:30–10:30pm.

Roaring Fork ✿✿ SOUTHWEST   I first fell in love with Robert McGrath's cooking in Scottsdale, Arizona, where I liked to meet friends at the original Roaring Fork for the terrific mulberry margaritas and kettles of savory green chile pork stew, served with big, buttery tortillas. Although McGrath earned his culinary chops in the Grand Canyon State, he's a native Texan, so nothing was lost in translation when he took his unique "American Western Bistro" fare back to the Lone Star state.

Every dish I sampled in the Austin branch was outstanding, from the appetizers of pan roasted scallops served with a black-bean tostada, and the crab cakes with chile slaw to the entrees of beef tenderloin with green beans in bacon sauce and jalapeño-rubbed shrimp. I didn't try the huge pork stew appetizer because I wanted to make room for the other dishes, but I can attest that the mulberry margaritas are as tasty as ever. Your appetite doesn't match your wallet? Come for happy hour and chow down on the Big Ass Bacon Cheeseburger.

701 Congress Ave. (in the InterContinental Stephen F. Austin). ✆ 512/583-0000. www.roaringfork.com. Reservations recommended. Main courses $17–$30. AE, DC, DISC, MC, V. Mon–Thurs 11:30am–2pm and 5–10pm; Fri 11:30am–2pm and 5–11pm; Sat 5–11pm; Sun 5–9pm.

Shoreline Grill ✿ SEAFOOD/NEW AMERICAN   Fish is the prime bait at this tony grill, which looks out over Town Lake and the Congress Avenue Bridge, but late spring through early fall, bats run a close second. During this period, when thousands of Mexican free-tailed bats emerge in unison from under the bridge at dusk, patio tables for viewing the phenomenon are at a premium.

When they're not going batty, diners focus on such starters as semolina-crusted oysters or venison chorizo quesadillas. Drum, a moist, meaty fish from the Gulf, is worth trying however it's prepared, and the roast salmon with tequila lime butter is excellent, too. Nonaquatic dishes include Parmesan-crusted chicken with penne pasta and prime rib with horseradish potatoes. Somehow this restaurant has been operating under the Austin foodie radar in recent years, with newer and trendier spots getting all the attention, but don't be deterred because this is still a fine downtown dining spot.

98 San Jacinto Blvd. ✆ 512/477-3300. www.shorelinegrill.com. Reservations recommended (patio seating can't be guaranteed but requests are taken). Main courses $19–$34. AE, DC, DISC, MC, V. Mon–Fri 11am–10pm; Sat 5–10pm; Sun 5–9pm.

MODERATE

Clay Pit ⚘ (Value) INDIAN   An elegant setting—a historic building with wood floors and exposed limestone walls, lit with soft lamps and votive candles, and sumptuous recipes, including creative curries and other sauces rich with nuts, raisins, and exotic spices—raise this brainchild of a husband-and-wife team and a New Delhi–trained chef to gourmet status. The starter of perfectly cooked coriander calamari is served with a piquant cilantro aioli. For an entree, consider *khuroos-e-tursh,* baked chicken breast stuffed with nuts, mushrooms, and onions and smothered in a cashew-almond cream sauce, or one of the many dazzling vegetarian dishes. A bargain buffet and a variety of wraps made with nan make this a great lunch stop while touring the nearby Capitol.

1601 Guadalupe St. ⓒ 512/322-5131. www.claypit.com. Reservations recommended. $6.95 lunch buffet; main courses $9–$16. AE, DC, DISC, MC, V. Mon–Thurs 11am–2pm and 5–10pm; Fri 11am–2pm and 5–11pm; Sat–Sun 5–11pm.

Manuel's MEXICAN/REGIONAL MEXICAN   One of the few moderate holdouts in a downtown dining scene that's rapidly heading uptown, price-wise, Manuel's is sleek, chic, and lively. Downtown executives are among the many who come to unwind at Manuel's lively happy hour (daily 4–7pm), with half-price hors d'oeuvres, discounted drinks, and salsa music (see "Only in Austin," later in this chapter, for the musical Sun brunch).

The food, which includes dishes from the interior of Mexico, is a creative cut above many Tex-Mex places. You can get well-prepared versions of the standards, but Manuel's also offers hard-to-find specialties such as the *chiles rellenos en nogada,* stuffed with pork and topped with walnut-cream brandy sauce. The excellent *enchiladas banderas* (cooked with green and red salsas) are arrayed in the colors of the Mexican flag: a green *tomatillo verde* sauce; a white chicken *suiza* (with sour cream and cheese); and a red *adobada* (marinated chicken), made with ancho chiles. A northwest branch, in Great Hills, 10201 Jollyville Rd. (ⓒ 512/345-1042), presents live music Thursday and Saturday nights.

310 Congress Ave. ⓒ 512/472-7555. www.manuels.com. Reservations accepted for 6 or more only. Main courses $7–$20. AE, DC, DISC, MC, V. Sun–Thurs 11am–10pm; Fri–Sat 11am–midnight.

Moonshine AMERICAN   I wasn't really wowed by the "duded up" home cooking I sampled here at lunchtime. The trout with cornbread was just okay, and the spicy popcorn that comes to the table automatically wasn't nearly spicy enough for me. On the other hand, the setting, a converted complex of 1850s buildings including a tree-shaded patio, was terrific, the service was excellent, and all the diners around me were happily tucking into their food. Enthusiastic recommendations from friends include the "corn dog" fried shrimp, the horse-radish-crusted salmon, the cornflake-fried chicken salad, and, for dessert, the peanut butter pie. Next time I plan to come for happy hour (Mon–Fri 3–6:30pm), try some half-price appetizers, and maybe share the signature Moonshine Jug of "white lightening" with peach and spice.

303 Red River St. ⓒ 512/236-9599. www.moonshinegrill.com. Reservations recommended. Salads and sandwiches $6–$9; main courses $11–$20. AE, DC, DISC, MC, V. Mon–Thurs 11am–10pm; Fri 11am–11pm; Sat 5–11pm.

Ranch 616 ⚘⚘ SOUTHWEST   The huge snake logo on the outside of an otherwise nondescript building—created by Bob "Daddy-O" Wade, best known for the oversized boots that front San Antonio's North Star Mall—is your first hint that this place might be a bit, well, different. Inside, cowboy kitsch, 1950s diner decor, and Mexican folk art mingle, as do workers from the nearby county offices, local movers and shakers, and anyone else looking for terrific food that, like the decor, defies easy categorization.

Call it South Texas Gourmet. You can really taste the chipotle chiles in the tartar sauce that comes with some of the best crispy oysters this side of the Mason-Dixon line, and the Gulf fish tacos are gussied—fired?—up with chile lime aioli and Tabasco jalapeño onions. No matter what you order (even the house salad, with its Texas pecans and picante dressing), your taste buds are going to wake up and cheer. More soothing and delicious are such desserts as the banana shortbread tart and any of the fried pies. In case you hadn't guessed from the description of the decor, this place is a hoot. Try to make it to Tequila Tuesday, where the fixed-price menu includes a drink of Sauza Hornitos, and everything is sided by live music.

616 Nueces St. (C) **512/479-7616.** http:/ranch616.citysearch.com. Reservations recommended. Lunch $7–$10; dinner $13–$22. AE, DC, DISC, MC, V. Mon–Thurs 11am–2:30pm and 5:30–10pm; Fri–Sat 11am–2:30pm and 5:30–11pm.

INEXPENSIVE

Chuy's *Kids* MEXICAN   One of the row of low-priced, friendly restaurants that line Barton Springs Road just east of Zilker Park, Chuy's stands out for its determinedly wacky decor—hubcaps lining the ceiling, Elvis memorabilia galore—and its sauce-smothered Tex-Mex food. You're not likely to leave hungry after specials like Chuy's special enchiladas, piled high with smoked chicken and cheese and topped with sour cream, or one of the "big as yo' face" burritos, stuffed with ground sirloin, say, and cheese and beans. This has been a local landmark since presidential daughter Jenna Bush got busted here for underage drinking (the margaritas *are* tempting . . .). There are two other Chuy's in town, one in the north on 10520 N. Lamar Blvd. ((C) **512/836-3218**), the other in the northwest on 11680 N. Research Blvd. ((C) **512/342-0011**).

1728 Barton Springs Rd. (C) **512/474-4452.** www.chuys.com. Reservations not accepted. Main courses $6–$9. AE, DC, DISC, MC, V. Sun–Thurs 11am–10pm; Fri–Sat 11am–11pm.

Frank & Angie's *Kids* ITALIAN/PIZZA   If you think pizza parlors should be low-key, colorful, corny—and, of course, have great pizza—you've come to the right place. This corrugated tin-roof building fronted by a neon sign and backed by a creek view patio is as casual as it gets, and you'll roll your eyes when you peruse the menu, chock-full of such groaners as "Corleone Calzones" and "Angiepasto." But, soon enough, the only thing you'll be groaning about is how full you'll feel after finishing one of the huge Italian grinders or downing too much of the delicious thin-crust pizza (though you can order it Brooklyn-style by the slice). Prices are reasonable and smiles are plentiful, and kids love the festive atmosphere.

508 West Ave. (between 5th and 6th sts., near Lamar). (C) **512/472-3535.** Sandwiches and calzones $5–$6.75; 18-in. pizzas $14–$17. AE, DISC, MC, V. Mon–Sat 11am–10pm; Sun 4–10pm.

Hut's Hamburgers *Value* AMERICAN   What with all the frou-frou, PC, and gourmet eateries you find in Austin, it's easy to forget sometimes that you're in Texas—or even America. This classic burger shack, which first opened its doors as Sammie's Drive-In in 1939, should serve as a reminder. Along with 19 types of burgers—many of them named after 1950s and 1960s rockers—you also find blue-plate specials of meatloaf, chicken-fried steak, and catfish. And the decor is early sports pennants. Still, you won't be entirely unaware of modern times since the burgers are served on whole-wheat buns and you can get a 100% fat-free veggie version.

807 W. 6th St. ✆ **512/472-0693.** Sandwiches and burgers $3.50–$6; plates $6–$7. AE, DISC, MC, V. Daily 11am–10pm.

The Iron Works ✿ BARBECUE   Some of the best barbecue in Austin is served in one of the most unusual settings. Until 1977, this building housed the ironworks of the Weigl family, who came over from Germany in 1913. You can see their ornamental craft all around town, including the State Capitol. Cattle brands created for Jack Benny ("Lasting 39"), Lucille Ball, and Bob Hope are displayed in front of the restaurant. The fall-off-the-bones-tender beef ribs are the most popular order, with the brisket running a close second. Lean turkey breast and juicy chicken are also smoked to perfection.

Red River and E. 1st sts. ✆ **800/669-3602** or 512/478-4855. www.ironworksbbq.com. Reservations accepted for large parties only. Sandwiches $2–$4.25; plates $6–$12; by the lb. $4.50–$16. AE, DC, MC, V. Mon–Sat 11am–9pm.

Katz's *Kids* DELI   Even if it doesn't quite achieve New York deli status—for one thing, the staff is not nearly rude enough, and for another, you can get jalapeños in your omelets—Katz's is as close as you'll come in Austin. The matzo balls are as light and the cheesecake as dense as they're supposed to be, and the pastrami sandwiches come in the requisite gargantuan portions. Katz's is a great place to come after hitting the Sixth Street clubs, whether you're craving scrambled eggs with lox, *kasha varnishkas* (noodle casserole), or (sigh) kosher-style tacos at 4am.

618 W. 6th St. ✆ **512/472-2037.** Reservations not accepted. Sandwiches $5.25–$9; main courses $7.50–$12. AE, DISC, MC, V. Daily 24 hr.

Las Manitas ✿ MEXICAN   This funky family-owned Mexican diner, decked out with local artwork and colorful booths and tables, is an Austin classic—don't leave town without checking it out. A rack of alternative newspapers at the door sets the political tone, but businesspeople and slackers alike pile into this small place for breakfasts of *migas con queso* (eggs scrambled with corn tortillas, cheddar cheese, and ranchero sauce) or *chilaquiles verdes* (tortilla strips topped with green tomatillo sauce, Jack cheese, and onions). The delicious refried beans are prepared with bacon but, this being Austin, most of the rest of the food is cooked in canola or olive oil; vegetarian items are highlighted, and smoothies as well as Mexican soft drinks and beers share the menu.

211 Congress Ave. ✆ **512/472-9357.** Reservations not accepted. Breakfast $2.95–$5.95; lunch $4.25–$7.95. AE, DC, DISC, MC, V. Mon–Fri 7am–4pm; Sat–Sun 7am–2:30pm.

Shady Grove ✿ AMERICAN   If your idea of comfort food involves chiles, don't pass up Shady Grove, one of Austin's quintessential relaxed restaurants. The inside dining area, with its Texas kitsch roadhouse decor and cushy booths, is plenty comfortable, but most people head for the large, tree-shaded patio when the weather permits. When your appetite is whetted by a day of fresh air at nearby Zilker Park, a hearty bowl of Freddie's Airstream chili might be just the thing. All the burgers are made with high-grade ground sirloin, and if you've never had a Fritos pie (Fritos topped with Airstream chili and cheese), this is the place to try one. Large salads—among them, noodles with Asian vegetables—or the hippie sandwich (grilled eggplant, veggies, and cheese with pesto mayonnaise) will satisfy the less carnivorous.

1624 Barton Springs Rd. ✆ **512/474-9991.** www.theshadygrove.com. Reservations not accepted. Main courses $7.25–$11. AE, DC, DISC, MC, V. Sun–Thurs 11am–10pm; Fri–Sat 11am–11pm.

3 South Austin

EXPENSIVE

Green Pastures ✿ CONTINENTAL   Peacocks strut their stuff among 225 live oaks surrounding this 1894 mansion, which was converted into a restaurant in 1945. The Southern graciousness and impeccable service have been retained over the years, but the new millennium brought a new chef, who gently moved the menu away from the Old World toward New America.

But this is still a premier "take your parents when they come to town" pick, with food that tends more toward creative classic than trendy. Although a grilled tofu entree and the requisite wasabi mashed potatoes are likely to turn up on the seasonally changing menu, you're equally likely to encounter smoked prime rib-eye with crab and avocado, or veal stuffed with shrimp. And the desserts have remained decidedly retro, including a Texas pecan ball (vanilla ice cream rolled in nuts and dripping fudge) and bananas Foster.

811 W. Live Oak Rd. ✆ 512/444-4747. www.greenpastures.citysearch.com. Reservations advised. Main courses $19–$32; Sunday brunch $28. AE, DC, DISC, MC, V. Daily 11am–2pm and 6–10pm (Sun brunch buffet 11am–2pm).

Uchi ✿✿ ASIAN/JAPANESE   Ooooh, Uchi. If you get as excited about sushi as I do—and even if you don't—this stylish restaurant will really float your boat. It's not just that the fish served here is superfresh, but that chef Tyson Cole comes up with such exciting things to do with it. For example, his Uchiviche— citrus-marinated whitefish and salmon mixed with tomato, peppers, cilantro, and Thai peppers—makes you wonder why no one ever thought of marrying Latin American and Japanese raw fish traditions before. It's not only the seafood that gets the culinary crossover treatment: Brie, pumpkin, shiitake mushrooms, and asparagus are among the food items that you can order tempura-style. And the skewered kobe beef should satisfy those who eschew vegetables and fish. Choose from a long list of cold sakes—especially the rare upmarket brands—for the perfect complement. The space, a converted 1930s bungalow done up in opulent Asian reds and blacks by two of the city's hottest designers, is at once cozy and eye-popping.

801 S. Lamar. ✆ 512/916-4808. Reservations accepted (and strongly suggested) for Mon–Thurs 5:30–9pm and Fri–Sat 5:30 to 6:30pm. Sushi (per piece) $2.25–$4.50; sashimi, hot and cold plates $5–$25. AE, DISC, MC, V. Mon–Thurs 5–10pm; Fri–Sat 5–11pm.

Vespaio ✿ ITALIAN   Still one of Austin's trendiest restaurants, Vespaio does-n't quite draw the long lines that it did when it first opened in the late 1990s, but the weird policy for reservations—they're accepted only for early hours on off-days—ensures that the see-and-be-seen bar is always packed. The swanked-up old storefront with lots of exposed brick and glass is a fun setting, and the food is worth waiting for, but you can drop quite a bit of dough on expensive wines while you're doing so. Your best bet is to get an order (they're huge) of the crispy calamari while you're waiting for a table. The spaghetti alla carbonara is super, as is the veal scaloppine with mushrooms. In the mood for a go-for-baroque pizza? Try the *boscaiola,* topped with wild boar sausage and Cambozola cheese. Among the 10 chalkboard specials offered nightly, the mixed meat and seafood grills are usually top-notch. In 2005, the restaurant is expanding next door, which should cut into waiting times considerably.

1610 S. Congress Ave. ✆ 512/441-6100. Reservations accepted for Tues–Thurs and Sun 5:30–6:30pm only. Pizzas and pastas $14–$19; main courses $14–$29. AE, DC, DISC, MC, V. Tues–Sun 5:30–10:30pm (bar 5pm–midnight).

Tips **Sweet Tooth**

Not only is Austin's homegrown brand of ice cream, **Amy's,** wonderfully rich and creamy, but watching the colorfully clad servers juggling the scoops is a kick. Amy's has nine Austin locations, including one on the west side of downtown, 1012 W. Sixth St. at Lamar Boulevard (© **512/ 480-0673**); one in SoCo, 1301 S. Congress Ave. (© **512/440-7488**); and one at the Arboretum, 10000 Research Blvd. (© **512/345-1006**). And if you don't have a chance to try it in town, you can catch this tasty treat at the airport.

MODERATE

Curra's Grill ★ *(Kids)* REGIONAL MEXICAN   You're likely to find this funky, colorful restaurant packed at any time of day, but it's worth the wait for the best interior Mexican food in South Austin (and, in the moderate price range, in the city). A couple of breakfast tacos and a cup of special Oaxacan dark roast coffee are a great way to jump-start your day. For lunch, consider the octopus ceviche and the *crema de calabaza* (cream of zucchini) soup, or perhaps the tacos *al pastor,* stuffed with chile-grilled pork. The chiles rellenos topped with cream pecan sauce make a super dinner entree, but if you're sharing, the tamale platter lets you sample from the five kinds available, including veggie and pecan-pineapple-coconut. The avocado and mango margaritas are tops in the potent potables department.

A Curra's in the northwest, 6801 Burnet Rd. (© **512/451-2560**), is not open for breakfast during the week and open only from 9am on the weekends.

614 E. Oltorf. © 512/444-0012. www.currasgrill.com. Reservations recommended for large parties. Main courses $5.25–$13. AE, DISC, MC, V. Sun–Thurs 7am–10pm; Fri–Sat 7am–11pm.

Güero's ★★ *(Kids)* MEXICAN/REGIONAL MEXICAN   Although the menu listings at this sprawling converted feed store, which serves as the unofficial center of the SoCo scene, are stylishly tongue-in-cheek—the entry for one pork dish describes it as being the same as the beef version "except piggish"—the food is seriously good, and the service both efficient and friendly. You can enjoy health-conscious versions of Tex-Mex standards as well as dishes from the interior of Mexico: snapper *a la veracruzana* (with tomatoes, green olives, and jalapeños), say, or Michoacán-style tamales. Lots of plates come topped with cheese, guacamole, and sour cream, but you can also opt for healthy choices like whole-wheat tortillas and soy chorizo. Come Sunday afternoon for a live music bonus.

1412 S. Congress. © 512/447-7688. www.guerostacobar.com. Reservations not accepted. Main courses $5.25–$14. AE, DC, DISC, MC, V. Mon–Fri 11am–11pm; Sat–Sun 8am–11pm.

Habana *(Value)* CUBAN   If you're looking for someplace exotic and fun to eat but don't like spicy food, this is your place. Traditional dishes like *ropa vieja* (shredded beef with tomato sauce) and amusing spins on tradition such as the *platano loco* (sliced plantain filled with roast pork, ham, and Swiss) are tasty without imparting that searing sensation many people associate with hot countries. (Those who thrive on that searing sensation can apply some of the good house-made salsas.) You have a choice of where to eat: a tropical shacklike main dining room; a funky front patio; grass-covered huts on the lawn; or behind the bar in the backyard, which really livens up after dark when the mojitos and Cuba Libres start flowing.

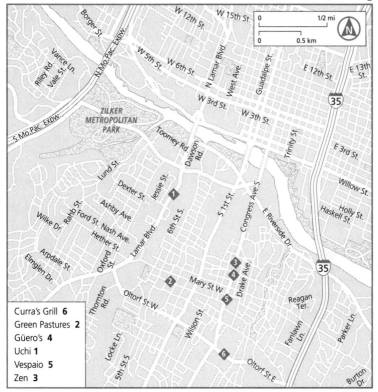

Curra's Grill **6**
Green Pastures **2**
Güero's **4**
Uchi **1**
Vespaio **5**
Zen **3**

Note: The restaurant moved from its South Congress locale to a new location (see below) in early 2005 after a fire.

709 E. Sixth St. ✆ **512/443-4252**. www.habana.com. Reservations recommended on weekends. Main courses $8.50–$14. AE, MC, V. Mon–Fri 7am–2am; Fri–Sat 9am–2am.

Matt's El Rancho MEXICAN   An oldie but a goodie. Lyndon Johnson hadn't been serving in the U.S. Senate very long when Matt's El Rancho first opened its doors. Although owner Matt Martinez outlived LBJ and other early customers, plenty of his original patrons followed when he moved his restaurant south of downtown in 1986. They came not out of habit, but because Matt (and now his son, Matt, Jr.) has been dishing up consistently tasty food since 1952.

Some of the items show the regulars' influence. For instance, you can thank former land commissioner Bob Armstrong for the tasty cheese, guacamole, and spiced-meat dip that bears his name. Chiles rellenos and shrimp Mexicana (smothered with peppers, onions, tomato, ranchero sauce, and Jack cheese) are perennial favorites. Although the place can seat almost 500, you might still have to wait for an hour on weekend nights. Just lounge out on the terrace, sip a fresh lime margarita, and chill. The once untouristed part of town where Matt's is located is becoming trendy as SoCo revitalization spreads south and to the thoroughfares running parallel to South Congress. Well, Matt's was always a bit ahead of the pack.

The branch at the Austin airport is not as atmospheric, nor is the menu as extensive, but you'll get a taste of what draws the crowds.

2613 S. Lamar Blvd. © **512/462-9333.** www.mattselrancho.com. Reservations not accepted for after 6pm on weekends, except for large groups. Main courses $6.75–$16. AE, DC, DISC, MC, V. Sun–Mon and Wed–Thurs 11am–10pm; Fri–Sat 11am–11pm.

The Salt Lick ⚓ *Kids* BARBECUE   It's 11½ miles from the junction of 290 West and FM 1826 (turn left) to The Salt Lick, but you'll start smelling the smoke during the last 5 miles of your trip. Moist chicken, beef, and pork, as well as terrific homemade pickles—not to mention the pretty, verdant setting—more than justify the drive. However, you'll be faced with a tough decision here: If you indulge in the all-you-can-eat family-style platter of beef, sausage, and pork ribs, you might have to pass on the fresh-baked peach cobbler, which would be a pity. In warm weather, seating is outside at picnic tables under oak trees; in winter, fireplaces blaze in a series of large, rustic rooms. Unlike many Texas barbecue places, The Salt Lick prides itself on its sauce, which has a sweet-and-sour tang. If you like your barbecue with a brew, you'll need to tote your own in a cooler, because Hays County is dry. Kids under 4 eat free. But you don't have to drive all the way out to the country for a smoked-meat fix. It's not quite as atmospheric as the original, but if you happen to be flying in or out of town, the Salt Lick's airport branch is convenient and quick. If you get hooked on the barbecue at either place, you can ship some brisket or smoked turkey back home.

18300 FM 1826, Driftwood. © **512/858-4959** or 888/SALT-LICK (mail order). http://saltlickbbq.com. Reservations for large parties only. Sandwiches $7–$8; plates $7–$15. No credit cards. Daily 11am–10pm.

INEXPENSIVE

Zen *Value Kids* JAPANESE   The food is flavorful, healthy, and inexpensive, the pared-down room light and welcoming—if you're looking for a nice, quick bite, it's hard to beat Zen. The poultry in such dishes as chicken teriyaki and veggies, for example, is steroid free, 25¢ gets you brown instead of white rice with your order, and the menu has so many heart-healthy symbols on it that it resembles a Valentine's card. Most of the food is typically Japanese—sushi, udon noodles, rice bowls, and teriyaki dishes—except, for some reason, for the Madison Mac & Cheese. No doubt it's a tongue-in-cheek touch, like the light fixtures that look like Chia pet doormats. You order at the counter and the food is brought to your table generally very quickly.

Two newer locations are at 2900 W. Anderson Lane, Suite 250 (© **512/451-4811**), and 3423 North Guadalupe (© **512/300-2633**).

1303 S. Congress Ave. © **512/444-8081.** www.eatzen.com. Reservations not accepted. $3.80–$7.95. DISC, MC, V. Daily 11am–10pm.

4 Central

VERY EXPENSIVE

Jeffrey's ⚓⚓ NEW AMERICAN   Jeffrey's has been garnering local acclaim since 1975, but it wasn't until 1991, when David Garrido came onboard, that it became a celebrity chef restaurant. That's why, when Garrido's time was divided between this original location and a newer one in Washington, D.C., regulars complained that the food in Austin was suffering from attention-deficit disorder.

But the D.C. restaurant is history, and Garrido is again concentrating on the food at this former storefront in artsy (translation: you don't need to get dressed up) Clarksville. Although the idea of using only the freshest ingredients and creating unlikely culinary combinations is no longer news, Jeffrey's still stands out. Flavors and textures dance wildly together and rarely trip. Appetizers might include ginger beef dumplings with spicy macadamias and—a signature dish

Veggie Heaven

Visitors to Austin who want to go meatless won't have to play second fiddle in the culinary orchestra. Not only do most fine dining rooms in town offer at least one good veggie option—not just the typical boring pasta dish, either—but the restaurants solely dedicated to vegetarians are a cut above those in most towns. These top picks all fall into the Inexpensive range:

Mother's Cafe & Garden   The crunchy granola crowd that frequents this Hyde Park cafe enjoys an international array of veggie dishes, with heavy south-of-the-border representation. You'll find classic chiles rellenos, burritos, and nachos, along with more unusual spicy tempeh enchiladas. The tropical shack–style back garden is appealing, and the young staff is friendly, but not nauseatingly so. There's a good, inexpensive selection of local beers and wines. 4215 Duval St. $\textcircled{C}$ **512/451-3994.** www.motherscafeaustin.com.

Mr. Natural   Only on Austin's East Side would you find a health food store/restaurant/bakery with an all Mexican-American staff, and dishes such as tofu *pipián* (in a red sauce), vegetarian chorizo, and zucchini *poblano* (with a chile/tomato sauce). Richard Linklater, Robert Rodriguez, and other successful hipsters are often spotted grazing at the lunchtime buffet. The more recently opened South Austin branch, at 2414 S. Lamar ($\textcircled{C}$ **512/916-9223**), has the same health-Mex menu but a more Anglo staff. 1901 E. First St. $\textcircled{C}$ **512/477-5228.** www.mrnatural-austin.com.

West Lynn Cafe   Although this sunny, soaring-ceiling restaurant, part homey, part techno-chic, is totally vegetarian, it doesn't attract only the Birkenstocks-with-socks set. Health-conscious sophisticates and artsy locals in the north-of-downtown neighborhood for which the restaurant is named also come to enjoy well-prepared dishes that range over the world's cuisine—everything from Thai red pepper curry and Szechuan stir-fry to pesto primavera, mushroom stroganoff, spanakopita, and artichoke enchiladas—accompanied by nice, reasonably priced wine. 1110 W. Lynn. $\textcircled{C}$ **512/482-0950.** www.westlynn.citysearch.com.

that never leaves the menu—crispy oysters topped with habanero honey aioli. Peppered venison loin with corn truffle pudding was among the entree successes on a recent menu. The wine list is outstanding. Two tasting menus, including one that offers three lighter courses, offer a (relatively) economical way to check that Garrido has indeed hit his stride again.

1204 W. Lynn. $\textcircled{C}$ 512/477-5584. www.jeffreysofaustin.com. Reservations strongly recommended. Main courses $25–$36; 4-course tasting menu $60; lighter prix-fixe menu $38. AE, DC, DISC, MC, V. Mon–Thurs 6–10pm; Fri–Sat 5:30–10:30pm; Sun 6–9:30pm.

EXPENSIVE

Fonda San Miguel $\underset{\star}{\star}\underset{\star}{\star}$ REGIONAL MEXICAN   Like American Southwest chefs who look to Native American staples such as blue corn for inspiration, Mexico City chefs have had their own back-to-the-roots movement. Such trends as using ancient Aztec ingredients have been carefully tracked and artfully translated at Fonda San Miguel, one of America's top fine-dining spots for Mexican regional cuisine since 1975 and still a standout. In 2004 it garnered the top Mexican food awards from both the *Austin Chronicle*'s critics and its readers.

The huge dining room, with its carved wooden doors, colorful paintings (many by famed Mexico artists), and live ficus tree, is a gorgeous backdrop to such appetizers as Veracruz-style ceviche or the traditional Sonoran salad of *nopalitos* (cactus pads). *Cochinita pibil* (pork baked in banana leaves) is one of the Yucatán offerings. Those with more traditional tastes will find familiar northern Mexican fare, extremely well prepared, on the menu.

2330 W. North Loop. © 512/459-4121 or 459-3401. www.fondasanmiguel.com. Reservations recommended. Main courses $13–$29. AE, DC, DISC, MC, V. Mon–Thurs 5:30–9:30pm; Fri–Sat 5:30–10:30pm (bar opens 30 min. earlier); Sun brunch 11am–2pm.

Wink ★★ *Finds* NEW AMERICAN   One of the darlings of the local foodie scene is a spare but attractive 17-table eatery in an unlikely strip center (at least its location, just north of Lamar and Sixth, is getting hipper by the minute). Chef/owners Stewart Scruggs and Mark Paul are fresh-ingredient fanatics and they train their staff well. Your server should be able to fill you in on every detail of the menu, down to the organic farm where the arugula and fennel in your rabbit confit salad came from. You never know what dishes will turn up unless— this being Austin—you check the daily listings on the restaurant's website, but expect a mix of such typical New American suspects as seared scallop on pancetta with baby sweet potatoes and more adventurous dishes like braised boar belly with apple cider sauce. The tasting menus, which include some off-menu surprises, are worth the splurge. Save some room (and dough) for desserts like the dreamy lemon curd cups.

1014 N. Lamar. © 512/482-8868. www.winkrestaurant.com. Reservations strongly suggested. Main courses $19–$26; 5-course tasting menu $65 ($95 with wine); 7-course tasting menu $85 ($125 with wine). AE, DC, DISC, MC, V. Mon–Thurs 6–11pm; Fri–Sat 5: 30–11pm.

MODERATE

Asti ★ *Value* ITALIAN   This is the Italian place everyone wants in their neighborhood: casual, consistently good, and reasonably priced. An open kitchen and retro Formica-topped tables create a hip, upbeat atmosphere. The designer pizzas make a nice light meal, and northern Italian specialties such as the Calabrese-style trout and the pan-seared halibut with green beans are winners. Save room for such desserts as the creamy espresso sorbet or the amazing bittersweet chocolate cannoli. For a little restaurant, Asti has an unexpectedly large and well-selected wine list (mostly Italian and Californian bottles). The beer list is smaller, but it's good to have one at all.

408C E. 43rd St. © 512/451-1218. www.astiaustin.com. Reservations recommended Thurs–Sat. Pizzas, pastas $7.50–$16; main courses $15–$16. AE, DC, DISC, MC, V. Mon–Thurs 11am–10pm; Fri 11am–11pm; Sat 5–11pm.

INEXPENSIVE

Cipollina ★ *Finds* ITALIAN/DELI   It's worth the short drive from downtown to have lunch or a light dinner at this casual chic neighborhood favorite, a large, open room with a deli case that could as easily be in Italy as in Clarksville. Everything's delicious: the thin-crust pizzas (especially the simple *margherita,* topped with mozzarella, tomato, and basil); creative grilled sandwiches such as lamb and sweet onion; and salads like the Mediterranean, with romaine, feta, olives, and oregano. Good coffee, a nice selection of wines by the glass, and excellent pastries round out the menu. There's a hot entree special every lunch and

---

(Kids) Family-Friendly Restaurants

Curra's (p. 184), **Güero's** (p. 184), **Hoover's** (p. 190), **Katz's** (p. 182), **Threadgill's** (p. 189), and **Zen** (p. 186) all have special menus for ages 12 and under, not to mention casual, kid-friendly atmospheres and food inexpensive enough to feed everyone without taking out a second mortgage. The separate Kid's Klub menu at Katz's also includes connect-the-dot, maze, and word games to keep youngsters occupied. **Chuy's** (p. 181) is great for teens and aspiring teens, who'll love the cool T-shirts, Elvis kitsch, and green iguanas crawling up the walls. And it provides a cautionary tale about underage drinking (or at least the perils of being related to the president). **Frank & Angie's** (p. 181) have delicious thin-crust pizza, and kids love the festive atmosphere. The **Salt Lick** (p. 186) serves all-you-can-eat family-style platters, and kids under 4 eat free. At the **County Line on the Hill** (p. 192), all-you-can-eat platters of meat (beef ribs, brisket, and sausage), and generous bowls of potato salad, cole slaw, and beans are just $5.95 for children under 12.

---

dinner, too. Come on your own with a good book, newspaper, or laptop (they offer free wi-fi). This is the kind of place where you'll immediately feel comfortable.

1213 W. Lynn. ℂ 512/477-5211. www.cipollina-austin.com. Reservations not accepted. Pizzas $7–$14; sandwiches $5.75–$6.95; salads $3.75–$5.95. AE, DC, DISC, MC, V. Mon–Sat 7am–9pm; Sun 7am–8pm.

Threadgill's (Kids) AMERICAN   If you want a hit of music history along with heaping plates of down-home food at good prices, this Austin institution is for you. When Kenneth Threadgill obtained Travis County's first legal liquor license after the repeal of Prohibition in 1933, he turned his Gulf gas station into a club. His Wednesday-night hootenannies were legendary in the 1960s, with performers like Janis Joplin turning up regularly. In turn, the Southern-style diner that was added on in 1980 became renowned for its huge chicken-fried steaks, as well as its vegetables. You can get fried okra, broccoli-rice casserole, garlic-cheese grits, black-eyed peas, and the like in combination plates or as sides.

Eddie Wilson, the current owner of Threadgill's, was the founder of the now-defunct Armadillo World Headquarters, Austin's most famous music venue (the downtown branch at 301 W. Riverside [ℂ **512/472-9304**] is called Threadgill's World Headquarters). Across the street from the old Armadillo, it's filled with music memorabilia from the club and a state-of-the-art sound system. Unlike the original location, it lays on a Sunday brunch buffet and, during the week, a "howdy" hour. Both branches still double as live music venues.

6416 N. Lamar Blvd. ℂ 512/451-5440. www.threadgills.com. Reservations not accepted. Sandwiches and burgers $5.95–$7.95; main courses $6.25–$15. DISC, MC, V. Mon–Sat 11am–10pm; Sun 11am–9pm.

5 East Side

MODERATE

Eastside Cafe AMERICAN   One of the earliest eateries to open in the rapidly trendifying area just east of the university and northeast of the capitol, Eastside Cafe remains popular with student herbivores and congressional carnivores alike. Diners enjoy eating on a tree-shaded patio or in one of a series of cheery, intimate rooms in a classic turn-of-the-century bungalow.

Not only is the crowd eclectic, but this restaurant gears its menu to all appetites. You can get half orders of such pasta dishes as the artichoke manicotti, of the mixed field green salad topped with warm goat cheese, and of entrees like the sesame-breaded catfish. Many of the main courses have a Southern comfort orientation—pork tenderloin with cornbread stuffing, say—and all come with soup or salad and a vegetable. Each morning, the gardener informs the head chef which of the vegetables in the restaurant's large organic garden are ready for active duty. An adjoining store carries gardening tools, cookware, and the cafe's salad dressings.

2113 Manor Rd. ✆ 512/476-5858. www.eastsidecafeaustin.com. Reservations recommended. Pastas $11–$14; main courses $13–$22. AE, DC, DISC, MC, V. Mon–Thurs 11:15am–9:30pm; Fri 11:15am–10pm; Sat 10am–10pm; Sun 10am–9:30pm (brunch Sat–Sun 10am–3pm).

INEXPENSIVE

Hoover's *Finds* *Kids* AMERICAN   Whether you call it down-home, Southern, or soul, the victuals heaped on your plate in this low-key East Side eatery will leave you feeling content. When native Austinite Alexander Hoover, long a presence on the local restaurant scene, opened up his own place near the neighborhood where he grew up, he looked to his mother's farm-grown recipes—a smidge of Cajun, a dollop of Tex-Mex—for inspiration. Fried catfish, meatloaf, gravy-smothered pork chops, chicken-fried steak, sides of mac and cheese or jalapeño-creamed spinach, peach cobbler—it's all authentic and it's all tasty. The crowd is a nice mix of the Eastside African-American community, UT students, and food lovers from all around town.

2002 Manor Rd. ✆ 512/479-5006. www.hooverscooking.com. Reservations not accepted. Sandwiches (with 1 side) $6.30–$7.30; plates (with 2 sides) $7–$12. DC, DISC, MC, V. Mon–Fri 11am–10pm; Sat–Sun 8am–10pm.

Vivo ✪ MEXICAN   A sure sign that the once-ethnic East Side has become a hip Anglo hangout is the fact that Vivo bills its food as "healthy Tex-Mex" and has brown rice and tofu on the menu. But that's not to suggest this place is boring. Far from it. Indoors, the walls are painted bright yellow, purple, and red, and hung with vibrant Mexican art. Outside, dining is on a tropical plant-decked patio fronted by a large stucco fountain.

Ah, and the food. . . . One dip of the house-made tortilla chips in the smoky, garlicky salsa made with skillet-blackened serrano chiles, and you know you're in expert hands. Vivo is known for its puffy tacos: cornmeal cakes that, instead of being flattened into tortillas, are fried (in canola oil of course) and filled with shredded beef, perhaps, or guacamole. They're delicious, and so are more typical Tex-Mex dishes like the enchiladas verdes, stuffed with chicken and cheese and topped with a sassy tomatillo sauce. In addition to its superlative list of margaritas and tequila shots, this place offers a drink rarely seen north of the border called "the michelada," which is beer poured over ice with fresh lime juice, Tabasco, and Worcestershire sauce. Viva Vivo!

2015 Manor Rd. ✆ 512/482-0300. Reservations recommended. Main courses and combination plates $6.50–$11. AE, DC, DISC, MC, V. Mon–Thurs 11am–10pm; Fri–Sat 11am–11pm.

6 Northwest

VERY EXPENSIVE

Eddie V's Edgewater Grille ✪ SEAFOOD/STEAK   This swanky Arboretum restaurant is one of the hottest dinner tickets in the Northwest. The supper club atmosphere—white tablecloths, lots of black accents, nightly live jazz in the lounge—is a contributing factor, but the main hook is the top-notch seafood.

The crispy calamari appetizer and lump crab cake make great starters, but you might be better off going for the less filling oysters-on-the-half-shell, because this place doesn't stint on portion sizes, and Parmesan-crusted lemon sole or smoked salmon with horseradish butter might not cut it as breakfast the next day. Besides, you want to leave room for the hot bread pudding soufflé, large enough for a table as long as you're not dining with an entourage. The downtown Eddie V's, 301 E. Fifth St. (✆ **512/472-1860**), has the same menu, the same decor, and the same "sea and be seen" cachet, but it doesn't have this room's Hill Country views at sunset. Both offer good happy hours (4:30–7pm), with half-price appetizers, and $1 off wines and cocktails.

9400B Arboretum Blvd. ✆ 512/342-6242. www.eddiev.com. Reservations recommended. Main courses $19–$32. AE, DC, DISC, MC, V. Mon–Sat 5–11pm; Sun 5–10pm.

EXPENSIVE

Z'Tejas Southwestern Grill ★ *Value* SOUTHWEST   An offshoot of a popular downtown eatery (and the second link in what became a small chain), this Arboretum restaurant is notable not only for its zippy Southwestern cuisine but also for its attractive dining space, featuring floor-to-ceiling windows, a soaring ceiling, sophisticated Santa Fe–style decor, and, in cool weather, a roaring fireplace. Grilled shrimp and guacamole tostada bites make a great starter, and if you see it on a specials menu, go for the smoked chiles rellenos made with apricots and goat cheese. Entrees include a delicious horseradish-crusted salmon and a pork tenderloin stuffed with chorizo, cheese, onions, and poblano chiles. Even if you think you can't eat another bite, order a piece of ancho chile fudge pie, too. It will miraculously disappear.

If you're staying downtown, try the original—and smaller—Z'Tejas at 1110 W. Sixth St. (✆ **512/478-5355**).

9400-A Arboretum Blvd. ✆ 512/346-3506. www.ztejas.com. Reservations recommended. Main courses $9.95–$25. AE, DC, DISC, MC, V. Mon–Thurs 11am–10pm; Fri 11am–11pm; Sat 10am–11pm; Sun 10am–10pm.

MODERATE

Chez Zee ★ *Finds* NEW AMERICAN   Many Northwest restaurants belong to over-produced "high concept" chains—you know, splashy decor, vaguely ethnic food—but this neighborhood bakery/bistro is a charming exception. The dining room, with its whimsical artwork, fairy light-draped windows, and enclosed front patio, is romantic without being formal. And it would be tough to bring someone here who couldn't find something to like on the eclectic menu—crunchy fried dill pickles, perhaps, or tasty tequila-lime grilled chicken. In fact, it's hard to find a culinary category in which Chez Zee doesn't shine. It topped the "Best American," "Best Dessert," and "Best Soup" categories in the 2004 *Austin Chronicle* Readers' poll. But this place is particularly renowned for its weekend brunches—Peach Bellinis with crème brûlée French toast, anyone?—and, yes, those stellar desserts. It's also open much later than most Austin restaurants, and features some of the best live jazz in town.

5406 Balcones. ✆ 512/454-2666. www.chez-zee.com. Main courses $12–$16. AE, DC, DISC, MC, V. Mon–Thurs 11am–10:30pm; Fri 11am–midnight; Sat 9am–midnight; Sun 9am–10pm.

Musashino ★ JAPANESE   This place has the freshest, best-prepared sushi in town and every Austin aficionado knows it—which is why, in spite of its inauspicious location (on the southbound access road of Mo-Pac in northwest Austin) and less-than-stunning setting (beneath a Chinese restaurant called Chinatown), it's always jammed. A combination of Musashino's local star status and its policy of not accepting reservations means you're likely to have to wait awhile for a table, especially on Friday and Saturday nights. If you don't mind not having the entire menu at your disposal, the cozy upstairs area, which has a sushi bar and table service, but a shorter menu, is a good substitute. Be sure to ask your server what's special before you order; delicacies not listed on the regular menu are often flown in.

3407 Greystone Dr. (C) **512/795-8593**. http://musashinosushi.com. Reservations not accepted. Sushi $2–$12 (including rolls); main courses $14–$28. AE, DC, DISC, MC, V. Mon–Fri 11:30am–2pm; Tues–Thurs and Sun 5:30–10pm; Fri–Sat 5:30–10:30pm.

7 West/Lakes

VERY EXPENSIVE

Hudson's on the Bend ★★ NEW AMERICAN   If you're game for game, served in a very civilized setting, come to Hudson's. Soft candlelight, fresh flowers, fine china, and attentive service combine with outstanding and out-of-the-ordinary cuisine to make this worth a special-occasion splurge. Sparkling lights draped over a cluster of oak trees draw you into a series of romantic dining rooms, set in an old house some 1½ miles southwest of the Mansfield Dam, near Lake Travis. The chipotle cream sauce was sufficiently spicy so that it was hard to tell whether the diamondback rattlesnake cakes tasted like chicken. But they were very good, as were the duck confit *gordita* (thick corn tortilla) and wild game tamale starters. Pecan-smoked duck breast and a mixed grill of venison, rabbit, quail, and buffalo are among the excellent entrees I've sampled; there's also a superb trout served with tangy mango-habanero butter.

One caveat to be aware of is that the charming but acoustically poor setting can make Hudson's indoor dining rooms noisy on weekends. Opt for the terrace if the weather permits.

3509 Hwy. 620 N. (C) **512/266-1369**. www.hudsononthebend.com. Reservations recommended, essential on weekends. Main courses $26–$45. AE, DC, DISC, MC, V. Sun 6–9pm; Mon–Thurs 6–9:30pm; Fri–Sat 5:30–10pm.

MODERATE

County Line on the Hill ★ *Kids* BARBECUE   The original of the County Line chain, opened in 1975, this place offers a taste of Texas history along with its BBQ. Some critics deride these smoked-meat outlets for their "suburban" barbecue, but Austinites have voted with their feet (or, rather, their cars). The crowds have lessened somewhat since this restaurant started opening for lunch, but if you don't get here before 6pm for dinner, you can wait as long as an hour to eat. Should this happen, sit out on the deck and soak in the views of the Hill Country, or look at the old advertising signs hung on the knotty-pine planks of this 1920s roadhouse, formerly a speak-easy and a brothel. In addition to the barbecue—oh-so-slowly-smoked ribs, brisket, chicken, or sausage—skewered meat or vegetable plates are available. Bring the family: All-you-can-eat platters of meat (beef ribs, brisket, and sausage), and generous bowls of potato salad, cole slaw, and beans are just $5.95 for children under 12. County Line on the Lake, near Lake Austin, 5204 FM 2222 ((C) **512/346-3664**), offers the same menu, and is also open for lunch and dinner.

6500 W. Bee Cave Rd. (C) **512/327-1742**. www.virtual-restaurants.com/countyline. Reservations not accepted. Plates $8–$17; all-you-can-eat platters $15–$20 ($6–$8 for children under 12). AE, DC, DISC, MC, V. Mon–Thurs 11:30am–2pm and 5–9pm; Fri 11:30am–2pm and 5–10pm; Sat 11:30am–10pm; Sun 11:30am–9:30pm (closing time is half-hour earlier in winter).

The Oasis AMERICAN/MEXICAN   This is the required spot for Austinites to take out-of-town guests at sunset. From the 40 multilevel decks nestled into the hillside hundreds of feet above Lake Travis, visitors and locals alike cheer—with toasts and applause—as the fiery orb descends behind the hills on the opposite bank. No one ever leaves unimpressed by the sunset. The food is another matter entirely: At best, it's erratic. Although different owners have tried over the years, so far no one has succeeded in getting it right all the time. Keep it simple—nachos, burgers (as opposed to, say, the crawfish étouffée enchiladas)—and you'll be okay. Then add a margarita, and kick back. It doesn't get much mellower than this.

6550 Comanche Trail, near Lake Travis. © 512/266-2442. www.oasis-austin.com. Reservations not accepted. Main courses $12–$20. AE, DC, DISC, MC, V. Mon–Thurs 11:30am–10pm; Fri 11:30am–11pm; Sat 11am–11pm; Sun 11am–10pm (brunch 11am–2pm); closing an hour earlier in fall/winter.

8 Only in Austin

For information on Austin's funky, original cafe scene, see "Late-Night Bites" in chapter 16.

A BAT'S-EYE VIEW

From late March through mid-November, the most coveted seats in town are the ones with a view of the thousands of bats that fly out from under the Congress Avenue Bridge in search of a hearty bug dinner at dusk. The **Shoreline Grill** (see earlier in this chapter) and the **Cafe at the Four Seasons,** 98 San Jacinto Blvd. (© **512/478-4500**), are the two toniest spots for observing this astounding phenomenon. **TGIF's** at the Radisson Hotel on Town Lake, 11 E. First St. (© **512/478-9611**), and **La Vista** at the Hyatt Regency Austin on Town Lake, 208 Barton Springs Rd. (© **512/477-1234**), offer more casual, collegial roosts.

MUSICAL BRUNCHES

For a religious experience on Sunday morning that doesn't require entering a church or temple, check out the gospel brunch at **Stubb's Bar-B-Q,** 801 Red River St. (© **512/480-8341**). The singing is heavenly, the pork ribs divine. At **Threadgill's World Headquarters** (p. 189), you can graze at a Southern-style buffet while listening to live inspirational sounds; find out who's playing at www.threadgills.com. If you worship at the altar of the likes of Miles Davis, the Sunday jazz brunches at both locations of **Manuel's** (p. 180) let you enjoy eggs with venison chorizo or corn gorditas with garlic and cilantro while listening to smokin' traditional or Latin jazz. Log on to www.manuels.com to find out who's gonna be sizzling while you're visiting.

COFFEEHOUSES

Austin has often been compared to Seattle for its music scene and its green, college-town atmosphere. Although the city isn't quite up to, er, speed when it comes to coffeehouses, there are enough homegrown versions these days to constitute a respectable presence around downtown and the university. All the following are wireless Internet hot spots.

Little City, 916 Congress Ave. (© **512/476-2489**), with its ultrachic design, is close to the downtown tourist sights, and the only local place to get a java fix near the capitol on Sunday. Another location, at 2604 Guadalupe, near the UT campus (© **512/467-2326**), roasts its own beans. Also near UT and also a roaster/grinder, **Mojo,** 2714 Guadalupe (© **512/477-6656**), provides java, pastry, and attitude 24/7. Musicians often turn up for the creative sandwiches and

Reel Barbecue

Forget cheap labor and right-to-work laws, one of the less-publicized inducements for filmmakers to come to Austin is the barbecue—slow-cooked over a wood-fueled fire, and so tasty it doesn't need sauce. Think in terms of an "Austin Barbecue Loop," a circle with a roughly 30-mile radius from the state capitol where hungry crews make the rounds. Sometimes the meat in joints within this loop comes on butcher paper rather than plates, and there's usually little ceremony in the service—if there's any service at all. But who cares about amenities when you're dealing with this kind of flavor and aroma?

Gary Bond, film liaison for the Austin Convention and Visitors Bureau, has the skinny on the celluloid-barbecue connection. According to Bond, the eastern portion of the Loop—where rolling prairies, farmland, and small towns conveniently pass for Everywhere, USA—has received rave reviews from location scouts, stars, and producers alike. **Rudy Mikeska's** (© 512/352-5561), in downtown Taylor, was featured in *The Hot Spot* as The Yellow Rose, the racy hangout of the Don Johnson character, while less than a block away, **Louie Mueller Barbecue** (© 512/352-6206) served as a location for *Flesh and Bone,* starring Dennis Quaid and James Caan. To the south, in Elgin, crews from movie segments, music videos, and commercials happily hit **Southside Market & BBQ** (© 512/281-4650) on breaks. Still farther south, three hot meat purveyors in Lockhart have Hollywood dealmakers bickering about which is best: **Kreutz Market** (in either of its two incarnations, one of which is called Smitty's; © 512/398-2361), **Black's Barbecue** (© 512/398-2712), or **Chisholm Trail** (© 512/398-6027).

As for the western part of the loop, the guys scouting for *Lolita* loved **Cooper's** (© 915/247-5713) open pit in Llano, while **The Salt Lick,** near Driftwood (p. 186), has hosted lots of wrap parties. In Austin itself, Nora Ephron couldn't tear herself away from **The Green Mesquite** (© 512/335-9885; various locations).

For more meaty locations, log on to **www.bbqfilm.com**, the website of "Barbecue: A Texas Love Story." This humorous film, narrated by former governor Ann Richards, travels all around Texas in search of the best you-know-what.

dark-roasted java drinks at **Jo's,** 1300 S. Congress (© **512/444-3800**), a hip outdoor hangout across the road from the Continental Club (every third Fri, there's a dog-friendly happy hour). At **Flipnotics,** 1601 Barton Springs Rd. (© **512/322-9750**), a two-story, indoor/outdoor "coffeespace," you can sip great caffeine drinks or beer while listening to acoustic singer/songwriters most nights. At **Spider House,** 2908 Fruth St. (© **512/480-9562**), just north of the UT campus, the likes of tempeh chili, Fritos pie, smoothies, all-natural fruit sangrias, and beer complement the coffee portion of the menu. The large, tree-shaded patio should get you mellow, too. Still, in the chill-out department, it's impossible to beat **Mozart's,** 3825 Lake Austin Blvd. (© **512/477-2900**), with killer views of Lake Austin and great white-chocolate-almond croissants.

14

Exploring Austin

Stroll up Congress Avenue and you'll see much the same sight visitors to Austin did more than 100 years ago: a broad thoroughfare, gently rising to the grandest of all state capitols. Long obsessed with its place in history, the city continues to honor that place today. The capitol underwent a complete overhaul in the 1990s, a grand new state history museum opened its doors near the capitol at the start of the new millennium, and downtown is turning back the clock with ongoing restorations. Austin is also on a cultural mission. Two multimillion-dollar complexes are being built to house the city's top art collections, and new galleries are opening all over town.

But it is Austin's myriad natural attractions that put the city on all the "most livable" lists. From bats and birds to Barton Springs, from the Highland Lakes to the hike-and-bike trails, Austin lays out the green carpet for its visitors. You'd be hard-pressed to find a city that has more to offer fresh-air enthusiasts.

It's also easy to sightsee here, even if you don't have a car. There's no charge for transportation on the city's seven 'Dillo lines, which cover most of the downtown tourist sites and the University of Texas. Other freebies include the Convention and Visitors Bureau's excellent guided walks and the state-sponsored tours of the governor's mansion and the state capitol.

SUGGESTED ITINERARIES

If You Have 1 Day

You'll see much of what makes Austin unique if you spend a day downtown. You might start out with a cup of coffee and a pastry at the **Little City Café,** then head over to the **Capitol Visitors Center,** a historic building that's an ideal place to begin your tour of the capitol complex. The **Capitol** and newer extension are next; you'll be impressed by the results of the costly restoration. You can go from here to the **governor's mansion** (keep in mind that the day's last tour begins at 11:40am, that tours are given Mon–Thurs only, and that you have to book in advance) and the nearby historic **Bremond**

block district for a taste of how the other half lived during the 19th century. Or visit the **Bob Bullock Texas State History Museum,** where you'll get the big picture (both figuratively and literally, via an IMAX theater).

Now head south, having lunch at one of the restaurants along Congress Avenue (La Traviata if you're up for Italian, Las Manitas if you prefer Mexican) or one on Riverside Drive (I'd vote for Shady Grove) near the shore of **Town Lake,** where you can rest under an oak tree or join the athletic hordes in perpetual motion on the hike-and-bike trail. Or, in fair weather, wait an hour and take a swim in **Barton**

Springs Pool. If you're in town from late March through October, book a table for dinner at the Shoreline Grill and **watch the bats** take off at dusk from under the Congress Avenue Bridge. Devote any energy you have left to hitting one—or several—of Austin's **live music** spots, perhaps the Continental Club or Antone's.

If You Have 2 Days

Day 1   Follow the itinerary outlined above.

Day 2   In the morning, head out to the **Lady Bird Johnson Wildflower Center** to see Texas's bountiful natural blooms. In the afternoon, visit the **LBJ Library** and **Harry Ransom Humanities Research Center** (or, if it has reopened, the **Blanton Museum of Art**) on the University of Texas campus. If you're traveling with youngsters, substitute the excellent **Children's Museum** or the **Austin Nature and Science Center.** At night, visit a different **live music club**—maybe the Broken Spoke, Stubb's, or La Zona Rosa.

If You Have 3 Days

Days 1 to 2   Same as Days 1 and 2 in "If You Have 2 Days."

Day 3   Scope out the cityscape from **Mount Bonnell,** the highest point in Austin, and then visit the nearby **Austin Museum of Art–Laguna Gloria.** After this, head for the historic **Hyde Park neighborhood,** including the **Elisabet Ney museum** (don't worry about cultural burnout as both museums are small and scenic). If the weather is nice, have lunch at one of the restaurants along Barton Springs Road, then spend the afternoon in **Zilker Park,** perhaps going for a stroll at the lovely Botanical Gardens. Or if you're interested in history, substitute the sights on Austin's East Side —the **George Washington Carver Museum,** the **State Cemetery,** and the **French Legation Museum.** There are a number of good, inexpensive Mexican restaurants in the area too. Alternatively, after Mt. Bonnell and AMOA-Laguna Gloria, you could head for **Lake Travis** and some serious water play. Just be sure to make it to **The Oasis** in time to applaud the sunset.

If You Have 4 Days

Days 1 to 3   Same as Days 1–3 in "If You Have 3 Days."

Day 4   Take a day trip to Fredericksburg or New Braunfels in the **Hill Country** (see chapter 17). Fredericksburg lays on the Germanic charm a bit more, but New Braunfels competes with watersports (and antiques aplenty).

If You Have 5 Days or More

Days 1 to 3   Follow the strategy in "If You Have 3 Days."

Days 4 to 5   Stay overnight at a bed-and-breakfast in **Fredericksburg** and visit the **LBJ Ranch, Enchanted Rock State Park,** and some nearby **Hill Country** towns (see chapter 17).

1 The Top Attractions

DOWNTOWN

The Bob Bullock Texas State History Museum ⭐ *Value* *Kids*   You'll get a quick course in Texas 101 at this museum, opened near the state capitol in 2001 and designed to echo some of its elements. Three floors of exhibits are arrayed around a huge rotunda centered by a 50-foot, polished granite map of Texas. It's

Downtown Austin Attractions

ArtHouse at Jones Center **13**
Austin Children's Museum **19**
Austin History Center **11**
Austin Museum of Art–Downtown **12**
Barton Springs Pool **23**
Bats **20**
Blanton Museum of Art **5**
Bob Bullock Texas State History
  Museum **6**
The Bremond Block **16**
Capitol Visitors Center **8**
Driskill Hotel **14**
Governor's Mansion **9**
Harry Ransom Humanities
  Research Center **2**

LBJ Library & Museum **4**
MEXIC-ARTE Museum **17**
Neill-Cochran Museum House **1**
O. Henry Museum **18**
Old Bakery & Emporium **10**
Philosopher's Rock **23**
Splash **23**
State Capitol **7**
Stevie Ray Vaughn Statue **21**
Texas Memorial Museum **3**
Treaty Oak **15**
Umlauf Sculpture Garden
  & Museum **22**
Zilker Zephyr Miniature Train **24**

Greater Austin Attractions

Austin Museum of Art–
  Laguna Gloria **2**
Austin Nature & Science Center **6**
Austin Zoo **11**
Covert Park at Mt. Bonnell **1**
Elisabet Ney Museum **4**
French Legation Museum **8**
Hyde Park **3**
Lady Bird Johnson Wildflower Center **10**
Moore/Andersson Compound **5**
Texas State Cemetery **9**
Zilker Botanical Garden **7**

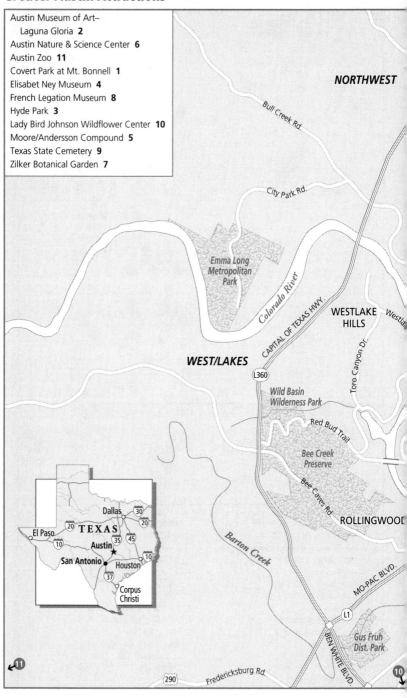

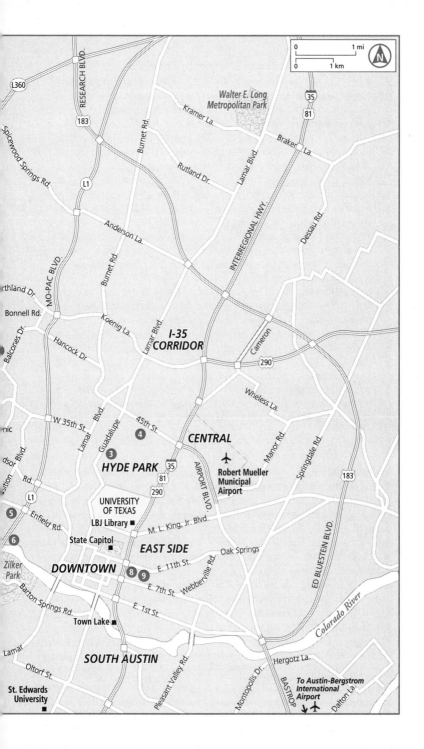

(Kids) Going Batty

Austin has the largest urban bat population in North America—much to the delight of Austinites. Some visitors are dubious at first, but it's impossible not to be impressed by the sight of 1.5 million of the creatures emerging en masse from under the Congress Avenue Bridge.

Each March, free-tailed bats migrate from central Mexico to various roost sites in the Southwest. In 1980, when a deck reconstruction of Austin's bridge created an ideal environment for bringing up babies, some 750,000 pregnant females began settling in every year. Each bat gives birth to a single pup, and by August these offspring take part in nightly forays west for bugs, usually around dusk. Depending on the size of the group, they might collectively munch on anywhere from 10,000 to 30,000 pounds of insects a night—one of the things that makes them so popular with Austinites. By November, these youngsters are old enough to hitch rides back south with their group on the winds of an early cold front.

While the bats are in town, an educational kiosk designed to dispel some of the more popular myths about them is set up each evening on the north bank of the river, just east of the bridge. You'll learn, for example, that bats are not rodents, they're not blind, and they're not in the least interested in getting in your hair. **Bat Conservation International** (② 512/327-9721; www.batcon.org), based in Austin, has lots of information—not to mention bat-related items for sale. Log on to the website or phone 800/538-BATS for a catalog. To find out when the bats are going to emerge from the bridge, call the *Austin American-Statesman* **Bat Hot Line** (② 512/416-5700, category 3636).

an impressive building, and the permanent displays—everything from Stephen F. Austin's diary to Neil Armstrong's spacesuit—and rotating exhibits are interesting enough but, for all the interactive video clips and engaging designs (lots of different rooms to duck into; varied floor surfaces), the presentations didn't strike me as dramatically different from those in history museums I toured as a kid. The real treat is the multimedia, special-effects Spirit Theater, the only one of its kind in Texas, where you can experience the high-speed whoosh of the great Galveston hurricane and feel your seats rattle as an East Texas oil well hits a gusher. Austin's only IMAX theater, with 3-D capabilities, is pretty dazzling too, though the films don't necessarily have a direct relation to Texas history. If you do everything (and at just $8.50 for a combination ticket for visitors ages 5–18, $6.50 for ages 3–4, you really should), plan to spend at least 2½ to 3 hours here.

1800 N. Congress Ave. ② 512/936-8746. www.TheStoryofTexas.com. Exhibit areas: $5.50 adults, $4.50 seniors 65 and over, $3 ages 5–18 (youth), free for children 4 and under. IMAX theater: $7 adults, $6 seniors, $5 youth. Texas Spirit Theater: $5 adults, $4 seniors, $3.50 youth. Combination tickets: Exhibits and IMAX $10/$8/$6/$5; exhibits and Spirit Theater $8.50/$6.50/$5/$3.50; exhibits and both theaters $14/$11/$8.50/$6.50 (children under 3 free to theaters if they sit in a parent's lap). Parking $3 with $5 minimum museum purchase, $5 otherwise (IMAX parking free after 6pm). Mon–Sat 9am–6pm; Sun noon–6pm. Phone or check website for additional IMAX evening hours. Closed Jan 1, Easter, Thanksgiving, and Dec 24–25. Bus: Orange or Blue 'Dillo.

State Capitol ★★ *Value*   The history of Texas's legislative center is as turbulent and dramatic as that of the state itself. The current 1888 capitol replaced an 1852 limestone statehouse that burned down in 1881. A land-rich but otherwise impecunious Texas government traded 3 million acres of public lands to contractors to finance its construction. Gleaming pink granite was donated to the cause, but a railroad had to be built to transport the material some 75 miles from Granite Mountain, near Marble Falls, to Austin. Texas convicts labored on the project alongside 62 stonecutters brought in from Scotland.

The result was the largest state capitol in the country, covering 3 acres and second only in size to the U.S. Capitol—but still, in typical Texas style, measuring 7 feet taller. The cornerstone alone weighs 16,000 pounds, and the total length of the wooden wainscoting runs approximately 7 miles. A splendid rotunda and dome lie at the intersection of the main corridors. The House and Senate chambers are located at opposite ends of the second level. Go up to the third-floor visitors' gallery during the legislative sessions if you want see how politics are conducted, Texas-style.

The building had become dingy and its offices warren-like over the past century, but a massive renovation and expansion in the 1990s—to the tune of $187.6 million—restored its grandeur. The expansion process itself is fascinating. Almost 700,000 tons of rock were chiseled from the ground to make way for an annex (often called the "inside-out, upside-down capitol"), constructed with similar materials and connected to the capitol and four other state buildings by tunnels. You can either opt for a 30- to 45-minute free guided tour or walk around on your own using self-guided tour pamphlets (one for the capitol, one for the grounds). Include the Capitol Visitors Center (see "More Attractions," below), and figure on spending a minimum of 2 hours here. Wear comfortable shoes; you'll be doing a lot of walking.

11th and Congress sts. ℂ **512/463-0063.** www.tspb.state.tx.us. Free admission. Mon–Fri 7am–10pm; Sat–Sun 9am–8pm; hours extended during legislative sessions (held in odd years, starting in Jan, for 140 straight calendar days). Closed all major holidays. Free guided tours. Mon–Fri 8:30am–4:30pm; Sat 9:30am–3:30pm; Sun noon–3:30. Bus: multiple bus lines; Orange, Red, Gold, or Blue 'Dillo.

CENTRAL

Barton Springs Pool ★★ *Kids*   If the University of Texas is the seat of Austin's intellect, and the state capitol is its political pulse, Barton Springs is the city's soul. The Native Americans who settled near here believed these waters had spiritual powers, and today's residents still place their faith in the abilities of the spring-fed pool to soothe and cool.

Each day, approximately 32 million gallons of water from the underground Edwards Aquifer bubble to the surface here, and at one time, this force powered several Austin mills. Although the original limestone bottom remains, concrete was added to the banks to form uniform sides to what is now a swimming pool of about 1,000 feet by 125 feet. Maintaining a constant 68°F (20°C) temperature, the amazingly clear water is bracing in summer and warming in winter, when many hearty souls brave the cold for a dip. Lifeguards are on duty for most of the day, and a large bathhouse operated by the Parks and Recreation Department offers changing facilities and a gift shop. For details about the Splash! environmental information center, see "Especially for Kids," later in this chapter.

Zilker Park, 2201 Barton Springs Rd. ℂ **512/476-9044.** www.ci.austin.tx.us/parks/bartonsprings.htm. Admission $3 adults, $2 ages 12–17, $1 seniors and children 11 and under (admission charged only after 9am Mar 13–Oct; free for early birds). Daily 5am–10pm except during pool maintenance (Thurs 9am–7pm). Lifeguard on duty Apr–Sept 8am–10pm; Oct to early Nov 8am–8pm; mid-Nov to Mar 9am–6pm. Gift shop and Splash! Tues–Fri noon–6pm; Sat–Sun 10am–6pm. Bus: 30 (Barton Creek Sq.).

LBJ Library and Museum ⭐ *Value* A presidential library may sound like a big yawn, but this one's almost as interesting as the 36th president to whom it's devoted. Lyndon Baines Johnson's popularity in Texas and his many successes in Washington are often forgotten in the wake of his resignation over the Vietnam War. The story of Johnson's long political career, starting with his early days as a state representative and continuing through to the Kennedy assassination and the groundbreaking Great Society legislation, is told through a variety of documents, mementos, and photographs. Johnson loved political cartoons, even when he was their butt, and examples from his large collection are among the museum's most interesting rotating exhibits. Other exhibits might include anything from photographs from the American Civil Rights era to a display of presidential holiday cards. Adults and kids alike are riveted by the animatronic version of LBJ. Dressed in his clothes and speaking with a tape recording of his voice, the life-size, gesticulating figure seems eerily alive from afar. From 1971, when it was dedicated, until his death in 1973, Johnson himself kept an office in this building, which commands an impressive campus view. A large, free parking lot next to the library makes it one of the few UT campus sights that's easy to drive up to.

University of Texas, 2313 Red River. ℂ 512/721-0200. www.lbjlib.utexas.edu. Free admission. Daily 9am–5pm. Closed Dec 25. Bus: 15; Blue or Orange 'Dillo; UT Shuttle.

SOUTH AUSTIN

Lady Bird Johnson Wildflower Center ⭐⭐⭐ Talk about fieldwork! The researchers at this lovely, colorful complex have 178 acres of wildflowers for their personal laboratory. Founded by Lady Bird Johnson in 1982, the center is dedicated to the study and preservation of native plants—and where better to survey them than in the Texas Hill Country, famous for its glorious spring blossoms?

The main attractions are naturally the display gardens—among them, one designed to attract butterflies—and the wildflower-filled meadow, but the native stone architecture of the visitor center and observation tower is attention grabbing, too. Included among the interesting indoor displays is one of Lady Bird's wide-brimmed gardening hats and a talking lawn mower with a British accent. There are usually free lectures and guided walks on the weekends—it's best to phone or check the website for current programs. The facility's research library is the largest in the United States for the study of native plants. The excellent gift shop sells packets of information about the species that are indigenous to your home state, as well as plant books and many creative botanical-related items. And you'll be buying for a good cause: Gift shop proceeds (as well as admission fees) all help fund the nonprofit organization. It'll take you at least a half-hour to drive here from central Austin, so plan to eat lunch here and spend a leisurely half-day.

4801 La Crosse Ave. ℂ 512/292-4200. www.wildflower.org. Admission $5 adults, $4 students and seniors 60 and up, $2 ages 5–12, free for children under 5. Tues–Sat 9am–5:30pm; Sun noon–5pm. (Mar–Apr rates go up to $7/$5 and grounds are open Mon.) Take Loop 1 (Mo-Pac) south to Slaughter Lane; drive ¾ mile to La Crosse Ave.

2 More Attractions

DOWNTOWN

ArtHouse at Jones Center An early-21st-century addition to downtown's art scene, the Jones Center is home to, and the exhibition venue for, ArtHouse (long known as Texas Fine Arts Association), which has promoted visual art in Texas since 1911. Its venerable history notwithstanding, this place is completely cutting edge. Genres range from representational to performance, and artists of all ethnicities are represented.

700 Congress Ave. © 512/453-5312. www.arthousetexas.org. Free admission. Tues–Wed and Fri 11am–7pm; Thurs 11am–9pm; Sat 10am–5pm; Sun 1–5pm. Bus: Red 'Dillo.

Austin History Center/Austin Public Library

Built in 1933, this Renaissance revival–style public library not only embodies some of the finest architecture, ironwork, and stone carving of its era, but also serves as the best resource for information about Austin from before the city's founding in 1839 to the present. The center also often hosts exhibitions drawn from its vast archives of historical photographs and sketches. And, of course, it's full of good books.

810 Guadalupe St. © 512/974-7480. www.ci.austin.tx.us./library. Free admission. Mon–Wed 10am–9pm; Sat 10am–6pm; Sun noon–6pm. Closed Thurs, Fri, and most holidays. Bus: 171; Blue or Silver 'Dillo.

Austin Museum of Art–Downtown

Plans for a major downtown museum of art have been in the works for more than 2 decades. This high-ceiling one-story space isn't it—plans are currently on hold, as art patrons were tapped out by contributing to the Blanton revamp (see below)—but this has developed into a cultural destination in its own right. Major-name shows—for example, Annie Liebovitz's music-related photographs in 2005—are complemented by exhibits of lesser-known local artists of consistently high quality.

823 Congress Ave. (at 9th St.). © 512/495-9224. www.amoa.org. Admission $5 adults, $4 seniors 55 and over and students, $1 for everyone Tues, free for children under 12. Tues–Wed and Fri–Sat 10am–6pm; Thurs 10am–8pm; Sun noon–5pm. Bus: Red, Gold, or Orange 'Dillo.

Bremond Block 🎯

"The family that builds together, bonds together" might have been the slogan of Eugene Bremond, an early Austin banker who established a mini real-estate monopoly for his own kin in the downtown area. In the mid-1860s, he started investing in land on what was once Block 80 of the original city plan. In 1874, he moved into a Greek revival home made by master builder Abner Cook. By the time he was through, he had created a family compound, purchasing and enlarging homes for himself, two sisters, a daughter, a son, and a brother-in-law. Some were destroyed, but those that remain on what is now known as the Bremond Block are exquisite examples of elaborate late-19th-century homes.

Between 7th and 8th, San Antonio and Guadalupe sts. Bus: Silver 'Dillo.

Capitol Visitors Center 🎯

The capitol wasn't the only important member of the state complex to undergo a face-lift. Texas also spent $4 million to gussy up its oldest surviving office building, the 1857 General Land Office. If the imposing German Romanesque structure looks a bit grand for the headquarters of an administrative agency, keep in mind that land has long been the state's most important resource. Among the employees of this important—and very political—office, charged with maintaining records and surveying holdings, was the writer O. Henry, who worked as a draftsman from 1887 to 1891. He based two short stories on his experiences here.

The building was rededicated as a visitor center for the Capitol Complex in the mid-1990s; the Texas Department of Transportation also distributes state travel information here. A Walter Cronkite–narrated video tells the history of the complex, and changing exhibits on the first floor highlight the Capitol

Preservation Project, while upstairs the displays focus on the Land Office and other aspects of Texas's past. A good gift shop carries lots of historical books and souvenirs.

112 E. 11th St. (southeast corner of Capitol grounds). ℂ **512/305-8400**. www.texascapitolvisitorscenter. com. Free admission. Daily 9am–5pm. Bus: Gold, Orange, Red, or Blue 'Dillo.

The Driskill   Col. Jesse Driskill was not a modest man. When he opened a hotel in 1886, he named it after himself, put busts of himself and his two sons over the entrances, and installed bas-relief sculptures of longhorn steers—to remind folks how he had made his fortune. Nor did he build a modest property. The ornate four-story structure, which originally boasted a sky-lit rotunda, has the largest arched doorway in Texas over its east entrance. It's so posh that the state legislature met here while the 1888 capitol was being built. The hotel has had its ups and downs over the years, but it was restored to its former glory in the late 1990s. You can pick up a history of the hotel at the front desk, and if the concierge has time, he'll be happy to help orient you.

604 Brazos St. ℂ **512/474-5911**. Bus: Silver, Blue, or Red 'Dillo.

Governor's Mansion ⭐   Although this is one of the oldest buildings in the city (1856), this opulent house is far from a mere symbol or museum piece. State law requires that the governor live here whenever he or she is in Austin. If the governor happens to be hosting a luncheon, you might notice warm smells wafting from the kitchen if you're on the last mansion tour of the day.

Living in the mansion isn't exactly a hardship, although it was originally built by Abner Cook without any indoor toilets (there are now seven). The house was beautifully restored in 1979, but you can still see the scars of nails that were hammered into the banister of the spiral staircase to break Governor Hogg's young son Tom of the habit of sliding down it. The nation's first female governor, Miriam "Ma" Ferguson, entertained her friend Will Rogers in the mansion, and Gov. John Connally recuperated here from gunshot wounds received when he accompanied John F. Kennedy on his fatal motorcade through Dallas. Among the many historical artifacts on display are a desk belonging to Stephen F. Austin and portraits of Davy Crockett and Sam Houston.

Tip: Only a limited number of visitors are allowed to tour the mansion, so make your required advance reservations as soon as you know when you're planning to visit—and at least 1 business day ahead of time.

1010 Colorado St. ℂ **512/463-5516** (recorded information) or **463-5518** (tour reservations). www.txfgm.org. Free admission. Tours generally offered every 20 min. Mon–Thurs 10–noon (last tour starts 11:40am). Closed Fri, weekends, some holidays, and at the discretion of the governor; call the 24-hr. information line to see if tours are offered the day you want to visit. Bus: Red, Blue, Gold, or Orange 'Dillo.

⌒**Fun Fact** **Old-Fashioned Moonlight**

Austin is the only city in the world to preserve its first public electric lights—17 of the original 31 "moonlight towers" from 1894 are still operating around the city. A special moonlight tower was erected for scenes in the movie *Dazed and Confused* when it was filmed in Austin by one of the state's native sons, Richard Linklater.

MEXIC-ARTE Museum   The first organization in Austin to promote multi-cultural contemporary art when it was formed in 1983, MEXIC-ARTE has a small permanent collection of 20th-century Mexican art, including photographs from the Mexican revolution and a fascinating array of masks from the state of Guerrero. It's supplemented by visiting shows—including some from Mexico, such as a recent survey of south-of-the-border contemporary art—and a back gallery of works of local Latino artists.

419 Congress Ave. ✆ 512/480-9373. www.mexic-artemuseum.org. Admission $5 adults, $4 seniors and students, $1 children under 12. Mon–Thurs 10am–6pm; Fri–Sat 10am–5pm; Sun 1–4pm for special exhibitions. Bus: Red 'Dillo.

O. Henry Museum   When William Sidney Porter, better known as O. Henry, lived in Austin (1884–98), he published a popular satirical newspaper called *Rolling Stone.* He also held down an odd string of jobs, including a stint as a teller at the First National Bank of Austin, where he was later accused of embezzling funds. It was while he was serving time for this crime that he wrote the 13 short stories that established his literary reputation. The modest Victorian cottage in which O. Henry lived with his wife and daughter from 1893 to 1895 showcases the family's bedroom furniture, silverware, and china, as well as the desk at which the author wrote copy for his failed publication. Temporary exhibits, which change throughout the year, include displays of O. Henry letters. Visitors are asked to wear flat, soft-soled shoes to prevent damage to the original pine floors.

409 E. 5th St. ✆ 512/472-1903. www.ci.austin.tx.us/parks/ohenry.htm. Free admission. Wed–Sun noon–5pm. Closed Thanksgiving, Dec 25, and Jan 1. Bus: Blue 'Dillo.

Old Bakery and Emporium   On the National Register of Historic Landmarks, the Old Bakery was built in 1876 by Charles Lundberg, a Swedish master baker, and continuously operated until 1936. You can still see the giant oven and wooden baker's spade inside. Rescued from demolition by the Austin Heritage Society, and now owned and operated by Austin's Parks and Recreation Department, the brick-and-limestone building is one of the few unaltered structures on Congress Avenue. It houses a gift shop, selling crafts handmade by seniors, a reasonably priced lunchroom (open 11am–1:30pm), and a hospitality desk with visitors' brochures.

1006 Congress Ave. ✆ 512/477-5961. www.ci.austin.tx.us/parks/bakery1.htm. Free admission. Mon–Fri 9am–4pm; first 3 Sat in Dec 10am–2pm. Closed most holidays. Bus: Red, Gold, or Orange 'Dillo.

Sixth Street   Formerly known as Pecan Street—all the east–west thoroughfares in Austin were originally named for trees—Sixth Street was once the main connecting road to the older settlements east of Austin. During the Reconstruction boom of the 1870s, the wooden wagon yards and saloons of the 1850s and 1860s began to be replaced by the more solid masonry structures you see today. After the new state capitol was built in 1888, the center of commercial activity began shifting toward Congress Avenue, and by the middle of the next century, Sixth Street had become a skid row.

Restoration of the 9 blocks designated a National Register District began in the late 1960s. In the 1970s, the street blossomed into a live-music center. Austin's former main street is now lined with restaurants, galleries, theaters, nightspots, and shops. The section east of Congress is still somewhat deserted during the day, when the roots of its sleazy past show in tattoo parlors and S&M leather shops. But that's changing, as wrecking balls seem to be swinging on every square inch of downtown. The streets west of Congress are seeing an increase in upscale business activity, and on weekend nights a mostly young crowd throngs the sidewalks of the entire stretch for club crawls.

Between Lavaca Ave. and I-35. Bus: Silver 'Dillo.

Treaty Oak   Legend has it that Stephen F. Austin signed the first boundary treaty with the Comanches under the spreading branches of this 500-year-old live oak, which once served as the symbolic border between Anglo and Indian territory. Whatever the case, this is the sole remaining tree in what was once a grove of Council Oaks—which made the well-publicized attempt on its life in the late 1980s especially shocking. But almost as dramatic as the story of the tree's deliberate poisoning by an attention-seeking Austinite is the tale of its rescue by an international team of foresters. The dried wood from major limbs that they removed was allocated to local artists, whose works were auctioned off for the tree's 500th anniversary in 1993. Now such items as pen sets, gavels, and clocks made out of the tree's severed limbs are for sale, with proceeds going to plant additional trees throughout public areas of Austin.

503 Baylor St., between W. 5th and 6th sts. ✆ 512/440-5194. www.ci.austin.tx.us/treatyoak. Bus: Silver 'Dillo.

CENTRAL

Austin Museum of Art–Laguna Gloria ★   Perched on 12½ palm- and pecan-shaded acres overlooking Lake Austin—believed by some to be part of a claim staked out for his retirement by Stephen F. Austin, who didn't live to enjoy the view—this lovely Mediterranean-style villa was built in 1916 by Austin newspaper publisher Hal Sevier and his wife, Clara Driscoll, best known for her successful crusade to save the Alamo from commercial development. The mansion was long used to host major traveling art shows, but, since it reopened in late 2003 following a $3.5 million renovation, the focus instead is on the historic aspects of the home and grounds. The lower-profile art exhibits held here no longer distract from the architecture and landscaping, which speak for themselves.

Tip: If the weather's nice, bring along a picnic lunch to enjoy by the lake. It's one of the prettiest spots in the city and, during the week, one of the most peaceful.

3809 W. 35th St. ✆ 512/458-8191. www.amoa.org. 1 mile past west end of 35th St. at the foot of Mt. Bonnell. Bus: 9 (Sat only).

Blanton Museum of Art   The Blanton is ranked among the top university art museums in the United States, featuring some of the most important art in the country. Most notable is the Suida-Manning Collection, a superb gathering of Renaissance works by such masters as Veronese, Rubens, and Tiepolo that was sought after by the Metropolitan museum, among others. Other permanent holdings include the Mari and James Michener collection of 20th-century American masters, the largest gathering of Latin American art in the United States, and a rare display of 19th-century plaster casts of monumental Greek and Roman sculpture.

Unfortunately, a new structure planned to highlight these impressive works isn't open yet. Scheduled to debut in early 2006 on MLK and Speedway (across from the Bob Bullock History Center), the new Blanton art space will help connect the university with the capitol complex. Meantime, you can still view portions of its impressive collection—albeit in a less than optimum setting inside a University of Texas building.

University of Texas, Art Building, 23rd St. and San Jacinto Blvd. ✆ 512/471-7324. www.blantonmuseum. org. Free admission. Tues–Thurs 10am–5pm (until 7pm Thurs); Sat–Sun 1–5pm. Closed university holidays. Bus: UT Shuttle.

Elisabet Ney Museum ⚐ Strong-willed and eccentric, German-born sculptor Elisabet Ney nevertheless charmed Austin society in the late 19th century. When she died, her admirers turned her Hyde Park studio into a museum. In the former loft and working area—part Greek temple, part medieval battlement—visitors can view plaster replicas of many of the artist's sculptures. Drawn toward the larger-than-life figures of her age, Ney had created busts of Schopenhauer, Garibaldi, and Bismarck by the time she was commissioned to make models of native Texas heroes Stephen F. Austin and Sam Houston for an 1893 Chicago exposition. William Jennings Bryan, Enrico Caruso, Jan Paderewski, and four Texas governors were among the many visitors to her Austin studio.

304 E. 44th St. ✆ **512/458-2255.** www.ci.austin.tx.us/elisabetney. Free admission. Wed–Sat 10am–5pm; Sun noon–5pm. Bus: 1 or 5.

Harry Ransom Humanities Research Center ⚐ The special collections of the Harry Ransom Center (HRC) contain approximately 1 million rare books (including a Gutenberg Bible, one of only five complete copies in the U.S.); 30 million literary manuscripts (including those by James Joyce, Ernest Hemingway, and Tennessee Williams); 5 million photographs, including the world's first; and more than 100,000 works of art, with several pieces by Diego Rivera and Frida Kahlo. Most of this wealth remains in the domain of scholars, although anyone can request a look at it, but since two new galleries were opened in 2003, visitors are treated to select portions of it in excellent rotating exhibitions. In 2004, for example, one display contrasted the lives and achievements of contemporaries Graham Greene and Evelyn Waugh, while another highlighted the manuscripts and prints of Walker Evans and James Agee. Check the website for the various lectures, plays, and poetry readings held here, too, and for displays at the affiliated Leeds Gallery.

University of Texas, Harry Ransom Center, 21st and Guadalupe sts. ✆ **512/471-8944.** www.hrc.utexas.edu. Free admission. Galleries Tues–Wed and Fri 10am–5pm; Thurs 10am–7pm; Sat–Sun noon–5pm; call for reading-room hours. Closed university holidays. Bus: Blue 'Dillo; UT Shuttle.

Hyde Park Unlike Eugene Bremond (see "Downtown," earlier in this chapter), developer Monroe Martin Shipe built homes for the middle, not upper, classes. In the 1890s, he created, and tirelessly promoted, a complex-cum-resort at the southwest edge of Austin. He even built an electric streetcar system to connect it with the rest of the city. By the middle of this century, Austin's first planned suburb had become somewhat shabby, but recent decades of gentrification have turned the tide. Now visitors can amble along pecan-shaded streets and look at beautifully restored residences, many in pleasing combinations of late Queen Anne and early craftsman styles. Shipe's own architecturally eclectic home, at 3816 Ave. G, is a bit grander than some of the others, but not much.

Between E. 38th and E. 45th, Duval and Guadalupe sts. Bus: 1 or 7.

Moore/Andersson Compound Architecture buffs won't want to miss the hacienda-like compound where Charles Moore spent the last decade of his life—when he wasn't traveling, that is. The peripatetic American architect, who kept a low profile but had a great influence on postmodernism, built five homes, but this one, which he designed with Arthur Andersson, perfectly demonstrates his combination of controlled freedom, whimsical imagination, and connection to the environment. The wildly colorful rooms are filled with folk art from around the world, while odd angles, bunks, and dividers render every inch of space fascinating. In the evening, the compound is now used as a conference and lecture center. Tours are led by enthusiastic graduate students in historic preservation at the University of Texas, where Moore held his last chair in architecture.

2102 Quarry Rd. ℂ **512/477-4557.** www.charlesmoore.org. Tours $10 adults, $4 students. By appointment only.

Neill-Cochran Museum House   Abner Cook, the architect-contractor responsible for the governor's mansion and many of the city's other gracious Greek Revival mansions, built this home in 1855. It bears his trademark portico with six Doric columns and a balustrade designed with crossed sheaves of wheat. Almost all its doors, windows, shutters, and hinges are original—which is rather astonishing when you consider the structure's history: The house was used as the city's first Blind Institute in 1856 and then as a hospital for Union prisoners near the end of the Civil War. The beautifully maintained 18th- and 19th-century furnishings are interesting, but many people come just to see the painting of bluebonnets that helped convince legislators to designate these native blooms as the state flower.

2310 San Gabriel St. ℂ **512/478-2335.** Admission $5 adults, free for children under 10. Wed–Sun 2–5pm; free 20-min. tours given (with admission). Bus: Gold 'Dillo; UT shuttle.

Texas Memorial Museum (Kids)   This museum, opened in 1936 to guard the natural and cultural treasures of the state, is now devoted to the natural sciences alone. Despite a major revamp in the early 2000s, it still seems oddly old-fashioned in parts, especially the lifeless dioramas and weird stuff in jars on the fourth floor. But kids will like first-floor Hall of Geology, with its huge Texas Pterosaur—the largest flying creature ever found—suspended from the ceiling. And the admission price is right, and the gift shop carries lots of good science toys.

University of Texas, 2400 Trinity St. ℂ **512/471-1604.** www.texasmemorialmuseum.org. Free admission (donations appreciated). Mon–Fri 9am–5pm; Sat 10am–5pm; Sun 1–5pm. Closed major holidays. Bus: 7, 103, 110, 127, 171, or 174; Orange 'Dillo.

Umlauf Sculpture Garden & Museum   This is a great museum for people who don't enjoy being cooped up in a stuffy, hushed space. An art instructor at the University of Texas for 40 years, Charles Umlauf donated his home, studio, and more than 250 pieces of artwork to the city of Austin, which maintains the lovely native garden where much of the sculpture is displayed. Umlauf, whose pieces reside in such places as the Smithsonian Institution and New York's Metropolitan Museum, worked in many media and styles. He also used a variety of models, though you'll probably recognize the portrait of Umlauf's most famous UT student, Farrah Fawcett. The museum video is captioned for those who are hearing-impaired, and with advance notice, "touch tours" can be arranged for those who are blind or visually impaired.

605 Robert E. Lee Rd. ℂ **512/445-5582.** www.umlaufsculpture.org. Admission $3.50 adults, $2.50 seniors, $1 students, free for children under 6. Wed–Fri 10am–4:30pm; Sat–Sun 1–4:30pm (Sat 10am–4:30pm June–Aug). Closed major holidays. Bus: 29 or 30.

University of Texas at Austin   In 1883, the 221 students and eight teachers who made up the newly established University of Texas in Austin had to meet in makeshift classrooms in the town's temporary capitol. At the time, the two million acres of dry west Texas land that the higher educational system had been granted barely brought in 40¢ an acre for grazing. Now, nearly 50,000 students occupy 120 buildings on UT's main campus alone, and that arid west Texas land, which blew a gusher in 1923, has raked in more than $4 billion in oil money—two-thirds of it directed to the UT school system.

The Texas Union Information Center, at 24th and Guadalupe (ℂ **512/475-6636**), is the best place to get information about the campus; it's open

Monday through Friday from 7am to 3am (really), Saturday from 10am to 3am, and Sunday from noon to 3am. In addition, you can pick up campus maps and other UT Austin–related materials at the ground floor of the Main building/UT Tower (near 24th and Whitis), which is also the point of departure for free campus tours—they're designed for prospective students and their families, but anyone can come. These leave weekdays at 11am and 2pm (only at 2pm in Dec and May) and Saturday at 2pm. Call ✆ **512/475-7399,** option 2, for recorded details. It's a lot tougher to get on the free Moonlight Prowl Tours, packed with amusing anecdotes of student life and campus lore, because they're held only a few evenings a month and they fill up quickly, but if you want to give it a try, log on to **www.utexas.edu/tours/prowl** and fill out the registration form.

See also "The Top Attractions," earlier in this chapter, for more on the LBJ Library and Museum; listings above in this section for the Harry Ransom Humanities Research Center, Blanton Museum of Art, and Texas Memorial Museum; the Walking Tour of university sights section, later; and information on visiting the UT Tower in the "Organized Tours" section, later in this chapter.

Guadalupe and I-35, Martin Luther King Jr. Blvd. and 26th St. ✆ **512/471-3434.** www.utexas.edu.

EAST SIDE

French Legation Museum   The oldest residence still standing in Austin was built in 1841 for Count Alphonse Dubois de Saligny, France's representative to the fledgling Republic of Texas. Although his home was very extravagant for the then-primitive capital, the flamboyant de Saligny didn't stay around to enjoy it for very long: He left town in a huff after his servant was beaten in retaliation for making bacon out of some pigs that had dined on the diplomat's linens. In the back of the house, considered the best example of French colonial–style architecture outside Louisiana, is a re-creation of the only known authentic Creole kitchen in the United States.

802 San Marcos. ✆ **512/472-8180.** www.frenchlegationmuseum.org. Admission $4 adults, $3 seniors, $2 students/teachers, free for children 5 and under. Tours Tues–Sun 1–4:30pm. Bus: 4 and 18 stop nearby (at San Marcos and 7th sts.); Silver 'Dillo. Go east on 7th St., then turn left on San Marcos St.; the parking lot is behind the museum on Embassy and 9th sts.

Texas State Cemetery ⚐   The city's namesake, Stephen F. Austin, is the best-known resident of this East Side cemetery, established by the state in 1851. Judge Edwin Waller, who laid out the grid plan for Austin's streets and later served as the city's mayor, also rests here, as do eight former Texas governors, various fighters in Texas's battles for independence, a woman who lived to tell the tale of the Alamo, and Barbara Jordan, the first black woman from the South elected to the U.S. Congress (in 1996, she became the first African American to gain admittance to these grounds). Perhaps the most striking monument, sculpted by Elisabet Ney (see "Central," above), commemorates Confederate general Albert Sidney Johnston, who died at the Battle of Shiloh.

You can pick up two self-guided-tour pamphlets at the visitor center/museum, which is designed to suggest the long barracks at the Alamo. The one published by the cemetery details the restorations completed in the 1990s and sketches the histories of some of the most important residents, while the one created by the Austin Convention and Visitors Bureau offers a wider historical context and gives some headstone highlights.

909 Navasota St. ✆ **512/463-0605.** www.cemetery.state.tx.us. Free admission. Grounds daily 8am–5pm; visitor center Mon–Fri 8am–5pm. Bus: 4 and 18 stop nearby.

AUSTIN OUTDOORS

LAKES

Highland Lakes   The six dams built by the Lower Colorado River Authority in the late 1930s through the early 1950s not only controlled the flooding that had plagued the areas surrounding Texas's Colorado River (not to be confused with the more famous river of the same name to the north), but also transformed the waterway into a sparkling chain of lakes, stretching some 150 miles northwest of Austin. The narrowest of them, Town Lake, is also the closest to downtown. The heart of urban recreation in Austin, it boasts a shoreline park and adjacent hike-and-bike trail. Lake Austin, the next in line, is more residential, but offers Emma Long Park (see "Parks & Gardens," below) as a public shore. Serious aquatic enthusiasts go all the way to Lake Travis, the longest lake in the chain, which offers the most possibilities for playing in the water. Together with the other Highland Lakes—Marble Falls, LBJ, Inks, and Buchanan, some of which are discussed in chapter 17—these compose the largest concentration of freshwater lakes in Texas. See also "Staying Active," later in this chapter, for activity and equipment-rental suggestions.

MOUNTAINS

Covert Park at Mount Bonnell ⭐   For the best views of the city and Hill Country, ascend this mountaintop park, at 785 feet the highest point in Austin. The oldest tourist attraction in town, it has also long been a favorite spot for romantic trysts, and rumor has it that any couple who climbed the 106 stone steps to the top together would fall in love (an emotion often confused with exhaustion). The peak was named for George W. Bonnell, Sam Houston's commissioner of Indian affairs in 1836, while the far-from-secret park at the summit gets its moniker from Frank M. Covert, Jr., who donated the land to the city in 1939.

3800 Mt. Bonnell Rd. No phone. Free admission. Daily 5am–10pm. Take Mt. Bonnell Rd. 1 mile past the west end of W. 35th St.

NATURE PRESERVES

For information on **Wild Basin Wilderness Preserve,** see "Organized Tours," later in this chapter.

City of Austin Nature Preserves   Highlights of the remarkably diverse group of natural habitats Austin boasts in its city-run nature preserves include **Blunn Creek** (1100 block of St. Edward's Dr.), 40 acres of upland woods and meadows traversed by a spring-fed creek. One of the two lookout areas is made of compacted volcanic ash. Spelunkers will like **Goat Cave** (3900 Deer Lane), which is honeycombed with limestone caves and sinkholes. You can arrange for cave tours by phoning the **Austin Nature Center** (© **512/327-8181**). Lovely **Mayfield Park** (3505 W. 35th St.) directly abuts the Barrow Brook Cove of Lake Austin. Peacocks and hens roam freely around lily ponds, and trails cross over bridges in oak and juniper woods. Visitors to the rock-walled ramada (a shaded shelter) at the **Zilker Preserve** (Barton Springs Rd. and Loop 1), with its meadows, streams, and cliff, can look out over downtown Austin. All the preserves are maintained in a primitive state with natural surface trails and no restrooms. The preserves are free, and open daily from dawn to dusk. For additional information, including directions, phone © **512/327-7723,** or log on to www.ci.austin.tx.us/preserves.

Westcave Preserve   If you don't like the weather in one part of Westcave Preserve, you might like it better in another: Up to a 25°F (–4°C) difference in temperature has been recorded between the highest area of this beautiful natural habitat, an arid Hill Country scrub, and the lowest, a lush woodland spread across a canyon floor. Because the ecosystem here is so delicate, the 30 acres on the Pedernales River may be entered only by guided tour. Reservations are taken for weekday visits, while on weekends, the first 30 people to show up at the allotted times are allowed in.

Star Rte. 1, Dripping Springs. ✆ 830/825-3442. www.westcave.org. Free admission Sat–Sun for tours at 10am, noon, 2pm, and 4pm (weather permitting). Take Hwy. 71 to Ranch Rd. 3238. Follow the signs 15 miles to Hamilton Pool, across the Pedernales River Bridge from the preserve.

OUTDOOR ART

Philosophers' Rock   Glenna Goodacre's wonderfully witty bronze sculpture of three of Austin's most recognized personalities from mid-century—naturalist Roy Bedichek, humorist J. Frank Dobie, and historian Walter Prescott Webb—captures the essence of the three friends who used to schmooze together at Barton Springs Pool. No heroic posing here: Two of the three are wearing bathing trunks, which reveal potbellies, wrinkles, and sagging muscles, and all three are sitting down in mid-discussion. The casual friendliness of the pose and the intelligence of the men's expressions have made this piece, installed in 1994, an Austin favorite.

Zilker Park, 2201 Barton Springs Rd., just outside the entrance to Barton Springs Pool.

Stevie Ray Vaughan Statue   In contrast to the Philosophers' Rock (see above), Ralph Roehming's bronze tribute to Austin singer/songwriter Stevie Ray Vaughan is artificial and awkward. Although he's wearing his habitual flat-brimmed hat and poncho, the stiffly posed Stevie Ray looks more like a frontiersman with a gun than a rock star with a guitar. But his devoted fans don't seem to mind, as evidenced by the flowers and devotions that almost always can be found at the foot of the statue.

South side of Town Lake, adjacent to Auditorium Shores.

PARKS & GARDENS

Emma Long Metropolitan Park   More than 1,100 acres of woodland and a mile of shore along Lake Austin make Emma Long Park—named after the first woman to sit on Austin's city council—a most appealing metropolitan space. Water activities revolve around two boat ramps, a fishing dock, and a protected swimming area, guarded by lifeguards on summer weekends. This is the only city park to offer camping, with permits ($6 for open camping, $15 utility camping in addition to entry fee) available on a first-come, first-served basis. If you hike through the stands of oak, ash, and juniper to an elevation of 1,000 feet, you'll get a view of the city spread out before you. Note that the park closes whenever its maximum capacity is reached.

1706 City Park Rd. ✆ 512/346-1831 or 346-3807. Admission $5 per vehicle Mon–Thurs; $8 Fri–Sun and holidays. Daily 7am–10pm. Exit I-35 at 290W, then go west (street names will change to Koenig, Allendale, Northland, and FM 2222) to City Park Rd. (near Loop 360). Turn south (left) and drive 6¼ miles to park entrance.

Zilker Botanical Garden ✿ *Kids*   There's bound to be something blooming at the Zilker Botanical Garden from March to October, but no matter what time of year you visit, you'll find this a soothing outdoor oasis to spend some time in. The Oriental Garden, created by the landscape architect Isamu Taniguchi when he was 70 years old, is particularly peaceful. Be sure to ask someone at the garden center to point out how Taniguchi landscaped the word "Austin" into a series of ponds in the design. A butterfly garden attracts gorgeous winged visitors during April and October migrations, and you can poke and prod the many plants in the herb garden to get them to yield their fragrances. One hundred million–year–old dinosaur tracks, discovered on the grounds in the early 1990s, are part of the 1.5-acre Hartman Prehistoric Garden, which includes plants from the Cretaceous Period and a 13-foot bronze sculpture of an Ornithomimus dinosaur.

2220 Barton Springs Rd. ⓒ 512/477-8672. http://zilkergarden.org. Free admission. Grounds dawn–dusk. Garden center Mon–Fri 8:30am–4pm; Sat 10am–5pm (Jan–Feb 1–5pm); Sun 1–5pm (sometimes open earlier on weekends for special garden shows; phone ahead). Bus: 30.

Zilker Park ⓡ *Kids*   Comprising 347 acres, the first 40 of which were donated to the city by the wealthy German immigrant for whom the park is named, this is Austin's favorite public playground. Its centerpiece is Barton Springs Pool (see "The Top Attractions," earlier in this chapter), but visitors and locals also flock to the Zilker Botanical Garden, the Austin Nature Preserves, and the Umlauf Sculpture Garden and Museum, all described in this chapter. See also the "Especially for Kids" and "Staying Active" sections for details about the Austin Nature and Science Center, the Zilker Zephyr Miniature Train, and Town Lake canoe rentals. In addition to its athletic fields (nine for soccer, one for rugby, and two multiuse), the park hosts a 9-hole disk (Frisbee) golf course and a sand volleyball court.

2201 Barton Springs Rd. ⓒ 512/476-9044. www.ci.austin.tx.us/zilker. Free admission. Daily 5am–10pm. Bus: 30.

3 Especially for Kids

The Bob Bullock Texas State History Museum and the **Texas Memorial Museum,** both described in earlier sections, are child-friendly, but outdoor attractions are still Austin's biggest draw for children. There's lots of room for children to splash around at **Barton Springs,** and even youngsters who thought bats were creepy are likely to be converted on further acquaintance with the critters. In addition, the following attractions are especially geared toward children.

Austin Children's Museum ⓡ   Located in a large, state-of-the-art facility, this excellent children's museum has something for people of all ages. Tots enjoy the low-key but creative playscapes, in between takes on a variety of "creation stations," and such grown-up environments as a studio sound stage (part of "Austin Kiddie Limits") please even incipient adolescents. Parents will get a kick out of the replica Austin city landscapes, including the recently introduced Rising Star Ranch, where a Hill Country pond is stocked with wooden musical frogs. Rotating exhibits, such as one on bats in 2004–05 ("If you could fly with your fingers, eat half your weight in bugs, see with your ears, and sleep upside down, you'd have your own exhibit too!") keep the museum continuously interesting.

Dell Discovery Center, 201 Colorado St. ⓒ 512/472-2499. www.austinkids.org. Admission $5.50, $3.50 for children 12–23 mo., free for children under 12 months. Tues–Sat 10am–5pm; Sun noon–5pm; donations only Wed 5–8pm, free Sun 4–5pm. Closed Mon and some holidays. Bus: 2, 10, 12, 15, 16, or 64; Red or Orange 'Dillo.

Austin Nature and Science Center ⓡ   Bats, bees, and crystal caverns are among the subjects of the Discovery Lab at this museum in the 80-acre Nature Center, which features lots of interactive exhibits. The tortoises, lizards, porcupine, and vultures in the Animal Exhibits—among more than 90 orphaned or injured creatures brought here from the wild—also hold kids' attention. An Eco-Detective trail highlights pond-life awareness. The Dino Pit, with its replicas of

Texas fossils and dinosaur tracks, is a lure for budding paleontologists. A variety of specialty camps, focusing on everything from caving to astronomy, are offered from late May through August.

Zilker Park, 301 Nature Center Dr. © 512/327-8181. www.ci.austin.tx.us/ansc. Donations requested; occasional special exhibits charge separately. Mon–Sat 9am–5pm; Sun noon–5pm. Closed July 4, Thanksgiving, and Dec 25. Bus: 30.

Austin Zoo   This small zoo, some 14 miles southwest of downtown, may not feature the state-of-the-jungle habitats of larger facilities, but it's easy to get up close and personal with the critters here. Most of the animal residents, who range from turkeys and potbellied pigs to marmosets and tigers, were mistreated, abandoned, or illegally imported before they found a home here. It costs $2.25 to board the 1½-mile miniature train for a scenic Hill Country ride, which lets you peer at some of the shyer animals. There are no food concessions here, just plenty of picnic tables.

10807 Rawhide Trail. © 512/288-1490. www.austinzoo.org. Admission $6 adults, $5 seniors, $4 children 2–12, free for children under 2. Daily 10am–6pm. Closed Thanksgiving and Dec 25. Take Hwy. 290W to Circle Dr., turn right, go 1.5 miles to Rawhide Trail, and turn right.

Splash! Into the Edwards Aquifer   The Edwards Aquifer, Austin's main source of water, is fed by a variety of underground creeks filtered through a large layer of limestone. You'll feel as though you're entering one of this vast ecosystem's sinkholes when you walk into the dimly lit enclosure—formerly the bathhouse at Barton Springs pool—where a variety of interactive displays grab kids' attention. Young visitors can make it rain on the city, identify water bugs, or peer through a periscope at swimmers. Although the focus is on the evils of pollution, the agenda is by no means heavy-handed.

Zilker Park, 2201 Barton Springs Rd. © 512/481-1466. www.ci.austin.tx.us./splash. Free admission. Tues–Sat 10am–5pm; Sun noon–5pm. Bus: 30 (Barton Creek Sq.).

Zilker Zephyr Miniature Train   Take a scenic 25-minute ride through Zilker Park on a narrow-gauge, light-rail miniature train, which takes you at a leisurely pace along Barton Creek and Town Lake. The train departs approximately every hour on the hour during the week and every half-hour on the weekend, weather permitting.

Zilker Park, 2100 Barton Springs Rd. (just across from the Barton Springs Pool). © 512/478-8286. Admission $2.75 adults, $1.75 under 12 and seniors, free for infants (under 1) on guardian's lap. Mon–Fri 10am–5pm; Sat–Sun 10am–7pm. Bus: 30.

4 Special-Interest Sightseeing

AFRICAN-AMERICAN HERITAGE

The many contributions of Austin's African-American community are highlighted at **George Washington Carver Museum and Cultural Center,** 1165 Angelina St. (© **512/472-4809;** www.ci.austin.tx.us/carver), the first in Texas devoted to black history. Rotating exhibits of contemporary artwork share the space with photographs, videos, oral histories, and other artifacts from the community's past. A number of other sites on the East Side are worth visiting, too. Less than 2 blocks from the Carver, on the corner of Hackberry and San Bernard streets, stands the **Wesley United Methodist Church.** Established at the end of the Civil War, it was one of the leading black churches in Texas. Diagonally across the street, the **Zeta Phi Beta Sorority,** Austin's first black Greek letter house, occupies the Thompson House, built in 1877, which is also the archival center for the Texas chapter of the sorority. Nearby, at the **State Cemetery** (see "More Attractions," earlier in this chapter), you can visit the gravesite of congresswoman and civil rights leader Barbara Jordan, the first African American to be buried here.

About a half-mile away, the sparsely furnished **Henry G. Madison Cabin** was built around 1863 by a black homesteader. When it was donated to the city in 1873, it was relocated to the grounds of the **Rosewood Park Recreation Center,** 2300 Rosewood Ave. (© **512/472-6838,** www.ci.austin.tx.us/parks/rosewood. htm). The cabin is being treated for termite damage but should be reopened to the public by spring 2005. You have to go across town, to the near west side, to explore the neighborhood known as **Clarksville,** which was founded by a former slave in 1871 as a utopian community for freed blacks, though it's an almost entirely white artists' enclave now.

For a more up-to-date look at the Austin scene, visit **Mitchie's Fine Art & Gift Gallery,** 6406 I-35 (Lincoln Village Shopping Center), Suite 2800 (© **512/323-6901;** www.mitchie.com), and **Bydee Arts & Gifts,** 412 E. Sixth St. (© **512/474-4343;** www.bydee.com), both offering a good selection of African-American painting and sculpture.

5 Strolling Around the University of Texas

No ivory tower (although it has several of them), the University of Texas is as integral to Austin's identity as it is to its economy. To explore the vast main campus is to glimpse the city's future as well as its past. Here, state-of-the-art structures—including information kiosks that can play the school's team songs—sit cheek by jowl with elegant examples of 19th-century architecture. The following tour points out many of the most interesting spots on campus. Unless you regularly trek the Himalayas, however, you'll probably want to drive or take a bus between some of the first seven sights. (Parking limitations were taken into account in this initial portion of the circuit.) For a walking-only tour, begin at stop 8; also note that stops 2, 5, 6, 12, and 20 are discussed earlier in this chapter, and stop 9 is detailed in the "Organized Tours" section, below.

WALKING TOUR   UT AUSTIN

Start:	The Arno Nowotny Building.
Finish:	The Littlefield Fountain.
Time:	1 hour, not including food breaks or museum visits.
Best Times:	On the weekends, when the campus is less crowded, more parking is available, and the Tower is open.
Worst Times:	Morning and midday during the week when classes are in session and parking is impossible to find. (**Beware:** Those tow-away zone signs mean business.)

In 1839, the Congress of the Republic of Texas ordered a site set aside for the establishment of a "university of the first class" in Austin. Some 40 years later, when the flagship of the new University of Texas system opened, its first two buildings went up on that original 40-acre plot, dubbed College Hill. Although there were attempts to establish master-design plans for the university from the turn of the century onward, they were only carried out in bits and pieces until 1930, when money from an earlier oil strike on UT land allowed the school to

1 Arno Nowotny Building

2 LBJ Library and Museum

3 Performing Arts Center

4 Darrell K. Royal/Texas Memorial Stadium

5 Art Building

6 Texas Memorial Museum

7 Santa Rita No. 1

8 Littlefield Memorial Fountain

9 Main Building and Tower

10 Garrison Hall

11 Battle Hall

12 Flawn Academic Center

13 Hogg Auditorium

14 Battle Oaks

15 Littlefield Home

16 The Drag

17 Texas Union Building

18 Goldsmith Hall

19 Sutton Hall

20 Harry Ransom Humanities
   Research Center

begin building in earnest. Between 1930 and 1945, consulting architect Paul Cret put his mark on 19 university buildings, most showing the influence of his education at Paris's Ecole des Beaux-Arts. If the entire 357-acre campus will never achieve stylistic unity, its earliest section has a grace and cohesion that make it a delight to stroll.

Though it begins at the oldest building owned by the university, this tour begins far from the original campus. At the frontage road of I-35 and the corner of Martin Luther King Jr. Boulevard, pull into the parking lot of:

❶ The Arno Nowotny Building

In the 1850s, several state-run asylums for the mentally ill and the physically handicapped arose on the outskirts of Austin. One of these was the State Asylum for the Blind, built by Abner Cook around 1856. The ornate Italianate-style structure soon became better known as the headquarters and barracks of General Custer, who had been sent to Austin in 1865 to reestablish order after the Civil War. Incorporated into the university and restored for its centennial celebration, the building is now used for administration.

Take Martin Luther King Jr. Boulevard to Red River, then drive north to the:

❷ LBJ Library and Museum

This library and museum offers another rare on-campus parking lot. (You'll want to leave your car here while you see sights 3–6.) The first presidential library to be built on a university campus, the huge travertine marble structure oversees a beautifully landscaped 14-acre complex. Among the museum's exhibits is a seven-eighths scale replica of the Oval Office as it looked when the Johnsons occupied the White House. In the adjoining Sid Richardson Hall are the Lyndon B. Johnson School of Public Affairs and the Barker Texas History Center, housing the world's most extensive collection of Texas memorabilia.

Stroll down the library steps across East Campus Drive to 23rd Street, where, next to the large Burleson bells on your right, you'll see the university's $41 million:

❸ Performing Arts Center

This arts center includes the 3,000-seat Bass Concert Hall, the 700-seat Bates Recital Hall, and other College of the Fine Arts auditoriums. The state-of-the-art acoustics at the Bass Concert Hall enhance the sounds of the largest tracker organ in the United States. Linking contemporary computer technology with a design that goes back some 2,000 years, it has 5,315 pipes—some of them 16 feet tall—and weighs 48,000 pounds.

From the same vantage point to the left looms the huge:

❹ Darrell K. Royal/Texas Memorial Stadium

The first of the annual UT–Texas A&M Thanksgiving Day games was played here in 1924. The upper deck directly facing you was added in 1972. In a drive to finance the original stadium, female students sold their hair, male students sold their blood, and UT alum Lutcher Stark matched every $10,000 they raised with $1,000 of his own funds. The stadium's mid-1990s name change to honor legendary Longhorns football coach Darrell K. Royal angered some who wanted the stadium to remain a memorial to Texas veterans, and confused others who wondered if Royal is still alive (he is).

Continue west on 23rd; at the corner of San Jacinto, a long staircase marks the entrance to the:

❺ Art Building

At press time, this was temporary home to the Blanton Museum of Art (see "More Attractions," earlier in this chapter), until its larger facility is completed on MLK and Speedway in early 2006.

Walk a short distance north on San Jacinto. A stampeding group of bronze mustangs will herald your arrival at the:

⑥ Texas Memorial Museum

This monumental art moderne building was designed by Paul Cret, and ground was broken for the institution by Franklin Roosevelt in 1936. Once home to the Capitol's original zinc goddess of liberty, which was moved to the Bob Bullock Texas State History Museum along with other historic treasures, this museum now focuses solely on the natural sciences.

Exit the building and take Trinity, which, curving into 25th Street, will bring you back to the parking lot of the LBJ Library and your car. Retrace your original route along Red River until you reach Martin Luther King Jr. Boulevard. Drive west, and at the corner of San Jacinto, you'll see:

⑦ Santa Rita No. 1

No. 1 is an oil rig transported here from west Texas, where liquid wealth first spewed forth from it on land belonging to the university in 1923. The money was distributed between the University of Texas system, which got the heftier two-thirds, and the Texas A&M system. Although not its main source of income, this windfall has helped make UT the second richest university in the country, after Harvard.

Continue on to University Avenue and turn left. There are public parking spaces around 21st Street and University, where you'll begin your walking tour at the:

⑧ Littlefield Memorial Fountain

This fountain was built in 1933. Pompeo Coppini, sculptor of the magnificent bronze centerpiece, believed that the rallying together of the nation during World War I marked the final healing of the wounds caused by the Civil War. He depicted the winged goddess Columbia riding on the bow of a battleship sailing across the ocean—represented by three rearing sea horses—to aid the Allies. The two

figures on the deck represent the Army and the Navy. This three-tiered fountain graces the most dramatic entrance to the university's original 40 acres. Behind you stands the state Capitol.

Directly ahead of you, across an oak-shaded mall lined with statues, is the:

⑨ Main Building and Tower

The university's first academic building was built here in 1884. The 307-foot-high structure that now rises above the university was created by Paul Cret in 1937. It's a fine example of the Beaux Arts style, particularly stunning when lit to celebrate a Longhorn victory. Sadly, the clock tower's many notable features—the small classical temple on top, say, or the 56-bell carillon, the largest in Texas—will probably always be dogged by the shadow of the carnage committed by Charles Whitman, who in August 1966 shot and killed 16 people and wounded 31 more from the tower before he was gunned down by a sharpshooter. Closed off to the public in 1975 after a series of suicide leaps from its observation deck, the tower reopened for supervised ascensions in 1999 (see "Organized Tours," below). If you climb the staircase on the east (right) side of the tower to the stone balustrade, you can see the dramatic sweep of the entire eastern section of campus, including the LBJ Library.

The first building in your direct line of vision is:

⑩ Garrison Hall

Garrison Hall is named for one of the earliest members of the UT faculty, and home to the department of history. Important names from Texas's past—Austin, Travis, Houston, and Lamar—are set here in stone. The walls just under the building's eaves are decorated with cattle brands; look for the carved cow skulls and cactuses on the balcony window on the north side.

If you retrace your steps to the western (left) side of the Main Building, you'll see:

⑪ Battle Hall

This building is regarded by many as the campus's most beautiful building. Designed in 1911 by Cass Gilbert, architect of the U.S. Supreme Court building, the hall was the first to be done in the Spanish Renaissance style that came to characterize so many of the structures on this section of campus (note the terra-cotta–tiled roof and broadly arched windows). On the second floor, you can see the grand reading room of what is now the Architecture and Planning Library.

Exit Battle Hall and walk left to the northern door, which faces the much newer:

⑫ Flawn Academic Center

A 200,000-volume undergraduate library shares space here with exhibits from the archives of the Humanities Research Center (see stop 20, below). Among the permanent displays in the Academic Center's Leeds Gallery is a cabin furnished with the effects of Erle Stanley Gardner, Perry Mason's creator. In front of the building, Charles Umlauf's *The Torch Bearers* symbolizes the passing of knowledge from one generation to the next.

Continue along the eastern side of the Academic Center, where you'll pass:

⑬ The Hogg Auditorium

This auditorium is another Paul Cret building, designed in the same monumental art moderne mode as his earlier Texas Memorial Museum, and recently renovated.

A few steps farther along, you'll come to the trees known as the:

⑭ Battle Oaks

The three oldest members of this small grove are said to predate the city of Austin itself. They survived the destruction of most of the grove to build a Civil War fortress and a later attempt to displace them with a new Biology Building. It was this last, near-fatal skirmish that earned them

their name. Legend has it that Dr. W. J. Battle, a professor of classics and an early university president, holed up in the largest oak with a rifle to protect the three ancient trees.

Look across the street. At the corner of 24th and Whitis, you'll see the:

⑮ Littlefield Home

This home was built in high Victorian style in 1894. Maj. George W. Littlefield, a wealthy developer, cattle rancher, and banker, bequeathed more than $1 million to the university on the condition that its campus not be moved to land that his rival, George W. Brackenridge, had donated. During the week, when the UT Development Office is open, you can enter through the east carriage driveway to see the house's gorgeous gold-and-white parlors, griffin-decorated fireplace, and other ornate details. On the weekend, just ogle the architecture and the shaggy, 35-foot-high deodar cedar, which Littlefield had shipped over from its native Himalayas.

TAKE A BREAK
O's Campus Cafe, in the A.C.E.S. building on 24th Street and Speedway (© **512/232-9060**; www.oscampuscafe.com), is brought to you by the same folks who created Jeffrey's and Cipollina (see chapter 13 for both) so you know it's going to be a notch up from standard campus fare. Its gourmet sandwiches, pizzas, and muffins don't disappoint. If you haven't stopped here en route to the central campus from stop 7, head east to Speedway along 24th Street. In the past couple of years, O's sprouted various to-go outlets, and an additional sit-down location at the McCombs School of Business. See website for details.

Backtrack to stop 15 and walk west about a block to Guadalupe to reach:

⑯ The Drag

As its name suggests, the Drag is Austin's main off-campus pedestrian strip. Bookstores, fast-food restaurants, and shops line the thoroughfare, which is usually crammed with students trying to grab a bite or a book between classes. On weekends, the pedestrian mall set aside for the 23rd Street Renaissance Market overflows with crafts vendors.

To get back to the university, cross Guadalupe at the traffic light in front of the huge Co-op, between 24th and 22nd streets. You'll now be facing the west mall.

On your left is the:

⑰ Texas Union Building

UT's student union building is yet another Paul Cret creation. A beautifully tiled staircase leads up to the second level, where, through the massive carved wooden doors, you'll see the Cactus Cafe, a popular coffeehouse and music venue (see chapter 16). This bustling student center hosts everything from a bowling alley to a formal ballroom.

Immediately across the mall to the right stands:

⑱ Goldsmith Hall

This is one of two adjacent buildings where architecture classes are held. Also designed by Paul Cret, this hall

has beautifully worn slate floors and a palm tree–dotted central courtyard.

Walk through the courtyard and go down a few steps. To your right is:

⑲ Sutton Hall

This hall was designed by Cass Gilbert in 1918 and is part of the School of Architecture. Like his Battle Hall, it is gracefully Mediterranean, with terracotta moldings, a red-tile roof, and large Palladian windows.

Enter Sutton Hall through double doors at the front and exit straight through the back. You are now facing the:

⑳ Harry Ransom Center

The Humanities Research Center (HRC) is housed here. The satirical portrait of a rich American literary archive in A. S. Byatt's best-selling novel *Possession* is widely acknowledged to have been based on HRC. On the first floor of this building, you can view the center's extremely rare Gutenberg Bible, one of just five complete copies in the U.S., as well as the world's first photograph, created by Joseph Nicèphore Nièpce in 1826.

Exit the building to 21st Street and the fountain where the tour began.

6 Organized Tours

See also chapter 16 for details on touring the *Austin City Limits* studio.

AN AMPHIBIOUS TOUR

Austin Duck Adventures   It's a hoot—or should I say a quack? Whether or not you opt to use the duck call whistle, included in the tour price, to blow at the folks you pass in the street, you'll get a kick out of this combination land and sea tour. You'll be transported in a six-wheel-drive amphibious vehicle (originally created for British troops during the Cold War) through Austin's historic downtown and the scenic west side before splashing into Lake Travis. Comedy writers helped devise the script for this 1½-hour tour, so it's funny as well as informative.

Boarding in front of the Austin Convention and Visitors Bureau, 209 E. 6th St. ✆ 512/4-SPLASH. www.austinducks.com. Tours $19 adults, $17 seniors and students, $13 ages 3–12. Daily tours; times change seasonally; call to check schedule.

BOAT TOURS

Capital Cruises   From March through October, Capital Cruises plies Town Lake with electric-powered boats heading out on a number of popular tours.

The bat cruises are especially big in summer, when warm nights are perfect for the enjoyable and educational hour-long excursions. The high point is seeing thousands of bats stream out from under their Congress Avenue Bridge roost. Dinner cruises, featuring fajitas from the Hyatt Regency's La Vista restaurant, are also fun on a balmy evening, and the afternoon sightseeing tours are a nice way to while away an hour on the weekend.

Hyatt Regency Town Lake boat dock. (℃ **512/480-9264.** www.capitalcruises.com. Bat and sightseeing cruises $8 adults, $6.50 seniors, $5 children 5–12; dinner cruises (including tax and tip) $30 adults, $19 children. Bat cruise daily ½ hour before sunset (call ahead for exact time), weather permitting; sightseeing cruise Sat–Sun at 1pm; dinner cruise Fri–Sun at 6pm. Reservations required for dinner cruises; for bat and sightseeing cruises, show up at the dock a minimum of 30 min. in advance.

Lone Star Riverboat   You'll set out against a backdrop of Austin's skyline and the state capitol on this riverboat cruise and move upstream past Barton Creek and Zilker Park. Along the way, you'll glimpse 100-foot-high cliffs and million-dollar estates. These scenic tours, accompanied by knowledgeable narrators, last 1½ hours. Slightly shorter bat-watching tours leave around half an hour before sunset, so call ahead to check.

South shore of Town Lake, between the Congress Ave. and S. 1st St. bridges, just next to the Hyatt. (℃ **512/327-1388.** http://www.lonestarriverboat.com. Scenic tours $9 adults, $7 seniors, $6 children 4–12; bat tours $8 adults, $6 seniors, $5 children 4–12. Scenic tours Sat–Sun 1pm Mar–Oct only. Bat tours nightly Apr–Oct only; call for exact times.

WALKING TOURS

Austin Ghost Tours   If you favor activities that are likely to keep you from sleeping, these tours are for you. Not only are the various outings held in the evening, but they're all concerned with ghouls. **The Ghosts of Austin Downtown Walking Tour** explores the stories of those that even death couldn't separate from downtown, while the tavern-crawl **Haunted Sixth Street Tour** capitalizes on the spirits that liked their spirits (and visitors who like both the spectral and the alcoholic manifestations). Austin Ghost Tours has also teamed up with the Austin Museum of Art for a special 90-minute **Haunted History Walking Tour,** featuring the museum exhibit "The Disembodied Spirit," the Wooten building, the Old Miller Opera House, and the Capitol. A variety of other tours are available as well, so be sure to check the website then call ahead to make the required reservations.

Tour departure points vary; check ahead. (℃ **512/853-9826.** www.austinghosttours.com. 90-min. Ghosts of Austin and 2-hr. Haunted Sixth Street tours $15. Tour schedules vary; call or check the website.

University of Texas Tower Observation Deck Tour   Off-limits to the public for nearly a quarter of a century, the infamous observation deck of the UT Tower (see "Strolling Around the University of Texas," earlier in this chapter)—where crazed gunman Charles Whitman went on a deadly shooting spree in 1966—was remodeled with a webbed dome and reopened in 1999. Billed as tours, these excursions to the top of the tower are really supervised visits, although a guide gives a short, informative spiel and stays on hand to answer questions. Frankly, it would probably be better if these visits—now about 30 minutes long—were half as short and half as expensive (I saw lots of people looking bored after about 10 minutes).

Deck tours are available by reservation only. Check the website or phone the numbers listed below on Monday to Friday 8am to 5pm to pin down the schedule and to find out how to get your tickets.

Note: You are permitted to bring along a camera, binoculars, or a camcorder to take advantage of the observation deck's spectacular, 360-degree view of the city and environs, but you must leave behind everything else, including purses, camera bags, tripods, strollers, and so forth. (Lockers are available at the Texas Union for $1.)

UT Campus, Texas Union Building. © 877/475-6633 (outside Austin) or 512/475-6633. www.utexas.edu/tower. Tours $5. Tours are offered Sat–Sun on the hour—starting as early as 11am and lasting until as late as 8pm—most of the year. Schedules vary according to the academic schedule; late May to late Aug, tours may be offered on Thurs and Fri evenings, and Sun tours eliminated.

Wild Basin Wilderness Preserve   The varied menu of guided tours at this preserve on a lovely 227-acre peninsula will keep nature and wildlife lovers happy, night and day. Native plants, birds, arrowheads, and snakes are among the topics covered (though not at the same time) during daylight walks. After dark, there are either also moonlight tours (coinciding with the full moon) or stargazing tours 3 or 4 days after the new moon. Call ahead or check the website for exact dates.

805 N. Capital of Texas Hwy. © 512/327-7622. www.wildbasin.org. Preserve admission $2 adults, $1 seniors and ages 5–12; 2-hour tours $3 adults, $1 ages 5–12, free for children under 5. Preserve daily dawn–dusk; office Mon–Fri 9am–4:30pm, Sat–Sun 8am–3pm. Hiking tours every weekend, weather permitting, stargazing tours twice monthly, weather permitting, generally 8 or 8:30pm to 9:30 or 10pm.

SELF-GUIDED TOURS

In addition to the guided walking tours offered by the **Austin Convention and Visitors Bureau** (see below), the ACVB publishes seven excellent, free self-guided tour booklets. Five tours (Bremond Block, Hyde Park, Congress Avenue and E. Sixth St., Texas State Cemetery, and Oakwood Cemetery) require foot power alone. The other two (West Austin and O. Henry Trail) combine walking and driving. They make for interesting reading even if you don't have time to follow the routes.

If you'd prefer to have a knowledgeable personal guide with you while you drive (along with, or as opposed to, a know-nothing friend, spouse, or significant other), consider buying the **Hit the Road Austin** audio tour CD ($19). You'll be escorted from downtown Austin through Zilker Park, along Wild Basin Preserve, to Mt. Bonnell, through Clarksville, the University of Texas, the Capitol, and various other points of interest. The narrators have the requisite Texas twang, and their stories are accompanied by such interesting audio effects as music, military drumbeats, and birdcalls. Along with the CD, you'll get a printed map of the tour route, so be nice because you might still have to rely on that person in the navigator seat. To order, call © **512/335-3300** or log on to www.hittheroadtours.com.

GUIDED WALKS

Whatever price you pay, you won't find better guided walks than the informative and entertaining **tours** ★★ offered free of charge by the **Austin Convention and Visitors Bureau (ACVB)** (© 866/GO-AUSTIN or 512/454-1545; www.austintexas.org), from March through November. Ninety-minute tours of the historic Bremond Block leave every Saturday and Sunday at 11am; Congress Avenue/East Sixth Street is explored for 1½ hours on Thursday, Friday, and Saturday starting at 9am, Sunday at 2pm. The hour-long Capitol Grounds tour is conducted on Saturday at 2pm and Sunday at 9am. All tours depart promptly from the south entrance of the capitol, weather permitting. Be warned, though: Come even a few minutes late and you'll miss out.

7 Staying Active

BALLOONING   For an uplifting experience, consider a hot-air balloon ride over Hill Country. **Austin Aeronauts Hot Air Balloons** (© 512/440-1492; www.austinaeronauts.com) and **Airwolf Adventures** (© 512/251-4024) are both reputable operators with FAA-licensed pilots. Their scenic excursions, including champagne breakfast, generally last about an hour.

BIKING   A city that has a "bicycle coordinator" on its payroll, Austin is a cyclist's dream. Contact **Austin Parks and Recreation,** 200 S. Lamar Blvd. (© 512/974-6700; www.ci.austin.tx.us/parks), for information on the city's more than 25 miles of scenic paths, the most popular of which are the Barton Creek Greenbelt (7.8 miles) and the Town Lake Greenbelt (10 miles). The **Veloway,** a 3.1-mile paved loop in Slaughter Creek Metropolitan Park, is devoted exclusively to bicyclists and in-line skaters.

You can rent bikes and get maps and other information from **University Cyclery,** 2901 N. Lamar Blvd. (© 512/474-6696, www.universitycyclery.com). A number of downtown hotels rent or provide free bicycles to their guests. For information on weekly road rides, contact the **Austin Cycling Association,** P.O. Box 5993, Austin, TX 78763 (© 512/282-7413; www.austincycling.org), which also publishes a monthly newsletter, *Southwest Cycling News,* though only local calls or e-mails are returned. For rougher mountain-bike routes, try the **Austin Ridge Riders.** Their website, www.austinridgeriders.com, will have the latest contact information.

BIRD-WATCHING   Endangered golden-cheeked warblers and black-capped vireos are among the many species you might spot around Austin. The **Travis Audubon Society** (© 512/926-8751; www.travisaudubon.org) organizes regular birding trips and even has a rare-bird hot line.

Texas Parks and Wildlife publishes *The Guide to Austin-Area Birding Sites,* which points you to the best urban perches. You should be able to pick up a copy at the Austin Visitor Center or at the offices of any of Austin's parks and preserves (see "More Attractions," earlier in this chapter). Avid birders should also enjoy *Adventures with a Texas Naturalist,* by Roy Bedichek. The author is one of the three friends depicted on the Philosophers' Rock, also listed in the "More Attractions" section, p. 211.

CANOEING   You can rent canoes at **Zilker Park,** 2000 Barton Springs Rd. (© 512/478-3852; www.fastair.com/zilker), for $10 an hour or $30 all day (Sat, Sun, and holidays only Oct–Mar). **Capital Cruises,** Hyatt Regency boat dock (© 512/480-9264; www.capitalcruises.com), also offers hourly rentals on Town Lake. If your paddling skills are a bit rusty, check out the instructional courses of UT's **Recreational Sports Outdoor Program** (© 512/471-3116).

FISHING   **Git Bit** (© 512/280-2861; www.gitbitfishing.com) provides guide service for half- or full-day bass-fishing trips on Lake Travis.

GOLF   For information about Austin's six municipal golf courses, call © 512/974-9350 or log on to www.ci.austin.tx.us/parks/golf.htm. Each offers pro shops and equipment rental, and their greens fees are very reasonable. Among them are the 9-hole **Hancock,** which was built in 1899 and is the oldest course in Texas, and the 18-hole **Lions,** where Tom Kite and Ben Crenshaw played college golf for the University of Texas.

HIKING   Austin's parks and preserves abound in nature trails; see "More Attractions," earlier in this chapter, for additional information. Contact the

Sierra Club (© 512/472-1767; www.texas.sierraclub.org/austin), if you're interested in organized hikes. **Wild Basin Wilderness Preserve** (see "Organized Tours," above) is another source for guided treks, offering periodic "Haunted Trails" tours along with its more typical hikes.

ROCK CLIMBING   Those with the urge to hang out on cliffs can call **Mountain Madness** (© 512/329-0309; www.mtmadness.com), which holds weekend rock-climbing courses at Enchanted Rock, a stunning granite outcropping in the Hill Country. **Austin Rock Gym** (© 512/416-9299; www.austin rockgym.com) offers two family-friendly indoor climbing facilities, as well as a variety of classes and guided outdoor trips.

SAILING   Lake Travis is the perfect place to let the wind drive your sails; among the operators offering sailboat rentals in the Austin area are **Commander's Point Yacht Basin** (© 512/266-2333), **Texas Sailing Academy** (© 512/ 261-6193; www.texassailing.com), and **Dutchman's Landing** (© 512/ 267-4289; www.dutchmanslanding.com); the first two companies also offer instruction.

SCUBA DIVING   The clarity of the limestone-filtered waters of Lake Travis makes it ideal for peeking around underwater. Boat wrecks and metal sculptures have been planted on the lake bottom of the private (paying) portion of **Windy Point Park** (© 512/266-3337; www.windypointpark.com), and Mother Nature has provided the park's advanced divers with an unusual underwater grove of pecan trees. Equipment rentals and lessons are available nearby from **Dive World** (© 512/219-1220; www.diveworldaustin.com), located at 12129 R.R. 620, #440.

SPELUNKING   The limestone country in the Austin area is rife with dark places in which to poke around. In the city, two wild caves you can crawl into with the proper training are **Airman's Cave** on the Barton Creek Greenbelt and **Goat Cave Preserve** in southwest Austin. Check the website of the Texas Speleological Association, www.cavetexas.org, and that of the University Speleological Society, www.utgrotto.org (you don't have to be a student to join), for links to statewide underground attractions. See also chapter 17 for other caves in nearby Hill Country.

SWIMMING   The best known of Austin's natural swimming holes is **Barton Springs Pool** (see "The Top Attractions," earlier in this chapter), but it's by no means the only one. Other scenic outdoor spots to take the plunge include **Deep Eddy Pool,** 401 Deep Eddy Ave. at Lake Austin Boulevard (© 512/ 472-8546), and **Hamilton Pool Preserve,** 27 miles west of Austin, off Texas 71 on FM 3238 (© 512/264-2740).

For lakeshore swimming, consider **Hippie Hollow** on Lake Travis, 2½ miles off FM 620, www.co.travis.tx.us/tnr/parks/hippie_hollow.asp, where you can let it all hang out in a series of clothing-optional coves, or **Emma Long Metropolitan Park** on Lake Austin (see "More Attractions," earlier in this chapter).

You can also get into the swim at a number of **free neighborhood pools;** contact the City Aquatics Department (© 512/476-4521; www.ci.austin.tx.us/ parks/aquatics.htm) for more information.

TENNIS   The very reasonably priced **Austin High School Tennis Center,** 2001 W. Cesar Chavez St. (© 512/477-7802), **Caswell Tennis Center,** 2312 Shoal Creek Blvd. (© 512/478-6268), and **Pharr Tennis Center,** 4201 Brookview Dr. (© 512/477-7773), all have enough courts to give you a good shot at getting one to play on. To find out about additional public courts, contact the Tennis Administration office (© **512/480-3020,** www.ci.austin.tx.us/parks/tennis.htm).

8 Spectator Sports

There are no professional teams in Austin, but a minor-league baseball team and a new arena football team have captured local attention. College sports are very big, particularly when the **University of Texas (UT) Longhorns** are playing. The most comprehensive source of information on the various teams is www.TexasSports.com, but you can phone the **UT Athletics Ticket Office** (© **512/471-3333**) to find out about schedules and **UTTM Charge-A-Ticket** (© **512/477-6060**) to order tickets.

BASEBALL The **University of Texas** baseball team goes to bat February through May at Disch-Falk Field (just east of I-35, at the corner of Martin Luther King Jr. Blvd. and Comal). Many players from this former NCAA championship squad have gone on to the big time, including two-time Cy Young award winner Roger Clemens.

Baseball Hall-of-Famer Nolan Ryan's **Round Rock Express,** a Houston Astros farm club, won the Texas League championship in 1999, their first year in existence (starting in the 2005 season, they'll compete in the Pacific Coast League). See them play at the Dell Diamond, 3400 E. Palm Valley Rd. in Round Rock (© **512/255-BALL** or 244-4209; www.roundrockexpress.com), a 8,688-seat stadium where you can choose from box seats or stadium seating—and an additional 3,000 fans can sit on a grassy berm in the outfield.

BASKETBALL The **University of Texas** Longhorn and Lady Longhorn basketball teams, both former Southwest Conference champions, play in the Frank C. Erwin Jr. Special Events Center (just west of I-35 on Red River between Martin Luther King Jr. Blvd. and 15th St.) November through March.

FOOTBALL It's hard to tell which is more central to the success of an Austin Thanksgiving: the turkey or the UT–Texas A&M game. Part of the Big 12 Conference, the **University of Texas** football team often fills the huge Darrell K. Royal/Texas Memorial Stadium (just west of I-35 between 23rd and 21st sts., E. Campus Dr., and San Jacinto Blvd.) during home games, played August through November.

Fans of smaller-field, indoor professional football welcomed the **Austin Wranglers** (© **512/491-6600;** www.austinwranglers.com) to the ranks of the Arena Football League in 2004, and were pleased with their 8-8 record—pretty good for a first season. The Wranglers play at the Erwin Center (see "Basketball," above).

GOLF Initiated in 2003 and boasting a $1.6 million purse, The **FedEx Kinko's Classic** (© **512/732-2666;** http://www.pgatour.com/tournaments/s610), part of the PGA's Champions Tour, will be held at the Hills Country Club at Lakeway Resort May 3 to 9 in 2005.

HOCKEY The **Austin Ice Bats** hockey team (© **512/927-PUCK;** www.icebats.com) has been getting anything but an icy reception from its Austin fans. This typically rowdy team plays at the Travis County Exposition Center, 7311 Decker Lane (about 15 min. east of UT). Tickets, which run from $10 to $35, are available at any UTTM outlet or from **Star Tickets** (© **888/597-STAR** or 512/469-SHOW; www.startickets.com). The team generally plays on weekends mid-October through late March; a phone call will get you the exact dates and times.

HORSE RACING   Pick your ponies at **Manor Downs,** 8 miles east of I-35 on U.S. 290 East (© **512/272-5581;** www.manordowns.com), Texas's oldest parimutuel horse racetrack. The track is open for quarter horse and thoroughbred live racing on Saturday and Sunday mid-February through May (general admission $2; main grandstand general seating $3; box seats or entrance to Turf Club restaurant/bar $5). The rest of the year, you can see simulcasts. Call or check the website for the current schedule.

SOCCER   August through December you can find the **University of Texas** women's soccer team working to defend their stellar record. In 2002 they garnered all the Big 12 soccer honors, including Player of the Year, Julie Gailey. Home games are played either Friday or Sunday at the Mike A. Myers Stadium and Soccer Field, just northeast of the UT football stadium at Robert Dedman Drive and Mike Myers Drive.

15

Shopping in Austin

When it comes to things intellectual, musical, and gustatory, Austin is a match for many cities twice its size. Shopping here may not quite have evolved into the art it has in glitzier big cities like Houston or Dallas, but this town still offers a more-than-adequate range of choices.

1 The Shopping Scene

The revitalization of Austin's urban retail scene, begun in the mid-1990s, is continuing apace. Downtown, specialty shops and art galleries continue to filter back to the renovated 19th-century buildings along **Sixth Street** and **Congress Avenue.** A little to the west, around Sixth Street and Lamar Boulevard, the **Market District,** anchored by a huge new Whole Foods Complex, is accelerating its expansion. Below Town Lake, **South Congress Avenue,** from Riverside south to Johanna Street, is still attracting trendy art galleries, boutiques, and antiques stores—many of them open late on the first Thursday of each month (see sidebar, below)—but these days the funkier, less expensive shops that characterized the area's initial retail resurgence are gravitating toward the (currently) lower rent **South First Street** and **South Lamar Boulevard.** In the vicinity of **Central Market,** between West 35th and 40th streets and Lamar and Mo-Pac, such small shopping centers as Jefferson Square draw locals in search of memorable buying experiences. Many stores on **the Drag**—the stretch of Guadalupe Street between Martin Luther King Jr. Boulevard and 26th Street, across from the University of Texas campus—are student-oriented, but a wide range of clothing, gifts, toys, and books can also be found here.

Still, much of Austin's shopping continues to move out to the suburban malls. In the northwest, three upscale shopping centers, **The Arboretum, The Arboretum Market,** and **The Gateway complex** (consisting of the Gateway Courtyard, the Gateway Market, and Gateway Square) have earned the area the nickname "South Dallas." Bargain hunters go farther afield to the huge collections of factory outlet stores in San Marcos and New Braunfels; see chapter 17 for details. That said, several new developments, including The Domain, anchored by Neiman-Marcus, are slated to open closer to Austin's center in 2006.

Specialty shops in Austin tend to open around 9 or 10am, Monday through Saturday, and close at about 5:30 or 6pm, and many have Sunday hours from noon to 6pm. Malls tend to keep the same Sunday schedule, but Monday through Saturday they don't close their doors until 9pm. Sales tax in Austin is 8.25%.

2 Shopping A to Z

ANTIQUES

In addition to the one-stop antiques markets listed below, a number of smaller shops line Burnet Road north of 45th Street. See also the **Travis County Farmers' Market** under "Food," below.

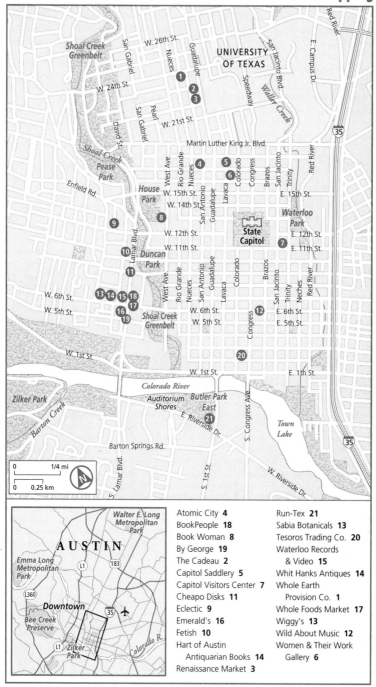

Downtown Austin Shopping

Greater Austin Shopping

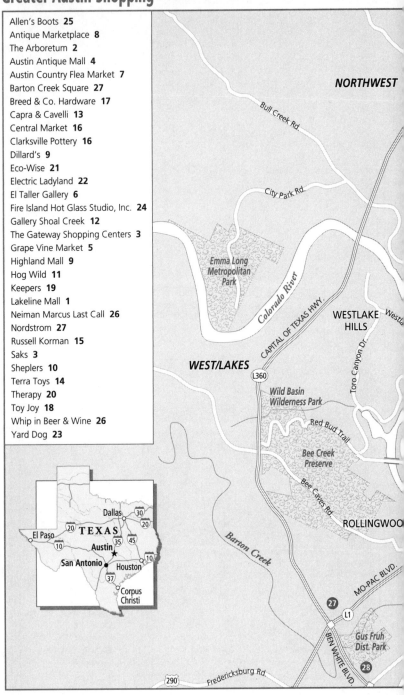

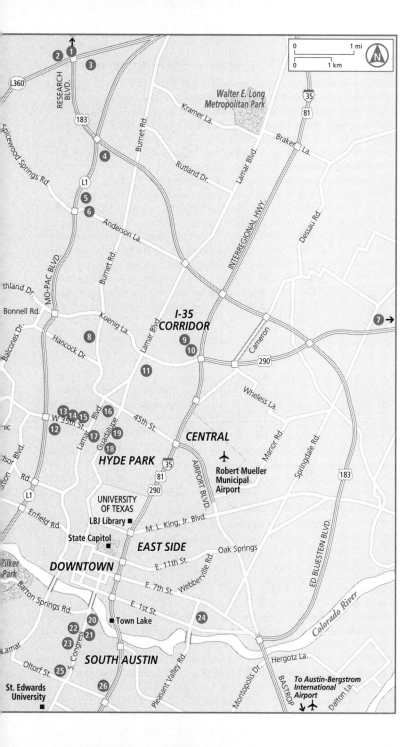

0   1 mi

0   1 km

N

L360

RESEARCH BLVD.

183

Spicewood Springs Rd

Walter E. Long Metropolitan Park

Kramer La.

Burnet Rd.

Rutland Dr.

Lamar Blvd

35

81

Braker La.

INTERREGIONAL HWY

Dessau Rd.

L1

Anderson La.

MO-PAC BLVD.

Burnet Rd.

thland Dr.

Bonnell Rd.

Balcones Dr.

Hancock Dr.

Koenig La.

Lamar Blvd

I-35 CORRIDOR

Cameron

290

Wheless La.

nic

W 35th St.

Lamar Blvd

Guadalupe

45th St.

CENTRAL

Manor Rd.

Springdale Rd.

183

HYDE PARK

35

81

290

AIRPORT BLVD.

✈ **Robert Mueller Municipal Airport**

thland Dr.

L1

Enfield Rd.

UNIVERSITY OF TEXAS

LBJ Library ■

State Capitol

M. L. King, Jr. Blvd.

EAST SIDE

Oak Springs

ED BLUESTEIN BLVD.

Zilker Park

DOWNTOWN

Barton Springs Rd.

E. 11th St.

E. 7th St.

Webberville Rd.

Colorado River

E. 1st St.

■ Town Lake

SOUTH AUSTIN

Pleasant Valley Rd.

Hergotz La.

Montopolis Dr.

BASTROP

To Austin-Bergstrom International Airport
↓ ✈

Lamar

Oltorf St.

S. Congress

St. Edwards University
■

Dalton La.

First Thursdays

As if there wasn't already enough street theater in Austin, the new millennium introduced a (semiorganized) monthly event to the roster. It's hard to say exactly how it started, but as early as 2001, merchants on trendy South Congress Avenue began keeping their doors open late and providing food, drinks, and, often entertainment on the first Thursday of every month. Soon impromptu open-air markets sprang up, and buskers, belly dancers, drum circles, and of course live bands performed indoors, outdoors, and in between.

As inevitably happens with any burgeoning phenomenon, First Thursday got out of hand. Merchants hosting the event soon learned the consequences of serving too much free alcohol—some wits began calling the event "First Thirsty"—and neighborhood homeowners complained about the crowds and parking shortages. For a time, it looked like First Thursday might disappear as quickly as it materialized. But the Mardi Gras–like atmosphere was toned down, and things have settled into a pleasant groove for merchants, shoppers, neighborhood residents, and scene makers alike. Long live First Thursday. To find out more, check www.firstthursday.info.

Antique Marketplace   For people who like antiques but don't enjoy speaking in hushed tones, the Antique Marketplace offers bargains and treasures in a friendly, relaxed atmosphere. You'll find a little bit of everything under the roof of this large warehouse-type building in central Austin: Czech glass, funky collectibles, and expensive furnishings. 5350 Burnet Rd. ℂ 512/452-1000.

Austin Antique Mall   You can spend anywhere from five bucks to thousands of dollars in this huge collection of antiques stores. More than 100 dealers occupying a 30,000-square-foot indoor space offer Roseville pottery, Fiesta dishes, Victorian furniture, costume jewelry, and much, much more. 8822 McCann Dr. ℂ 512/459-5900. www.antiquetexas.com.

Whit Hanks Antiques   More than a dozen independent dealers gather at tony Whit Hanks, just across the street from Treaty Oak. This is Austin's premier outlet for fine antiques. Even if you can't afford to buy anything, it's fun to ogle items from fine crystal and vases to Chinese cabinets and neoclassical columns. 1009 W. 6th St. ℂ 512/478-2101.

ART GALLERIES

It's not exactly SoHo, but the area just northwest of the Capitol and south of the University of Texas—specifically, the block bounded by Guadalupe and Lavaca to the west and east and 17th and 18th streets to the south and north—has a large concentration of galleries. They include the group clustered in the **Guadalupe Arts Building,** 1705 Guadalupe; **D. Berman,** next door at 1701 Guadalupe; and Women & Their Work Gallery (see below).

For additional information about other galleries and art exhibits and events in Austin, call **City Art Link** at ℂ 512/452-7773 or log on to www.cityartlink.com.

El Taller Gallery   Located just east of Mo-Pac, this appealing showcase for Southwestern art sells Santa Fe pieces at Austin prices. Amado Peña, Jr., who once owned the gallery, is represented here, and you'll also find work by R. C. Gorman and other Native American artists, as well as whimsical Western paintings by Darryl Willison. Handmade Pueblo pottery and vintage Southwestern jewelry are among the gallery's other interesting offerings. 2438 W. Anderson Lane. © 800/234-7362 or 512/302-0100. www.eltallergallery.com.

Gallery Shoal Creek   Since it opened in 1965, Shoal Creek has moved away from an exclusive emphasis on Western art to encompass work from a wide range of American regions. The focus is on contemporary painting in representational or Impressionist styles—for example, Jerry Ruthven's Southwest landscapes or Nancy McGowan's naturalist watercolors. Like El Taller, this is an Austin outlet for many artists who also have galleries in Santa Fe. 1500 W. 34th St. © 512/454-6671. www.gshoalcreek.com.

Wild About Music   Austin's commitment to music makes it a perfect location for this gallery and shop, strictly devoted to items with a musical theme. Some of the pieces are expensive, but nearly all of them are fun. Items run the gamut from books, posters, and musician-designed T-shirts to musical instruments and furniture. 115 E 6th St. © 512/708-1700. www.wildaboutmusic.com.

Women & Their Work Gallery   Founded in 1978, this nonprofit gallery is devoted to more than visual art—it also promotes and showcases women in dance, music, theater, film, and literature. Regularly changing exhibits have little in common except innovation. This art space got the nod for "Best Gallery" from the *Austin Chronicle* in 2004. The gift shop has a great selection of unusual crafts and jewelry created by female artists. 1710 Lavaca St. © 512/477-1064. www.womenandtheirwork.org.

Yard Dog Folk Art   "Outsider" art, created in the deep, rural South, usually by the poor and sometimes by the incarcerated, is not for everyone, but for those interested in contemporary American folk art, this gallery is not to be missed. Naturally, it's in the hip South Congress area, where no one would be so uncool as to admit they find some of this stuff less than extraordinary. 1510 S. Congress Ave. © 512/912-1613. www.yarddog.com.

BOOKSTORES

As might be expected, many of Austin's bookstores are concentrated in the University of Texas area, and specifically on the Drag. Along with discounted reading matter, new and used, **Half-Price Books,** 3110 Guadalupe St. (© 512/451-4463; www.halfpricebooks.com; four other locations), also carries CDs, cassettes, and videos.

The **University Co-Op,** 2244 Guadalupe St. (© 512/476-7211; www.coopbookstore.com; five other smaller outlets), opened in 1896, has many volumes of general interest, along with the requisite orange-and-white Longhorn T-shirts, mugs, and other UT souvenirs.

Note: A longtime presence on the Drag, Barnes & Noble closed its Guadalupe store in early 2005, leaving its three other locations to take up the literary and audio slack.

BookPeople   Expanded in the mid-1990s from its New Age roots but remaining stubbornly quirky and independent, this store stocks more than 250,000 titles ranging over a wide variety of subjects. BookPeople also has an extensive array of self-help videos, books on tape, and gift items (the KEEP AUSTIN WEIRD T-shirt is their bestseller). Lots of intimate sitting areas and an espresso bar prevent this huge store—the largest in Texas—from feeling overwhelming. More than 200 author signings and special events are held here every year. 603 N. Lamar Blvd. ✆ 800/853-9757 or 512/472-5050. www.bookpeople.com.

BookWoman Offering the largest selection of books by and about women in Texas, this store is also one of the best feminist resource centers, the place to find out about women's organizations and events statewide. Readings and discussion groups are regularly held here, too. BookWoman also carries a great selection of T-shirts, cards, posters, and music. 918 W. 12th St. ✆ 512/472-2785. www.ebook woman.com.

Hart of Austin Antiquarian Books You'll have to enter the Whit Hanks complex (see Antiques, above) to locate this excellent repository of rare books, maps, and prints, many of them devoted to Texas subjects—no outside sign alerts you to its presence (perhaps a side effect of focusing on the past?). 1009 W. 6th St. ✆ 512/477-7755.

CRAFTS

Eclectic A dazzling panoply of hand-painted furniture, pottery, and art—new and old—from around the world is beautifully presented in this large store (with a bonus parking lot in back). An outstanding jewelry section includes pieces from Mexico, Africa, Indonesia, Afghanistan, and other exotic places. 700 N. Lamar. ✆ 512/477-1816.

Tesoros Trading Co. If you like exotic tchotchkes, be prepared to lose all sense of time when you enter this store. Colorful hand-woven cloth from Guatemala, intricate weavings from Peru, glassware, jewelry, and tinwork from Mexico—all these and more are available at Tesoros, which (in addition to its high-quality folk art) also offers a limited selection of furniture, dishes, and housewares from Latin America. Plenty of reasonably priced items mingle with expensive treasures. 209 Congress Ave. ✆ 512/479-8377. www.tesoros.com.

DEPARTMENT STORES

Dillard's This Little Rock–based chain, spread throughout the Southwest, carries a nice variety of mid- to high-range merchandise. In Highland Mall, there are two separate outlets, one focusing on home furnishings and women's clothing, the other devoted to men's and children's wear. All the stores have country shops with good selections of stylish Western fashions. Two other locations are at the Barton Creek Square Mall (✆ 512/327-6100) and the Lakeline Mall (✆ 512/257-8740). Highland Mall. ✆ 512/452-9393. www.dillards.com.

Nordstrom First Saks arrived, and now Nordstrom has come. Fashion- and status-conscious Austin shoppers—the segment of the city not devoted to keeping Austin weird—were all aflutter when this huge (144,000 sq. ft.) store debuted in Barton Creek Square in 2003. 2901 S. Capitol of Texas Hwy. ✆ 512/691-3500. www.nordstrom.com.

Saks Acquisition-wise, Austin came of age in the late 1990s with the opening of a link in this golden chain. Although smaller than many of the other Saks stores, it offers the high-tone fashions and accouterments you'd expect, as well as a personal shopper service. 9722 Great Hills Trail. ✆ 512/231-3700. www.saksfifthavenue.com.

DISCOUNT SHOPPING

Neiman Marcus Last Call ✪ Fans of Texas-grown Neiman Marcus will want to take advantage of Last Call, which consolidates fashions from 27 of the chain's department stores and sells them here at prices 50% to 75% off retail. New merchandise shipments arrive every week, and not only can you find great bargains, but you needn't sacrifice the attention for which Neiman Marcus is famous because the staff here is as helpful as at any other branch and a personal shopper service is available as well. Brodie Oaks Shopping Center, 4115 S. Capital of Texas Hwy. at S. Lamar. ℭ 512/447-0701. www.neimanmarcus.com.

ECO-WARES

Eco-wise It's hard to typecast a shop that sells everything from greeting cards, natural insect repellent, and hand-woven purses to building materials and home decorating supplies. The common denominator? Everything you'll find here is created with an eye toward the environment—that is, it's recycled, made from natural fabrics, and/or chemical free. Staff is knowledgeable and helpful, and customers are passionately loyal. The store offers baby and wedding-shower registries for earth-friendly brides and grooms or moms and dads. 110 W. Elizabeth. ℭ 512/326-4474. www.ecowise.com.

ESSENTIAL OILS

Sabia Botanicals All those soothing oils and lotions in their pretty bottles on the shelves seem to whisper, "Buy me, I'll make you feel better." This is aromatherapy central, but along with New Age products, the store also carries old-time herbal lines, such as Kiehl's. 500 N. Lamar, Suite 150. ℭ 512/469-0447. www.sabia.com.

FASHIONS

For children's clothing, see **Terra Toys** under "Toys," p. 238.

MEN

See also **By George** under "Women," below.

Capra & Cavelli Funny radio ads—not to mention hip and classic fashions— draw image-conscious guys (and gals) into this west Austin store. And talk about service: C&C will bring items to your home or office for your perusing pleasure. 3500 Jefferson, Suite 110. ℭ 512/450-1919. www.capracavelli.com.

Keepers Austinites seeking to make the transition from geek to fashion chic turn to this locally owned men's specialty store for friendly but expert advice and the latest in well-made men's clothing. You'll find an "image consultant" and expert tailors on the premises. 1004 W. 38th St. ℭ 512/302-3664. www.keepersclothing.com.

OUTDOOR

Run-Tex Owned by the footwear editor for *Runner's World* magazine—and serving as the official wear test center for that publication—this store not only has a huge inventory of shoes and other running gear, but also does everything it can to promote healthful jogging practices, even offering free running classes and a free injury-evaluation clinic. The staff will make sure any footwear you buy is a perfect fit for your feet and running style. There's a larger Run-Tex in Gateway Market, 9901 Capital of Texas Hwy. (ℭ 512/343-1164); a location at 2201 Lake Austin Blvd. (ℭ 512/477-9464); and a related WalkTex at 4001 N. Lamar (ℭ 512/454-WALK). But this downtown store is best: It's near that runner's Mecca, Town Lake. 422 W. Riverside Dr. ℭ 512/472-3254. www.runtex.com.

WOMEN

See also **The Cadeau,** listed under "Gifts/Souvenirs," below, and Capra & Cavelli, under "Men," above.

By George In its various incarnations, By George has long been a prime pick for Austin fashion victims, and now the men's and women's outlets have been consolidated into a single huge clothing emporium. Both genders like the mix of well-established and up-and-coming designers with (somewhat) less pricey off-the-rack clothing here with the common denominator of hip, contemporary fashions in natural fabrics. There's also another, more casual women's store for the college crowd on the Drag at 2346 Guadalupe St. (✆ **512/472-2731**). 524 N. Lamar Blvd. ✆ **512/472-5951.**

Emeralds It's young, it's hip, it's got Carrie Bradshaw shoes by the dozens, plus racks of outrageous party dresses to wear them with. And—should your friends have the same tastes as Carrie's do—you can also buy cards, candles, aromatherapy bath salts, and funky jewelry here. 624 N. Lamar Blvd. ✆ **512/476-3660.**

Fetish At this shoe fashionista heaven, featuring footwear from the classical to the fanciful, you can also find plenty of trendy and elegant stuff to wear from the ankles up—dresses, tops, skirts, pants, lingerie, jewelry, and more. 1112 N. Lamar. ✆ **512/457-1007.**

Therapy Many of Austin's top singer/songwriters come to this hip SoCo boutique to seek out clothing as clever as the store's name (any shopper worth her credit card knows the value of retail therapy). A small but constantly changing inventory of inventive styles by local designers—everything from purses and casual halters to flowing skirts and evening gowns—is sold at prices that fall well below what you'd find at the large national stores. Feeling better yet? 1113 S. Congress Ave. ✆ **877/326-2331** or 512/326-2331. www.therapyclothing.com.

VINTAGE

Electric Ladyland/Lucy in Disguise with Diamonds Feather boas, tutus, flapper dresses, angel wings, and the occasional gorilla suit overflow the narrow aisles of Austin's best-known costume and vintage clothing outlet. The owner, who really *does* dress like that all the time, is a walking advertisement for her fascinating store. The store carries more-or-less subdued clothing like floral-print dresses and striped shirts, but you're likely to get sidetracked by rack after rack of outrageousness. At Halloween, this is costume-rental central. 1506 S. Congress Ave. ✆ **512/444-2002.**

FOOD

In addition to hosting some of the nation's most impressive megagroceries, Austin also has an abundance of farmers' markets. Perhaps the most notable of them, **Austin Farmers' Market,** held downtown at Republic Square Park, Fourth Street at Guadalupe, every Saturday from 9am to 1pm March through November (✆ **512/236-0074;** www.austinfarmersmarket.com), not only features food products but also live music, cooking demonstrations, kids' activities, and workshops on everything from organic gardening to aromatherapy.

South Congress Organic Farmers' Market, held Saturday from 8am to 1pm in the parking lot of El Gallo Restaurant, 2910 S. Congress Ave. (✆ **512/281-4712;** www.austinfarm.org/safm), is smaller, but you've got the guarantee that all the goods are locally grown without chemicals.

A bit farther afield—literally—is the **Travis County Farmers' Market,** 6701 Burnet Rd. (✆ **512/454-1002**), which hosts monthly festivals honoring particular crops and/or growing seasons. It also boasts three restaurants, a bakery, a store selling country-primitive antiques, and long hours; open from 8am to 6pm daily.

For a good overview of the other fresh produce purveyors in town, check out **www.agr.state.tx.us/picktexas/farm_market/austin.htm**.

Central Market 🏵🏵   Aah, foodie heaven! Not only can you buy every imaginable edible item at these gourmet megamarkets—fresh or frozen, local or imported—but you also can enjoy the cooking of a top-notch chef in the restaurant section, which features cowboy, bistro, Italian, vegetarian—you name it—cuisines. Moreover, prices are surprisingly reasonable. A monthly newsletter announces what's fresh in the produce department, which jazz musicians are entertaining on the weekend, and which gourmet chef is holding forth at the market's cooking school. The newer Westgate Shopping Center branch, 4477 S. Lamar (𝄏 **512/899-4300**), in South Austin, is as impressive as its history-making sibling north of UT. 4001 N. Lamar. 𝄏 **512/206-1000**. www.centralmarket.com.

Whole Foods Market   The first link in what is now the world's largest organic and natural foods supermarket chain is celebrating its 25th birthday in early 2005 by opening an 80,000-square-foot store near its original downtown location (as well as an adjacent office tower to serve as corporate headquarters). From chemical-free cosmetics to frozen tofu burgers, Whole Foods has long covered the entire (organic) enchilada, and now it's looking to compete with Central Market (see above) in the food-entertainment arena by creating a 600-seat amphitheater, a playscape, gardens, on-site massages, a cooking school, and more. The northwest store in Gateway Market, 9607 Research Blvd. (𝄏 **512/345-5003**), will not be subject to this extreme makeover. 525 N. Lamar Blvd. 𝄏 **512/476-1206**. www.wholefoods.com.

GIFTS/SOUVENIRS

See also **Wild About Music,** listed under "Art Galleries," p. 231, and **Emeralds,** listed under the "Women" subsection of the "Fashions" section, above.

The Cadeau   *Cadeau* means "gift" in French, and this is the perfect place to find one, whether it be beautiful contemporary kitchenware, pottery, jewelry, clothing, bibelots, tchotchkes, or knickknacks. Be forewarned: Just when you think you've narrowed down your choice, you may suddenly realize you've missed two whole rooms full of goodies to choose from. To add to the dilemma, there's a second location, at 4001 N. Lamar Blvd. (𝄏 **512/453-6988**), near Central Market. 2316 Guadalupe St. (the Drag). 𝄏 **512/477-7276**.

Capitol Visitors Center   Over the years, visitors have admired—sometimes excessively—the intricately designed door hinges of the capitol. The gift shop at the visitor center sells brass bookends made from the original models used, during the capitol's renovation, to cast replacements for hinges that were cadged over the years. Other Texas memorabilia includes paperweights made from reproductions of the capitol's Texas seal doorknobs and local food products. There are also a variety of educational toys and an excellent selection of historical books. 112 E. 11th St. (southeast corner of Capitol grounds). 𝄏 **512/305-8400**. www.texascapitolvisitorscenter.com.

GLASS & POTTERY

Clarksville Pottery & Galleries   This pottery emporium, filled with lovely pieces created by local artisans, has long been transplanted from its namesake location in the artsy section of downtown to a prime spot near Central Market (see "Food," above). You'll find everything ceramic, from candleholders to bird feeders, as well as handblown glass, woodcarvings, and contemporary jewelry in a variety of media; there's a unique selection of Judaica, too. An additional outlet, in the Arboretum Market, 9828 Great Hills Trail, Suite 110 (© **512/794-8580**), carries equally impressive stock. 4001 N. Lamar, Suite 200. © **512/454-9079**. www. clarksvillepottery.com.

Fire Island Hot Glass Studio, Inc. This glass blowing studio, about 2 miles east of I-35, is a bit off the beaten track, but it's a treat to watch the owners/artists, Matthew LaBarbera and his wife, Teresa Ueltschey, at their delicate craft. Demonstrations are given every Saturday morning from 9am to noon (other times by appointment). Other galleries around Austin carry the couple's elegant perfume bottles, oil lamps, bowls, and paperweights, but this showroom naturally has the largest selection. If you have a certain design in mind, you can special order a set of goblets. 3401 E. 4th St. © **512/389-1100**. www.fireislandglass.com.

HARDWARE & MORE

Breed & Co. Hardware You don't have to be a power-drill freak to visit Breed & Co. How many hardware stores, after all, have bridal registries where you can sign up for Waterford crystal? This darling of Austin DIY has everything from nails to tropical plants, organic fertilizer, gardening book and cookbooks, pâté molds, and cherry pitters. There's a newer branch in the chic Westlake Hills area, 3663 Bee Cave Rd. (© **512/328-3960**). 718 W. 29th St. © **512/474-6679**. www.breedandco.com.

JEWELRY

See also **Eclectic** and **Tesoros,** under "Crafts," above, and **Clarksville Pottery,** under "Glass & Pottery," above.

Russell Korman You'd never know it from his current elegant digs, but Russell Korman got his start in Austin's jewelry trade by selling beads on the Drag. Although he's moved on to fine 14-karat gold, platinum, and diamond pieces, along with fine pens and watches—there's an experienced watchmaker on the premises—his store still has a considerable collection of more casual sterling silver from Mexico. Prices are very competitive, even for the most formal baubles. 3806 N. Lamar Blvd. © **512/451-9292**.

MALLS/SHOPPING CENTERS

The Arboretum The retail anchor of the far northwest part of town is a shopping center so chic that it calls itself a market, not a mall. This two-level collection of outdoor boutiques doesn't include any department stores, but it does have a Barnes & Noble Superstore and a huge Pottery Barn. You'll find your basic selection of yuppie shops—everything from upscale clothing stores to a cigar humidor. The second floor features art galleries, a custom jeweler, and crafts shops. Dining options, including a Cheesecake Factory, a T.G.I. Friday's, and an outlet for Amy's—Austin's local favorite ice cream—tend to be on the casual side, but there's also a good local steakhouse, Dan McKlusky's. 10000 Research Blvd. (Hwy. 183 and Loop 360). © **512/338-4437**. www.shopsimon.com.

Barton Creek Square Set on a bluff with a view of downtown, Barton Creek tends to be frequented by upscale West Siders; the wide-ranging collection of more than 180 shops is anchored by Nordstrom, Dillard's, Foley's, Sears, and JCPenney. One of the newer malls in Austin, it's refined and low-key, but the presence of Frederick's of Hollywood and Victoria's Secret lingerie boutiques makes one wonder if the daytime soaps might not be onto something about the bored rich. At least they've got a sense of humor: There's also a jewelry store called Filthy Rich of Austin. 2901 S. Capital of Texas Hwy. © **512/327-7040**. www.bartoncreeksquare.com.

Gateway Shopping Centers   Comprising three not-so-distinct shopping areas, the Gateway Courtyard, the Gateway Market, and Gateway Square, this large, open complex includes mainly national chains such as Crate & Barrel, REI, Old Navy, and CompUSA. There are also branches of Austin-based stores, including Run-Tex and Whole Foods Market, discussed individually in this chapter. 9607 Research Blvd. at Hwy. 183 and Capital of Texas Hwy. ℂ **512/338-4755.** www.simon.com/mall.

Highland Mall   Austin's first mall, built in the 1970s, is still one of the city's most popular places to shop. It's located at the south end of the hotel zone near the old airport, just minutes north of downtown on I-35. Reasonably priced casual-clothing stores like Gap and Express vie with higher-end shops such as Ann Taylor. Dillard's (two of 'em!), Foley's, and JCPenney department stores coexist with specialty stores like Papyrus and the Warner Bros. Studio Store. The tonier Lincoln Plaza shops are just to the south, on I-35. The food court is impressive, where you can choose from the likes of cheesesteaks, baked potatoes, pizza, hamburgers, Thai food, and wraps. 6001 Airport Blvd. ℂ **512/454-9656.** www.highlandmall.com.

Lakeline Mall   Austin's newest shopping mecca, in an upscale far northwest location, is notable for its attention-grabbing design, featuring lots of colorful murals and detailed reliefs of the city. The shops, including Foley's, Dillard's, Mervyn's, Sears, JCPenney, Brookstone, the Bombay Company, and Best Buy, are not nearly so unusual, but there are some interesting smaller shops, from Dollar Tree, where everything costs a buck, to the Stockpot, with state-of-the art cookware. 11200 Lakeline Mall Dr., Cedar Park. ℂ **512/257-SHOP.** www.lakelinemall.com.

MARKETS

Austin Country Flea Market   Every Saturday and Sunday year-round, more than 550 covered spaces are filled with merchants selling all the usual flea market goods and then some—new and used clothing, fresh herbs and produce, electronics, antiques. This is the largest flea market in central Texas, covering more than 130 paved acres. There's live music every weekend—generally a spirited Latino band—to step up the shopping pace. 9500 Hwy. 290 E. (4 miles east of I-35). ℂ **512/928-2795** or 928-4711.

Renaissance Market   Flash back or be introduced to tie-dye days at this hippie-ish crafts market, where vendors are licensed by the city of Austin (read: no commercial schlock). Billed as the only continuously operated, open-air crafts market in the United States, it's theoretically open daily 8am to 10pm, but most of the merchants turn up only on the weekends. You'll find everything from silver jewelry and hand-carved flutes to batik T-shirts. Many of the artisans come in from small towns in the nearby Hill Country. W. 23rd St. and Guadalupe St. (the Drag). ℂ **512/397-1456.**

MUSIC

Following a national trend, four music stores—Sound Exchange, Tower Records, 33 Degrees, and Jupiter Music—have closed in Austin in the past 2 years. Only one independent, Waterloo, is still in operation at this writing. A bit sad for the Live Music Capital of the World, no?

Cheapo Discs   In spite of being an import, Cheapo has carved out a niche in the hearts of Austin music lovers. It's *the* place to buy, sell, and trade new and used CDs, and thanks to the knowledgeable (if often surly) staff, there are always treasures to be found in its half-acre of bins. 914 N. Lamar. ℂ **512/477-4499.** www.cheapotexas.com.

Waterloo Records and Video   Carrying a huge selection of sounds, Waterloo is always the first in town to get the new releases. If they don't have something on hand, they'll order it for you promptly. The store offers preview listening, compilation tapes of Austin groups, and tickets to all major-label shows around town. It also hosts frequent in-store promotional performances by both local and mid-sized national bands. There's a video annex just west of the record store (℃ **512/474-2525**) and, for purists, a vinyl section. 600A N. Lamar Blvd. ℃ 512/474-2500. www.waterloorecords.com.

OUTDOOR GEAR

See also **Run-Tex,** listed under "Fashions," p. 233.

The Whole Earth Provision Co.   Austin's large population of outdoor enthusiasts flocks to this store to be outfitted in the latest gear and earth-friendly fashions. If you wouldn't think of hiking without a two-way radio or a Magellan positioning navigator, you can find them here. The Austin-based chain also carries gifts, housewares, educational toys, and travel books. There are additional locations at 1014 N. Lamar Blvd. (℃ **512/476-1414**) and Westgate Shopping Center, 4477 S. Lamar (℃ **512/899-0992**). 2410 San Antonio St. ℃ **512/478-1577**. www.wholeearthprovision.com.

TOYS

Atomic City   Playthings—including a sizable collection of vintage metal wind-up toys—are just one component of the merchandise at this funky, eclectic store in a deceptively prim-looking house near the University of Texas. You'll also find a sizable collection of cult classic film and TV memorabilia, and, in the back, hundreds of styles of shoes and boots for the ultrahip rockabilly crowd. It's all a bit surreal—but in a good way. 1700 San Antonio St. ℃ **512/477-0293**.

Hog Wild   Always regretted throwing out that Howdy Doody lunch box? You can get it back—for a few more bucks, of course—at this nostalgia-inducing little toyshop on the edge of Hyde Park. Photos of celebrity customers such as Quentin Tarantino and Mira Sorvino hang on the wall. 100A E. North Loop Blvd. ℃ **512/467-9453**.

Terra Toys   Steiff teddy bears, the wooden Playmobil world, and other high-quality imported toys are among the kiddie delights at Terra, which, along with its children's-apparel component, **Dragonsnaps** (℃ **512/445-4497**), recently moved to the north side of town, now sharing a single space. The store also carries a variety of miniatures, train sets, books, and kites. 2438 W. Anderson Lane. ℃ **800/247-TOYS** or 512/445-4489. www.terratoys.com.

Toy Joy   The name says it all! The only question is whether kids or grown-ups will have more Toy Joy here. Ambi and Sailor Moon are among the appealing children's lines sold in the large back room. Out front, things like lava lamps, yo-yos, and cartoon-character watches keep both GenXers and boomers fascinated. Amazingly, it's open until midnight on Friday and Saturday. 2900 Guadalupe St. ℃ **512/320-0090**.

WESTERN STORES

Allen's Boots   Name notwithstanding, Allen's sells a lot more than just footwear. Come here too for hats, belts, jewelry, and other boot-scootin' accouterments, and bring the young 'uns too. This store, in now trendy SoCo—which explains the appearance of tie-dyed KEEP AUSTIN WEIRD T-shirts with the Allen's logo—has been around since 1970. Its staying power through the area's sleazy years is a testament to its quality and fair prices. 1522 S. Congress St. ℃ **512/447-1413**.

Capitol Saddlery   The custom-made boots of this classic three-level Western store near the capitol were immortalized in a song by Jerry Jeff Walker. Run by the same family for 7 decades, this place is a bit chaotic, but it's worth poking around to see the hand-tooled saddles, belts, tack, and altogether functional cowboy gear. 1614 Lavaca St. (C) 512/478-9309. www.capitolsaddlery.com.

Sheplers   Adjacent to Highland Mall, the huge Austin branch of this chain of Western-wear department stores has everything the well-dressed urban cowboy or cowgirl might require. If you're already back home and you get a sudden urge for a concho belt or bolo tie, the mail-order and online business can see you through any cow-fashion crisis. 6001 Middle Fiskville Rd. (C) 512/454-3000 or 800/835-4004 (mail order). www.sheplers.com.

WINE & BEER

See also **Central Market** and **Whole Foods Market** in "Food," p. 235.

Grape Vine Market   This warehouse-size wine store, with an expert staff, a huge selection of bottles at good prices, and a large menu of wine tastings and classes, is yet another sign that Austin is coming of yuppie age. If you're seeking a unique wine gift, this is definitely the place to come. There's a good selection of brews and spirits here, too. 7938 Great Northern Blvd. (C) 512/323-5900. www.grapevinemarket.com.

Whip In Beer and Wine *(Finds)*   Beginning life as a convenience store just off the freeway, this place doesn't have much in the way of atmosphere. What it does have is an amazing selection of beer: At a conservative estimate, Whip In has almost 400 different types of brews at any given time, and even more come Oktoberfest or other special beer-producing seasons. In 2003 one of the members of the family that owns Whip In opened **Travis Heights Beverage World,** which features a terrific selection of wines and spirits of all varieties, weekly wine and spirit tastings, and fine cigars. It's right next door to Whip In at 1948 S. I-35 ((C) **512/440-7778;** www.travisheightsbevworld.com). 1950 S. I-35, Woodland Avenue exit on southbound service road. (C) 512/442-5337. www.whipin.com.

Wiggy's   If liquor and tobacco are among your vices, Wiggy's can help you indulge in high style. In addition to its extensive selection of wines (more than 1,500 in stock) and single-malt scotches, this friendly West End store also carries a huge array of imported smokes, including humidified cigars. Prices are reasonable, and the staff is very knowledgeable. The newer location at 1104 N. Lamar ((C) **512/479-0045**) is smaller and doesn't have the congenial neighborhood feel of the downtown branch. 1130 W. 6th St. (C) 512/474-**WINE.**

16

Austin After Dark

It's hard to imagine an itch for entertainment, high or low, that Austin couldn't scratch. The city's live music scene rivals those of Seattle and Nashville, and the performing arts run the gamut from classic lyric opera to high-tech modern dance. Ironically, the source of much of the city's high culture is literally crude: When an oil well on land belonging to the University of Texas system blew in a gusher in 1923, future money for the arts was all but assured.

The best sources for what's on around town are the *Austin Chronicle* and *XLent,* the entertainment supplement of the *Austin-American Statesman.* Both are free and available in hundreds of outlets every Thursday.

The **Austin Circle of Theaters Hot Line** (© 512/416-5700, ext. 1603; www.acotonline.org) can tell you what's on the boards each week. If you want to know who's kicking around, phone **Danceline** (© 512/416-5700, ext. 3262).

The University of Texas is the locus for many of the city's performing arts events. You can reach Texas Box Office at www.TexasBoxOffice.com or © 512/477-6060; there are also outlets in most HEB grocery stores. For other major venues, call © 512/494-1800.

Some of the concerts at La Zona Rosa, the Backyard, and Austin Music Hall, and selected shows at the Paramount Theatre, can be booked through **Star Tickets Plus** (© 888/597-STAR or 512/469-SHOW; www.premier.star tickets.com), with outlets in most Albertson's grocery stores.

The **Austix Box Office,** 3423 Guadalupe (© **512/474-8497** or 416-5700, ext. 1603; www.austix.com), handles phone charges for many of the smaller theaters in Austin, as well as half-price ticket sales. Call for a recorded listing of what's currently being discounted, then pick up tickets at the Austix Box Office or at the **Austin Visitors Center,** 209 E. Sixth (at the corner of Brazos) Tuesday through Thursday from noon to 6pm, Friday and Saturday from noon to 7pm. Half-price tickets are also on sale at **Bookpeople,** 603 N. Lamar Blvd. (© 512/472-5050), on Thursday from 4 to 7pm.

The newest ticket service in town, **Front Gate Tickets** (© **512/389-0315;** www.frontgatetickets.com), handles Austin City Limits Festival tickets as well as those for some of the larger shows at Stubb's, Antone's, La Zona Rosa, the Parish, and the Vibe.

FREE ENTERTAINMENT

Starting in late April or early May, the city sponsors 10 weeks of free **Wednesday night concerts** at Waterloo Park, which range from rock and reggae to Latin and country-and-western, as well as **Sunday concerts** at dusk at Wooldridge Park, Ninth and Guadalupe, featuring the Austin Symphony Orchestra. Call © 512/442-2263 for current schedules of these two series and of the free **Zilker Park Jazz Festival** in September. Every other Wednesday

But There Are No Limits on the Entertainment

PBS's longest-running television program (it first aired in 1975), *Austin City Limits* has showcased such major talent as Lyle Lovett, Willie Nelson, Garth Brooks, Mary Chapin Carpenter, the Dixie Chicks, and Phish. Originally pure country, it has evolved to embrace blues, zydeco, Cajun, Tejano—you name it. The show is taped live from August through February at the KLRU-TV studio, 2504B Whitis St. (near Dean Keeton, 1 block in from Guadalupe), but the schedule is very fluid, so you have to be vigilant to nab the free tickets, which are distributed on a first-come, first-served basis on the day of the taping. Log on to **www.pbs.org/klru/austin** for details of how to get tickets, or phone the show's hot line at ℂ **512/475-9077**.

You don't have to plan in advance to get a free tour of the recording studio, where you can watch an interesting video clip of the show's highlights, stroll through the control room, and get up on the studio stage and play air guitar. Tours are offered at the KLRU studio at 10:30am every Friday except holidays (call ℂ **512/471-4811** to verify the schedule around holidays).

You do, however, have to plan ahead if you want to attend the **Austin City Limits Music Festival,** which debuted in September 2002. Performers at this hugely successful premiere event included Emmylou Harris, Los Lobos, Shawn Colvin, Jimmie Vaughan, and Patty Griffin. For information on future festivals, log on to **www.aclfestival.com** or call ℂ **888/597-7827;** for tickets, call 512/389-0315. This festival is becoming more massive each year, with acts arriving early to make surprise appearances in clubs around town. Locals say it's beginning to resemble South by Southwest (see the "Label It Successful" box, below), but without the stuffy conference part.

night from June through August, **Blues on the Green** is held at Zilker Park Rock Island, 2100 Barton Springs Rd. Contact sponsor KGSR (ℂ **512/390-KGSR;** www.kgsr.com) for information. Some 75,000 people turn out to cheer the 1812 Overture and the fireworks at the Austin Symphony's **Fourth of July Concert** at the northeast triangle of Zilker Park (ℂ **512/476-6064;** www.austinsymphony.org).

From mid-July through late August, the **Beverly F. Sheffield Zilker Hillside Theater,** across from Barton Springs Pool, hosts a summer musical (Zilker Theater Productions, ℂ **512/479-9491;** www.zilker.org). Started in the late 1950s, this is the longest-running series of its type in the United States. The summer **Austin Shakespeare Festival** is often held at the theater, too; for up-to-date information, call ℂ **512/454-BARD** or log on to www.austinshakespeare.org. More than 5,000 people can perch on the theater's grassy knoll to watch performances. Seating is first-come, first-served, so bring your own blanket or lawn chairs.

For information about the huge block party called **First Thursday,** see chapter 15.

1 The Performing Arts

Austin has its own symphony, theater, ballet, lyric opera, and modern dance companies, but it also draws major international talent to town. Much of the action, local and imported, goes on at the University of Texas's Performing Arts Center, but some terrific outdoor venues take advantage of the city's abundant greenery and mild weather.

OPERA & CLASSICAL MUSIC

In addition to putting on performances and sponsoring high-caliber visiting artists, the **Austin Chamber Music Center,** 4930 Burnet Rd., Suite 203 (© **512/454-7562** or 454-0026; www.austinchambermusic.org), holds an annual summer festival. Its popular Intimate Concert series is held at elegant private homes. Austin's first professional opera company, founded in 1985, **Austin Lyric Opera,** 901 Barton Springs Rd. (© **800/31-OPERA** or 512/472-5992 [box office]; www.austinlyricopera.org), currently presents three productions a year at the Bass Concert Hall. Major national and international artists hit the high notes in such operas as *Tosca, Elektra,* and *Marriage of Figaro* in the 2004–05 season.

Austin Symphony   A resident in Austin since 1911, the symphony performs most of its classical works at Bass Concert Hall, although a new hall, which will also host Ballet Austin, the Austin Lyric Opera, and other arts organizations, is slated for completion in 2007. The informal Pops shows (such as Glen Campbell in 2005) play to a picnic table–seated crowd at the Palmer Events Center. In addition, in June and July at Symphony Square, every Wednesday from 9:30am to about 11:30am, kids can try out various orchestral instruments in the symphony's version of a petting zoo. Symphony Square is a complex comprising an outdoor amphitheater and four historic structures dating from 1871 to 1877. Narrow Waller Creek runs between the seats and the stage of the amphitheater. Box office is open Monday to Friday 9am to 5pm; concert days noon to 5pm.1101 Red River St. © 888/4-MAESTRO or 512/476-6064. www.austinsymphony.org. Tickets $19–$35 classical, $20 and $37 pops.

THEATER

The **State Theater Company,** 719 Congress Ave. (© **512/472-5143** or 472-7134; www.austintheatre.org), which performs at the beautiful old theater for which it is named, is Austin's most professional troupe, and their recent repertoire ran the gamut from *A Christmas Carol* to *Nickel and Dimed.* Austin's oldest theater, incorporated in 1933, the **Zachary Scott Theatre Center** (© **512/476-0541** [box office] or 476-0594; www.zachscott.com), makes use of two adjacent venues at the edge of Zilker Park: the John E. Whisenhunt Arena at 1510 Toomey Rd., and the theater-in-the-round Kleburg at 1421 W. Riverside Dr. The rich and varied offerings, including *Crown,* Elton John's *Aida,* and *Keepin' It Weird* (yes, a local Austin production) in 2004–05, are supplemented by holiday productions like David Sedaris's *Santaland Diaries.*

Other theaters in town tend toward the smaller and, in some cases, more offbeat. Top players include the intimate **Hyde Park Theatre,** 511 W. 43rd St. (© **512/479-PLAY** [box office] or 479-7530; www.hydeparktheatre.org), focused on Austin writers, actors, and designers. It's the venue for the Short Fringe performances at the annual 5-week-long FronteraFest, the largest fringe theater/performance art festival in the Southwest. At the thriving theater department at St. Edward's University, the **Mary Moody Northen Theatre,**

Kids A Venerable Venue

The Marx Brothers, Sarah Bernhardt, Helen Hayes, and Katharine Hepburn all entertained at the **Paramount Theatre,** 713 Congress Ave. (© **512/472-5470** [box office] or 472-2901; www.austintheatre.org), a former vaudeville house, which opened as the Majestic Theatre in 1915 and functioned as a movie palace for 50 years. Restored to its original opulence at the end of the 20th century, the Paramount now hosts a diverse roster of nationally touring plays, visiting celebrity performers and lecturers, film festivals and series, and local dance and theatrical productions.

3001 S. Congress Ave. (© **512/448-8484** [box office] or 448-8483; www. stedwards.edu/hum/thtr/mmnt.html), gets support for its performances from a variety of professional directors and guest actors. It's tough to typecast **One World Theatre,** 7701 Bee Cave Rd. (© **512/330-9500;** www.oneworldtheatre. org), where performers might range from *Tangokinesis* to Judy Collins, but you couldn't find a more appealing venue for them than this intimate (300-seat) Tuscan castle–style theater in countrified West Austin.

East Austin is becoming the increasingly gentrified home of many experimental performance and film venues. The most established in that area is **The Vortex,** 2307 Manor Rd. (© **512/478-LAVA;** www.vortexrep.org), home to the Vortex Repertory Company. You can tell by the titles alone—*The Dark Poet's Binge,* say, or *St. Enid and the Black Hand*—that you're well into the fringe. Others to look out for are **The Off Center,** 2211 Hidalgo St. (© **512/567-7833,** www. rudemechs.com/offcente), and **The Blue Theater,** 916 Springdale Rd. (© **512/927-1118,** www.bluetheater.org). The latter hosts such annual events as the full-length FronteraFest performances and Flicker Fest film screenings.

DANCE

The two dozen professional dancers of **Ballet Austin,** 3004 Guadalupe St. (© **512/476-2163** [box office] or 476-9051; www.balletaustin.org), leap and bound in such classics as *The Nutcracker* and *Swan Lake,* as well as in the more avant-garde pieces of the trendsetting *Director's Choice* series, which pairs the work of various contemporary choreographers with the music of popular local Latin musicians and singer-songwriters. When in town, the troupe performs at Bass Concert Hall or the Paramount Theatre. An aptly high-tech ensemble for plugged-in Austin, **Sharir + Bustamante Dance Works,** 3724 Jefferson St., Suite 201 (© **512/236-1296** or 477-6060 [box office], www.sbdanceworks. org), stretches the boundaries of dance toward virtual reality by including video projections and computer-generated images in its choreography. Most of the Austin performances are held at UT's Performing Arts Center, but there are also site-specific environmental pieces. In addition, **Dance Umbrella,** 3710 Cedar St. (© **512/450-0456,** www.danceumbrella.com), sponsors and presents performances by national and international touring acts.

2 The Club & Music Scene

The appearance of country-and-western "outlaw" Willie Nelson at the Armadillo World Headquarters in 1972 united hippies and rednecks in a common musical cause, and is often credited with the birth of the live-music scene on Austin's **Sixth Street.** The city has since become an incubator for a wonderfully vital, crossbred alternative sound that mixes rock, country, folk, and blues. Although the Armadillo is defunct and Sixth Street is long past its creative prime—with some notable exceptions, it caters pretty much to a rowdy college crowd—live music in Austin is very much alive, just more geographically diffuse. There's always something happening downtown in the **Warehouse District,** on the west side, and, most recently, on the stretch of **Red River** between 6th and 10th streets. Some venues, like the Continental Club, have long been off the beaten path, while others, like the Backyard, more recently expanded the boundaries of Austin's musical terrain. It's best to have fun and poke around as you can never tell which dive might turn up the latest talent (Janis Joplin, Stevie Ray Vaughan, and Jimmie Dale Gilmore all played local gigs). If you're here during S×SW (see box, below), you'll see the town turn into one huge, music-mad party.

Note: Categories of clubs in a city known for crossover are often very rough approximations, so those that completely defy typecasting are dubbed "eclectic." Cover charges range from $5 to $15 for well-liked local bands. Note, too, that in addition to the clubs detailed below, several of the restaurants discussed in chapter 13, including **Threadgill's** (p. 189) and **Manuel's** (p. 180), offer live music regularly.

CLUB/DANCE

Oslo   This series of narrow rooms, done in black and white with retro minimalist furnishings, is *the* place to see and be seen in Austin for those who've long eschewed Sixth Street. A sophisticated crowd sips the most creative drinks in town and nibbles intriguing appetizers which are served until 10pm, when things start kicking inside and the line begins to stack up outside. Oslo regularly exhibits the work of local experimental artists and plays host to a strong roster of the city's finest DJs, as well as live performers like regular Tuesday-night torch singer, Hedda Layne. 301 W. 6th Street. © **512/480-9433**. www.oslo-austin.com. No cover most nights.

FOLK & COUNTRY

Broken Spoke ⭐⭐   This is the genuine item, a Western honky-tonk dating from 1964 with a wood-plank floor and a cowboy-hatted, two-steppin' crowd. Still, it's in Austin, so don't be surprised if the band wears Hawaiian shirts, or if tongues are firmly in cheek for some of the songs. Photos of Hank Williams, Tex Ritter, and other country greats line the walls of the club's "museum." You can eat in a large, open room out front (the chicken-fried steak can't be beat), or bring your long necks back to a table overlooking the dance floor. 3201 S. Lamar Blvd. © **512/442-6189**. www.brokenspokeaustintx.com. Cover $5–$15.

Continental Club ⭐   Although it also showcases rock, rockabilly, and new wave sounds, the Continental Club holds on to its traditional country roots by celebrating events such as Hank Williams's and Elvis's birthdays. A small, smoky club with high stools and a pool table in the backroom, this is a not-to-be-missed Austin classic. It's considered by many to have the best happy hour music in town, and the folksy Tuesday blues with Toni Price is a real crowd pleaser. 1315 S. Congress Ave. © **512/441-2444**. www.continentalclub.com. Cover $5–$20.

Jovita's   A winning recipe, Jovita's is part Mexican restaurant, part nightclub, part Mexican-American cultural center—and all South Austin landmark. How can you beat a place that's got terrific flautas and enchiladas, tasty margaritas,

Label It Successful—Austin's S×SW

Started in 1987 as a way to showcase unsigned Texas bands, S×SW soon became *the* place for fledgling musicians from around the world to come to schmooze music-industry bigwigs. In the mid-1990s, film and interactive (high-tech and Internet) components were added to the event, and now they're almost as important as the original musical showcases. A list of festival participants could easily be mistaken for a *Rolling Stone* or *People* magazine table of contents.

Even if you're not looking to make it in the music, film, or Internet industries, this is still the hottest conference ticket around. Programs might include as many as 60 panels and workshops and 900 musical appearances at more than 40 venues around town. Prices for 2005 range from $150 (if you register early for the film or interactive aspects alone) to $810 for the walk-up Platinum rate, which affords access to all conference and music events.

The **South by Southwest (S×SW) Music and Media Conference & Festival** (its full name) is held during UT's spring break, usually the third week of March. For current schedules and speakers/performers, check the website at **www.sxsw.com** or call ✆ **512/467-7979**.

and some of the best sounds in town, ranging from salsa to country? 1619 S. 1st St. ✆ **512/447-7825.** Cover $5–$10.

JAZZ & BLUES

Antone's ⋆ Although Willie Nelson and crossover country-and-western bands like the Austin Lounge Lizards have been known to turn up at Clifford Antone's place, the club owner's name has always been synonymous with the blues. Stevie Ray Vaughan used to be a regular, and when major blues artists like Buddy Guy, Etta James, or Edgar Winter venture down this way, you can be sure they'll either be playing Antone's or stopping by for a surprise set. The owner's incarceration (for selling marijuana) and the club's relocation to the warehouse district haven't changed anything—this is still where you come to hear the bad, sad songs. 213 W. 5th St. ✆ **512/320-8424.** www.antones.net. Cover $8–$35 (depending on performer).

Elephant Room Stars on location in Austin mingle with T-shirted students and well-dressed older aficionados at this intimate downtown venue, as dark and smoky as a jazz bar should be. The focus is on contemporary and traditional jazz, although the bill branches out to rock on occasion. 315 Congress Ave. ✆ **512/473-2279.** www.natespace.com/elephant/. Cover $5–$15.

LATIN & REGGAE

Flamingo Cantina One of the only Sixth Street clubs most serious music lovers still go to, the Flamingo attracts local and touring acts in all subgenres of reggae—dancehall, ska, rocksteady, and dub—as well as a range of local Latin bands and DJs. Lounge around one of several bars and open-air decks when you're not sitting on the comfy carpeted bleachers listening to the performers. 515 E. 6th St. ✆ **512/494-9336.** www.flamingocantina.com. Cover $5–$20.

ROCK

Emo's   Austin's last word in alternative music, Emo's draws acts of all sizes and flavors, from Johnny Cash to Green Day. It primarily attracts college kids, but you won't really feel out of place at any age. The front room holds the bar, pool tables, and pinball machines. You'll have to cross the outside patio to reach the backroom where the bands play. 603 Red River St. ℂ 512/477-EMOS. www.emosaustin.com. Cover $8–$15.

The Red Eyed Fly   A good representative of the hot new music scene along Red River north of Sixth Street, the Fly showcases Texas's top hard rock, pop, and punk bands—as well as national touring acts—at its great outdoor stage. Inside, the jukebox rocks with local sounds. 715 Red River St. ℂ 512/474-1084. www.redeyedfly.com. Cover $5–$12.

SINGER-SONGWRITER

Cactus Cafe ☞   A small, dark cavern with great acoustics and a fully stocked bar, UT's Cactus Cafe is singer-songwriter heaven, a place where dramatic stage antics take a back seat to engaged showmanship. The crowd's attentive listening attracts talented solo artists like Alison Krauss, Townes Van Zandt, and Suzanne Vega, along with well-known acoustic combos. The adjacent **Texas Union Ballroom** (ℂ 512/475-6645) draws larger crowds with big names like the Dixie Chicks. Texas Union, University of Texas campus (24th and Guadalupe). ℂ 512/475-6515. www.utexas.edu/student/txunion/ae/cactus. Cover $10–$35.

Ego's   Located in the parking garage of an apartment building, this '60s clubhouse is dark, smoky, seedy, and loads of fun. Locals throng here for the strong drinks and live nightly music, from piano to honky-tonk country. A couple of run-down pool tables and video games add to the funky charm. You can shoot pool free after 10pm nightly. 510 S. Congress Ave. ℂ 512/474-7091. Cover $3–$8.

Saxon Pub   You'll recognize the Saxon Pub by the giant knight in shining armor in the parking lot, an old friend among lots of new faces along South Lamar Boulevard. This is a long-standing home to South Austin's large community of singer-songwriters. Don't be put off by the medieval kitsch outside—inside, the atmosphere is comfortable and no-nonsense. 1320 S. Lamar Blvd. ℂ 512/448-2552. www.thesaxonpub.com. Cover $5–$15.

Speakeasy   The walk down a dark alley in the warehouse district to reach this multilevel club is all part of the 1920s Prohibition theme, which, mercifully, is not taken to an obnoxious extreme. Lots of dark wood and red velvet drapes help create a swanky atmosphere. Walk up two flights of narrow stairs to enjoy a drink or dance on the romantic Evergreen terrace, which overlooks downtown. The booze is not bootleg, the music (mostly of the singer-songwriter type) is fine, and there's no prohibition on good times. 412 Congress Ave. ℂ 512/476-8086. www.speakeasyaustin.com. Cover $5–$15.

Girl Power

The Austin sound may have long been dominated by names like Willie, Stevie Ray, and Jerry Jeff (Janis was a too-brief blip on the all-male radar screen), but that's changing. Austin is now becoming known as the home of such prominent female performers as Sara Hickman, Shawn Colvin, Patrice Pike, Kelly Willis, Eliza Gilkyson, and the Dixie Chicks.

ECLECTIC

The Backyard ⭐⭐   A terrific sound system and a casual country atmosphere have helped make this one of Austin's hottest venues, although it rarely hosts local bands anymore. Since it opened in the early 1990s, the Allman Brothers, Joan Baez, Chicago, Elvis Costello, Norah Jones, k.d. lang, Lyle Lovett, Bonnie Raitt, and Brian Wilson have all played the terraced outdoor amphitheater, which is shaded by ancient live oaks. Be sure to come early for dinner to the Waterloo Ice House, which serves a Texas menu, including barbecue from The Iron Works (see chapter 13). The food's all good and reasonably priced. Hwy. 71 W. at R.R. 620, Bee Cave. ℂ 512/263-4146; 888/597-STAR or 469-SHOW for tickets. www. thebackyard.net. Tickets $6–$12 local acts, $20–$50 national acts.

Carousel Lounge   In spite of (or maybe because of) its out-of-the-way location and bizarre circus theme—complete with elephant and lion-tamer murals and an actual carousel behind the bar—the Carousel Lounge is a highly popular local watering hole. You never know what will turn up onstage—this place has hosted everything from smaller musical acts to belly dancers. 1110 E. 52nd St. ℂ 512/452-6790. Cover no more than $5.

La Zona Rosa ⭐⭐   Another Austin classic, LZR has departed from its funky roots a bit to go upmarket, featuring bigger names and bigger covers than in the past. But the venue has remained the same—a renovated garage brightly painted with monsters and filled with kitschy memorabilia—and this is still a fun place to listen to good bands, from the Gourds to Greg Allman and Friends. 612 W. 4th St. ℂ 512/263-4146; 888/597-STAR or 512/469-SHOW for tickets. www.lazonarosa.com. Tickets $8–$12 local acts, $20–$50 national acts.

The Parish   Formerly called "The Mercury," this hall atop Jazz Restaurant on Sixth Street is known locally as the best place to see the cream of the local crop alongside the best midsize national acts in a range of genres—hip-hop, rock, funk, reggae, Latin, and electronic. 214 E. 6th. ℂ 512/478-6372. www.theparishroom. com. Tickets $5–$12 local acts, $13–$20 national acts.

Stubb's Bar-B-Q   Within the rough limestone walls of a renovated historic building you'll find great barbecue and country Texas fare and three friendly bars—plus terrific music, ranging from singer-songwriter solos to hip-hop open mics to all-out country jams. Out back, the Waller Amphitheater hosts some of the bigger acts. See also chapter 13 for Stubb's Sunday gospel brunches. 801 Red River St. ℂ 512/480-8341. www.stubbsaustin.com. Cover $6–$25.

COMEDY CLUBS

Cap City Comedy   Top ranked on the stand-up circuit, Cap City books nationally recognized comedians like Dave Chapell, Carlos Mencia, and Bobcat Goldwaith. The cream of the crop turn up on Friday and Saturday, of course, but you'll find plenty to laugh at (including lower cover charges) the rest of the week. Performances are nightly 8pm with additional performances Friday and Saturday at 10:30pm. 8120 Research Blvd., Suite 100. ℂ 512/467-2333. www.capcitycomedy.com. Tickets $4.50–$12.

Esther's Follies   You might miss a couple of the punch lines if you're not in on the latest twists and turns of local politics, but the no-holds-barred Esther's Follies doesn't spare Washington, either. It's very satirical, very irreverent, very Austin. Performances are Thursday 8pm; Friday through Saturday 8 and 10pm. 525 E. 6th St. ℂ 512/320-0553. www.esthersfollies.com. Tickets $18–$23; $2 off for students and seniors.

Velveeta Room For one-stop comedy consumption, go straight from Esther's to the Velveeta Room next door, a deliberately cheesy club serving more generic stand-up, local and national, as well as, on Thursday night, an open mic. Open-mic night is Thursday at 10pm; performances Friday to Saturday are 9:30 and 11pm. 521 E. 6th St. ℰ **512/469-9116.** www.thevelveetaroom.com. Tickets $5–$10.

3 The Bar Scene

BREWPUBS

Bitter End B-Side Lounge & Tap Room Adjoining the Bitter End Bistro & Brewery, this intimate gathering spot serves up (canned) swing, jazz, and blues along with its excellent home brews. Additional yuppie draws are a cask-conditioned beer tap and a separate cigar room. 311 Colorado St. ℰ **512/478-5890** or 478-2337.

Copper Tank Brewing Company Within the confines of these thick limestone walls, sports fans catch games on one of the two large screens, couples dine from an eclectic menu, and singles hopefully scan the crowd, while beer aficionados of all stripes savor the light Whitetail Ale or the Big Dog Stout. A small courtyard provides a haven from the madding crowd. 504 Trinity St. ℰ **512/ 478-8444.**

BRITISH & IRISH PUBS

Dog & Duck Pub I have it on the authority of British friends that this is the real deal, a comfy "local" (British pub) with a relaxing atmosphere. You'll be touring all the British Isles with the mix of darts, Irish jams, bagpipes, and hearty brews. The bangers and mash taste authentic, too—not that that's necessarily a good thing. 406 W. 17th St. ℰ **512/479-0598.** www.doganduckpub.com.

Mother Egan's It's no blarney to boast that this pub's got something for everyone. The weekday happy hour is genuinely happy, animated by lively, friendly banter and a general atmosphere of bonhomie, while on the weekends, the bar welcomes patrons from the open-air artists' market next door. There's no shortage of classic pub entertainment, either, with a healthy mix of TV football, live music in the singer-songwriter vein, and tournaments for trivia and Texas Hold 'Em–style poker. The Irish classics (corned beef and cabbage, shepherd's pie, and so on) and American pub grub are crowd pleasers, too. 715 W. 6th St. ℰ **512/478-7747.** www.motheregansirishpub.com.

GAY BARS

Oilcan Harry's Its name notwithstanding—it's known locally as The Can—this slick warehouse-district bar attracts a clean-cut, upscale, mostly male crowd. Consistently voted Austin's Best Gay Club by readers of the *Austin Chronicle,* this is the place to go if you're looking for a buttoned-down, Brooks Brothers kind of guy. There's dancing, but not with the same frenzy as at many of the other clubs. 211 W. 4th St. ℰ **512/320-8823.** www.oilcanharrys.com.

Impressions

There is a very remarkable number of drinking and gambling shops [in Austin], but not one book store.

—Frederick Law Olmsted, *A Journey Through Texas* (1853)

Late-Night Bites

If it's 3am and you have a hankering for a huge stack of pancakes to soak up that last Shiner you probably shouldn't have downed, Austin has you covered. Part Texas roadhouse, part all-night diner, Austin's cafes offer extra-late hours, funky atmosphere, and large quantities of hippie food. To call them cafes is a bit misleading—there's nothing remotely resembling Gallic, or even Seattle, chic here—but it's as good a term as any for these Austin originals.

One of the earliest on the scene and still hugely popular is **Kerbey Lane,** 3704 Kerbey Lane (🌑 **512/451-1436,** www.kerbeylanecafe.com). Sunday mornings, locals spill out on the porch of the comfortable old house, waiting for a table so they can order the signature "pancakes as big as your head." Musicians finishing up late-night gigs at the Continental Club usually head over to the **Magnolia Cafe South,** 1920 S. Congress Ave. (🌑 **512/445-0000;** www.cafemagnolia.com). On nice nights, enjoy the Love Veggies sautéed in garlic butter or the Deep Eddy burrito on an outdoor deck. Both cafes are open 24 hours daily. Kerbey Lane has three other locations, and Magnolia Cafe has one clone, but the originals are far more interesting.

Rainbow Cattle Co. This is Austin's prime gay country-western dance hall. It's about 75% male, but also attracts a fair share of lesbian two-steppers, especially on Thursday, which is Ladies Night. 305 W. 5th St. 🌑 **512/472-5288.** www.rainbow cattleco.com.

A HISTORIC BAR

Scholz Garten 🌟 Since 1866, when councilman August Scholz first opened his tavern near the state capitol, every Texas governor has visited it at least once (and many quite a few more times). In recent years, Texas's oldest operating biergarten was sold to the owners of the popular Green Mesquite BBQ, giving it new life. The extensive menu now combines barbecue favorites with traditional bratwurst and sauerkraut; a state-of-the-art sound system cranks out the polka tunes; and patio tables as well as a few strategically placed TV sets help Longhorn fans cheer on their team—a Scholz's tradition in and of itself. All in all, a great place to drink in some Austin history. 1607 San Jacinto Blvd. 🌑 **512/474-1958.**

LOCAL FAVORITES

Cedar Door Think "Cheers" with a redwood deck in downtown Austin. In spite of the fact that it keeps changing location—it's moved four times in its 26-year history—the Cedar Door remains Austin's favorite neighborhood bar, drawing a group of potluck regulars ranging from hippies to journalists and politicos. The beer's cold, the drinks are strong, and to lots of folks (no doubt those whose families moved a lot when they were kids), it feels like home. 201 Brazos. 🌑 **512/473-3712.** www.cedardooraustin.com.

Club de Ville This is one of the few bars in the area where you can actually have a conversation without shouting. Settle in on one of the couches inside—the low red light is both atmospheric and flattering—or lounge under the stars, where a natural limestone cliff creates a private walled patio. The cliff is also a great acoustical barrier for the bands that occasionally play here. 900 Red River. 🌑 **512/457-0900.**

A PIANO BAR

The Driskill Sink into one of the plush chairs arrayed around a grand piano and enjoy everything from blues to show tunes in the upper-lobby bar of this newly opulent historic hotel. A pianist accompanies the happy hour hors d'oeuvres (nightly 5–7pm), but the ivory thumping doesn't get going in earnest until 9pm Tuesday through Saturday. 604 Brazos St. ℂ 512/391-7162. www.driskillgrill.com/bar.html.

A WINE & TAPAS BAR

Málaga Come to this sleek, sophisticated spot to sip fine wines at good prices—50 selections by the glass—and nibble Spanish appetizers (the swordfish bites are especially tasty). An important caveat to bear in mind is that this place is not for the smoke-sensitive. 208 W. 4th St. ℂ 512/236-8020.

4 Films

Not surprisingly, you can see more foreign films in Austin than anywhere else in the state. Nearly every cinema in town devotes at least one screen to something off Hollywood's beaten track. In the university area, the largest concentration of art films can be found at the **Dobie Theatre,** 2025 Guadalupe St., on the Drag

Celluloid Austin

Austin has long had an undercover Hollywood presence. During the past 3 decades, more than 90 films were shot in the city and its vicinity. But you'd be hard-pressed to identify Texas's capital in any of them. Because it has such a wide range of landscapes, Austin has filled in for locations as far-flung as Canada and Vietnam.

The city has less of an identity crisis behind the camera. It first earned its credentials as an indie director–friendly place in 1982, when the Coen brothers shot *Blood Simple* here. And when University of Texas graduate Richard Linklater captured some of the loopier members of his alma mater in *Slackers*—adding a word to the national vocabulary in the process—Austin arrived on the *cinéaste* scene. Linklater is often spotted around town with Robert Rodriguez, who shot all or part of several of his films (*Alienated, The Faculty,* and the *Spy Kids* series) in Austin, and with Quentin Tarantino, who owns property in town. Mike Judge, of *Beavis and Butthead* and *King of the Hill* fame, lives in Austin, too.

Of the many cinematic events held in town, October's **Austin Film Festival** is among the more interesting. Held in tandem with the Heart of Films Screenwriters Conference, it focuses on movies with great scripts. For current information, contact the Austin Film Festival, 1604 Nueces, Austin, TX 78701 (ℂ **800/310-FEST** or 512/478-4795; fax 512/478-6205; www.austinfilmfestival.com). And the come-lately film component of S×SW (see sidebar earlier in this chapter) gets larger every year. Panelists have included Linklater and John Sayles, whose film *Lone Star* had its world premiere here.

See also chapter 10 for information on the Austin Gay and Lesbian International Film Festival.

(© 512/472-FILM), and at the two venues of the **Texas Union Film Series,** UT campus, Texas Union Building and Hogg Auditorium (© 512/475-6656). If you'd like something a little more substantial than popcorn with your flicks, check out the **Alamo Drafthouse,** 409 Colorado St. (© 512/476-1320; www. drafthouse.com), offering an inexpensive casual menu nightly as well as such specials as Chinese food and Chinese beer to accompany kung fu films. In addition to films (generally of the alternative or cult variety) and food, there are lectures by celebrity guests—anyone from James Ellroy to Pauly Shore—as well as the live film spoofs of Mr. Sinus Theater. The two newer northern locations, Alamo Village, 2700 W. Anderson Lane, and Alamo Lake Creek, 13729 Research Blvd. at Hwy. 183 in the Lake Creek Shopping Center, do variations on the downtown themes (both can be reached at the same number as the downtown branch).

17

Touring the Texas Hill Country

A rising and falling dreamscape of lakes, rivers, springs, and caverns, the Hill Country is one of Texas's prettiest regions—especially in early spring, when wildflowers daub it with every pigment in nature's palette. Dotted with old dance halls, country stores, and quaint Teutonic towns—more than 30,000 Germans emigrated to Texas during the great land-grant years of the Republic—and birthplace to one of the U.S.'s more colorful recent presidents, the region also lays out an appealing tableau of the state's history.

San Antonio lies at the southern edge of the Hill Country, while Austin is the northeastern gateway to the region. The following tour traces a roughly circular route from San Antonio, but it's only 80 miles between the two cities. Distances in this area are sufficiently short that you can design excursions based on your point of origin and your particular interests.

Note: Driving in the Hill Country can be a delight, but the speed limit on some roads is 70 mph. If you want to enjoy the scenery, move onto the nice, wide shoulders provided for slower drivers and let others pass. It's considered part of Texas road courtesy.

The highlights of the Texas Hill Country are covered here, but those with extra time will find far more to explore. For additional information about the area, contact the **Texas Hill Country Visitor Center,** 803 W. Hwy. 281 S., Johnson City, TX 78636 (© **830/868-5700;** www.hillcountry info.com). The **Heart of Texas Wildlife Trail West** map, which details loop routes covering a variety of the region's natural attractions, is available free at most Hill Country town visitor centers. You can also order the map in advance for $3 by logging on to **http:// tcebookstore.org** or by calling © **888/ 900-2577.**

1 Boerne ⚹

From downtown San Antonio, it's a straight shot north on I-10 to Boerne (rhymes with "journey"). It's a good base for travelers, as it's near both a big city (just 30 miles from San Antonio) and some very rural areas. A popular health resort in the 1880s, the little (2¼ miles long) town near Cibolo Creek was first settled 30 years earlier by freedom-seeking German intellectuals, including firebrand journalist Ludwig Börne, for whom it was named. A gazebo with a Victorian cupola in the center of the main plaza often hosts concerts by the Boerne Village Band, the oldest continuously operating German band in the world outside Germany (it first tuned up in 1860). A number of the town's 19th-century limestone buildings house small historical museums, boutiques, and restaurants, and old-fashioned lampposts and German street signs add atmosphere. But Boerne's biggest draw is the crafts and antiques shops lining the *Hauptstrasse,* or main street. For details, stop in at the **Greater Boerne Chamber of Commerce,** 126 Rosewood Ave., Boerne, TX 78006 (© **888/842-8080** or 830/249-8000; www.boerne.org).

SEEING THE SIGHTS

Those who want to spend their time outdoors can explore four distinct ecosystems—grassland, marshland, woodland, and river bottom—via short treks on the **Cibolo Nature Center,** City Park Road, off Hwy. 46 East next to the Kendall County Fairgrounds (© **830/249-4616;** www.cibolo.org). Dinosaur tracks trace the route of *Acrocanthosaurus atokensis* and friends, whose fossilized footprints were uncovered when the area was flooded in 1997. If you like your strolls to include sand traps, the top-rated **Tapatio Springs Golf Course,** Johns Road exit off I-10 West (© **800/999-3299** or 830/537-4611; www.tapatio.com), is your place.

One of the most popular nearby attractions is **Cascade Caverns** (© **830/ 755-8080;** www.cascadecaverns.com); drive about 3 miles south of Boerne on I-10, take exit 543, and drive a little over 2⅓ miles east. This active cave boasts huge chambers, a 100-foot underground waterfall, and comfortable walking trails; guides provide 45-minute to 1-hour interpretive tours every 30 minutes. It's open Memorial Day through mid-August daily 9am to 6pm; off season Monday through Friday 10am to 4pm, Saturday and Sunday 9am to 5pm. Admission is $13 adults, $7.95 children. Another popular underground attraction is the stalactite- and stalagmite-filled **Cave Without a Name,** 325 Kreutzberg Rd., 12 miles northeast of Boerne (© **830/537-4212;** www. cavewithoutaname.com). A little boy who wrote that it was too pretty to name won a naming contest held when the cavern was discovered in 1939, and happily the $500 he earned put him through college (where maybe he learned how to name things). Hour-long tours of the six chambers are offered throughout the day. Open Memorial Day through Labor Day daily 9am to 6pm; off season daily 10am to 5pm. Admission $11 adults, $6 children.

Rafters and canoeists like **Guadalupe River State Park,** some 13 miles east of Boerne, off Hwy. 46 on P.R. 31 (© **830/438-2656;** www.tpwd.state.tx.us/ park/guadalup/), comprising more than 1,900 acres surrounding a lovely cypress-edged river. Keep an eye out and you might spot white-tailed deer, coyotes, armadillos, or even a rare golden-cheeked warbler. The gate is open daily from 8am to 10pm, and the entrance fee is $5 adults, $3 seniors; 12 and under are free.

If your tastes run to the aboveground and Epicurean, drive 12 miles north of Boerne on FM 1376 to the **Sister Creek Vineyards** (© **830/324-6704;** www.sistercreekvineyards.com), located in a converted century-old cotton gin on the main—actually the only—street in Sisterdale (pop. 50). Traditional French wines are made using traditional French techniques, but the attitude is Texas friendly. Open 11am to 5pm Monday through Saturday, Sunday noon to 5pm. Weave down the road afterward to the **Sisterdale General Store** (© **830/ 324-6767**), opened in 1954 and featuring a beautiful old handcrafted bar made of East Texas pine.

WHERE TO STAY

Now an appealing B&B in the heart of town, **Ye Kendall Inn,** 128 W. Blanco, Boerne, TX 78006 (© **800/364-2138** or 830/249-2138; www.yekendallinn.com), opened as a stagecoach lodge in 1859. The rooms ($109–$139) and suites ($140–$190) are individually—and attractively—decorated, some with Victorian antiques, others with American rustic pieces. Historic cabins ($140–$190) transported to the grounds are available too.

The Texas Hill Country

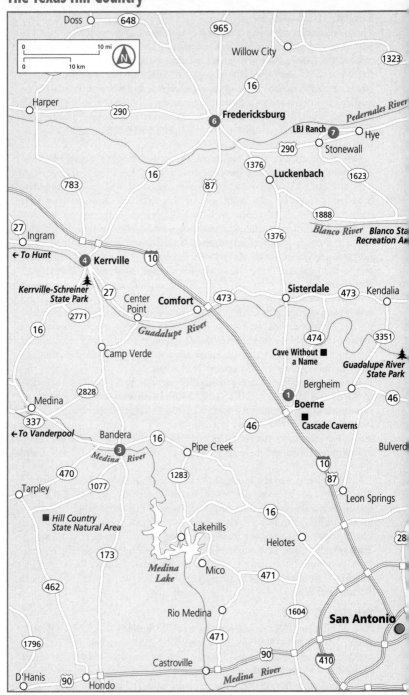

Doss · 648 · 965 · Willow City · 1323

10 mi
10 km

Harper · 290 · Fredericksburg · Pedernales River · LBJ Ranch · Hye · Stonewall · 290 · 1376 · Luckenbach · 1623

16 · 783 · 16 · 87 · 1888 · 1376 · Blanco River · Blanco Sta Recreation Ar

27 · Ingram · 10 · Kerrville · Sisterdale · 473 · Kendalia · ← To Hunt · Kerrville-Schreiner State Park · 27 · Center Point · Comfort · 473 · 474 · 3351 · 2771 · 16 · Guadalupe River · Cave Without a Name · Guadalupe River State Park · Camp Verde · Bergheim · 46 · 2828 · Boerne · Medina · Cascade Caverns · 337 · ← To Vanderpool · Bandera · 16 · Pipe Creek · 46 · 10 · Bulverd · Medina River · 87 · 470 · 1077 · 1283 · Leon Springs · Tarpley · Hill Country State Natural Area · 16 · Lakehills · Helotes · 28 · 173 · Medina Lake · Mico · 471 · 462 · Rio Medina · 1604 · San Antonio · 1796 · 471 · 90 · 410 · Castroville · D'Hanis · 90 · Hondo · Medina River

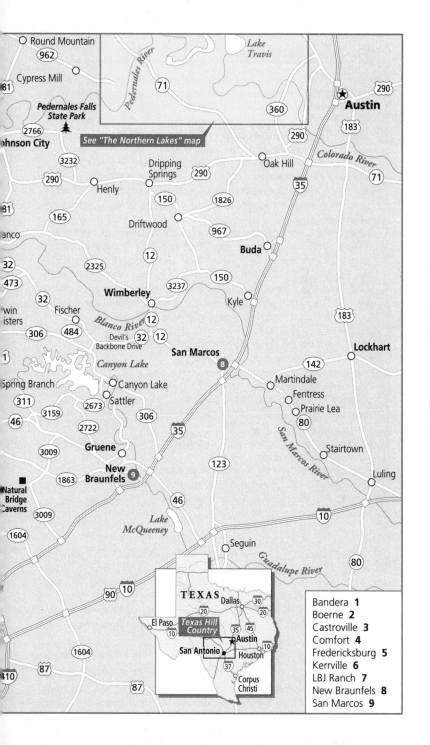

Round Mountain
962
Cypress Mill
81

**Pedernales Falls
State Park**
2766
ohnson City

Pedernales River
71
*Lake
Travis*

★ **Austin**
290
183

3232
290
Henly

Dripping
Springs
290

Oak Hill
290
Colorado River
35
71

See "The Northern Lakes" map

360

81
165
anco

150
Driftwood

1826
967

Buda
150

32
473

2325

12

150
3237
Kyle

183

32
win
isters
Fischer
306
484

Blanco River 12
Devil's 32 12
Backbone Drive

Wimberley

San Marcos
8

142

Lockhart

Canyon Lake

Spring Branch
311
46
3159
2673
Sattler
2722

Canyon Lake
306
35

Martindale
Fentress
Prairie Lea
80

Stairtown

Luling

Gruene
3009
1863
**New
Braunfels**
9

123

San Marcos River

■
**Natural
Bridge
Caverns**
3009

46

*Lake
McQueeney*

10

1604

90 10

Seguin

Guadalupe River
80

1604

87

410

87

TEXAS
Dallas
20
30
20
El Paso
*Texas Hill
Country*
10
35 45
■ **Austin**
San Antonio ■
Houston
10
37
Corpus
Christi

Bandera	**1**
Boerne	**2**
Castroville	**3**
Comfort	**4**
Fredericksburg	**5**
Kerrville	**6**
LBJ Ranch	**7**
New Braunfels	**8**
San Marcos	**9**

A Taste of Alsace in Texas

For a town just 20 miles from San Antonio (via U.S. 90 W.), Castroville has maintained a rural atmosphere. Henri Castro, a Portuguese-born Jewish Frenchman who received a 1.25-million-acre grant from the Republic of Texas in exchange for his commitment to colonize the land, founded it on a scenic bend of the Medina River in 1842. Second only to Stephen F. Austin in the number of settlers he brought over, Castro recruited most of his 2,134 immigrants from the Rhine Valley, especially from the French province of Alsace. You can still hear Alsatian, an unwritten dialect of German, spoken by some of the older members of town, though the language is likely to die out in the area when they do.

Get some insight into the town's history at the **Landmark Inn State Historic Site,** 402 E. Florence St., Castroville, TX 78009 (© **830/ 931-2133;** www.tpwd.state.tx.us/park/landmark/landmark.htm), which also counts a nature trail, an old gristmill, and a stone dam among its attractions. The park's centerpiece, the **Landmark Inn** offers eight simple rooms decorated with early Texas pieces dating up until the 1940s.

For a delicious taste of the past, visit **Haby's Alsatian Bakery,** 207 U.S. 90 East (© **830/931-2118**), owned by the Tschirhart family since 1974 and featuring apple fritters, strudels, stollens, breads, and coffeecakes. Open Monday to Saturday 5am to 7pm.

For additional information, contact the **Castroville Chamber of Commerce,** 802 London St., P.O. Box 572, Castroville, TX 78009 (© **800/ 778-6775** or 830/538-3142; www.castroville.com), where you can pick up a walking-tour booklet of the town's historical buildings, as well as a map that details the local boutiques and antiques shops (they're not concentrated in a single area). It's open 9am to noon and 1 to 3pm Monday through Friday.

Note: Castroville tends to close down on Monday and Tuesday, and some places are shuttered on Wednesday and Sunday as well. If you want to find everything open, come on Thursday, Friday, or Saturday.

The **Guadalupe River Ranch Resort and Spa,** P.O. Box 877, Boerne, TX 78006 (© **800/460-2005;** www.guadaluperiverranch.com), was owned by actress Olivia de Havilland in the 1930s, and served as an art colony for a time. This gorgeous spread offers abundant activities ranging from river rafting and porch sitting to getting wrapped and polished at the spa. The rooms—arrayed in a variety of buildings, including stone cottages and an adobe hacienda—range from $104 to $234, double.

WHERE TO DINE

The Limestone Grill, in Ye Kendall Inn (see above), 128 W. Blanco (© **830/ 249-9954**), sets an elegant tone for its eclectic Southwestern/American menu. It's open for lunch Monday through Saturday, dinner Tuesday to Saturday, brunch only Sunday; entrees are moderate to expensive. An adjoining wine bar made the scene in late 2004. The more casual **Bear Moon Bakery,** 401 S. Main St. (© **830/816-BEAR**), is ideal for a hearty breakfast or light lunch. Organic ingredients and locally grown produce enhance the flavor of the inventive soups, salads, sandwiches, and wonderful desserts. It's open Tuesday to Saturday 6am to 5pm, Sunday 8am to 4pm, and is inexpensively priced. The food is mix and match—a variety of portion sizes and ethnic origins—and somewhat hit-and-miss at the **Dodging Duck Brewhaus,** 402 River Rd. (© **830/248-DUCK**) but you can't beat the views of Cibolo Creek from the front deck, and the beer, handcrafted on the premises, is top-notch. Prices are generally moderate. You can have lunch or dinner at the Duck Tuesday through Sunday.

2 Bandera

Bandera is a slice of life out of the Old West, a town that could serve as a John Ford film set. Established as a lumber camp in 1853, this popular guest-ranch center still has the feel of the frontier. Not only are many of its historic buildings intact, but people are as genuinely friendly as any you might imagine from America's small-town past. True, the roads are getting more crowded each year, but once you hunker down, you're unlikely to need to do much driving around.

WHAT TO SEE & DO

Interested in delving into the town's roots? Pick up a self-guided tour brochure of historic sites—including **St. Stanislaus** (1855), the country's second-oldest Polish parish—at the **Bandera County Convention and Visitors Bureau,** 1206 Hackberry St., Bandera, TX 78003 (© **800/364-3833** or 830/796-3045; www.banderacowboycapital.com), open weekdays 9am to 5:30pm, Saturday 9am to 2pm. Or explore the town's living traditions by strolling along Main Street, where a variety of crafters work in the careful, hand-hewn style of yesteryear. Shops include **Kline Saddlery** (© **830/460-4303**), featuring belts, purses, briefcases, and flask covers as well as horse wear; the **Stampede** (© **830/ 796-7650**), a good spot for Western collectibles; and the huge **Love's Antique Mall** (© **830/796-3838**), a one-stop shopping center for current local crafts as well as things retro. Off the main drag, buy beautiful customized belt buckles, spurs, and jewelry at **Hy O Silver,** 715 13th St. (© **830/796-7961**). Naturally, plenty of places in town such as **The Cowboy Store,** 302 Main St. (© **830/ 796-8176**), can outfit you in Western duds.

If you want to break those clothes in, the Convention and Visitors Bureau can direct you to the outfitter who can match you with the perfect mount; most of the guest ranches (see "Staying at a Guest Ranch," below) offer rides for day-trippers; one I recommend is **Desert Hearts Cowgirl Club** (© **830/796-7001** or 534-5750 [cell]). Check the CVB, too, to find out if any rodeos or roping exhibitions are in the area. (They occur often in summer and less regularly in fall.)

THE GREAT OUTDOORS

You don't have to go farther than **Bandera Park** (© **830/796-3765**), a 77-acre green space within city limits, to enjoy nature, whether you want to stroll along the River Bend Native Plant Trail or picnic by the Medina River. Or you can canter through the **Hill Country State Natural Area,** 10 miles southwest of Bandera (© **830/796-4413;** www.tpwd.state.tx.us/park/hillcoun/), the largest state park in Texas allowing horseback riding. A visit to the nonprofit **Brighter Days Horse Refuge,** 682 Krause Rd., Pipe Creek, about 9 miles northeast of Bandera (© **830/510-6607;** www.brighterdayshorserefuge.org), will warm any animal lover's heart. The price of admission to this rehabilitation center for abandoned and neglected horses is a bag of carrots or apples; donations are also very welcome.

About 20 miles southeast of town (take Hwy. 16 to R.R. 1283), **Bandera County Park at Medina Lake** (✆ **830/796-3765;** http://wildtexas.com/parks/medinalk.php) is the place to hook crappie, white or black bass, and especially huge yellow catfish; the public boat ramp is on the north side of the lake, at the end of P.R. 37. The Bandera Convention and Visitors Bureau can provide the names of various outfitters for those who want to kayak, canoe, or tube the Medina River.

Most people visit the **Lost Maples State Natural Area,** about 40 miles west of Bandera in Vanderpool (✆ **830/966-3413,** www.tpwd.state.tx.us/park/lostmap), in autumn, when the leaves put on a brilliant show. But birders come in winter to look at bald eagles, hikers like the wildflower array in spring, and anglers try to reduce the Guadalupe bass population of the Sabinal River in summer.

STAYING AT A GUEST RANCH

Accommodations in this area range from rustic cabins to upscale B&Bs, but for the full flavor of the region, plan to stay at one of Bandera's many guest ranches (you'll find a full listing of them, as well as of other lodgings, on the Bandera website). Note that most of them have a 2-night (or more) minimum stay. You wouldn't want to spend less time at a dude ranch, anyway; it'll take at least half a day to start to unwind. Expect to encounter lots of European visitors. These places are great for cultural exchange, and you'll learn about all the best beers in Texas—and Germany.

Rates at all the following are based on double occupancy and include three meals, two trail rides, and most other activities.

At the **Dixie Dude Ranch,** P.O. Box 548, Bandera, TX 78003 (✆ **800/375-YALL** or 830/796-4481; www.dixieduderanch.com), a longtime favorite retreat, you're likely to see white-tailed deer or wild turkeys as you trot on horseback through a 725-acre spread. The down-home, friendly atmosphere keeps folks coming back year after year. Rates are $94 to $114 per adult per night.

Tubing on the Medina River and soaking in a hot tub are among the many activities at the **Mayan Ranch,** P.O. Box 577, Bandera, TX 78003 (✆ **830/796-3312** or 460-3036; www.mayanranch.com), another well-established family-run place ($125–$135 per adult); corporate groups often come for a bit of loosening up. The ranch provides plenty of additional Western fun for its guests during high season—things like two-step lessons, cookouts, hayrides, singing cowboys, or trick-roping exhibitions.

The owner of **Silver Spur Guest Ranch,** 9266 Bandera Creek Rd., Bandera, TX 78003 (✆ **830/796-3037** or 460-3639; www.ssranch.com), used to be a bull rider, so the equestrian expertise of the staff is especially high ($125 per adult). So is the comfort level. The rooms in the main ranch house and the separate cabins are individually decorated, with styles ranging from Victorian pretty to country rustic. The ranch, which abuts the Hill Country State Natural Area, also boasts the region's largest swimming pool, some roaming buffalo, and a great kids' play area.

WHERE TO DINE

Those not chowing down at a guest ranch might want to put on the feed bag on Main Street's **O.S.T.** (✆ **830/796-3836**), named for the Old Spanish Trail that used to run through Bandera. Serving up down-home Texas and Tex-Mex victuals since 1921, this cafe has a room dedicated to The Duke and other cowboy film stars. It's open daily for breakfast, lunch, and dinner; entrees are inexpensive to moderate.

Billy Gene's, 1105 Main St. (© **830/460-3200**), lays on huge platters of down-home country standards like chicken-fried steak or meatloaf for seriously retro prices. Less health-defying dishes such as huge salads are available here, too. An open deck and huge windows afford excellent Medina River vistas. It's open daily for breakfast, lunch, and dinner; meals are inexpensive to moderate.

The setting, in a motel at the edge of town, is nothing special, but the **Bandera Star Steakhouse,** 700 State Hwy. 16 S. (© **830/796-3093**), serves some of the best big meat in town. Small meat too: Half-size portions of, say, pork chops, come with all the sides (salad, veggies, rolls) but aren't as hard on the wallet or waistline. The same menu is served at the more casual and very friendly Morgan's bar next door. Lunch and dinner are served Monday through Friday, dinner only on Saturday. Prices are moderate to expensive.

It's not easy to find a seat inside **Mac and Ernie's,** a quirky, semigourmet eatery in a shack some 12 miles west of Bandera in Tarpley (© **830/562-3250**). But that's okay, because the picnic tables out back are the perfect setting for the outstanding steaks, catfish, and specials like quail in ancho honey, served on paper plates with plastic utensils. Hours are very limited (lunch Wed, lunch and dinner Fri–Sat), and prices are moderate.

SOME LOCAL HONKY-TONKS

Don't miss **Arkey Blue & The Silver Dollar Bar** 👣👣 (© **830/796-8826**), a genuine spit-and-sawdust cowboy honky-tonk on Main Street usually called Arkey's. When there's no live music, plug a quarter in the old jukebox and play a country ballad by the owner. And look for the table where Hank Williams, Sr., carved his name.

No one who tends toward the PC should enter the tiny **11th Street Cowboy Bar,** 307 11th St. (© **830/796-4849**), what with all the bras hanging off the rafters. But you can always retreat to the spacious deck out back, and listen to Cajun and country bands.

At the **Bandera Saloon,** 401 Main St. (© **830/796-3699**), the deck is out front and overlooks the town's main drag, but the boot scootin' to live rockabilly and country music takes place inside the large barnlike structure.

EN ROUTE TO KERRVILLE

Each of the roads from Bandera to Kerrville has its distinct allure. The longer Hwy. 16 route—37 miles compared to 26—is one of the most gorgeous in the region, its scenic switchbacks introducing a new forest, river, or rolling ranchland vista at every turn (don't worry, the road is curvy but not precipitous and you're at river level most of the time). Go this way and you'll also pass through Medina. You won't doubt the little town's self-proclaimed status as Apple Capital of Texas when you come to **Love Creek Orchards Cider Mill and Country Store** (© **800/449-0882** or 830/589-2588; www.lovecreekorchards.com) on the main street. Along with apple pies and other fresh-baked goods, you can buy apple cider, apple syrup, apple butter, apple jam, apple ice cream—you can even have an apple sapling shipped back home. Not feeling fruity? The restaurant out back serves some of the best burgers in the area.

Military buffs and souvenir seekers might want to take the more direct but also scenic Hwy. 173, which passes through **Camp Verde,** the former headquarters (1856–69) of the short-lived U.S. Army camel cavalry. Widespread ignorance of the animals' habits and the onset of the Civil War led to the abandonment of the attempt to introduce "ships of the desert" into dry Southwest terrain, but the commander of the post had great respect for his humpbacked recruits. There's little left of the fortress itself, but you can tour the **1877 General Store and Post Office** (© 830/634-7722), purveying camel memorabilia and artifacts as well as country-cute contemporary crafts. The store also sells fixings for picnics at the pleasant roadside park nearby.

3 Kerrville

With a population of about 20,000, Kerrville is larger than the other Hill Country towns detailed here. Now a popular retirement and tourist area, it was founded in the 1840s by Joshua Brown, a shingle maker attracted by the area's many cypress trees (and a friend of Maj. James Kerr, who never actually saw the town and county named after him). A rough-and-tumble camp surrounded by more civilized German towns, Kerrville soon became a ranching center for longhorn cattle and, more unusually, for Angora goats, eventually turning out the most mohair in the United States. After it was lauded in the 1920s for its healthful climate, Kerrville began to draw youth camps, sanitariums, and artists.

SEEING THE SIGHTS

It's a good idea to make your first stop the **Kerrville Convention and Visitors Bureau,** 2108 Sidney Baker, Kerrville, TX 78028 (© **800/221-7958** or 830/792-3535; www.kerrvilletexascvb.com), where you can get a map of the area as well as of the historic downtown district. Open weekdays 8:30am to 5pm, Saturday 9am to 3pm, Sunday 10am to 3pm.

Tip: If you're planning to come to Kerrville around Memorial Day weekend, when the huge, 18-day **Kerrville Folk Festival** kicks off and the **Official Texas State Arts and Crafts Fair** is held, book far in advance.

For your second stop, head to the restored downtown, flanked by the Guadalupe River and a pleasant park. Its historic buildings, most of them concentrated on Earl Garrett and Water streets, host a variety of restaurants and shops, many selling antiques and/or country cutesy knickknacks. Among the most impressive structures is the mansion built of native stone by Alfred Giles for pioneer rancher and banker Capt. Charles Schreiner. It's now home to the **Hill Country Museum,** 226 Earl Garrett St. (© **830/896-8633;** www.kerr downtown.com/hillcountrymuseum), open Monday to Saturday 10am to 4pm; admission $5 adults, $2 students. Highlights include a collection of antique ball gowns. Those interested in updating their own wardrobe of party clothes might consider visiting **Schreiner's,** 736 Water St. (© **830/896-1212**), established in 1869 and continuously operating since then as a general merchandise store. The 1935 post office now hosts the **Kerr Arts & Cultural Center,** 228 Earl Garrett St. (© **830/895-2911,** www.kacckerrville.com), where local artists and artisans strut—and sell—their stuff.

You'll need to drive about 3½ miles north of town to visit the headquarters of **James Avery Craftsman,** Harper Road (© **830/895-1122**), where you can watch artisans work on silver and gold jewelry designs, many of which incorporate Christian symbols. Naturally, there's an adjoining retail shop.

Whether or not you think you like Western art, the **Museum of Western Art** (formerly the Cowboy Artists of America Museum), 1550 Bandera Hwy. (© **830/896-2553;** www.museumofwesternart.org), is not to be missed. Lying just outside the main part of town, the high-quality collection is housed in a striking Southwestern structure. Open Monday to Saturday 9am to 5pm, Sunday 1 to 5pm from Memorial Day through Labor Day; closed Monday the rest

A Bit of Old England in the Old West

Several attractions, some endearingly offbeat, plus beautiful vistas along the Guadalupe River, warrant a detour west of Kerrville. Drive 5 miles from the center of town on Hwy. 27 West to reach tiny **Ingram.** Take Hwy. 39 West to the second traffic light downtown. After about ¼ mile, you'll see a sign for the Historic Old Ingram Loop, once a cowboy cattle droving route and now home to rows of **antiques shops, crafts boutiques, and art galleries** and **studios.** Back on Hwy. 39, continue another few blocks to the **Hill Country Arts Foundation** (© **800/459-4223** or 830/367-5121; www.hcaf.com), a complex comprising two theaters, an art gallery, and studios where arts-and-crafts classes are held. Every summer since 1948, a series of musicals has been offered on the outdoor stage. Continue 7 miles west on Hwy. 39 to the junction of FM 1340, where you'll find **Hunt,** which pretty much consists of a combination general store, bar, and restaurant that would look right at home in any Western. Now head west on FM 1340 for about ¼ mile. *Surprise:* There's a replica of **Stonehenge** sitting out in the middle of a field. It's not as large as the original, but this being Texas, it's not exactly diminutive, either. A couple of reproduction Easter Island heads fill out the ancient mystery sculpture group commissioned by Al Shepherd, a wealthy eccentric who died in the mid-1990s.

of the year; $5 adults, $3.50 seniors, $2 ages 15 to 18 and students, $1 ages 6 to 14. Outdoor enthusiasts will enjoy the nearby **Kerrville-Schreiner Park,** 2385 Bandera Hwy. (© **830/257-5392;** www.tpwd.state.tx.us/park/kerrvill/), a 500-acre green space boasting 7 miles of hiking trails, as well as swimming and boating on the Guadalupe River.

A NEARBY RANCH

You'll need a reservation to visit the **Y.O. Ranch,** 32 miles from Kerrville, off Hwy. 41, Mt. Home, TX 78058 (© **800/YO-RANCH** or 830/640-3222; www.yoranch.com). Originally comprising 550,000 acres purchased by Charles Schreiner in 1880, the Y.O. Ranch is now a 40,000-acre working ranch known for its exotic wildlife (1½- to 2-hr. tours cost $28 per person) and Texas longhorn cattle. Daily activities include everything from organized hunts—not a good idea for those taking the wildlife tours to contemplate—to horseback rides and hayrides. A variety of overnight accommodations are available, too.

WHERE TO STAY

The **Y.O. Ranch Resort Hotel and Conference Center,** 2033 Sidney Baker, Kerrville, TX 78028 (© **877/YO-RESORT** or 830/257-4440; www.yoresort.com)—not near the Y.O. Ranch (see above), but in Kerrville itself—offers large and attractive Western-style quarters. Its Branding Iron dining room features big steaks as well as continental fare, and the gift shop has a terrific selection of creative Western-theme goods. Double rooms range from $79 to $119, depending on the season.

Inn of the Hills Resort, 1001 Junction Hwy., Kerrville, TX 78028 (© **800/ 292-5690** or 830/895-5000; www.innofthehills.com), looks like a motel from the outside, but it has the best facilities in town, including tennis courts, three swimming pools, a putting green, two restaurants, a popular pub, and free access to the excellent health club next door. Rates for double rooms range seasonally from $80 to $95.

The **River Run Bed and Breakfast Inn,** 120 Francisco Lemos St., Kerrville, TX 78028 (© **800/460-7170** or 830/896-8533; www.riverrunbb.com), was built in the late 20th century, but its native limestone and sloping tin roof hearken back to 19th-century German Hill Country architecture. A welcoming front porch, proximity to the Guadalupe River, rooms done in Texas country style, and big down-home breakfasts make you feel you're in a remote rural retreat, but whirlpool tubs and TVs with (in the suites) VCRs remind you you're actually near the civilized center of town. Room rates are $100 to $105; suites cost $139.

WHERE TO DINE

The setting—a beautifully restored 1915 depot with a lovely patio out back—is not the only thing outstanding about **Rails,** 615 Schreiner (© **830/257-3877**), which serves some of the best food in the Hill Country. Everything, from the creative salads and Italian panini sandwiches to a small selection of hearty entrees, is made with the freshest ingredients, many bought locally. The restaurant is open for lunch and dinner Monday through Saturday, and prices are moderate. In warm weather, there's live classic jazz on the patio from Thursday to Saturday.

The name is Italian, but the menu is eclectic, with lots of nods toward Mexico, at **Francisco's,** 201 Earl Garrett St. (© **830/257-2995**), housed in the 1890s Weston building. A downtown business crowd samples soup and salad combos at lunchtime; many return on weekend evenings for such mix-it-up entrees as cilantro lime shrimp or teriyaki chipotle chicken (which I'm told tastes a lot better than it sounds). Francisco's is open for lunch Monday through Saturday, dinner Thursday through Saturday. Prices range from moderate to expensive.

If you missed the pie at Love Creek (see "En Route to Kerrville," above), you can enjoy a slice at **Adams Apple,** 225 Earl Garret (© **830/896-1277**). A variety of inexpensive soups, salads, and sandwiches—including peanut better and Love Creek jelly—are available for lunch Monday through Saturday, but you're likely to have a hard time leaving without a slice of that pie or maybe a fresh-baked triple-chocolate cookie.

TAKING TIME OUT FOR COMFORT

The most direct route from Kerrville to Fredericksburg is via Hwy. 16 North, but antiques lovers and architectural buffs will want to detour some 18 miles southeast along Hwy. 27 to seek Comfort. It has been said that the freethinking German immigrants who founded the town in 1852 were originally going to call it Gemütlichkeit—a more difficult-to-pronounce native version of its current name—when they arrived at this welcoming spot after an arduous journey from New Braunfels. The story is probably apocryphal, but it's an appealing explanation of the name, especially as no one is quite sure what the truth is.

The rough-hewn limestone buildings in the center of Comfort may compose the most complete 19th-century business district in Texas. Architect Alfred Giles, who also left his distinctive mark on San Antonio's streets, designed some of the offices. These days, most of these structures, and especially those on High Street, host high-quality (and generally high-priced) antiques shops. More than

Kids Bats & Ostriches Along a Back Road to Fredericksburg

If you missed the bats in Austin, you've got a chance to see even more in an abandoned railroad tunnel supervised by the Texas Parks and Wildlife Department. From Comfort, take Hwy. 473 North 4 or 5 miles. When the road winds to the right toward Sisterdale, keep going straight on Old Hwy. 9. After another 8 or 9 miles, you'll spot a parking lot and a mound of large rocks on top of a hill. During migration season (May–Oct), you can watch as many as 3 million Mexican free-tailed bats set off on a food foray around dusk. There's no charge to witness the phenomenon from the Upper Viewing Area, near the parking lot; it's open daily. If you want a closer view and an educational presentation lasting about 30 minutes to an hour, come to the Lower Viewing Area, open from Thursday through Sunday ($5 adults, $3 seniors, $2 children 6–16). There are 60 seats, filled on a first-come, first-served basis. Contact the **Old Tunnel Wildlife Management Area** (© **830/990-2860;** www.tpwd.state.tx.us/wma/find_a_wma/list/?id=17) to find out when its occupants are likely to flee the bat cave, as well as other information.

Even if you don't stop for the bats, this is a wonderfully scenic route to Fredericksburg. You won't see any road signs, but have faith—this really will take you to town, eventually. You're likely to spot grazing goats and cows and even some strutting ostriches.

30 dealers gather at the **Comfort Antique Mall,** 734 High St. (© **830/995-4678**). The nearby complex of antiques shops known as **Comfort Common,** 717 High St. (© **830/995-3030**), also doubles as a bed-and-breakfast. If you're in town Thursday to Sunday from 11am to 3:30pm, combine shopping and noshing at **Arlene's Café and Gift Shop,** 426 Seventh St., just off High Street (© **830/995-3330**). The tasty soups, sandwiches, and desserts are freshly made on the premises.

The **Comfort Chamber of Commerce,** on Seven and High streets (**830/995-3131,** www.comfort-texas.com), has very limited hours, but who knows—you might be lucky enough to arrive when it's open (I never have been). Alternatively, try the **Ingenhuett Store,** 830–834 High St. (© **830/995-2149**), owned and operated by the same German-American family since 1867. Along with groceries, outdoor gear, and sundries, the store carries maps and other sources of tourist information.

4 Fredericksburg

San Antonians and Austinites flock to Fredericksburg in droves on the weekends—and with good reason. The town has outstanding shopping, lots of historic sites (so you can pretend you're not just there to shop), and some of the most unusual accommodations around, all in a pretty rural setting.

Fredericksburg may have become fairly yuppified, but it also remains devoted to its European past. Baron Ottfried Hans von Meusebach was one of 10 nobles who formed a society designed to help Germans resettle in Texas, where they would be safe from political persecution and economic hardship. In 1846, he took 120 settlers in ox-drawn carts from New Braunfels to this site, which he named for Prince Frederick of Prussia. The town's mile-long main street is still wide enough for a team of oxen to turn around in (although that hasn't been tested lately). The permanent peace treaty Meusebach negotiated with the Comanches in 1847, claimed to be the only one in the United States that was ever honored, and the gold rush of 1849—Fredericksburg was the last place California-bound prospectors could get supplies—both helped the town thrive. Fredericksburg became and remains the seat of Gillespie County, the largest peach-producing county in the state—which explains the many roadside stands selling the fruit from late May through mid-August, and the profusion of peachy products found around this area.

SEEING THE SIGHTS
IN TOWN

For a virtual preview, go to **www.fredericksburg-texas.com**. Once you're in town, the **Visitor Information Center,** 302 E. Austin St., Fredericksburg, TX 78624 (© **888/997-3600** or 830/997-6523), can direct you to the many points of interest in the town's historic district. Open weekdays 8:30am to 5pm, Saturday 9am to noon and 1 to 5pm, Sunday noon to 4pm. Points of interest include a number of little **Sunday Houses,** built by German settlers in distant rural areas because they needed a place to stay overnight when they came to town to trade or attend church. You'll also notice many homes built in the Hill Country version of the German *fachwerk* design, made out of limestone with diagonal wood supports.

The unusual octagonal **Vereins Kirche (Society Church)** in Market Square once functioned as a town hall, school, and storehouse. A 1935 replica of the original 1847 building now holds the archives of the Gillespie County Historical Society. Open 10am to 4pm Monday to Saturday, 1 to 4pm Sunday, admission $1 per person. The Historical Society also maintains the **Pioneer Museum Complex,** 309 W. Main St., anchored by the 1849 Kammlah House, which was a family residence and general store until the 1920s. Open Monday to Saturday 10am to 5pm, Sunday 1 to 5pm; the admission price, $4 for ages 12 and up, also includes entry to the Vereins Kirche. Among the other historical structures here are a one-room schoolhouse and a blacksmith's forge. For information on both places and on the other historical structures in town, phone © **830/997-2835** or log on to www.pioneermuseum.com.

The 1852 Steamboat Hotel, originally owned by the grandfather of World War II naval hero Chester A. Nimitz, is now part of the **National Museum of the Pacific War** ☆☆, 311 E. Austin St. (© **830/997-4379;** www.nimitz-museum.org), a 9-acre Texas State Historical Park and the world's only museum focusing solely on the Pacific theater. It just keeps expanding and getting better. In addition to the exhibits in the steamboat-shaped hotel devoted to Nimitz and his comrades (currently closed for repairs until 2006), there are also the Japanese Garden of Peace, a gift from the people of Japan; the Memorial Wall, the equivalent of the Vietnam wall for Pacific War veterans; the life-size Pacific Combat Zone (2½ blocks east of the museum), which replicates a World War II battle scene; and the George Bush Gallery, where you can see a captured Japanese midget submarine and a multimedia simulation of a bombing raid on Guadalcanal. The Center for Pacific War Studies, a major research facility, is

Fredericksburg

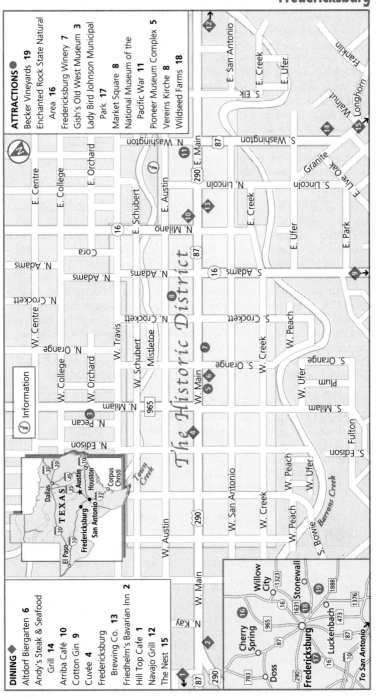

DINING ◆

Altdorf Biergarten **6**
Andy's Steak & Seafood
Grill **14**
Arriba Café **10**
Cotton Gin **9**
Cuvée **4**
Fredericksburg
Brewing Co. **13**
Friedhelm's Bavarian Inn **2**
Hill Top Cafe **1**
Navajo Grill **12**
The Nest **15**

ATTRACTIONS ●

Becker Vineyards **19**
Enchanted Rock State Natural
Area **16**
Fredericksburg Winery **7**
Gish's Old West Museum **3**
Lady Bird Johnson Municipal
Park **17**
Market Square **8**
National Museum of the
Pacific War **11**
Pioneer Museum Complex **5**
Vereins Kirche **8**
Wildseed Farms **18**

slated to open by the end of the decade as part of an expansion that will double the exhibition area of the George Bush Gallery. Until then, limited access to the library archives can be arranged by special request. Indoor exhibits open daily from 10am to 5pm, outdoor exhibits daily from 8am to 5pm; closed Christmas. Adult admission is $5, students pay $3, and children under 6 enter free.

If you're interested in saddles, chaps, spurs, sheriffs' badges, and other cowboy-o-bilia, visit **Gish's Old West Museum,** 502 N. Milam St. (© 830/ 997-2794). A successful illustrator for Sears & Roebuck, Joe Gish started buying Western props to help him with his art. After more than 40 years of trading and buying with the best, he has gathered a very impressive collection. Joe opens the museum when he's around (he generally is), but if you don't want to take a chance, phone ahead to make an appointment.

NEARBY

One of the many attractions in the Fredericksburg vicinity is **Lady Bird Johnson Municipal Park,** 2 miles southwest of town off Hwy. 16 (© 830/ 997-4202; www.fbgtx.org/departments/ladybirdpark.htm). It features an 18-hole golf course; a baseball field; basketball, volleyball, and tennis courts; an Olympic-size swimming pool (open summer only); a lake for fishing; and a wilderness trail.

A visit to the **Wildseed Farms** ⭐, 7 miles east on Hwy. 290 (© 830/ 990-1393; www.wildseedfarms.com), will disabuse you of any naive notions you may have had that wildflowers grew wild. At this working wildflower farm, from April through July, beautiful fields of blossoms are harvested for seeds that are sold throughout the world. During the growing season, for $5 you can grab a bucket and pick bluebonnets, poppies, or whatever's blooming when you visit. There are a gift shop and the Brew-Bonnet beer garden, which sells light snacks. Entry to the grounds, open 9:30am to 6pm daily, is free but you'll have to pay ($4 adults, $3.50 seniors and ages 4–12) to visit the latest addition, the Butterfly Haus, featuring pretty flitters native to Texas.

For a scenic loop drive, head northwest to **Willow City.** The 13-mile route, which leads back to Hwy. 16, is especially spectacular in wildflower season.

Note: The loop is also seriously clogged with traffic when the flowers put in their springtime appearance. You might want to avoid the route at that time of year, and just use your blooming imagination.

Wine Not?

Sonoma has nothing to sweat about yet, but Texas has got a grape thing going these days, and many of the state's wineries are cropping up in the Hill Country. The Fredericksburg area alone hosts eight of them. In the heart of town, the family-run **Fredericksburg Winery,** 237 W. Main St. (© 830/990-8747), sells its own hand-bottled, hand-corked, and hand-labeled vintages, and specializes in dessert wines. Perhaps the most respected winemaker in the vicinity is **Becker Vineyards,** 10 miles east of town on Hwy. 290, off Jenschke Lane (© 830/644-2681). All the region's wineries offer tours and tastings. For more details, pick up a free copy of the **Texas Hill Country Wine Trail** brochure in the Fredericksburg Visitor Center, or log on to **www.texaswinetrail.com.**

Take FM 965 some 18 miles north to reach **Enchanted Rock State Natural Area** 🏃🏃 (© **325/247-3903;** www.tpwd.state.tx.us/park/enchantd), a 640-acre, pink-granite dome that draws hordes of hikers. The creaking noises that emanate from it at night—likely caused by the cooling of the rock's outer surface—led the area's Native American tribes to believe that evil spirits inhabited the rock. Because of the rock's popularity, a limit is placed on visitors. If the park is considered full—which frequently occurs on weekends and holidays—you will be asked to return around 5pm. It's best to call in advance to check. The park is open daily 8am to 10pm; day-use entrance fees are $5 adults, $3 seniors, 12 and under free.

SHOPPING

Ladies and gentleman, start your acquisition engines. If you're pressed for time, concentrate on Main Street between Elk and Milam (although the blocks west of Market Square, recently dubbed Uptown, are fast becoming prime retail estate, too). *Warning:* You may OD on cuteness. More than 100 specialty shops, many of them in mid-19th-century houses, feature work by Hill Country artisans. You'll find candles, lace coverlets, cuckoo clocks, hand-woven rugs, even dulcimers. At **Homestead,** 230 E. Main (© **830/997-5551;** www.home steadstores.com), an ultrafashionable, three-story home furnishings emporium, European rural retro (chain-distressed wrought-iron beds from France, for example) meets contemporary natural fabrics. Pooch people will go barking mad over **Dogologie,** 148b W. Main St. (© **830/997-5855;** www.dogologie.com), carrying everything the fashionable canine might need. For something less effete, check out **Texas Jack's,** 117 N. Adams St. (© **830/997-3213;** www.texas jacks.com), which has outfitted actors for Western films and TV shows, including *Lonesome Dove, Tombstone,* and *Gunsmoke.* This is the place to stock up on red long johns. Interest in the handcrafted wares of **Chocolat,** 330 W. Main St. (© **800/842-3382** or 830/990-9382), tends to transcend all gender and political divides.

Becoming increasingly well-known via its mail-order business is the **Fredericksburg Herb Farm,** 405 Whitney St. (© **800/259-HERB** or 830/997-8615; www.fredericksburgherbfarm.com), just a bit south of town. You can visit the flower beds that produce salad dressings, teas, fragrances, and air fresheners (including lavender, one of the area's major crops these days), and then sample some of them in the on-site restaurant (lunch only; moderate), B&B, and day spa.

WHERE TO STAY

Perhaps even more than for its shopping, Fredericksburg is well-known for its appealing accommodations. In addition to the usual rural motels, the town boasts more than 300 bed-and-breakfasts and *gastehauses* (guest cottages). If you choose one of the latter, you can spend the night in anything from an 1865 homestead with its own wishing well to a bedroom above an old bakery or a limestone Sunday House. Most *gastehauses* are romantic havens complete with robes, fireplaces, and even spas. And, unlike the typical B&B, these places ensure privacy because either breakfast is provided the night before—the perishables are left in a refrigerator—or guests are given coupons to enjoy breakfast at a local restaurant. *Gastehauses* are comparatively reasonable; for about $110 to $175, you can get loads of history and charm. The four main services that book this type of lodging are **Be My Guest,** 110 N. Milam (© **866/997-7227** or 830/ 997-7227; www.bemyguestfredericksburgtexas.com); **First Class Bed & Breakfast Reservation Service,** 909 E. Main (© **888/991-6749** or 830/997-0443;

www.fredericksburg-lodging.com); **Gästehaus Schmidt,** 231 W. Main St. (℘ **866/ 427-8374** or 830/997-5612; www.fbglodging.com); **Hill Country Lodging & Reservation Service,** 215 W. Main St. (℘ **800/745-3591** or 830/990-8455; www.fredericksburgbedbreakfast.com); and **Main Street B&B Reservation Service,** 337 E. Main (℘ **888/559-8555** or 830/997-0153; www.travelmainstreet. com). Specializing in the more familiar type of B&B is **Fredericksburg Traditional Bed & Breakfast Inns** (℘ **800/494-4678;** www.fredericksburgtrad.com).

A recent addition to the Fredericksburg lodging scene, the delightful **Hangar Hotel,** 155 Airport Rd., Fredericksburg, TX 78624 (℘ **830/997-9990;** www. hangarhotel.com), banks on nostalgia for the World War II flyboy era. Located, like the name suggests, at the town's tiny private airport, this hotel hearkens back to the 1940s with its clean-lined art moderne–style rooms, as well as an officer's club (democratically open to all) and retro diner. The re-creation isn't taken too far: Rooms have all the mod-cons. Rates—which include one $5 "food ration," good at the diner, per night—run from $139 to $149 on weekends, $109 during the week.

See also Rose Hill Manor, in the "Lyndon B. Johnson Country" section, below.

WHERE TO DINE

Fredericksburg's dining scene is very diverse, catering to the traditional and the trendy alike. The former tend to frequent the **Altdorf Biergarten,** 301 W. Main St. (℘ **830/997-7865**), open Wednesday to Monday for lunch and dinner, Sunday for brunch, and **Friedhelm's Bavarian Inn,** 905 W. Main St. (℘ **830/997-6300**), open Tuesday to Sunday for lunch and dinner, both featuring moderately priced, hearty schnitzels, dumplings, and sauerbraten, and large selections of German beer. The **Fredericksburg Brewing Co.,** 245 E. Main St. (℘ **830/997-1646**), offers its own home brews and, in addition to the typical pub food, dishes up lots of lighter selections. Book one of the rooms upstairs and you can crawl into bed after a pizza and a pint of Pedernales Pilsner. It's open daily for lunch and dinner; prices are moderate. For blue-plate specials and huge breakfasts of eggs, biscuits, and gravy, locals converge on **Andy's Steak & Seafood Grill,** 413 S. Washington St. (℘ **830/ 997-3744**), open since 1957. Andy's is open daily for breakfast and lunch, for dinner Monday through Saturday; meals are inexpensive to moderate.

Theoretically geared toward those seeking lighter fare, **Arriba Cafe,** 249 E. Main St. (℘ **830/990-0498**), serves huge sandwiches (take advantage of the half sizes) and salads—not to mention incredible pastries from the Rather Sweet bakery downstairs. Lunch is offered Monday through Saturday, and the bakery is open on those days from 8am to 5pm. Local foodies like to roost in **The Nest,** 607 S. Washington St. (℘ **830/990-8383**), which features updated American cuisine in a lovely old house Thursday through Monday evenings; meals are expensive. Equally popular and a bit more cutting edge, the contemporary-chic **Navajo Grill,** 803 E. Main St. (℘ **830/990-8289**), offers food inspired by New Orleans, the Southwest, and occasionally the Caribbean. Open nightly for dinner and on Sunday for brunch; expensive. Oenophiles will adore **Cuvée,** 342 W. Main St. (℘ **830/990-1600**), with its excellent selection of wines by the glass and weekly changing menu (anything from a Middle Eastern platter designed to be shared to full steak dinners). It's open for lunch Thursday through Saturday, for dinner Tuesday through Sunday. Prices range from moderate to expensive. Call or log on to www.cuveewine.net to check about wine and food classes.

Straddling the line between gourmet and *gemütlich,* the **Cotton Gin,** 2805 S. Hwy. 16 (℘ **830/990-5734**), dishes up fare that's just plain good—and plenty of it. Dishes tend toward Tex-Mex (say, shrimp simmered with chilies and

Going Back (in Time) to Luckenbach

About 11 miles southeast of Fredericksburg on R.R. 1376, but light-years away in spirit, the town of **Luckenbach** (pop. 25) was immortalized in song by Waylon Jennings and Willie Nelson. The town pretty much consists of a dance hall and a post office/general store/bar. But it's a very mellow place to hang out. Someone's almost always strumming a guitar, and on weekend afternoons and evenings, Jerry Jeff Walker or Robert Earl Keen might be among the names who turn up at the dance hall. Tying the knot? You can rent the dance hall—or even the entire town. Call © 830/997-3224 for details. And to get a feel for the town, log on to www.luckenbachtexas.com.

Whenever you visit, lots of beer is likely to be involved, so consider staying at the **Full Moon Inn,** 3234 Luckenbach Rd., Fredericksburg, TX 78624 (© 800/997-1124 or 830/997-2205; www.luckenbachtx.com), just ½ mile from the action on a rise overlooking the wildflower-dotted countryside. The best of the accommodations, which range in price from $125 to $200, is the 1800s log cabin, large enough to sleep four. Rooter Boy, the resident pot-bellied pig, is usually around to greet guests.

smothered in cheese and bacon) but also include crossovers like eggplant pirogi. There's a lunch buffet during the week, and dinner is served Monday through Saturday. Entrees range from moderate to expensive.

NIGHTLIFE

Yes, Fredericksburg's got nightlife, or at least what passes for it in the Hill Country. Some of the live music action takes place a bit outside of the center of town. At the **Hill Top Café,** about 11 miles north of town on I-87 (© 830/997-8922), you might find the owner, a former member of the band Asleep at the Wheel, very much awake at the piano, jamming with friends. (The Cajun and Greek food's good too.) Luckenbach (see sidebar, above) also hosts lots of good bands.

And lately, Fredericksburg's main (and side) streets have also come alive with the sound of music—everything from rockabilly and jazz to oompah—especially from Thursday through Saturday nights. An offshoot of The Luckenbach Dancehall, **Hondo's on Main,** 312 W. Main St. (© 830/997-1633), also tends to feature Texas roots bands. Several of the places listed in the "Where to Dine" section, above (including Andy's, the Fredericksburg Brewing Co., and Cuvée) also double as live music venues. Check with the Visitor Information Center for a complete weekly listing.

5 Lyndon B. Johnson Country

Welcome to Johnson territory, where the forebears of the 36th president settled almost 150 years ago. Even before he attained the country's highest office, Lyndon Baines Johnson was a local hero whose successful fight for funding a series of dams provided the region with inexpensive water and power. Try to make a day out of a visit to LBJ's boyhood home and the sprawling ranch that became known as the Texas White House. Even if you're not usually drawn to the past, you're likely to find yourself fascinated by Johnson's frontier lineage.

LBJ HISTORICAL PARKS

From Fredericksburg, take U.S. 290 East for 16 miles to the entrance of the **Lyndon B. Johnson State and National Historical Parks at LBJ Ranch** ☆, near Stonewall, jointly operated by the Texas Parks and Wildlife Department (**830/644-2252;** www.tpwd.state.tx.us/park/lbj) and the National Park Service (℡ **830/868-7128;** www.nps.gov/lyjo). Tour buses depart regularly from the state park visitor center, which displays interesting memorabilia from Johnson's boyhood, to the still-operating Johnson Ranch. You probably won't spot Lady Bird Johnson, who spends about a third of her time here, but don't be surprised to see grazing longhorn cattle.

Crossing over the swiftly flowing Pedernales River and through fields of phlox, Indian blanket, and other wildflowers, you can easily see why Johnson used the ranch as a second, more comfortable White House, and why, discouraged from running for a second presidential term, he came back here to find solace and, eventually, to die. A reconstruction of the former president's modest birthplace lies close to his (also modest) final resting place, shared with five generations of Johnsons.

On the side of the river from which you started out, period-costumed "occupants" of the **Sauer-Beckmann Living History Farm** give visitors a look at typical Texas-German farm life at the turn of the century. Chickens, pigs, turkeys, and other farm animals roam freely or in large pens, while the farmers go about their chores, which might include churning butter, baking, or feeding the animals. The midwife who attended LBJ's birth grew up here. As interesting as Colonial Williamsburg, but much less known (and thus not as well funded), this is a terrific place to come with kids. Nearby are nature trails, a swimming pool (open only in summer), and lots of picnic spots. Bring your pole (or rent one in Austin) if you want to fish in the Pedernales River.

Bus tours—the only way to see the ranch—cost $6 for ages 18 to 61, $3 for ages 7 to 17 and over 62; children 6 and under are free. All other areas are free. All state park buildings, including the visitor center, are open daily 8am to 5pm; the Sauer-Beckmann Living History Farm is open daily 8am to 4:30pm. The Nature Trail, grounds, and picnic areas are open until dark every day. National Park Service tours of the LBJ Ranch, lasting from 1 to 1½ hours, depart from the state park visitor center daily 10am to 4pm (tours may be shortened or canceled due to excessive heat and humidity). All facilities in both sections of the park are closed Thanksgiving, Christmas, and New Year's Day.

It's 14 miles farther east along U.S. 290 to **Johnson City,** a pleasant agricultural town named for founder James Polk Johnson, LBJ's first cousin once removed. The **Boyhood Home** ☆—the house on Elm Street where Lyndon was raised after age 5—is the centerpiece of this unit of the **Lyndon B. Johnson National Historical Park.** The modest white clapboard structure the family occupied from 1913 on was a hub of intellectual and political activity: LBJ's father, Sam Ealy Johnson, Jr., was a state legislator, and his mother, Rebekah, was one of the few college-educated women in the country at the beginning of the 20th century. From here, be sure to walk over to the **Johnson Settlement,** where LBJ's grandfather, Sam Ealy Johnson, Sr., and his great-uncle, Jessie, engaged in successful cattle speculation in the 1860s. The rustic dogtrot cabin out of which they ran their business is still intact. Before exploring the two sites, stop at the **visitor center** (℡ **830/868-7128**); from U.S. 290, which turns into

Main Street, take F Street to Lady Bird Lane, and you'll see the signs—where a number of excellent interactive displays and two half-hour-long films (one about Johnson's presidency, and the other about Lady Bird) provide background for the buildings you'll see.

The Boyhood Home, visitor center, and Johnson Settlement are all open 8:45am to 5pm daily except Christmas, Thanksgiving, and New Year's Day. Admission is free. The Boyhood Home can be visited only by tours, offered every half-hour from 9 to 11:30am, and 1 to 4:30pm.

BEYOND LBJ: WHAT TO DO, WHERE TO EAT & STAY

Johnson City has attractions that have little to do with the 36th president, although you can claim that shopping for antiques is also a history-oriented activity (hey, it's worth a try). Several low-key antiques shops dot Main Street; perhaps the best is the **Old Lumber Yard,** 209 E. Main St. (© **830/868-2381**), selling reasonably priced items from a variety of eras, including the present one. One of the highlights of the complex is the **Silver K Café** (© **830/868-2911**), where creative soups, salads, and sandwiches are served at lunchtime from Monday to Saturday. From Thursday through Saturday evenings, you might dine on Gulf Coast cioppino, perhaps, or pan-grilled top sirloin with mustard sauce. Prices range from moderate to expensive. If you prefer your meats more portable, visit **Whittington's,** 602 Hwy. 281 S. (© **877/868-5501**), renowned around Texas for its beef and turkey jerky (just drop in for a sample; fresh jerky bears little resemblance to the convenience store kind).

The area's top place to dine—and to bed down—isn't in Johnson City, however, but about 16 miles to the west. You'll drive down a rural back road to reach **Rose Hill Manor,** 2614 Upper Albert Rd., Stonewall, TX 78671 (© **877/ ROSEHIL** or 830/644-2247; www.rose-hill.com), a reconstructed southern manse. Light and airy accommodations—four in the main house, and six in separate cottages—are beautifully but comfortably furnished with antiques. All offer porches or patios and great Hill Country views. Rates run from $145 to $165. The inn's New American cuisine, served Wednesday through Sunday evenings in an ultraromantic dining room, is outstanding. Reservations are essential; prices are expensive.

The **Johnson Chamber of Commerce and Tourism Bureau,** 604 Hwy. 281 S., Johnson City, TX 78636 (© **830/868-7684;** www.johnsoncity-texas.com), can provide information about other local dining, lodging, and shopping options.

If you're heading on to Austin, take a short detour from U.S. 290 to **Pedernales Falls State Park,** 8 miles east of Johnson City on F.R. 2766 (© **830/ 868-7304;** www.tpwd.state.tx.us/park/pedernal). When the flow of the Pedernales River is normal to high, the stepped waterfalls that give the 4,860-acre park its name are quite dramatic.

6 The Northern Lakes

Nature lovers and those seeking a slice of rural Texas should consider detouring even farther from Johnson City en route to Austin to visit the northernmost of the Highland Lakes (see chapter 14): Lake Marble Falls, Lake LBJ, Inks Lake, and Lake Buchanan. One of the nice things about touring this area is that you have to take it slow: All that water forces you to meander along rural roads rather than drive directly to your destination. And of course engaging with that water—whether submerging in it or just gazing at it—is what most people come here for. For additional information about where to kayak, sail, swim, or fish, check with the chambers of commerce and visitor centers listed in this section.

From Johnson City, it's 23 miles north on Hwy. 281 to the town of **Marble Falls,** renowned for two natural features, only one of which still exists. The cascades for which the town was named once descended some 20 feet along a series of marble ledges, but they were submerged when the Max Starcke Dam, which created Lake Marble Falls, was completed in 1951. (You can occasionally get a peek at the falls when the Lower Colorado River Authority lowers the water level to repair the dam.) The town's other natural claim to fame is the still very visible Granite Mountain, from which the pink granite used to create the state capitol in Austin was quarried.

The main reason most people come to Marble Falls these days is its three parks and its two lakes (Lake LBJ lies a little upstream), but it's also pleasant to wander around the center of town, where there are a number of historic homes, antiques shops, and the (new) Old Oak shopping complex, featuring such whimsical gift boutiques as It's All About Me.

One of the town's other attractions is also the place to get details on what to see and do in the area: The **Marble Falls/Lake LBJ Visitor Center,** 801 Hwy. 281 (© **800/759-8178** or 830/693-4449; www.marblefalls.org), is located in the Historic Depot Building, built to serve the railroad spur used to transport granite to Austin. The visitor center is open Monday to Friday from 8am to 5pm.

Trains no longer make it to Marble Falls, but they do go to **Burnet,** some 14 miles to the north. The Austin Steam Train Association restored the five historic coaches and the 1916 locomotive that you can board for the **Hill Country Flyer Steam Train Excursion** (© **512/477-8468;** www.austinsteamtrain.org), a leisurely 33-mile tootle from Cedar Park, northwest of Austin. The train runs Saturday and Sunday March through May, Saturday only June to November, and selected December evenings. Fares are $25 adults, $22 seniors, and $15 for children in coach.

The train makes a 3-hour layover on Burnet's historic town square, which, with its impressive county courthouse—not to mention its collectibles shops and cafes—is also a good spot for visitors who drive into town to explore (*beware:* a gunfight is staged at 2:30pm on most Saturdays when the train comes in). Burnet grew up around a U.S. Army post established in 1849, and you can still visit the **Fort Croghan Grounds and Museum,** 703 Buchanan Dr. (Hwy. 29 W.) (© **512/756-8281;** www.fortcroghan.org), home to several historic outbuildings and more than 1,200 historic artifacts from around the county. Admission is free; the museum is open April through August, Thursday through Saturday, from 10am to 5pm. In the same complex (but not in a historic building and open year-round) is the **Burnet Chamber of Commerce** (© **512/756-4297;** www.burnetchamber.org). Here, among other things, you can find out why Burnet calls itself the Bluebonnet Capitol of Texas—and when you should come to see if it lives up to that claim. The chamber is open 8:30am to 5:30pm Monday through Friday.

Some 11 miles southwest of Burnet, **Longhorn Cavern State Park,** Park Road 4, 6 miles off U.S. 281 (© **877/441-CAVE** or 830/598-CAVE), has as its centerpiece one of the few river-formed caverns in Texas. Its past visitors included Ice Age animals, Comanche Indians, Confederate soldiers, and members of the Civilian Conservation Corps, who built the stairs that descend into the main room in the 1930s. The cave's natural and human history is detailed

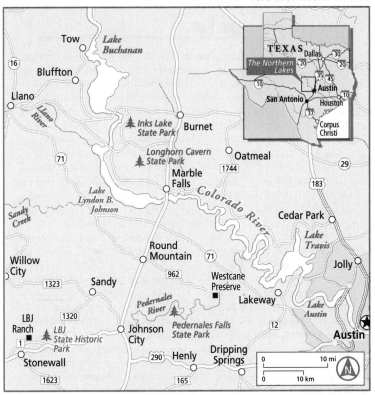

on narrated tours—the only way you can visit—that last about an hour and a half; they're offered from Labor Day to Memorial Day Monday to Thursday at 11am, 1pm, and 3pm, Friday to Sunday from 10am to 4pm every hour on the hour. In summer, tours run every day on the hour from 10am to 4pm. Admission is $11 adults, $9.95 for children ages 13 to 19, $5.95 ages 2 to 12.

Continue north on Park Road 4, beyond where it intersects with R.R. 2342, and you'll reach **Inks Lake State Park,** 3630 Park Road 4 W. (© **512/793-2223;** www.tpwd.state.tx.us/park/inks), offering some 1,200 acres of recreational facilities on and adjacent to the lake for which it's named: hiking trails, canoe and paddle-boat rentals, swimming, fishing—even golf on an 18-hole course. Don't miss Devil's Waterhole, flanked by pink granite boulders and a waterfall. You can canoe through it, hike to it, or just view it from a scenic overlook on Park Road 4.

Those with limited time might want to skip Inks Lake in favor of the oldest, most remote, and largest of the Highland Lakes, the 32-mile-long Lake Buchanan. The best way to see it—and the highlight of any trip to this area—is the **Vanishing Texas River Cruise** ★★ (© **800/4-RIVER-4** or 512/756-6986; www.vtrc.com), which departs from the Canyon of the Eagles Lodge & Nature Park (see "Where to Stay & Dine," below), at the end of R.R. 2341 on the lake's north shore (call for directions, or check the website). The lake's banks are still startlingly pristine (though private development may soon

Driving the Bluebonnet Trail

Call it *lupinus subcarnosus*, *lupinus texensis*, buffalo clover, wolf flower, even *el conejo*: A bluebonnet by any other name still smells as sweet, and looks as pretty. So when the official state flower of Texas puts in an appearance—starting in March and peaking in April—hordes of people descend on the Hill Country to ogle and photograph the fields of flowers (think East Coast leaf-watching in autumn, only more in a more concentrated area and time frame).

Several parts of the Hill Country offer good wildflower viewing opportunities, but the official Bluebonnet Trail starts in Austin and winds its way through several of the northern Highland Lakes communities, including Llano, Burnet, and Marble Falls. Like the bluebonnets, the trail itself is ephemeral: The signage for this route exists for only two weekends, usually the first couple in April (see "The Bluebonnet Trail" map). Burnet even hosts a **Bluebonnet Festival** on the second weekend in April, with live entertainment and food and crafts vendors (✆ **512/756-4297**).

But bluebonnets aren't the only show in town. The **Texas Hill Country Wildflower Trail** was created by 10 Hill Country communities to celebrate the natural roadside beauty from late March through June. In addition to bluebonnets, you'll see Texas paintbrush, sunflowers, coreopsis, and black-eyed Susans. For more information on event listings, locations, and activities along the, contact the **Wildflower Trail Headquarters** at ✆ **866/TEX-FEST** or go to www.tex-fest.com. For more on the Bluebonnet Trail and other wildflower-related events, contact the **Wildflower Hotline** (aka the National Wildflower Research Center in Austin; see Chapter 16) at ✆ **512-929-3600**.

make the "vanishing" part of the cruise's name too true), and no matter what time of year you come you're bound to see some wildlife. From November through March, bald eagles troll the skies, while the rest of the year wild turkeys and deer abound. These expertly narrated tours, which offer a lot of historical as well as natural information, vary season by season; prices range from about $17 for adults for the basic 2½-hour naturalist tours to $25 for sunset dinner cruises. Reservations are recommended.

If you want to get more up close and personal with the water, book one of the kayaking tours run by **Lake Buchanan Adventures** (✆ **512/756-9911;** www.lakebuchananadventures.com), which depart from the same north Lake Buchanan dock as the river cruises. A 4-hour trip, which includes a deli lunch at the scenic Fall Creek waterfalls, and all equipment, gear, and experienced guides, runs $65 for adults. Hiking and kayaking trips, overnight camping trips, and boat rentals are available too. Reservations are essential.

Both the Vanishing Texas River Cruise and Lake Buchanan Adventures include excursions to a winery on their rosters (usually in spring), but you can also visit **Fall Creek Vineyards** (✆ **915/379-5361;** www.fcv.com) by land. From Marble Falls, go west on R.R. 1431; after 20 miles, it meets Hwy. 261.

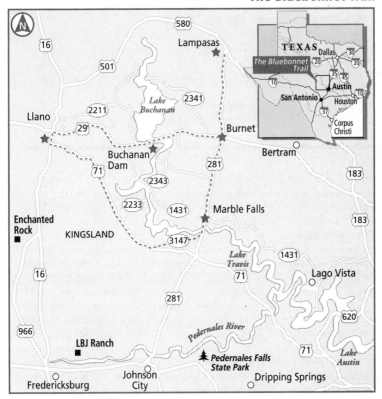

Turn left (north) on Hwy. 261 and drive 6 miles along Lake Buchanan to Bluffton, then take a right on R.R. 2241, which will trail off after about 8 miles (2¼ miles beyond the town of Tow) into the winery. The bottles produced by these 65 acres of lakeside vineyards won't excite real oenophiles—and you can buy some of the wines for less at the HEB supermarket in Burnet—but it's a pretty drive over to the tasting room. Best bets: the Chardonnays and Rieslings. The vineyards are open Monday to Friday from 11am to 4pm; Saturday from noon to 5pm; and Sunday from noon to 4pm.

WHERE TO STAY & DINE

Rustic lakeside cabins and small motels dot this entire area, but two lodgings stand out. If you head 15 miles east of Marble Falls on FM 1431, you'll reach the town (such as it is) of Kingsland and **The Antlers,** 1001 King St., Kingsland, TX 78639 (ⓒ **800/383-0007** or 916/388-4411, www.theantlers.com), a restored turn-of-the-century resort occupying 15 acres on Lake LBJ. You've got a choice of bedding down in one of six antiques-filled suites in the 1901 railroad hotel, as President William McKinley did ($120–$140); in one of three colorful converted train cabooses ($120) or a converted railroad coach ($130–$140), parked on a piece of original track; or in one of seven appealing cabins scattered around the grounds ($130–$220). Some of the accommodations sleep four or six people comfortably, and one of the lodges accommodates up to eight. Activities include

Speaking Northern Lake-ese, 1, 2, 3

Want to talk like a local?

1. For Buchanan, lake or dam, say "*Buck*-anon," not "*Byou*-kanon." The body of water was named after congressman James Buchanan, who got federal funds to complete the dam in the 1930s, not after the U.S. president.
2. The town of Tow rhymes with "now."
3. Burnet, town and county, is pronounced "*Burn*-it" (as in "Durnit, can't you learnit?").

strolling several nature trails, boating or fishing on the lake, or browsing the antiques shop in the main hotel building. For fortification, cross the road to the Kingsland Old Town Grill, a good place for steak, regular or chicken-fried. Look eerily familiar? This 1890s Victorian house served as the film set for the original *Texas Chainsaw Massacre.*

Opened in 1999 on 940 acres owned by the Lower Colorado River Authority—most of it still wilderness preserve—the **Canyon of the Eagles Lodge & Nature Park,** 16942 R.R. 2341, Burnet, TX 78611 (© **800/977-0081** or 512/756-8787; www.canyonoftheeagles.com), is ideal for those seeking serious escape. You can indulge in the Lake Buchanan excursions or adventures described in the previous section, hike the property's trails, stargaze at the lodge's observatory, or just kick back on your porch and watch birds flitting by. The Canyon Room restaurant offers everything from Fredericksburg bratwurst to pecan-crusted trout. Rates for the rooms, which are country-style rustic but feature such conveniences as phones with dataports (in case your escape is not *that* serious) and, in the Cottage Rooms, minifridges and microwaves, range from $99 to $159. A minimum of 2 nights is required for popular weekends, but you wouldn't want to stay less time than that anyway.

In addition to the Kingsland Old Town Grill and the Canyon Room—the latter has the advantage of being BYOB and the disadvantage of being far from most everywhere if you're not staying at the lodge—I'd recommend two places in Marble Falls, which fall at the opposite ends of the history (and sophistication) spectrum. **Blue Bonnet Cafe,** 211 Hwy. 281 (© **830/693-2344;** www.bluebonnetcafe.net), first opened its doors in 1929 and has been receiving accolades for its down-home country food—chicken-fried steak, pot roast, fried okra—ever since: It was recently voted the number one place to eat breakfast in Texas by the readers of *Texas Monthly* magazine. It's open every day for breakfast and lunch, and serves dinner every day except Sunday. Prices are inexpensive to moderate. **Café 909,** 909 Second St. (© **830/693-2126;** www.cafe909.com), which debuted in 2003, showcases the New American cuisine of chef/owner Mark Schmidt, who has cooked at some of the top restaurants in Dallas and Santa Fe. In a pared-down but intimate limestone building, enjoy the likes of seared divers scallops with roasted eggplant purée, followed, perhaps, by pan roasted breast of pheasant with spaghetti squash carbonara. Don't skip the stellar desserts. Café 909 is open for dinner Tuesday through Saturday. Prices are expensive, and reservations are requested.

Barbecue lovers—especially those en route to or from Fredericksburg—might want to make the pilgrimage to Llano, where the Wootan family has been smoking big meat in a big pit forever at **Cooper's,** 505 W. Dallas St. (© **325-247-5713;**

www.coopersbbq.com). The huge pork chop is the signature pig-out dish, but you won't go wrong with any of the cuts you choose from the grill before you enter the restaurant to pay and pick up your sides of coleslaw, beans, and white bread. Cooper's is open 10:30am to 8pm Sunday through Thursday, until 9pm Friday and Saturday. Prices are inexpensive to moderate.

7 San Marcos

Some 26 miles south of Austin via I-35, San Marcos was first settled by a tribe of nomadic Native Americans around 12,000 years ago. Some scholars claim it is the oldest continuously inhabited site in the Western Hemisphere. Temporary home to two Spanish missions in the late 1700s, as well as to Comanches and Apaches (which explains the "temporary" part), this site at the headwaters of the San Marcos River was permanently settled by Anglos in the middle of the 19th century. Now host to Texas State University—San Marcos (formerly Southwest Texas State University), the alma mater of LBJ, and the only university in the state to graduate a future president—San Marcos has the laid-back feel of a college town. It's also fast becoming a bedroom community of Austin, only half an hour away.

WHAT TO SEE & DO

In the center of town—and, clearly, the reason for its existence—more than 1,000 springs well up from the Balcones Fault to form Spring Lake; its astonishingly clear waters maintain a constant temperature of 72°F (22°C). On the lake's shore sits the **Aquarena Center** 𝄐𝄐, 1 Aquarena Springs Dr. (© **512/ 245-7575;** www.aquarenacenter.com), an exemplar of tourism trends. The first theme park to be opened in Texas, and once home to Ralph the Swimming Pig, it was purchased in the mid-1990s by Texas State University, which then spent $16 million to convert it into an environmental research center. Glass-bottom boat tours, which allow you to view the lake's rare flora and fauna, cost $7 for adults, $6 for seniors 55 and older, and $5 for children 4 to 14. In addition, there are environmental tours (2 weeks advance arrangement required), an endangered species exhibit, a natural aquarium, hikes, and a boardwalk over the wetlands, where more than 100 species of birds have been spotted. You can also visit the log home of Gen. Edward Burleson, who built the dam that created Spring Lake to power his gristmill.

The **San Marcos River,** which begins at Spring Lake, is also getting (somewhat) eco-conscious. Log on to www.sanmarcosriver.org to find out about conservation measures taken by the San Marcos River Foundation. Not-so-rare species on the river include canoeists and rafters: Between May and September, the local Lions Club (© **512/396-LION;** www.centuryinter.net/smlc/ tuberental.html) rents inner tubes and operates a river shuttle at City Park; check the website for a schedule and rates.

When the Balcones Fault was active some 30 million years ago, an earthquake created the cave at the center of **Wonder World,** 1000 Prospect St., off Bishop (© **877/492-4657** or 512/392-3760; www.wonderworldpark.com). If you're short on time, don't go out of your way to visit this much-hyped attraction. (Skip the petting farm, for example, which is essentially a tram ride through an enclosure of depressed-looking deer.) A tour of the cave eventually takes you to the so-called Anti-Gravity House, where you can see water flowing upward. The cave ($11 adults, $9 children 4–11) is okay, but the Anti-Gravity House ($3 all ages) is just tacky. This attraction is open daily from June through August from

8am to 8pm; Monday through Friday from 9am to 5pm, Saturday and Sunday from 9am to 6pm the rest of the year; it is closed Christmas Eve and Christmas.

San Marcos's entire downtown area is listed in the National Register of Historic Places. Its hub is **Courthouse Square,** where several turn-of-the-century buildings are being restored. The **State Bank and Trust Building,** dating back to the late 1800s, was robbed by the Newton Gang in 1924 and (most likely) by Machine Gun Kelly in 1933; *The Getaway,* starring Steve McQueen and Ali McGraw, was shot here in 1972. See "Where to Stay & Dine," below, for the building's latest incarnation.

To get an inside look at one of the town's two tree-lined residential districts, make an appointment to view the **Millie Seaton Collection of Dolls and Toys,** 1104 W. Hopkins ((C) **512/396-1944**), housed in the opulent 1908 Augusta Hofheinz mansion. Thousands of tiny eyes peer at you from the three stories crammed with figurines that Mrs. Seaton has been collecting since 1965, including some rare historical specimens. You're likely to recognize a few of them from your childhood. Admission is free.

Texas State University's Albert B. Alkek Library isn't old, but it's home to some of the state's most important literary artifacts as well as to a gem of a gallery. The **Southwestern Writers Collection** ⟨⟩, on the seventh floor of the library at 601 University Dr. ((C) **512/245-3861;** www.library.swt.edu/swwc), showcases materials donated by the region's leading filmmakers, musicians, and wordsmiths. You might see anything from a 1555 printing of the journey of Spanish adventurer Cabeza de Vaca to a songbook created by an 11-year-old Willie Nelson to the costumes worn by Tommy Lee Jones and Robert Duvall in *Lonesome Dove.* (The collection was founded by screenwriter Bill Wittliff, who wrote the script for that TV miniseries as well as for *Legends of the Fall* and *A Perfect Storm.*) The collection is generally open to the public Monday, Tuesday, and Friday 8am to 5pm, Wednesday and Thursday 8am to 7pm, Saturday 9am to 5pm, Sunday 2 to 6pm, but hours change with university holidays and breaks; phone ahead or check the website. The **Wittliff Gallery of Southwestern & Mexican Photography** ⟨⟩ ((C) **512/245-2313**) exhibits not only works from an excellent permanent collection, but also temporary shows by other renowned photographers. Call ahead for directions to the building and parking garage; hours are the same as for the Southwestern Writers Collection.

OUTLET SHOPPING

If truth be told, lots of people bypass San Marcos altogether and head straight for the two factory outlet malls a few miles south of downtown—the biggest discount shopfest in Texas. Take exit 200 from I-35 for both the **Tanger Factory Outlet Center** ((C) **800/408-8424** or 512/396-7446; www.tangeroutlet.com) and the larger and tonier **Prime Outlets** ((C) **800/628-9465** or 512/396-2200; www. primeoutlets.com) right next door. Among the almost 150 stores, you'll find everything from Dana Buchman, Anne Klein, and Brooks Brothers to Coach, Samsonite, and Waterford/Wedgwood. There's also a Saks Fifth Avenue outlet.

The **San Marcos Convention and Visitors Bureau,** 202 N. C. M. Allen Pkwy., San Marcos, TX 78666 ((C) **888/200-5620** or 512/393-5900; www. sanmarcoscharms.com), can provide you with information on mall bus transportation, as well as a complete list of places to eat and stay in town.

WHERE TO STAY & DINE

The **Crystal River Inn,** 326 W. Hopkins, San Marcos, TX 78666 ((C) **888/ 396-3739** or 512/396-3739; www.crystalriverinn.com), offers something for everyone. Nine rooms and three suites, beautifully decorated with antiques, occupy a large 1883 Victorian main house and two smaller historic structures behind it. There's also a fully furnished executive apartment across the street. Rates, which range from a low of $90 for a room during the week to a high of $160 for a two-bedroom suite on the weekend, include a full breakfast. The elaborately scripted (and enthusiastically acted) murder-mystery weekends are extremely popular.

The prettiest place to have a meal in town is the courtyard at **Palmer's,** 216 W. Moore (© **512/353-3500;** www.palmerstexas.com), where you can sit among lovely native plants and trees and enjoy dishes ranging from penne pasta Alfredo with artichoke hearts and sun-dried tomatoes or charbroiled ahi tuna to a hefty Kansas City strip steak. Save room for the delicious Key lime or chocolate satin pies. The restaurant is open for lunch and dinner daily, and meals are moderate to expensive.

For a bit of history with your meal, you can't beat the **Hill Country Grill,** 100 W. Hopkins St. (© **512/396-6100;** www.hillcountrygrill.com), in the old State Bank and Trust Building. Dine on such well-prepared standards as grilled salmon or rib-eye in a couple of the former vaults—they're windowless, so the claustrophobic might opt for the airy exterior dining room—or sip such cocktails as Getaway Gold at a bar that incorporates the bank counter. The restaurant is open for lunch and dinner Monday through Saturday; prices are moderate to expensive.

NEARBY WIMBERLEY

A river resort town some 15 miles northwest of San Marcos, Wimberley attracts Austinites with a slew of bed-and-breakfasts—it's a favorite setting for family reunions—and a concentration of resident artists. From April through December, the first Saturday of each month is **Market Day,** a huge crafts gathering on Lion's Field; check http://visitwimberly.com/marketdays for additional information.

If you like artsy and craftsy (and, especially, country cutesy) stuff, you could spend all day browsing the shops and boutiques on and near the town square. But one of the most interesting places to visit is 1½ miles south of the town center: **Wimberley Glass Works,** Spoke Hill Road (© **512/847-9348;** www.wgw.com), stands out for its rainbow-like array of blown glassware. The jewelry, made with shards of broken glass, is outstanding. You can watch owner/artist Tim de Jong at work much of the time (except Tues, when the furnaces are refilled).

Right next door is another great reason to come to Wimberley. The **Blair House,** 100 Spoke Hill Rd., Wimberley, TX 78676 (© **877/549-5450** or 512/847-8828; www.blairhouseinn.com), is a luxurious property on 85 Hill Country acres, offering eight beautifully decorated rooms and two separate cottages in a Texas limestone ranch complex. What with a cooking school on the premises, you know the breakfasts—and dinners, offered to outsiders as well as guests every Saturday night ($58)—are going to be good. Rates run $135 to $235 for double rooms, $275 to $285 for the cottages. The cooking classes and dinners are very popular with Austinites (and others), so book in advance if you want to attend.

For information about other places to stay, eat, or shop in Wimberley, contact the **Chamber of Commerce,** 14100 R.R. 12, just north of the town square (© **512/847-2201;** www.wimberley.org). Another resource for accommodations is **All Wimberley Lodging,** 400 River Rd. (© **800/460-3909** or 512/847-3909; www.texashillcountrylodging.com).

A MEATY DETOUR TO LOCKHART

The scenic loop from San Marcos to Lockhart and back (or up to Austin) is a must for those who love barbecue. Take Hwy. 80 some 27 miles east to Luling and the junction of Hwy. 183. It's 15 miles north to Lockhart, Texas's smoked-meat mecca. Many people swear by the barbecue at **Kreuz Market** ✿, 619 N. Colorado (② **512/398-2361**), where the brisket, prime rib, and sausage come with little other than some white bread; your food is slapped down on butcher paper, and the seating is family-style. It's open for lunch and dinner Monday to Saturday. Those who enjoy side dishes such as homemade coleslaw and pinto beans—or prefer eating off plates on tables that aren't shared with other diners—will be happier at **Black's Barbecue,** 215 N. Main St. (② **512/398-2712;** blacksbbq.com), open daily for lunch and dinner. Although these two are the main contenders, **Chisholm Trail Barbecue,** 1323 S. Colorado (② **512/398-6027**), also has its die-hard defenders; its niceties extend to a salad bar. It is open Monday to Saturday for lunch and dinner. And then there's **Smitty's Market,** 208 S. Commerce (② **512/398-9344**), the product of sibling rivalry: When the owner of Kreuz Market died, his son inherited the business, his daughter the building (and the ability to create good barbecue). It's open daily for lunch and dinner. Kreuz's was established in 1900, Black's in 1932, Chisholm Trail in 1978, Smitty's in 1999. All four are inexpensively priced.

But there's more to Lockhart than just barbecue. At the center of town, the 1893 **Caldwell County Courthouse** ✿ is said to be the most photographed town hall in Texas. Though it's impossible to verify or refute the claim, there's no question that the ornate French Second Empire–style structure is photogenic: Its film credits include *The Great Waldo Pepper, What's Eating Gilbert Grape,* and *Waiting for Guffman.* You can pick up a guide to downtown Lockhart's historic structures, many of which house antiques shops, at the **Lockhart Chamber of Commerce,** 205 S. Main St. at Prairie Lea (② **512/398-2818;** www.lockhart-tx.org).

PICKING OUT A HAT IN BUDA

There's not a whole lot happening in the town of Buda (pronounced *Byou*-duh), but if you get off I-35 at the Buda exit (exit 220, about halfway between Austin and San Marcos), you'll see **Texas Hatters** (② **800/421-HATS** or 512/295-4287; www.texashatters.com) on the access road on the east side of the highway. In business for more than 50 years, this Western hatter has had an unlikely mix of famous customers, from Tip O'Neill, George Bush, and the king of Sweden to Al Hirt, Willie Nelson, Chuck Norris, and Arnold Schwarzenegger—to name just a few.

A LITERARY ASIDE

Pulitzer Prize–winning author Katherine Anne Porter, best known for her novel *Ship of Fools,* spent most of her childhood just a few miles south of Buda, in the town of Kyle. In 2001, the 1880 **Katherine Anne Porter House,** 508 W. Center St. (② **512/268-6637;** www.english.swt.edu/kap), was dedicated and opened to the public, as well as to a visiting writer chosen by the Texas State University–San Marcos. The house, which was restored and furnished with period antiques, hosts Porter's works and a collection of her photographs. There's no admission charge, but you need to call ahead for an appointment.

8 New Braunfels

Some 16 miles south of San Marcos on I-35, New Braunfels sits at the junction of the Comal and Guadalupe rivers. German settlers were brought here in 1845 by Prince Carl of Solms-Braunfels, the commissioner general of the Society for the Protection of German Immigrants in Texas, the same group that later founded Fredericksburg. Although Prince Carl returned to Germany within a year to marry his fiancée, who refused to join him in the wilderness, his colony prospered. By the 1850s, New Braunfels was the fourth-largest city in Texas after Houston, San Antonio, and Galveston. Although you have to look a little to find its quainter side today, this is a good place to enjoy a bit of Germanic history—and a lot of watersports.

WHAT TO SEE & DO

At the **New Braunfels Chamber of Commerce,** 390 S. Seguin, New Braunfels, TX 78130 (© **800/572-2626** or 830/625-2385; www.nbjumpin.com), open weekdays 8am to 5pm, you can pick up a pamphlet detailing the 40-point **historic walking tour** of midtown. Highlights include the Romanesque-Gothic Comal County Courthouse (1898) on Main Plaza; the nearby Jacob Schmidt Building (193 W. San Antonio), built on the site where William Gebhardt, of canned chili fame, perfected his formula for chili powder in 1896; and the 1928 Faust Hotel (240 S. Seguin), believed by some to be haunted by its owner. These days, draughts pulled from the microbrewery on the Faust's premises help allay even the most haunting anxieties. **Henne Hardware,** 246 W. San Antonio (© **830/606-6707**), established in 1857, sells modern bits and bobs, but maintains its original tin-roof ceiling, rings for hanging buggy whips, and an old pulley system for transporting cash and paperwork through the back business office. It's said to be the oldest hardware store in Texas. **Naeglin's,** 129 S. Seguin Ave. (© **830/625-5722**), opened in 1868, stakes its claim as the state's longest-running bakery. It's the place to try some *kolaches*—Czech pastries filled with cheese, fruit, poppy seeds, sausage, or ham, among other delicious fillings.

Several small museums are worth a visit. Prince Carl never did build a planned castle for his sweetheart, Sophia, on the elevated spot where the **Sophienburg Museum,** 401 W. Coll St. (© **830/629-1572;** www.nbtx.com/sophienburg), now stands, but it's nevertheless an excellent place to learn about the history of New Braunfels and other Hill Country settlements. Open Monday to Saturday 10am to 5pm, Sunday 1 to 5pm; $5 adults, students under 18 free. The **Museum of Texas Handmade Furniture** ⚘, 1370 Church Hill Dr. (© **830/629-6504;** www.nbheritagevillage.com), also sheds light on local domestic life of the 19th century with its beautiful examples of Texas Biedermeier by master craftsman Johan Michael Jahn. They're displayed at the gracious 1858 Breustedt-Dillon Haus. The 11-acre Heritage Village complex also includes an 1848 log cabin and a barn that houses a reproduction cabinetmaker's workshop. The museum is open Tuesday through Sunday from 1 to 4pm from February 1 through November 30, closed December and January. The last tour begins at 3:30pm. Admission costs $5 for adults, $4 for seniors, $1 for children ages 6 to 12.

You can tour other historic structures, including the original 1870 schoolhouse and such transported shops as a tiny music studio, at the nearby **Conservation Plaza,** 1300 Church Hill Dr. (© **830/629-2943**), centered around a gazebo and garden with more than 50 varieties of antique roses. Guided tours (included in admission) are offered every day except Monday. It's open Tuesday to Friday, 10am to 3pm, and Saturday and Sunday, 2 to 5pm; adult admission costs $2.50, while children 6 to 17 pay 50¢. Also owned by the New Braunfels Conservation Society, the 1852 **Lindheimer Home** ✷, 491 Comal Ave. (✆ **830/608-1512**), is probably the best example of an early *fachwerk* house still standing in New Braunfels. Ferdinand J. Lindheimer, one of the town's first set-tlers—he scouted out the site for Prince Solms—was an internationally recog-nized botanist and editor of the town's German-language newspaper. Museum hours are limited—in summer, it's open Thursday to Tuesday from 2 to 5pm; the rest of the year, it's only open weekends from 2 to 5pm—but you can wan-der the lovely grounds planted with Texas natives (38 species of plant were named for Lindheimer) even if you can't get in to see the house.

HISTORIC GRUENE ✷✷

You can get a more concentrated glimpse of the past at Gruene (pronounced "Green"), 4 miles northwest of downtown New Braunfels. First settled by Ger-man farmers in the 1840s, Gruene was virtually abandoned during the Depres-sion in the 1930s. It remained a ghost town until the mid-1970s, when two investors realized the value of its intact historic buildings and sold them to busi-nesses rather than raze them. These days, tiny Gruene is crowded with day-trip-pers browsing the specialty shops in the wonderfully restored structures, which include a smoked-meat shop, lots of cutesy gift boutiques, and several antiques shops.

The **New Braunfels Museum of Art & Music** ✷, 1259 Gruene Rd., on the river behind Gruene Mansion (✆ **800/456-4866** or 830/625-5636; www.nbmuseum.org), focuses on popular arts in the West and South (as opposed to, say, high culture and the classics). Subjects of recent exhibits, which change quarterly and combine music and art components, have included Texas accordion music, central Texas dance halls, and cowboy art and poetry; the 2005 season kicked off with a multimedia exhibit celebrating Austin City Limits's 30th anniversary. Live music throughout the year includes an open mic on Sun-day afternoons, and the recording of *New Braunfels Live* radio show of roots music on Thursday evenings. The museum is open Wednesday through Sunday from noon to 6pm from September 1 through April 30; Monday through Thursday from 10am to 6pm, Friday and Saturday from 10am to 8pm, Sunday noon to 8pm the rest of the year. No admission; donations gratefully accepted (and you can contribute by shopping at the museum's excellent gift shop).

A brochure detailing the town's retailers, restaurants, and accommodations is available from the New Braunfels Chamber of Commerce (see above) or at most of Gruene's shops. You can also get information on the town's website, www.gruene.net.

WATERSPORTS

Gruene also figures among the New Braunfels area's impressive array of places to get wet, most of them open only in summer. Outfitters who can help you ride the Guadalupe River rapids on raft, tube, canoe, or inflatable kayak include **Rockin' R River Rides** (✆ **800/553-5628** or 830/629-9999; www.rockinr.com) and **Gruene River Company** (✆ **888/705-2800** or 830/625-2800; www.toobing.com), both on Gruene Road just south of the Gruene Bridge.

You can go tubing, too, at **Schlitterbahn** ✪, Texas's largest water park and one of the best in the country, 305 W. Austin St. in New Braunfels (© **830/ 625-2351;** www.schlitterbahn.com). If there's a way to get wet 'n' wild, this place has got it. Six separate areas feature gigantic slides, pools, and rides, including Master Blaster, one of the world's steepest uphill water coasters. The combination of a natural river-and-woods setting and high-tech attractions make this splashy 65-acre play land a standout. The park usually opens in late April and closes in mid-September; call or check the website for the exact dates. All-day passes cost $30 for adults, $25 for children 3 to 11; children under 3 enter free.

Those who like their water play a bit more low-key might try downtown New Braunfels's **Landa Park** (© 830/608-2160), where you can either swim in the largest spring-fed pool in Texas or calmly float in an inner tube down the Comal River—at 2½ miles the "largest shortest" river in the world, according to *Ripley's Believe It or Not.* There's also an Olympic-size swimming pool, and you can rent paddle boats, canoes, and water cycles. Even if you're not prepared to immerse yourself, you might take the lovely 22-mile drive along the Guadalupe River from downtown's Cypress Bend Park to **Canyon Lake,** whose clarity makes it perfect for scuba diving.

For more details about all the places where camping, food, and water toys are available along the Guadalupe River, pick up the *Water Recreation Guide* pamphlet at the New Braunfels Visitors Center.

Perhaps you want to buy your own toys—and learn how to use them. The 70-acre **Texas Ski Ranch,** 6700 I-35 N. (© **830/627-2843;** www.texasskiranch. com), is paradise for those interested in wake, skate, and motor sports. Features of this new and expanding complex include a cable lake, boat lake, skate park, and motor track—at all of which you can test the equipment you want to purchase or rent (you can also bring your own), and show off the latest athletic clothing, sold here, too. Training clinics and private lessons for a variety of sports are offered. It costs $4 (free for over 65 and under 6) to use the recreation areas. The complex is open Tuesday through Thursday from 10am to 8pm, Friday and Saturday 10am to 9pm, Sunday 10am to 6pm.

NEARBY CAVERNS & ANIMALS

Natural Bridge Caverns, 26495 Natural Bridge Caverns Rd. (© **210/651-6101;** www.naturalbridgecaverns.com), 12 miles west of New Braunfels, is named for the 60-foot limestone arch spanning its entryway. More than a mile of huge rooms and passages is filled with stunning, multihued formations—still being formed, as the dripping water attests. Tours of the Jeremy Room, recently opened to the public, are restricted to small groups who tour with flashlights. The daring—and physically fit—can opt to join one of the Adventure Tours, which involve crawling and, in some cases, rappelling, in an unlighted cave not open to the general public ($125 for 3–4 hours), while those who prefer their adventures outdoors can opt for the new Watchtower Challenge, a 40-foot climbing tower with a zipline (prices vary, subject to weather and availability). The caverns are open 9am to 7pm June through Labor Day, 9am to 4pm the rest of the year; closed Thanksgiving Day, Christmas Day, and New Year's Day; general admission costs $15 adults, $14 seniors 60 and older, $9 ages 4 to 12; Jeremy Room $17/ $15/$9.50; combination ticket $25/$17/$15.

Just down the road, the **Natural Bridge Wildlife Ranch,** 26515 Natural Bridge Caverns Rd. (© **830/438-7400;** www.nbwildliferanchtx.com), lets you get up close and personal—from the safety of your car—with some 50 threatened and endangered species from around the world; there's also a shorter (and equally safe) walking safari. Packets of food sold at the entryway inspire even some generally shy types to amble over to your vehicle. It is open daily 9am to 5pm, with extended summer hours 'til 6:30pm; admission costs $14 adults, $12 seniors 65 and older, $6.50 ages 3 to 11.

WHERE TO STAY IN NEW BRAUNFELS & GRUENE

The **Prince Solms Inn,** 295 E. San Antonio St., New Braunfels, TX 78130 (© **800/625-9169** or 830/625-9169; www.princesolmsinn.com), has been in continuous operation since it opened its doors to travelers in 1898. A prime downtown location, tree-shaded courtyard, downstairs piano bar, and gorgeously florid, High Victorian–style sleeping quarters have put accommodations at this charming bed-and-breakfast in great demand. Three Western-themed rooms in a converted 1860 feed store next door are ideal for families, and there's an ultraromantic separate cabin in the back of the main house. Rates range from $125 to $175.

For history with a river view, consider the **Gruene Mansion Inn,** 1275 Gruene Rd., New Braunfels, TX 78130 (© **830/629-2641;** www.gruenemansioninn. com). The barns that once belonged to the opulent 1875 plantation house were converted to rustic elegant cottages with decks; some also offer cozy lofts (if you don't like stairs, request a single-level room). Accommodations for two go from $149 to $169 per night, including breakfast served in the plantation house. Two separate lodges, suitable for families, are available, too ($209–$229).

The nearby **Gruene Apple Bed and Breakfast,** 1235 Gruene Rd. (© **830/643-1234;** www.grueneapple.com), set on a bluff overlooking the Guadalupe River, is less historic, more upscale. This opulent limestone mansion, built expressly to serve as an inn, hosts 14 luxurious theme rooms, from "Wild West" and "Shady Lady" to the more decorous "1776"; many look out on the river from private balconies. On-site recreation includes a natural stone swimming pool, hot tub, pool table, player piano—even a small movie theater. Doubles range from $160 to $210; midweek discounts available.

If you're planning to come to town during the *Wurstfest* sausage festival (late Oct to early Nov), be sure to book well in advance, no matter where you stay— that is high season here.

WHERE TO DINE IN NEW BRAUNFELS & GRUENE

The **New Braunfels Smokehouse,** 140 Hwy. 46 S., at I-35 (© **830/625-2416;** www.nbsmokehouse.com), opened in 1951 as a tasting room for the meats it started hickory smoking in 1943. Savor it in platters or on sandwiches, or have some shipped home as a savory souvenir. It's open daily for breakfast, lunch, and dinner; prices are moderate. The far newer **Huisache Grill,** 303 W. San Antonio St. (© **830/620-9001;** www.huisache.com), has an updated American menu that draws foodies from as far as San Antonio. The pecan-crusted pork-chop catfish and Yucatán chicken are among the excellent entrees. Lunch and dinner are served daily; prices are moderate to expensive. An even more recent arrival on downtown's fine dining scene, **Myron's,** 136 Castell Rd. (© **830/624-1024;** myronsprimesteakhouse.com), serves perfectly prepared Chicago prime steak in a retro swank dining room (a converted 1920s movie palace). Prices are big-city expensive (all the sides are extra, for example), but the outstanding food and service, combined with the atmosphere, make any meal here a special occasion. Myron's is open for dinner nightly. Reservations are recommended for dinner at both the Huisache Grill and Myron's.

In Gruene, the **Gristmill River Restaurant & Bar,** 1287 Gruene Rd. (© **830/625-0684;** www.gristmillrestaurant.com), a converted 100-year-old cotton gin, includes burgers and chicken-fried steak as well as healthful salads on its Texas-casual menu. Kick back on one of its multiple decks and gaze out at the Guadalupe River. Lunch and dinner daily; prices are moderate.

NEW BRAUNFELS & GRUENE AFTER DARK

Lyle Lovett and Garth Brooks are just a few of the big names who have played **Gruene Hall** ★★, Gruene Road, corner of Hunter Road (© **830/629-7077;** www.gruenehall.com), the oldest country-and-western dance hall in Texas and still one of the state's most outstanding spots for a live-music fix. Some of the scenes in *Michael,* starring John Travolta, were shot here. By itself, the hall is worth a detour; when in town, if there's live music playing, it is an absolute must—just remember to wear your cowboy boots and hat.

At the **Brauntex Performing Arts Theatre,** 290 W. San Antonio (© **830/ 627-0808;** www.brauntex.org), a restored 1942 movie theater in midtown New Braunfels, you can expect to see anything from Frula, an eastern European folk-dancing extravaganza that played Carnegie Hall, to such local acts as the Flying J. Wranglers.

Appendix A:
San Antonio & Austin in Depth

Texans, who consider their state the center of the universe, are surprised when not everyone knows exactly what went on at the Alamo, or what the latest tech developments are in Austin. You won't learn everything there is to know about these two cities from this necessarily brief overview, but at least you'll be armed with some background information.

1 San Antonio Past & Present

San Antonio's past is the stuff of legend, the Alamo being but the most famous episode. If it were a movie, the story of the city would be an epic with an improbably packed plot, encompassing the end of a great empire, the rise of a republic, and the rescue of the river with which the story began.

ON A MISSION

Having already established an empire by the late 17th century—the huge viceroyalty of New Spain, which included, at its high point, Mexico, Guatemala, and large parts of the southwestern United States—Spain was engaged in the far less glamorous task of maintaining it. The remote regions of east Texas had been coming under attack by the native Apache and Comanche, and now with rumors flying of French forays into the Spanish territory, search parties were dispatched to investigate.

On one of these search parties in 1691, regional governor Domingo Teran de los Ríos and Father Damian Massenet came upon a wooded plain fed by a fast-flowing river. They named the river—called Yanaguana by the native Coahuiltecan Indians— San Antonio de Padua, after the saint's day on which they arrived. When, some decades later, the Spanish Franciscans proposed building a new mission halfway between the ones on the Rio Grande and those more recently

Dateline

- **1691** On June 13, feast day of St. Anthony of Padua, San Antonio River discovered and named by the Spanish; governor of Spanish colonial province of Texas makes contact with Coahuiltecan Indians.
- **1718** Mission San Antonio de Valero (later nicknamed the Alamo) founded; presidio San Antonio de Béxar established to protect it and other missions to be built nearby.
- **1720** Mission San José founded.
- **1731** Missions Concepción, San Juan Capistrano, and Espada relocated from East Texas to San Antonio area; 15 Canary Island families sent by Spain to help populate Texas establish the first civil settlement in San Antonio.
- **1793–94** The missions are secularized by order of the Spanish crown.
- **1820** Moses Austin petitions Spanish governor in San Antonio for permission to settle Americans in Texas.
- **1821** Mexico wins independence from Spain.
- **1835** Siege of Béxar: first battle in San Antonio for Texas independence from Mexico.
- **1836** The Alamo falls after 13-day siege by Mexican general Santa Anna; using "Remember the Alamo" as a rallying cry, Sam Houston defeats Santa Anna at San Jacinto.
- **1836** Republic of Texas established.
- **1845** Texas annexed to the United States.
- **1861** Texas secedes from the Union.
- **1876** Fort Sam Houston established as new quartermaster depot.

established in east Texas, the abundant water and friendliness of the local population made the plain near the San Antonio River seem like a good choice.

And so it was that in 1718, Mission San Antonio de Valero—later known as the Alamo—was founded. To protect the religious complex from Apache attack, the presidio (fortress) of San Antonio de Béxar went up a few days later. In 1719, a second mission was built nearby, and in 1731, three ill-fated east Texas missions, nearly destroyed by French and Indian attacks, were moved hundreds of miles to the safer banks of the San Antonio River. Also, in March 1731, 15 weary families arrived from the Spanish Canary Islands with a royal dispensation from Philip V to help settle his far-flung New World kingdom. Near the protection of the presidio, they established the village of San Fernando de Béxar.

Thus, within little more than a decade, what is now downtown San Antonio became home to three distinct, though related, settlements: a mission complex, the military garrison designed to protect it, and the civilian town known as Béxar (pronounced "bear"), which was officially renamed San Antonio in 1837. To irrigate their crops, the early settlers were given narrow strips of land stretching back from the river and from the nearby San Pedro Creek, and centuries later, the paths connecting these strips, which followed the winding waterways, were paved and became the city's streets.

- **1877** The railroad arrives in San Antonio, precipitating new waves of immigration.
- **1880s** King William, first residential suburb, begins to be developed by German immigrants.
- **1939–40** Works Project Administration builds River Walk, based on plans drawn up in 1929 by architect Robert H. H. Hugman.
- **1968** HemisFair exposition—River Walk extension, Convention Center, Mansión del Rio, and Hilton Palacio del Rio completed for the occasion, along with Tower of the Americas and other fair structures.
- **1988** Rivercenter Mall opens.
- **1989** Premier of the newly refurbished Majestic Theatre.
- **1993** Alamodome, huge new sports complex, completed.
- **1995** Southbank and Presidio complexes open on the river.
- **1998** Opening of the Nelson A. Rockefeller Center for Latin American Art, a three-story, $11 million addition to the San Antonio Museum of Art; reopening of the Empire Theatre.
- **1999** San Antonio Spurs outgrow the Alamodome; funding approved for the new SBC Center.
- **2001** Completion of Convention Center expansion.
- **2002** Opening of SBC Center, new home to the Spurs, the rodeo, and more.
- **2003** Spurs win the NBA championship.
- **2005** Opening of Museo Americano Smithsonian, part of the Alameda National Center for Latino Arts and Culture. Opening of the San Antonio Museum of Art's Lenora and Walter F. Brown Asian Art Wing.

REMEMBER THE ALAMO

As the 18th century wore on, the missions came continuously under siege by hostile Indians, the mission Indians fell victim to a host of European diseases against which they had no natural resistance, and by the end of the 1700s, the Spanish mission system itself was nearly dead. In 1794, Mission San Antonio de Valero was secularized, its rich farmlands redistributed. In 1810, recognizing the military potential of the thick walls of the complex, the Spanish authorities turned the former mission into a garrison. The men recruited to serve here all hailed from the Mexican town of San José y Santiago del Alamo de Parras. The name of their station was soon shortened to the Alamo (Spanish for "cottonwood tree").

By 1824, all five missions had been secularized and Spain was, once again, worried about Texas. Apache and Comanche roamed the territory freely, and with the incentive of converting the native populations eliminated, it was next to impossible to persuade Spaniards to live there. Although the Spanish were rightly suspicious of Anglo-American designs on their land, when land agent Moses Austin arrived in San Antonio in 1820, the government reluctantly gave him permission to settle some 300 Anglo-American families in the region. Austin died before he could see his plan carried out, however. And Spain lost its hold on Mexico in 1821, when the country gained its independence after a decade of struggle. But Moses's son Stephen convinced the new government to honor the terms of the original agreement.

By 1830, however, the Mexicans were growing nervous about the large numbers of Anglos descending on their country from the north. Having already repealed many of the tax breaks they had initially granted the settlers, they now prohibited all further U.S. immigration to the territory. When, in 1835, Gen. Antonio López de Santa Anna abolished Mexico's democratic 1824 constitution, Tejanos (Mexican Texans) and Anglos alike balked at his dictatorship, and a cry rose up for a separate republic.

The first battle for Texas independence fought on San Antonio soil fell to the rebels when Mexican general Martín Perfecto de Cós surrendered after a short, successful siege of the town in December 1835. But it was the return engagement, that glorious, doomed fight against all odds, that forever captured the American imagination. From February 23 through March 6, 1836, some 180 volunteers—among them Davy Crockett and Jim Bowie—serving under the command of William Travis, died trying to defend the Alamo fortress against a vastly greater number of Santa Anna's men. One month later, Sam Houston spurred his troops on to victory at the Battle of San Jacinto with the cry "Remember the Alamo," thus securing Texas's freedom.

AFTER THE FALL

Ironically, few Americans came to live in San Antonio during Texas's stint as a republic (1836–45), but settlers came from overseas in droves: By 1850, 5 years after Texas joined the United States, Tejanos (Mexican Texans) and Americans were outnumbered by European, mostly German, immigrants. The Civil War put a temporary halt to the city's growth—in part because Texas joined the Confederacy and most of the new settlers were Union sympathizers—but expansion picked up again soon afterward. As elsewhere in the West, the coming of the railroad in 1877 set off a new wave of immigration. Riding hard on its crest, the King William district of the city, a residential suburb named for Kaiser Wilhelm, was developed by prosperous German merchants.

Some of the immigrants set up Southern-style plantations, others opened factories and shops, and more and more who arrived after the Civil War earned their keep by driving cattle. The Spanish had brought Longhorn cattle and

---

Impressions

From all manner of people, business men, consumptive men, curious men, and wealthy men, there came an exhibition of profound affection for San Antonio. It seemed to symbolize for them the poetry of life in Texas.

—Stephen Crane, *Patriot Shrine of Texas* (1895)

Fun Fact **The Lay of the Land**

Three geographical zones meet in San Antonio: The Balcones Fault divides the farms and forests of east Texas from the scrubby brush land and ranches of west Texas, and the Edwards Plateau drops off to the southern coastal plains. Frederick Law Olmsted's description in his 1853 *A Journey Through Texas* is more poetic. San Antonio, he writes, "lies basking on the edge of a vast plain, through which the river winds slowly off beyond where the eye can reach. To the east are gentle slopes toward it; to the north a long gradual sweep upward to the mountain country, which comes down within five or six miles; to the south and west, the open prairies, extending almost level to the coast, a hundred and fifty miles away."

vaqueros (cowboys) from Mexico into the area, and now Texas cowboys drove herds north on the Chisholm Trail from San Antonio to Kansas City, where they were shipped east. Others moved cattle west, for use as seed stock in the fledgling ranching industry.

Over the years, San Antonio had never abandoned its role as a military stronghold. As early as 1849, the Alamo was designated a quartermaster depot for the U.S. Army, and now in 1876 the much larger Fort Sam Houston was built to take over those duties. Apache chief Geronimo was held at the clock tower in the fort's Quadrangle for 40 days in 1886, en route to exile in Florida, and Teddy Roosevelt outfitted his Rough Riders—some of whom he recruited in San Antonio bars—at Fort Sam 12 years later.

As the city marched into the 20th century, Fort Sam Houston continued to expand. In 1910, it witnessed the first military flight by an American, and early aviation stars like Charles Lindbergh honed their flying skills here. From 1917 to 1941, four Army air bases—Kelly Field, Brooks Field, Randolph Field, and Lackland Army Air Base—shot up, making San Antonio the largest military complex in the United States outside the Washington, D.C., area. Although Kelly was downsized and privatized, the military remains the city's major employer today.

A RIVER RUNS THROUGH IT

As the city moved farther and farther from its agrarian roots, the San Antonio River became much less central to the economy and by the turn of the century, its constant flooding made it a downright nuisance. When a particularly severe storm caused it to overflow its banks in 1921, killing 50 people and destroying many downtown businesses, there was serious talk of cementing over the river.

In 1925, the newly formed San Antonio Conservation Society warned the city council against killing the goose that was laying the golden eggs of downtown economic growth. And in 1927, Robert H. H. Hugman, an architect who had lived in New Orleans and studied that city's Vieux Carré district, came up with a detailed plan for saving the waterway. His proposed River Walk, with shops, restaurants, and entertainment areas buttressed by a series of floodgates, would render the river profitable as well as safe, and also preserve its natural beauty. The Depression intervened, but in 1941, with the help of a federal Works Project Administration (WPA) grant, Hugman's vision became a reality.

Still, for some decades more, the River Walk remained just another pretty space and it was not until the 1968 HemisFair exposition drew record crowds to the rescued waterway that the city really began banking on its banks.

SAN ANTONIO TODAY

The eighth largest city in the United States (its population is approximately 1.2 million), and one of the oldest, is undergoing a metamorphosis. For a good part of the past century, San Antonio was a military town that happened to have a nice river promenade running through its decaying downtown area. Now, with the continuing growth in tourism, San Antonio's number two industry—it has an annual economic impact of approximately $7.2 billion—the city is increasingly perceived by outsiders as a place with a terrific river walk.

Although the city's outlying theme parks and central area attractions are also benefiting from increased visitation, and work continues on the redevelopment of the River Walk for 13 miles from Brackenridge Park to Mission Espada, downtown is by far the most affected section. The city's Henry B. Gonzalez Convention Center doubled in size at the end of the 1990s, and its $187 million expansion was completed in the beginning of the new century. And, as though the Alamodome, the state-of-the-arts sports arena built in the last decade of the 20th century, wasn't high-tech enough for the Spurs, the huge new SBC Center opened nearby in 2002 (the Spurs apparently took to their new home, winning the NBA championship in 2003). But the biggest trend is recycling: Suddenly historic is hot. The Majestic Theatre was restored and reopened in the late 1980s, the Empire Theatre followed in the late 1990s, and the Aztec Theater should be ready to welcome audiences again in 2006. And every time you turn around it seems as though another old building has been converted into a hotel.

Middle-class residential growth still lags a bit behind commercial development in this area. San Antonians who moved downtown in the past decade initially patted themselves on the back for their prescience, but many are now beginning to second-guess the changes they helped bring about. Not only are there few residential services (the area still has no major supermarket, for example), but the huge success of the riverside Southbank and Presidio complexes, opened in the mid-1990s, destroyed what little quiet there was at night. The result was ordinances to cut down on late-night noise and the opening up of a dialogue between residents and businesses.

This is not to suggest there's no growth in any business sectors besides tourism. The city's number one industry, healthcare and bioscience, has a total economic impact of at least $12.9 billion, including medical conferences and the many people who travel to San Antonio for medical treatment. Boeing and Lockheed Martin are among the aviation companies that have been attracted to the former Kelly Air Force Base, now KellyUSA, while other businesses like SBC (formerly Southwestern Bell) moved their headquarters to San Antonio in the mid 1990s. And an $800 million Toyota truck manufacturing plant, which should bring at least 2,000 jobs into the area, is slated to be completed in 2006.

The North American Free Trade Agreement (NAFTA), signed in 1994, was also a boon for the city, which hosts the North American Development Bank—the financial arm of NAFTA—in its downtown International Center. Representatives from the various states of Mexico are housed in the same building as part of the "Casas" program. With its large Hispanic population, regular flights to Mexico City, cultural attractions such as the Latin American wing of the San

---

> **Fun Fact   Did You Know?**
>
> - More jars of salsa than ketchup are consumed in the United States today.
> - The first military flight by an American took place at Fort Sam Houston in 1910; in 1915, the entire U.S. Air Force—six reconnaissance planes—resided at the fort.
> - Barbed wire was first demonstrated in San Antonio's Military Plaza.

Antonio Museum of Art, and the Centro Alameda project—the first cornerstone of which, the Museo Americano Smithsonian, is opening in 2005—and a history of strong business relations with Mexico, San Antonio is ideally positioned to take advantage of the economic reciprocity between the two nations. And the fact that Meximerica Media, which is starting a chain of Spanish-language newspapers, established its headquarters in San Antonio in 2004 strengthens the city's status as a major center for marketing and media aimed at the U.S. Hispanic population, including some of the country's top Hispanic advertising firms.

Even with its rosy outlook, the city is facing some major problems, ones it shares with other rapidly growing Southwest urban centers. San Antonio and Austin are 80 miles and political light-years apart, but the two cities are growing ever closer. Although they haven't yet melded to form the single, huge metropolis that futurists predict, the increasing suburban sprawl and the growth of New Braunfels and San Marcos, two small cities that lie between San Antonio and Austin, are causing a great deal of congestion on I-35, which connects all four cities.

An even more serious concern is the city's water supply. Currently, the Edwards Aquifer is the city's only source of water, and ominously, no one knows exactly how many years' worth of water it contains. Even that supply is being threatened by development: Although the original plans to build a vast new golf complex, PGA Village, were scrapped as a result of an outcry by environmentalists—they contended that the project, slated to be built on the aquifer's recharge zone, would have a negative impact on the city's water supply—a new version, said to be more environmentally sensitive, is currently under consideration. At this writing, the outcome is undetermined, but don't be surprised if professional golf comes out the winner this time.

2 Austin Past & Present

A vast territory that threw off foreign rule to become an independent nation—remember the Alamo?—Texas has always played a starring role in the romance of the American West. So it's only fitting that Texas's capital should spring, full-blown, from the imagination of a man on a buffalo hunt.

Dateline

- 1730 Franciscans build a mission at Barton Springs, but abandon it within a year.
- 1836 Texas wins independence from Mexico; Republic of Texas established.

continues

A CAPITAL DILEMMA

The man was Mirabeau Buonaparte Lamar, who had earned a reputation for bravery in Texas's struggle for independence from Mexico. In 1838, when our story begins, Lamar was vice-president of the 2-year-old Republic of Texas, and Sam Houston, the even more renowned hero of the Battle of San Jacinto, was president. Although they shared a strong will, the two men had very different ideas about the future of the republic. Houston tended to look eastward, toward union with the United States, while Lamar saw independence as the first step to establishing an empire that would stretch to the Pacific.

That year, an adventurer named Jacob Harrell set up a camp called Waterloo at the western edge of the frontier. Lying on the northern banks of Texas's Colorado River (not to be confused with the larger waterway up north), it was nestled against a series of gentle hills. Some 100 years earlier, the Franciscans had established a temporary mission here. In the 1820s, Stephen F. Austin, Texas's earliest and greatest land developer, had the area surveyed for the smaller of the two colonies he was to establish on Mexican territory.

But the place had otherwise seen few Anglos before Harrell arrived, though for thousands of years, mainly nomadic Indian tribes, including the Comanches, Lipan Apaches, and Tonkawas, had visited it. Thus, it was to a rather pristine spot that, in the autumn of 1838, Harrell invited his friend Mirabeau Lamar to take part in a shooting expedition. The buffalo hunt proved extremely successful, and when Lamar gazed at the rolling, wooded land surrounding Waterloo, he saw that it was good.

In December of the same year, Lamar became president of the Republic. He ordered the congressional

- **1838** Jacob Harrell sets up camp on the Colorado River, calling the settlement Waterloo; Mirabeau B. Lamar succeeds Sam Houston as president of Texas.
- **1839** Congressional commission recommends Waterloo as site for new capital of the republic. Waterloo's name changes to Austin.
- **1842** Sam Houston succeeds Lamar as president, reestablishes Houston as Texas's capital, and orders nation's archives moved there. Austinites resist.
- **1844** Anson Jones succeeds Houston as president and returns capital to Austin.
- **1845** Constitutional convention in Austin approves annexation of Texas by the United States.
- **1850s** Austin undergoes a building boom; construction of the capitol (1853), Governor's Mansion (1856), and General Land Office (1857).
- **1861** Texas votes to secede from the Union (Travis County, which includes Austin, votes against secession).
- **1865** General Custer is among those who come to restore order in Austin during Reconstruction.
- **1871** First rail line to Austin completed.
- **1883** University of Texas opens.
- **1923** Santa Rita No. 1, an oil well on University of Texas land, strikes a gusher.
- **1937** Lyndon Johnson elected U.S. representative from Tenth Congressional District, which includes Austin.
- **Late 1930s to early 1950s** Six dams built on the Colorado River by the Lower Colorado River Authority, resulting in formation of the Highland Lakes chain.
- **1960s** High-tech firms, including IBM, move to Austin.
- **1972** Willie Nelson moves back to Texas from Nashville; helps spur live-music scene on Sixth Street.
- **1976** PBS's *Austin City Limits* airs for the first time.
- **1980s** Booming real-estate market goes bust, but South By Southwest (S×SW) Music Festival debuts (1987).
- **1993** S×SW adds interactive (tech) and film components to its festival.

commission that had been charged with the task of selecting a site for a permanent capital, to be named after Stephen F. Austin, to check out Waterloo. Much to the dismay of residents of Houston—home to the temporary capital—who considered Waterloo a dangerous wilderness outpost, the commission recommended Lamar's pet site.

In early 1839, Lamar's friend Edwin Waller was dispatched to plan a city—the only one in the United States besides Washington, D.C., designed to be an independent nation's capital. The first public lots went on sale on August 1, 1839, and by November of that year, Austin was ready to host its first session of Congress.

Austin's position as capital was far from entrenched, however. Attacks on the republic by Mexico in 1842 gave Sam Houston, now president again, sufficient excuse to order the national archives to be relocated out of remote

- 1995 Capitol, including new annex, reopens after massive refurbishing.
- 1997 Completion of the refurbishing of the capitol's grounds and of the Texas State Cemetery.
- 1999 Opening of Austin-Bergstrom International Airport.
- 2000 The Driskill revamp completed, the Stephen F. Austin Hotel reopens, and plans to turn Robert Mueller Airport into film production studio approved.
- 2001 The Bob Bullock Texas State History Museum opens.
- 2002 The tech recession hits, but Austin's still partying like it's 2000, as the Austin City Limits Music Festival debuts.
- 2003 Samsung announces major 3-year expansion.
- 2004 Debut of Austin's tallest building, the Frost Bank Tower, on Congress Avenue. *Austin City Limits* celebrates 30 years on-air as the longest-running music program in American TV history.

Austin. Resistant Austinites greeted the 26 armed men who came to repossess the historic papers with a cannon. After a struggle, the men returned empty-handed, and Houston abandoned his plan, thus ceding to Austin the victory in what came to be called the Archive War.

Although Austin won this skirmish, it was losing a larger battle for existence. Houston refused to convene Congress in Austin. By 1843, Austin's population had dropped down to 200 and its buildings lay in disrepair. Help came in the person of Anson Jones, who succeeded to the presidency in 1844. The constitutional convention he called in 1845 not only approved Texas's annexation to the United States, but also named Austin the capital until 1850, when voters of what was now the state of Texas would choose their governmental seat for the next 20 years. In 1850, Austin campaigned hard for the position and won by a landslide.

A CAPITAL SOLUTION

Austin thrived under the protection of the U.S. Army. The first permanent buildings to go up during the 1850s construction boom following statehood included an impressive limestone capitol. Two of the buildings in its complex, the General Land Office and the Governor's Mansion, are still in use today.

The boom was short-lived, however. Although Austin's Travis County voted against secession, Texas decided to join the Confederacy in 1861. By 1865, Union army units—including one led by Gen. George Armstrong Custer—were sent to restore order in a defeated and looted Austin.

But once again Austin rebounded. With the arrival of the railroad in 1871, the city's recovery was sealed. The following year, when Austin won election as state capital, it was delivered.

Impressions

Like the ancient city of Rome, Austin is built upon seven hills, and it is impossible to conceive of a more beautiful and lovely situation.
—George W. Bonnell, Commissioner of
Indian Affairs of the Republic of Texas (1840)

Still, there were more battles for status to be fought. Back in 1839, the Republic of Texas had declared its intention to build a "university of the first class," and in 1876, a new state constitution mandated its establishment. Through yet another bout of heavy electioneering, Austin won the right to establish the flagship of Texas's higher educational system on its soil. In 1883, the classrooms not yet completed, the first 221 members of what is now a student body of more than 50,000 met the eight instructors of the University of Texas.

The university wasn't the only Austin institution without permanent quarters that year. The old limestone capitol had burned in 1881, and a new, much larger home for the legislature was being built. In 1888, after a series of mishaps—the need to construct a railroad branch to transport the donated building materials, among them—the current capitol was completed. The grand red-granite edifice looking down upon the city symbolized Austin's arrival.

DAMS, OIL & MICROCHIPS

The new capitol notwithstanding, the city was once again in a slump. Although some believed that quality of life would be sacrificed to growth—a view still strongly argued today—most townspeople embraced the idea of harnessing the fast-flowing waters of the Colorado River as the solution to Austin's economic woes. A dam, they thought, would not only provide a cheap source of electricity for residents, but also supply power for irrigation and new factories. Dedicated in 1893, the Austin Dam did indeed fulfill these goals—but only temporarily. The energy source proved to be limited, and when torrential rains pelted the city in April 1900, Austin's dreams came crashing down with its dam.

Another dam, attempted in 1915, was never finished. It wasn't until the late 1930s that a permanent solution to the water power problem was found. The successful plea to President Roosevelt for federal funds on the part of young Lyndon Johnson, the newly elected representative from Austin's Tenth Congressional District, was crucial to the construction of six dams along the lower Colorado River. These dams not only afforded Austin and central Texas all the hydroelectric power and drinking water they needed, but also created the seven Highland Lakes—aesthetically appealing and a great source of recreational revenue.

Still, Austin might have remained a backwater capital seat abutting a beautiful lake had it not been for the discovery of oil on University of Texas (UT) land in 1923. The huge amounts of money that subsequently flowed into the Permanent University Fund—worth some $4 billion today—enabled Austin's campus to become truly first-class. While most of the country was cutting back during the Depression, UT went on a building binge and began hiring a faculty as impressive as the new halls in which they were to hold forth.

The indirect effects of the oil bonus reached far beyond College Hill. UT scientists and engineers founded Tracor, the first of Austin's more than 250 high-tech companies, in 1955. Lured by the city's natural attractions and its access to a growing bank of young brainpower, many outside companies soon arrived:

IBM (1967), Texas Instruments (1968), and Motorola's Semiconductor Products Section (1974). In the 1980s, two huge computer consortiums, MCC and SEMATECH, opted to make Austin their home. And wunderkind Michael Dell, who started out selling computers from his dorm room at UT in 1984 and is now the CEO of the hugely successful Austin-based Dell Computer Corporation, spawned a new breed of local "Dellionaires" by rewarding his employees with company stock.

Willie Nelson's return to Austin from Nashville in 1972 didn't have quite as profound an effect on the economy, but it certainly had one on the city's live-music scene. Hippies and country-and-western fans could now find common ground at the many clubs that began to sprout up along downtown's Sixth Street, which had largely been abandoned. These music venues, combined with the construction that followed in the wake of the city's high-tech success, helped spur a general downtown resurgence.

AUSTIN TODAY

During the 1990s, Austin's population increased by 41% (from 465,600 to 656,600), as high-paying tech jobs drew out-of-staters—quite a few of them Californians with much disposable cash. Many of the new residents moved to the suburban west and northwest, but the economic expansion also fueled a resurgence in the older central city.

Downtown projects at the end of the last century included the restoration of the capitol and its grounds; the refurbishing of the State Theatre; and the renovation of the Driskill Hotel and the reopening of the Stephen F. Austin Hotel, two grand historic properties. The convention center doubled in size and the Bob Bullock Texas History Center, a major tourist attraction, opened in 2001. And now downtown's skyline has begun to transform, too. In early 2004, both the high-rise Hilton Austin Convention Center Hotel and the chic Art Deco–style Frost Bank Tower, the city's tallest building, were completed.

The ongoing conversion of former warehouses and commercial lofts into residential housing is an even more crucial sign that downtown is returning to the land of the living—and, especially, the eating. A popular farmer's market has sprouted up Saturday mornings on Republic Square, and the opening of the huge new headquarters of the Austin-grown Whole Foods chain on Sixth and Lamar in early 2005 is bound to nurture the growth of downtown's west side.

In addition, the debut of the Austin-Bergstrom International Airport south of downtown in 1999 enhanced the development of an area that had already

---

(*Fun Fact* **And the Beat Goes On . . .**

Both Janis Joplin, who attended the University of Texas for a short time, and Stevie Ray Vaughan, enshrined in a statue overlooking Town Lake, got their starts in Austin clubs in the 1960s. During the 1970s the area was a hotbed for "outlaw" country singers Willie Nelson, Waylon Jennings, and Jerry Jeff Walker. During the 1980s there was a national surge of interest in local country-folk artists Lyle Lovett, Eric Taylor, Townes Van Zandt, Darden Smith, Robert Earl Keen, and Nanci Griffith. And the tradition continues with Austin's current musical residents including Grammy Award winners Shawn Colvin and the Dixie Chicks, among others.

started to make a comeback. South Congress Street (aka SoCo, of course) continues to draw hip galleries and boutiques, many of which stay open late once a month to take part in the new First Thursdays block party. As SoCo gets more mainstream, South Lamar and South First—not yet dubbed SoLa or SoFi—have begun to take up the alternative slack, opening stores of the type that characterized South Congress in its earlier, less expensive incarnation. And, in an ultimate Austin act of recycling, the abandoned hangars of the old Robert Mueller airport were transformed into a film production studio in 2000, which has meant more jobs and more activity in a once-decaying north-central neighborhood.

But there are many signs that Austin is becoming a victim of its own success. There's now a gated residential complex right down the street from the famed Continental Club, and, with the rise in rents, many of the struggling musicians who gave Austin's music scene its vitality can no longer afford to live here. Many of Austin's new restaurants are owned by groups of outside investors, and some funky midtown eateries like Kerbey Lane have spun characterless counterparts in the city's soulless northwest. And although the new airport prides itself on its use of local concessionaires, the restaurants and hotels that are springing up alongside the facility are chains. Indeed, locals are sufficiently worried about the city's evolving character that they've spawned a small industry of bumper stickers and T-shirts pleading KEEP AUSTIN WEIRD.

One of the most pressing problems is out-of-control traffic. Formerly bicycle-friendly streets are no longer as hospitable to two-wheelers. And although the freeways are perpetually being expanded, they can't keep pace with the ever-burgeoning population, while in downtown, construction is forcing detours on already choked narrow streets. In 2004, voters approved a commuter rail system that will run from the northern satellite of Cedar Park to downtown, but it will be many years before it might begin to provide relief of the auto glut.

The tech recession halted some of the new construction for a while, but signs of yet another tech boom are evident: In 2003, Samsung Austin Semiconductor, established in 1996 as the company's only semiconductor fabrication plant outside Korea, announced a 3-year, $500 million upgrade and expansion of its facilities. And in 2004, citing the presence in town of such nanotechnology businesses as NanoCoolers and Molecular Imprints—not to mention a highly educated and tech-savvy workforce—NanoVance Inc. announced the start-up of a major nanotechnology device manufacturer in Austin. No doubt about it: This comeback-kid of cities, which became capital because of its hubris and feistiness, never stays down for long.

Appendix B:
For International Visitors

Whether it's your 1st visit or your 10th, a trip to the United States may require an additional degree of planning. This chapter will provide you with essential information, helpful tips, and advice for the more common problems that some visitors encounter.

1 Preparing for Your Trip

ENTRY REQUIREMENTS

Check at any U.S. embassy or consulate for current information and requirements. You can also obtain a visa application and other information online at the **U.S. State Department**'s website, at **www.travel.state.gov.**

VISAS The U.S. State Department has a **Visa Waiver Program** allowing citizens of certain countries to enter the United States without a visa for stays of up to 90 days. At press time these included Andorra, Australia, Austria, Belgium, Brunei, Denmark, Finland, France, Germany, Iceland, Ireland, Italy, Japan, Liechtenstein, Luxembourg, Monaco, the Netherlands, New Zealand, Norway, Portugal, San Marino, Singapore, Slovenia, Spain, Sweden, Switzerland, and the United Kingdom. Citizens of these countries need only a valid passport and a round-trip air or cruise ticket in their possession upon arrival. If they first enter the United States, they may also visit Mexico, Canada, Bermuda, and/or the Caribbean islands and return to the United States without a visa. Further information is available from any U.S. embassy or consulate. Canadian citizens may enter the United States without visas; they need only proof of residence.

Citizens of all other countries must have (1) a valid passport that expires at least 6 months later than the scheduled end of their visit to the United States, and (2) a tourist visa, which may be obtained without charge from any U.S. consulate.

To obtain a visa, the traveler must submit a completed application form (either in person or by mail) with a 1½-inch-square photo, and must demonstrate binding ties to a residence abroad. Usually you can obtain a visa at once or within 24 hours, but it may take longer during the summer rush from June through August. If you cannot go in person, contact the nearest U.S. embassy or consulate for directions on applying by mail. Your travel agent or airline office may also be able to provide you with visa applications and instructions. The U.S. consulate or embassy that issues your visa will determine whether you will be issued a multiple- or single-entry visa and any restrictions regarding the length of your stay.

British subjects can obtain up-to-date visa information by calling the **U.S. Embassy Visa Information Line** (*✆* **0891/200-290**) or by visiting the "Consular Services" section of the American Embassy London's website at www. usembassy.org.uk.

Irish citizens can obtain up-to-date visa information through the **Embassy of the USA Dublin,** 42 Elgin Rd., Dublin 4, Ireland (*✆* **353/1-668-8777**), or by checking the "Consular Services" section of the website at http://dublin. usembassy.gov.

Australian citizens can obtain up-to-date visa information by contacting the **U.S. Embassy Canberra,** Moonah Place, Yarralumla, ACT 2600 (© **02/6214-5600**), or by checking the U.S. Diplomatic Mission's website at http://usembassy-australia.state.gov/consular.

Citizens of **New Zealand** can obtain up-to-date visa information by contacting the **U.S. Embassy New Zealand,** 29 Fitzherbert Terr., Thorndon, Wellington (© **644/472-2068**), or get the information directly from the "For New Zealanders" section of the website at http://usembassy.org.nz.

MEDICAL REQUIREMENTS   Unless you're arriving from an area known to be suffering from an epidemic (particularly cholera or yellow fever), inoculations or vaccinations are not required for entry into the United States. If you have a medical condition that requires **syringe-administered medications,** carry a valid signed prescription from your physician—the Federal Aviation Administration (FAA) no longer allows airline passengers to pack syringes in their carry-on baggage without documented proof of medical need. If you have a disease that requires treatment with **narcotics,** you should also carry documented proof with you—smuggling narcotics aboard a plane is a serious offense that carries severe penalties in the U.S.

For **HIV-positive visitors,** requirements for entering the United States are somewhat vague and change frequently. According to the latest publication of *HIV and Immigrants: A Manual for AIDS Service Providers,* the Immigration and Naturalization Service (INS) doesn't require a medical exam for entry into the United States, but INS officials may stop individuals because they look sick or because they are carrying AIDS/HIV medicine.

If an HIV-positive noncitizen applies for a nonimmigrant visa, the question on the application regarding communicable diseases is tricky no matter which way it's answered. If the applicant checks "no," INS may deny the visa on the grounds that the applicant committed fraud. If the applicant checks "yes" or if INS suspects the person is HIV-positive, it will deny the visa unless the applicant asks for a special waiver for visitors. This waiver is for people visiting the United States for a short time, to attend a conference, for instance, to visit close relatives, or to receive medical treatment. It can be a confusing situation. For up-to-the-minute information, contact **AIDSinfo** (© **800/448-0440** or 301/519-6616 outside the U.S.; www.aidsinfo.nih.gov) or the **Gay Men's Health Crisis** (© **212/367-1000;** www.gmhc.org).

DRIVER'S LICENSES   Foreign driver's licenses are mostly recognized in the U.S., although you may want to get an international driver's license if your home license is not written in English.

PASSPORT INFORMATION

Safeguard your passport in an inconspicuous, inaccessible place like a money belt. Make a copy of the critical pages, including the passport number, and store it in a safe place, separate from the passport itself. If you lose your passport, visit the nearest consulate of your native country as soon as possible for a replacement. Passport applications are downloadable from the websites listed below.

Note: The International Civil Aviation Organization has recommended a policy requiring that *every* individual who travels by air have a passport. In response, many countries are now requiring that children must be issued their own passport to travel internationally, whereas before those under 16 or so may have been allowed to travel on a parent or guardian's passport.

FOR RESIDENTS OF CANADA

You can pick up a passport application at one of 28 regional passport offices or most travel agencies. Canadian children who travel must have their own passport. However, if you hold a valid Canadian passport issued before December 11, 2001, that bears the name of your child, the passport remains valid for you and your child until it expires. Passports cost C$85 for those 16 years and older (valid 5 years), C$35 for children 3 to 15 (valid 5 years), and C$20 for children under 3 (valid 3 years). Applications, which must be accompanied by two identical passport-sized photographs and proof of Canadian citizenship, are available at travel agencies throughout Canada or from the central **Passport Office,** Department of Foreign Affairs and International Trade, Ottawa, ON K1A 0G3 (© **800/567-6868;** www.dfait-maeci.gc.ca/passport). Processing takes 5 to 10 days if you apply in person, or about 3 weeks by mail.

FOR RESIDENTS OF THE UNITED KINGDOM

As a member of the European Union, you need only an identity card, not a passport, to travel to other EU countries. However, if you already possess a passport, it's always useful to carry it. To pick up an application for a standard 10-year passport (5-year passport for children under 16), visit the nearest Passport Office, major post office, or travel agency. You can also contact the **United Kingdom Passport Service** at © **0870/571-0410** or visit its website at www.passport.gov.uk. Passports are £33 for adults and £19 for children under 16, with another £30 fee if you apply in person at a Passport Office. Processing takes about 2 weeks (1 week if you apply at the Passport Office).

FOR RESIDENTS OF IRELAND

You can apply for a 10-year passport, costing €57, at the **Passport Office,** Setanta Centre, Molesworth Street, Dublin 2 (© **01/671-1633;** www.irlgov.ie/iveagh). Those under age 18 and over 65 must apply for a €12 3-year passport. You can also apply at 1A South Mall, Cork (© **021/272-525**), or over the counter at most main post offices.

FOR RESIDENTS OF AUSTRALIA

You can get an application from your local post office or any branch of Passports Australia, but you must schedule an interview at the passport office to present your application materials. Call the **Australian Passport Information Service** at © **131-232,** or visit the government website at www.passports.gov.au. Passports for adults are A$144 and for those under 18 are A$72.

FOR RESIDENTS OF NEW ZEALAND

You can pick up a passport application at any New Zealand Passports Office or download it from their website. Contact the **Passports Office** at © **0800/225-050** in New Zealand or 04/474-8100, or log on to www.passports.govt.nz. Passports for adults are NZ$80 and for children under 16 are NZ$40.

CUSTOMS
WHAT YOU CAN BRING IN

Every visitor more than 21 years of age may bring in, free of duty, the following: (1) 1 liter of wine or hard liquor; (2) 200 cigarettes, 100 cigars (but not from Cuba), or 3 pounds of smoking tobacco; and (3) $100 worth of gifts. These exemptions are offered to travelers who spend at least 72 hours in the United States and who have not claimed them within the preceding 6 months.

It is altogether forbidden to bring into the country foodstuffs (particularly fruit, cooked meats, and canned goods) and plants (vegetables, seeds, tropical plants, and the like). Foreign tourists may bring in or take out up to $10,000 in U.S. or foreign currency with no formalities; larger sums must be declared to U.S. Customs on entering or leaving, which includes filing form CM 4790. For more specific information regarding U.S. Customs and Border Protection, contact your nearest U.S. embassy or consulate, or the **U.S. Customs** office (✆ **202/ 927-1770** or www.customs.ustreas.gov).

WHAT YOU CAN TAKE HOME

U.K. citizens returning from a non-EU country have a customs allowance of the following: 200 cigarettes; 50 cigars; 250g of smoking tobacco; 2 liters of still table wine; 1 liter of spirits or strong liqueurs (over 22% volume); 2 liters of fortified wine, sparkling wine, or other liqueurs; 60cc (ml) of perfume; 250cc (ml) of toilet water; and £145 worth of all other goods, including gifts and souvenirs. People under 17 cannot have the tobacco or alcohol allowance. For more information, contact **HM Customs & Excise** at ✆ **0845/010-9000** (from outside the U.K., 020/8929-0152), or consult their website at www.hmce.gov.uk.

For a clear summary of **Canadian** rules, request the booklet *I Declare,* issued by the **Canada Customs and Revenue Agency** (✆ **800/461-9999** in Canada, or 204/983-3500; www.ccra-adrc.gc.ca). Canada allows its citizens a C$750 exemption, and you're allowed to bring back duty-free one carton of cigarettes, 1 can of tobacco, 40 imperial ounces of liquor, and 50 cigars. In addition, you're allowed to mail gifts to Canada valued at less than C$60 a day, provided they're unsolicited and don't contain alcohol or tobacco (write on the package "Unsolicited gift, under $60 value"). All valuables should be declared on the Y-38 form before departure from Canada, including serial numbers of valuables you already own, such as expensive foreign cameras. *Note:* The $750 exemption can be used only once a year and only after an absence of 7 days.

The duty-free allowance in **Australia** is A$400 or, for those under 18, A$200. Citizens age 18 and over can bring in 250 cigarettes or 250 grams of loose tobacco, and 1,125 milliliters of alcohol. If you're returning with valuables you already own, such as foreign-made cameras, you should file form B263. A helpful brochure available from Australian consulates or Customs offices is *Know Before You Go.* For more information, call the **Australian Customs Service** at ✆ **1300/363-263,** or log on to www.customs.gov.au.

The duty-free allowance for **New Zealand** is NZ$700. Citizens over 17 can bring in 200 cigarettes, 50 cigars, or 250 grams of tobacco (or a mixture of all three if their combined weight doesn't exceed 250g); plus 4.5 liters of wine and beer, or 1.125 liters of liquor. New Zealand currency does not carry import or export restrictions. Fill out a certificate of export, listing the valuables you are taking out of the country; that way, you can bring them back without paying duty. Most questions are answered in a free pamphlet available at New Zealand consulates and Customs offices: *New Zealand Customs Guide for Travellers, Notice no. 4.* For more information, contact **New Zealand Customs,** The Customhouse, 17–21 Whitmore St., Box 2218, Wellington (✆ **0800/428-786** or 04/473-6099; www.customs.govt.nz).

HEALTH INSURANCE

Although it's not required of travelers, health insurance is highly recommended. Unlike many European countries, the United States does not usually offer free or low-cost medical care to its citizens or visitors. Doctors and hospitals are expensive, and in most cases will require advance payment or proof of coverage before they render their services. Policies can cover everything from the loss or theft of your baggage and trip cancellation to the guarantee of bail in case you're arrested. Good policies will also cover the costs of an accident, repatriation, or death. See "Insurance" in chapter 2 for more information. Packages such as **Europ Assistance's "Worldwide Healthcare Plan"** are sold by European automobile clubs and travel agencies at attractive rates. **Worldwide Assistance Services, Inc.** (© 800/821-2828; www.worldwideassistance.com), is the agent for Europ Assistance in the United States.

Though lack of health insurance may prevent you from being admitted to a hospital in nonemergencies, don't worry about being left on a street corner to die: The American way is to fix you now and bill the living daylights out of you later.

INSURANCE FOR BRITISH TRAVELERS   Most big travel agents offer their own insurance and will probably try to sell you their package when you book a holiday. Think before you sign. **Britain's Consumers' Association** recommends that you insist on seeing the policy and reading the fine print before buying travel insurance. **The Association of British Insurers** (© 020/7600-3333; www.abi.org.uk) gives advice by phone and publishes *Holiday Insurance,* a free guide to policy provisions and prices. You might also shop around for better deals: Try **Columbus Direct** (© 020/7375-0011; www.columbusdirect.net).

INSURANCE FOR CANADIAN TRAVELERS   Canadians should check with their provincial health-plan offices or call **Health Canada** (© 613/957-2991; www.hc-sc.gc.ca) to find out the extent of their coverage and what documentation and receipts they must take home in case they are treated in the United States.

MONEY

CURRENCY   The U.S. monetary system is very simple: The most common **bills** are the $1 (colloquially, a "buck"), $5, $10, and $20 denominations. There are also $2 bills (seldom encountered), $50 bills, and $100 bills (the last two are usually not welcome as payment for small purchases). All the paper money was recently redesigned, making the famous faces adorning them disproportionately large. The old-style bills are still legal tender.

There are seven denominations of coins: 1¢ (1 cent, or a penny); 5¢ (5 cents, or a nickel); 10¢ (10 cents, or a dime); 25¢ (25 cents, or a quarter); 50¢ (50 cents, or a half dollar); the gold-colored "Sacagawea" coin worth $1; and, prized by collectors, the rare, older silver dollar.

Note: The "foreign-exchange bureaus" so common in Europe are rare even at airports in the United States, and nonexistent outside major cities. It's best not to change foreign money (or traveler's checks denominated in a currency other than U.S. dollars) at a small-town bank, or even a branch in a big city; in fact, leave any currency other than U.S. dollars at home—it may prove a greater nuisance to you than it's worth.

TRAVELER'S CHECKS   Though traveler's checks are widely accepted, make sure that they're denominated in U.S. dollars, as foreign-currency checks are often difficult to exchange. The three traveler's checks that are most widely recognized—and least likely to be denied—are **Visa, American Express,** and **Thomas Cook.** Be sure to record the numbers of the checks, and keep that information in a separate place in case they get lost or stolen. Most businesses are pretty good about taking traveler's checks, but you're better off cashing them in at a bank (in small amounts, of course) and paying in cash. *Remember:* You'll need identification, such as a driver's license or passport, to change a traveler's check.

CREDIT CARDS & ATMS   Credit cards are the most widely used form of payment in the United States: **Visa** (Barclaycard in Britain), **MasterCard** (Euro-Card in Europe, Access in Britain, Chargex in Canada), **American Express, Diners Club,** and **Discover.** There are, however, a handful of stores and restaurants that do not take credit cards, so be sure to ask in advance. Most businesses display a sticker near their entrance to let you know which cards they accept. (*Note:* Businesses may require a minimum purchase, usually around $10, to use a credit card.)

It is strongly recommended that you bring at least one major credit card. You must have a credit or charge card to rent a car. Hotels and airlines usually require a credit card imprint as a deposit against expenses, and in an emergency a credit card can be priceless.

You'll find **automated teller machines (ATMs)** on just about every block—at least in almost every town—across the country. Some ATMs will allow you to draw U.S. currency against your bank and credit cards. Check with your bank before leaving home, and remember that you will need your personal identification number (PIN) to do so. Most accept Visa, MasterCard, and American Express, as well as ATM cards from other U.S. banks. Expect to be charged up to $3 per transaction, however, if you're not using your own bank's ATM.

One way around these fees is to ask for cash back at grocery stores that accept ATM cards and don't charge usage fees. Of course, you'll have to purchase something first.

ATM cards with major credit card backing, known as "debit cards," are now a commonly acceptable form of payment in most stores and restaurants. Debit cards draw money directly from your checking account. Some stores enable you to receive "cash back" on your debit card purchases as well.

SAFETY
GENERAL SUGGESTIONS   Although tourist areas are generally safe, U.S. urban areas tend to be less safe than those in Europe or Japan. You should always stay alert. This is particularly true of large American cities. If you're in doubt about which neighborhoods are safe, don't hesitate to make inquiries with the hotel front desk staff or the local tourist office.

Avoid deserted areas, especially at night, and don't go into public parks after dark unless there's a concert or similar occasion that will attract a crowd.

Avoid carrying valuables with you on the street, and keep expensive cameras or electronic equipment bagged up or covered when not in use. If you're using a map, try to consult it inconspicuously—or better yet, study it before you leave your room. Hold onto your pocketbook, and place your billfold in an inside pocket. In theaters, restaurants, and other public places, keep your possessions in sight.

Travel Tip
Be sure to keep a copy of all your travel papers separate from your wallet or purse, and leave a copy with someone at home should you need it faxed in an emergency.

SIZE CONVERSION CHART

Women's Clothing

American	4	6	8	10	12	14	16	
French	34	36	38	40	42	44	46	
British	6	8	10	12	14	16	18	

Women's Shoes

American	5	6	7	8	9	10
French	36	37	38	39	40	41
British	4	5	6	7	8	9

Men's Suits

American	34	36	38	40	42	44	46	48
French	44	46	48	50	52	54	56	58
British	34	36	38	40	42	44	46	48

Men's Shirts

American	14½	15	15½	16	16½	17	17½
French	37	38	39	41	42	43	44
British	14½	15	15½	16	16½	17	17½

Men's Shoes

American	7	8	9	10	11	12	13
French	39½	41	42	43	44½	46	47
British	6	7	8	9	10	11	12

Always lock your room door—don't assume that once you're inside the hotel you are automatically safe and no longer need to be aware of your surroundings. Hotels are open to the public, and in a large hotel, security may not be able to screen everyone who enters.

You may want to contact the **San Antonio Convention and Visitors Bureau,** 203 S. St. Mary's St., 2nd fl., San Antonio, TX 78205 (© **800/207-6700;** www.sanantoniovisit.com), or the **Austin Visitors Center**, 209 E. Sixth St., Austin, TX 78701 (© **866/GO-AUSTIN;** www.austintexas.org), ahead of time for additional advice on safety precautions. See also the "Safety" sections of "Fast Facts: San Antonio," in chapter 3, p. 40, and "Fast Facts: Austin," in chapter 11, p. 155.

DRIVING SAFETY   Driving safety is important too, and carjacking is not unprecedented. Question your rental agency about personal safety and ask for a traveler-safety brochure when you pick up your car. Obtain written directions—or a map with the route clearly marked—from the agency showing how to get to your destination. (Many agencies now offer the option of renting a cellphone for the duration of your car rental; check with the rental agent when you pick up the car. Otherwise, contact **InTouch USA** at © **800/872-7626** or www.intouchusa.com for short-term cellphone rental.) And, if possible, arrive and depart during daylight hours.

If you drive off a highway and end up in a dodgy-looking neighborhood, leave the area as quickly as possible. If you have an accident, even on the highway, stay in your car with the doors locked until you assess the situation or until the police arrive. If you're bumped from behind on the street or are involved in a minor accident with no injuries, and the situation appears to be suspicious, motion to the other driver to follow you. Never get out of your car in such situations. Go directly to the nearest police precinct, well-lit service station, or 24-hour store.

Park in well-lit and well-traveled areas whenever possible. Always keep your car doors locked, whether the vehicle is attended or unattended. Never leave any packages or valuables in sight. If someone attempts to rob you or steal your car, don't try to resist the thief/carjacker. Report the incident to the police department immediately by calling ✆ **911.**

2 Getting to the U.S.

Houston and Dallas–Forth Worth are the hubs for international flights into Texas. **Air Canada** (✆ **888/247-2262;** www.aircanada.com) offers daily nonstop flights from Toronto and Calgary to Houston and from Toronto to Dallas–Fort Worth. **American Airlines** (✆ **800/433-7300;** www.aa.com), **British Airways** (✆ **845/773-3377;** www.britishairways.com), **Continental** (✆ **800/523-3273;** www.continental.com), and **Delta Airlines** (✆ **800/221-1212;** www.delta.com) all offer nonstop service from London (either Heathrow or Gatwick) to either Dallas–Fort Worth or Houston or both. **Aerolitoral** (✆ **01800/021-26622;** www.aerolitoral.com), Continental (✆ **01800/900-5000;** www.continental.com), and **Mexicana** (✆ **800/531-7921;** www.mexicana.com) offer service from Mexico to San Antonio.

For more information about travel to San Antonio and Austin, see the "Getting There" sections of chapters 2 and 10.

AIRLINE DISCOUNTS The smart traveler can find numerable ways to reduce the price of a plane ticket simply by taking time to shop around. For example, overseas visitors can take advantage of the APEX (advance purchase excursion) reductions offered by all major U.S. and European carriers. For more money-saving airline advice, see "Getting There," in chapters 2 and 10. For the best rates, compare fares and be flexible with the dates and times of travel.

IMMIGRATION & CUSTOMS CLEARANCE Visitors arriving by air, no matter what the port of entry, should cultivate patience and resignation before setting foot on U.S. soil. Getting through immigration control can take as long as 2 hours on some days, especially on summer weekends, so be sure to carry this guidebook or something else to read. This is especially true in the aftermath of

---

Tips Prepare to Be Fingerprinted

Since January 2004, many international visitors traveling on visas to the United States have been photographed and fingerprinted at Customs in a new program created by the Department of Homeland Security called **US-VISIT.** Non–U.S. citizens arriving at airports and on cruise ships must undergo an instant background check as part of the government's ongoing efforts to deter terrorism by verifying the identity of incoming and outgoing visitors. Exempt from the extra scrutiny are visitors entering by land or those from 28 countries (mostly in Europe) that don't require a visa for short-term visits. For more information, go to the Homeland Security website at **www.dhs.gov/dhspublic/.**

the World Trade Center attacks, when security clearances have been considerably beefed up at U.S. airports.

People traveling by air from Canada, Bermuda, and certain countries in the Caribbean can sometimes clear Customs and Immigration at the point of departure, which is much quicker.

3 Getting Around the U.S.

BY PLANE   Some large airlines (for example, Northwest and Delta) offer travelers on their transatlantic or transpacific flights special discount tickets under the name **Visit USA,** allowing mostly one-way travel from one U.S. destination to another at very low prices. These discount tickets are not on sale in the United States and must be purchased abroad in conjunction with your international ticket. This system is the best, easiest, and fastest way to see the United States at low cost. You should obtain information well in advance from your travel agent or the office of the airline concerned, since the conditions attached to these discount tickets can be changed without advance notice.

BY TRAIN   International visitors (excluding Canada) can also buy a **USA Rail Pass,** good for 15 or 30 days of unlimited travel on Amtrak (© **800/USA-RAIL;** www.amtrak.com). The pass is available through many overseas travel agents. Prices in 2004 for a 15-day pass were $295 off-peak, $440 peak; a 30-day pass costs $385 off-peak, $550 peak. With a foreign passport, you can also buy passes at some Amtrak offices in the United States, including locations in San Francisco, Los Angeles, Chicago, New York, Miami, Boston, and Washington, D.C. Reservations are generally required and should be made for each part of your trip as early as possible. Regional rail passes are also available.

BY BUS   Although bus travel is often the most economical form of public transit for short hops between U.S. cities, it can also be slow and uncomfortable—certainly not an option for everyone (particularly when Amtrak, which is far more luxurious, offers similar rates). **Greyhound/Trailways** (© **800/231-2222;** www.greyhound.com), the sole nationwide bus line, offers an **International Ameripass** that must be purchased before coming to the United States, or by phone through the Greyhound International Office at the Port Authority Bus Terminal in New York City (© **212/971-0492**). The pass can be obtained from foreign travel agents or through Greyhound's website (order at least 21 days before your departure to the U.S.) and costs less than the domestic version. Passes for 2004 cost as follows: 4 days $160, 7 days $219, 10 days $269, 15 days $329, 21 days $379, 30 days $439, 45 days $489, or 60 days $599. You can get more info on the pass at the website, or by calling © **402/330-8552.** In addition, special rates are available for seniors and students.

BY CAR   Unless you plan to spend the bulk of your vacation time in a city where walking is the best and easiest way to get around (read: New York City or New Orleans), the most cost-effective, convenient, and comfortable way to travel around the United States is by car. The interstate highway system connects cities and towns all over the country; in addition to these high-speed, limited-access roadways, there's an extensive network of federal, state, and local highways and roads. Some of the national car-rental companies include **Alamo** (© 800/462-5266; www.alamo.com), **Avis** (© 800/230-4898; www.avis.com), **Budget** (© 800/527-0700; www.budget.com), **Dollar** (© 800/800-3665; www.dollar.com), **Hertz** (© 800/654-3131; www.hertz.com), **National** (© 800/227-7368; www.national-car.com), and **Thrifty** (© 800/847-4389; www.thrifty.com).

If you plan to rent a car in the United States, you probably won't need the services of an additional automobile organization. If you're planning to buy or borrow a car, automobile-association membership is recommended. **AAA, the American Automobile Association** (© **800/222-4357**), is the country's largest auto club and supplies its members with maps, insurance, and, most important, emergency road service. The cost of joining runs from $63 for singles to $87 for two members, but if you're a member of a foreign auto club with reciprocal arrangements, you can enjoy free AAA service in America.

FAST FACTS: **For the International Traveler**

Automobile Organizations Auto clubs will supply maps, suggested routes, guidebooks, accident and bail-bond insurance, and emergency road service. The **American Automobile Association (AAA)** is the major auto club in the United States. If you belong to an auto club in your home country, inquire about AAA reciprocity before you leave. You may be able to join AAA even if you're not a member of a reciprocal club; to inquire, call AAA (© **800/222-4357**). AAA is actually an organization of regional auto clubs, so look under "AAA Automobile Club" in the White Pages of the telephone directory. AAA has a nationwide emergency road service telephone number (© 800/AAA-HELP).

Business Hours Offices are usually open weekdays from 9am to 5pm. Banks are open weekdays from 9am to 3pm or later and sometimes Saturday mornings. Stores typically open between 9 and 10am and close between 5 and 6pm from Monday through Saturday. Stores in shopping complexes or malls tend to stay open late—until about 9pm on weekdays and weekends—and many malls and larger department stores are open on Sunday.

Currency & Currency Exchange See "Entry Requirements" and "Money" under "Preparing for Your Trip," earlier in this chapter.

Drinking Laws The legal age for purchase and consumption of alcoholic beverages is 21; proof of age is required and often requested at bars, nightclubs, and restaurants, so it's always a good idea to bring ID when you go out. Beer and wine can be purchased in supermarkets in Texas. See "Liquor Laws" in "Fast Facts: San Antonio," in chapter 3, and "Fast Facts: Austin," in chapter 11.

Do not carry open containers of alcohol in your car or any public area that isn't zoned for alcohol consumption. The police can fine you on the spot. And nothing will ruin your trip faster than getting a citation for DUI ("driving under the influence"), so don't even think about driving while intoxicated.

Electricity Like Canada, the United States uses 110–120 volts AC (60 cycles), compared to 220–240 volts AC (50 cycles) in most of Europe, Australia, and New Zealand. If your small appliances use 220–240 volts, you'll need a 110-volt transformer and a plug adapter with two flat parallel pins to operate them here. Downward converters that change 220–240 volts to 110–120 volts are difficult to find in the United States, so bring one with you.

Embassies & Consulates All embassies are located in the nation's capital, Washington, D.C. Some consulates are located in major U.S. cities, and most nations have a mission to the United Nations in New York City. If your country isn't listed below, call for directory information in Washington, D.C. (© **202/555-1212**) or log on to **www.embassy.org/embassies**.

The embassy of **Australia** is at 1601 Massachusetts Ave. NW, Washington, DC 20036 (© **202/797-3000**; www.austemb.org). There are consulates in New York, Honolulu, Houston, Los Angeles, and San Francisco.

The embassy of **Canada** is at 501 Pennsylvania Ave. NW, Washington, DC 20001 (© **202/682-1740**; www.canadianembassy.org). Other Canadian consulates are in Buffalo (NY), Detroit, Los Angeles, New York, and Seattle. There's a **Canadian Consulate** in Dallas at 750 N. St. Paul St., Suite 1700, Dallas, TX 75201 (© **214/922-9806**).

The embassy of **Ireland** is at 2234 Massachusetts Ave. NW, Washington, DC 20008 (© **202/462-3939**; www.irelandemb.org). Irish consulates are in Boston, Chicago, New York, and San Francisco.

The embassy of **Japan** is at 2520 Massachusetts Ave. NW, Washington, DC 20008 (© **202/238-6700**; www.embjapan.org). Japanese consulates are located in many cities, including Atlanta, Boston, Detroit, New York, San Francisco, and Seattle.

The embassy of **New Zealand** is at 37 Observatory Circle NW, Washington, DC 20008 (© **202/328-4800**; www.nzemb.org). New Zealand consulates are in Los Angeles, Salt Lake City, San Francisco, and Seattle.

The embassy of the **United Kingdom** is at 3100 Massachusetts Ave. NW, Washington, DC 20008 (© **202/462-1340**; www.britainusa.com). Other British consulates are in Atlanta, Boston, Chicago, Cleveland, Houston, Los Angeles, New York, San Francisco, and Seattle. Houston is home to a consulate for the United Kingdom at 1000 Louisiana St., Suite 1900, Houston, TX 77002 (© **713/659-6270**).

Emergencies Call © **911** to report a fire, call the police, or get an ambulance anywhere in the United States. This is a toll-free call. (No coins are required at public telephones.)

If you encounter serious problems, contact the **Traveler's Aid International** (© **202/546-1127**; www.travelersaid.org) to help direct you to a local branch. This nationwide, nonprofit, social-service organization geared to helping travelers in difficult straits offers services that might include reuniting families separated while traveling, providing food and/or shelter to people stranded without cash, or even emotional counseling. If you're in trouble, seek them out.

Gasoline (Petrol) Petrol is known as gasoline (or simply "gas") in the United States, and petrol stations are known as both gas stations and service stations. Gasoline costs about half as much here as it does in Europe (about $2 per gallon at press time), and taxes are already included in the printed price. One U.S. gallon equals 3.8 liters or .85 Imperial gallons.

Holidays Banks, government offices, post offices, and many stores, restaurants, and museums are closed on the following legal national holidays: January 1 (New Year's Day), the third Monday in January (Martin Luther King, Jr., Day), the third Monday in February (Presidents' Day/Washington's Birthday), the last Monday in May (Memorial Day), July

4th (Independence Day), the first Monday in September (Labor Day), the second Monday in October (Columbus Day), November 11 (Veterans' Day/Armistice Day), the fourth Thursday in November (Thanksgiving Day), and December 25 (Christmas). Also, the Tuesday following the first Monday in November is Election Day and is a federal government holiday in presidential-election years (held every 4 years, and next in 2008).

Legal Aid If you are "pulled over" for a minor infraction (such as speeding), never attempt to pay the fine directly to a police officer; this could be construed as attempted bribery, a much more serious crime. Pay fines by mail, or directly into the hands of the clerk of the court. If accused of a more serious offense, say and do nothing before consulting a lawyer. Here the burden is on the state to prove a person's guilt beyond a reasonable doubt, and everyone has the right to remain silent, whether he or she is suspected of a crime or actually arrested. Once arrested, a person can make one telephone call to a party of his or her choice. Call your embassy or consulate.

Mail If you aren't sure what your address will be in the United States, mail can be sent to you, in your name, c/o General Delivery at the main post office of the city or region where you expect to be. (Call © **800/275-8777** for information on the nearest post office.) The addressee must pick up mail in person and must produce proof of identity (driver's license, passport, and so on). Most post offices will hold your mail for up to 1 month, and are open Monday to Friday from 8am to 6pm, and Saturday from 9am to 3pm.

Generally found at intersections, mailboxes are blue with a red-and-white stripe and carry the inscription U.S. MAIL. If your mail is addressed to a U.S. destination, don't forget to add the five-digit postal code (or zip code), after the two-letter abbreviation of the state to which the mail is addressed. This is essential for prompt delivery.

At press time, domestic postage rates were 23¢ for a postcard and 37¢ for a letter. For international mail, a first-class letter of up to one-half ounce costs 80¢ (60¢ to Canada and Mexico); a first-class postcard costs 70¢ (50¢ to Canada and Mexico); and a preprinted postal aerogramme costs 70¢.

Measurements See the chart on the inside front cover of this book for details on converting metric measurements to U.S. equivalents.

Taxes The United States has no value-added tax (VAT) or other indirect tax at the national level. Every state, county, and city has the right to levy its own local tax on all purchases, including hotel and restaurant checks, airline tickets, and so on. See the taxes section of "Fast Facts: San Antonio," in chapter 3, and "Fast Facts: Austin," in chapter 11.

Telephone, Telegraph, Telex, & Fax The telephone system in the United States is run by private corporations, so rates, especially for long-distance service and operator-assisted calls, can vary widely. Generally, hotel surcharges on long-distance and local calls are astronomical, so you're usually better off using a **public pay telephone,** which you'll find clearly marked in most public buildings and private establishments as well as on the street. Convenience grocery stores and gas stations always have them. Many convenience groceries and packaging services sell **prepaid calling cards** in denominations up to $50; these can be the least expensive way to call home. Many public phones at airports now accept American

Express, MasterCard, and Visa credit cards. **Local calls** made from public pay phones in most locales cost 50¢. Pay phones do not accept pennies, and few will take anything larger than a quarter.

You may want to look into leasing a cell-phone for the duration of your trip.

Most long-distance and international calls can be dialed directly from any phone. **For calls within the United States and to Canada,** dial 1 followed by the area code and the seven-digit number. **For other international calls,** dial 011 followed by the country code, city code, and the telephone number of the person you are calling.

Calls to area codes **800, 888, 877,** and **866** are toll-free. However, calls to numbers in area codes **700** and **900** (chat lines, bulletin boards, "dating" services, and so on) can be very expensive—usually a charge of 95¢ to $3 or more per minute, and they sometimes have minimum charges that can run as high as $15 or more.

For **reversed-charge or collect calls,** and for person-to-person calls, dial 0 (zero, not the letter O) followed by the area code and number you want; an operator will then come on the line, and you should specify that you are calling collect, or person-to-person, or both. If your operator-assisted call is international, ask for the overseas operator.

For **local directory assistance** ("information"), dial 411; for long-distance information, dial 1, then the appropriate area code and 555-1212.

Telegraph and telex services are provided primarily by Western Union. You can bring your telegram into the nearest Western Union office (there are hundreds across the country) or dictate it over the phone (© **800/ 325-6000**). You can also telegraph money, or have it telegraphed to you, very quickly over the Western Union system, but this service can cost as much as 15 to 20 percent of the amount sent.

Most hotels have **fax machines** available for guest use (be sure to ask about the charge to use it). Many hotel rooms are even wired for guests' fax machines. A less expensive way to send and receive faxes may be at stores such as **The UPS Store** (formerly Mail Boxes Etc.), a national chain of retail packing service shops. (Look in the Yellow Pages directory under "Packing Services.")

There are two kinds of telephone directories in the United States. The so-called **White Pages** list private households and business subscribers in alphabetical order. The inside front cover lists emergency numbers for police, fire, ambulance, the Coast Guard, poison-control center, crime-victims hotline, and so on. The first few pages will tell you how to make long-distance and international calls, complete with country codes and area codes. Government numbers are usually printed on blue paper within the White Pages. Printed on yellow paper, the so-called **Yellow Pages** list all local services, businesses, industries, and houses of worship according to activity with an index at the front or back. (Drugstores/pharmacies and restaurants are also listed by geographic location.) The Yellow Pages also include city plans or detailed area maps, postal zip codes, and public transportation routes.

Time The continental United States is divided into **four time zones:** Eastern Standard Time (EST), Central Standard Time (CST), Mountain Standard Time (MST), and Pacific Standard Time (PST). Alaska and Hawaii have their own zones. For example, noon in New York City (EST) is 11am in Chicago (CST), 10am in Denver (MST), 9am in Los Angeles (PST), 8am in Anchorage (AST), and 7am in Honolulu (HST). San Antonio and Austin (but not all of the rest of Texas, which is huge) are in the Central Time zone.

Daylight saving time is in effect from 1am on the first Sunday in April through 1am on the last Sunday in October, except in Arizona, Hawaii, most of Indiana, and Puerto Rico. Daylight saving time moves the clock 1 hour ahead of standard time.

Tipping Tips are a very important part of certain workers' income, and gratuities are the standard way of showing appreciation for services provided. (Tipping is certainly not compulsory if the service is poor!) In hotels, tip **bellhops** at least $1 per bag ($2–$3 per bag if you have a lot of luggage) and tip the **chamber staff** $1 to $2 per day (more if you've left a disaster area for him or her to clean up). Tip the **doorman** or **concierge** only if he or she has provided you with some specific service (for example, calling a cab for you or obtaining difficult-to-get theater tickets). Tip the **valet-parking attendant** $1 every time you get your car.

In restaurants, bars, and nightclubs, tip **service staff** 15% to 20% of the check, tip **bartenders** 10% to 15%, tip **checkroom attendants** $1 per garment, and tip **valet-parking attendants** $1 per vehicle.

As for other service personnel, tip **cab drivers** 15% of the fare; tip **skycaps** at airports at least $1 per bag ($2–$3 per bag if you have a lot of luggage); and tip **hairdressers** and **barbers** 15% to 20%.

Toilets You won't find public toilets or "restrooms" on the streets in most U.S. cities, but they can be found in hotel lobbies, bars, restaurants, museums, department stores, railway and bus stations, and service stations. Large hotels and fast-food restaurants are probably the best bet for good, clean facilities. If possible, avoid the toilets at parks and beaches, which tend to be dirty; some may be unsafe. Restaurants and bars in resorts or heavily visited areas may reserve their restrooms for patrons. Some establishments display a notice indicating this. You can ignore this sign or, better yet, avoid arguments by paying for a cup of coffee or a soft drink, which will qualify you as a patron.

Appendix C:
Useful Toll-Free Numbers
& Websites

AIRLINES

Aeromar Airlines
✆ 888/627-0207 in the U.S.
www.aeromarairlines.com

Air Canada
✆ 888/247-2262
www.aircanada.ca

Alaska Airlines
✆ 800/252-7522
www.alaskaair.com

America West Airlines
✆ 800/235-9292
www.americawest.com

American Airlines
✆ 800/433-7300
www.aa.com

ATA Airlines
✆ 800/I-FLY-ATA
www.ata.com

British Airways
✆ 800/247-9297
✆ 0845/773-3377 in the U.K.
www.ba.com

Continental Airlines
✆ 800/525-0280
www.continental.com

Delta Air Lines
✆ 800/221-1212
www.delta.com

Frontier Airlines
✆ 800/432-1359
www.frontierairlines.com

Mexicana Airlines
✆ 800/531-7921 in the U.S.
www.mexicana.com

Midwest Airlines
✆ 800/452-2022
www.midwestairlines.com

Northwest Airlines
✆ 800/225-2525
www.nwa.com

Qantas
✆ 800/227-4500 in the U.S.
✆ 13-13-13 in Australia
www.qantas.com

Southwest Airlines
✆ 800/435-9792
www.iflyswa.com

United Airlines
✆ 800/241-6522
www.united.com

US Airways
✆ 800/428-4322
www.usairways.com

CAR-RENTAL AGENCIES

Advantage
✆ 800/777-5500
www.advantagerentacar.com

Alamo
✆ 800/327-9633
www.alamo.com

Avis
✆ 800/331-1212
www.avis.com

Budget
✆ 800/527-0700
www.budget.com

Dollar
✆ 800/800-4000
www.dollarcar.com

Enterprise
✆ 800/325-8007
www.enterprise.com

Hertz
✆ 800/654-3131
www.hertz.com

National
✆ 800/CAR-RENT
www.nationalcar.com

Payless
✆ 800/PAYLESS
www.paylesscar.com

Rent-A-Wreck
✆ 800/944-7501
www.rentawreck.com

Thrifty
✆ 800/367-2277
www.thrifty.com

MAJOR HOTEL & MOTEL CHAINS

Best Western International
✆ 800/780-7234
www.bestwestern.com

Clarion Hotel
✆ 800/CLARION
www.hotelchoice.com

Comfort Inn
✆ 800/228-5150
www.hotelchoice.com

Courtyard by Marriott
✆ 800/321-2211
www.courtyard.com

Days Inn
✆ 800/325-2525
www.daysinn.com

Doubletree Hotels
✆ 800/222-TREE
www.doubletree.com

Econo Lodge
✆ 800/55-ECONO
www.hotelchoice.com

Embassy Suites Hotels
✆ 800/EMBASSY
www.embassy-suites.com

Fairfield Inn by Marriott
✆ 800/228-2800
www.fairfieldinn.com

Hampton Inn
✆ 800/HAMPTON
www.hampton-inn.com

Hilton Hotels
✆ 800/HILTONS
www.hilton.com

Holiday Inn
✆ 800/HOLIDAY
www.holiday-inn.com

Howard Johnson
✆ 800/I-GO-HOJO
www.hojo.com

Hyatt Hotels & Resorts
✆ 888/591-1234
www.hyatt.com

InterContinental Hotels & Resorts
✆ 888/567-8725
www.intercontinental.com

La Quinta Inns
✆ 800/531-5900
www.laquinta.com

Marriott Hotels
✆ 888/236-2427
www.marriott.com

Motel 6
✆ 800/4-MOTEL6
www.motel6.com

Omni Hotels
✆ 800/THE-OMNI
www.omnihotels.com

Quality
✆ 800/228-5151
www.hotelchoice.com

Radisson Hotels
✆ 888/201-1717
www.radisson.com

Ramada
✆ 888/298-2054
www.ramada.com

Red Roof Inns
© 800/RED-ROOF
www.redroof.com

Residence Inn by Marriott
© 800/331-3131
www.residenceinn.com

Rodeway Inn
© 800/228-2000
www.hotelchoice.com

Sheraton Hotels & Resorts
© 888/625-5144
www.sheraton.com

Super 8 Motels
© 800/800-8000
www.super8.com

Travelodge
© 800/578-7878
www.travelodge.com

Westin Hotels & Resorts
© 800/937-8461
www.westin.com

Index

See also Accommodations and Restaurant indexes, below.

ACCOMMODATIONS —SAN ANTONIO

ACCOMMODATIONS —AUSTIN

A Guide for Every Type of Traveler

FROMMER'S® COMPLETE GUIDES

For independent leisure or business travelers who value complete coverage, candid advice, and lots of choices in all price ranges.

These are the most complete, up-to-date guides you can buy. Count on Frommer's for exact prices, savvy trip planning, sightseeing advice, dozens of detailed maps, and candid reviews of hotels and restaurants in every price range. All Complete Guides offer special icons to point you to great finds, excellent values, and more. Every hotel, restaurant, and attraction is rated from zero to three stars to help you make the best choices.

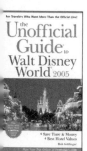

UNOFFICIAL GUIDES

For honeymooners, families, business travelers, and anyone else who values no-nonsense, *Consumer Reports*–style advice.

Unofficial Guides are ideal for those who want to know the pros and cons of the places they are visiting and make informed decisions. The guides rank and rate every hotel, restaurant, and attraction, with evaluations based on reader surveys and critiques compiled by a team of unbiased inspectors.

FROMMER'S® IRREVERENT GUIDES

For experienced, sophisticated travelers looking for a fresh, candid perspective on a destination.

This unique series is perfect for anyone who wants a cutting-edge perspective on the hottest destinations. Covering all major cities around the globe, these guides are unabashedly honest and down-right hilarious. Decked out with a retro-savvy feel, each book features new photos, maps, and neighborhood references.

FROMMER'S® WITH KIDS GUIDES

For families traveling with children ages 2 to 14.

Here are the ultimate guides for a successful family vacation. Written by parents, they're packed with information on museums, outdoor activities, attractions, great drives and strolls, incredible parks, the liveliest places to stay and eat, and more.

Visit Frommers.com

Frommer's is a registered trademark of Arthur Frommer, used under exclusive license.

WILEY
Now you know.

A Guide for Every Type of Traveler

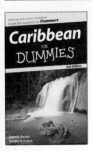

FOR DUMMIES® TRAVEL GUIDES

For curious, independent travelers.

The ultimate user-friendly trip planners, combining the broad appeal and time-tested features of the For Dummies guides with Frommer's accurate, up-to-date information and travel expertise. Written in a personal, conversational voice, For Dummies Travel Guides put the fun back into travel planning. They offer savvy, focused content on destinations and popular types of travel, with current and extensive coverage of hotels, restaurants, and attractions.

SUZY GERSHMAN'S BORN TO SHOP GUIDES

For avid shoppers seeking the best places to shop worldwide.

These savvy, opinionated guides, all personally researched and written by shopping guru Suzy Gershman, provide detailed descriptions of shopping neighborhoods, listings of conveniently located hotels and restaurants, easy-to-follow shopping tours, accurate maps, size conversion charts, and practical information about shipping, customs, VAT laws, and bargaining. The handy pocket size makes it easy to carry them in your purse while you shop 'til you drop.

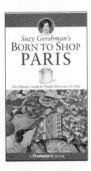

FROMMER'S® $-A-DAY GUIDES

For independent travelers who want the very best for their money without sacrificing comfort or style.

The renowned series of guides that gave Frommer's its start is the only budget travel series for grown-ups—travelers with limited funds who still want to travel in comfort and style. The $-a-Day Guides are for travelers who want the very best values, but who also want to eat well and stay in comfortable hotels with modern amenities. Each guide is tailored to a specific daily budget and is filled with money-saving advice and detailed maps, plus comprehensive information on sightseeing, shopping, nightlife, and outdoor activities.

FROMMER'S® PORTABLE GUIDES

For short-term travelers who insist on value and a lightweight guide, including weekenders and convention-goers.

Frommer's inexpensive, pocket-sized Portable Guides offer travelers the very best of each destination so that they can make the best use of their limited time. The guides include all the detailed information and insider advice for which Frommer's is famous, but in a more concise, easy-to-carry format.

Visit Frommers.com

WILEY
Now you know.

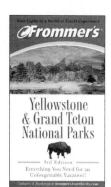
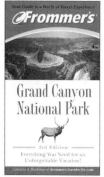
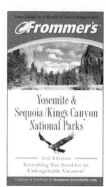

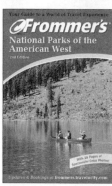
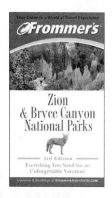
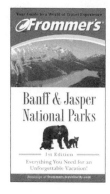
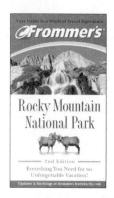

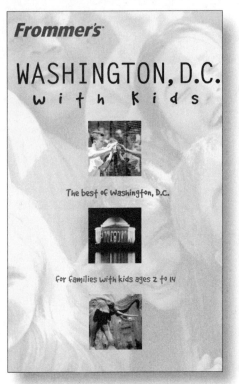

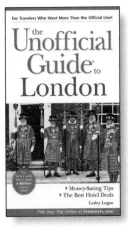
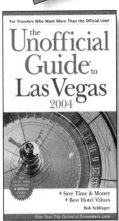
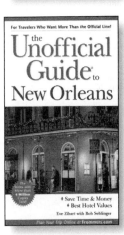

FROMMER'S® COMPLETE TRAVEL GUIDES

FROMMER'S® DOLLAR-A-DAY GUIDES

FROMMER'S® PORTABLE GUIDES

FROMMER'S® NATIONAL PARK GUIDES

Algonquin Provincial Park
Banff & Jasper
Family Vacations in the National
  Parks

Grand Canyon
National Parks of the American
  West
Rocky Mountain

Yellowstone & Grand Teton
Yosemite & Sequoia/Kings
  Canyon
Zion & Bryce Canyon

FROMMER'S® MEMORABLE WALKS

Chicago
London

New York
Paris

San Francisco

FROMMER'S® WITH KIDS GUIDES

Chicago
Las Vegas
New York City

Ottawa
San Francisco
Toronto

Vancouver
Walt Disney World® & Orlando
Washington, D.C.

SUZY GERSHMAN'S BORN TO SHOP GUIDES

Born to Shop: France
Born to Shop: Hong Kong,
  Shanghai & Beijing

Born to Shop: Italy
Born to Shop: London

Born to Shop: New York
Born to Shop: Paris

FROMMER'S® IRREVERENT GUIDES

Amsterdam
Boston
Chicago
Las Vegas
London

Los Angeles
Manhattan
New Orleans
Paris
Rome

San Francisco
Seattle & Portland
Vancouver
Walt Disney World®
Washington, D.C.

FROMMER'S® BEST-LOVED DRIVING TOURS

Austria
Britain
California
France

Germany
Ireland
Italy
New England

Northern Italy
Scotland
Spain
Tuscany & Umbria

THE UNOFFICIAL GUIDES®

Beyond Disney
California with Kids
Central Italy
Chicago
Cruises
Disneyland®
England
Florida
Florida with Kids
Inside Disney

Hawaii
Las Vegas
London
Maui
Mexico's Best Beach Resorts
Mini Las Vegas
Mini Mickey
New Orleans
New York City
Paris

San Francisco
Skiing & Snowboarding in the
  West
South Florida including Miami &
  the Keys
Walt Disney World®
Walt Disney World® for
  Grown-ups
Walt Disney World® with Kids
Washington, D.C.

SPECIAL-INTEREST TITLES

Athens Past & Present
Cities Ranked & Rated
Frommer's Best Day Trips from London
Frommer's Best RV & Tent Campgrounds
  in the U.S.A.
Frommer's Caribbean Hideaways
Frommer's China: The 50 Most Memorable Trips
Frommer's Exploring America by RV
Frommer's Gay & Lesbian Europe
Frommer's NYC Free & Dirt Cheap

Frommer's Road Atlas Europe
Frommer's Road Atlas France
Frommer's Road Atlas Ireland
Frommer's Wonderful Weekends from
  New York City
The New York Times' Guide to Unforgettable
  Weekends
Retirement Places Rated
Rome Past & Present

Travel Tip: He who finds the best hotel deal has more to spend on facials involving knobbly vegetables.

Hello, the Roaming Gnome here. I've been nabbed from the garden and taken round the world. The people who took me are so terribly clever. They find the best offerings on Travelocity. For very little cha-ching. And that means I get to be pampered and exfoliated till I'm pink as a bunny's doodah.

travelocity®

1-888-TRAVELOCITY | travelocity.com | America Online Keyword: Travel

Travel Tip: Make sure there's customer service for any change of plans — involving friendly natives, for example.

One can plan and plan, but if you don't book with the right people you can't seize le moment and canoodle with the poodle named Pansy. I, for one, am all for fraternizing with the locals. Better yet, if I need to extend my stay and my gnome nappers are willing, it can all be arranged through the 800 number at, oh look, how convenient, the lovely company coat of arms.

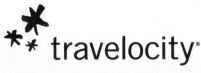

travelocity®